OXFORD HISTORICAL MONOGRAPHS

Editors

M. G. BROCK	BARBARA HARVEY
H. M. MAYR-HARTING	H. G. PITT
A. F. THOMPSON	H. R. TREVOR-ROPER

GW00771031

History

CORN, CASH, COMMERCE

The Economic Policies of the
Tory Governments 1815–1830

by
BOYD HILTON
Fellow of Trinity College, Cambridge

OXFORD UNIVERSITY PRESS

Oxford University Press, Walton Street, Oxford OX2 6DP

OXFORD LONDON GLASGOW NEW YORK
TORONTO MELBOURNE WELLINGTON CAPE TOWN
IBADAN NAIROBI DAR ES SALAAM LUSAKA ADDIS ABABA
KUALA LUMPUR SINGAPORE JAKARTA HONG KONG TOKYO
DELHI BOMBAY CALCUTTA MADRAS KARACHI

© *Oxford University Press 1977*

All rights reserved. No part of this publication may be reproduced, stored in a retrieval system, or transmitted, in any form or by any means, electronic, mechanical, photocopying, recording or otherwise, without the prior permission of Oxford University Press

British Library Cataloguing in Publication Data

Hilton, Boyd
    Corn, cash, commerce. — (Oxford historical monographs).
    1. Great Britain — Economic policy
    I. Title II. Series
    330. 9'41'074   HC255

ISBN 0-19-821884-2

First published 1977
Reprinted as paperback 1980

Printed in Great Britain by
Lowe & Brydone Printers Ltd
Thetford, Norfolk

To MY PARENTS

PREFACE

British governments in the late eighteenth century made no attempts to control the spontaneous and uncoordinated processes known as the 'first Industrial Revolution'. Helpless in the teeth of gale-force growth, they did not know whether they should be putting the vessel back to port or letting her loose on an ocean of change, and rather than navigate the economy they eagerly endorsed the new ideas of *laissez-faire* and a minimum state. But after Waterloo, events forced ministers to commit themselves on economic issues. No doubt some of their new philosophy was simply veneer to obscure political motives or to furbish traditional policies handed down by Pitt, but the extremity of post-war distress was making pundits of all men and compelling a positive response. Indeed its eagerness to abdicate responsibility even pushed Lord Liverpool's government towards positive reforms in the direction of free trade, if only to eliminate some protected interests and official patronage. But beyond this, strict ministerial impartiality was no longer possible. For example, Liverpool's government thought that the recent heady growth of cotton manufacturing, prices, and population was to a large extent an artificial consequence of war and monetary depreciation, and it restored the currency to its pre-war or 'natural' state partly in order to neutralize the effects of the nation's long struggle against France. Intended therefore as an act of retrospective justice to those economic groups that had done badly out of the war, resumption nevertheless disrupted the affairs of a whole generation that had never known the *antebellum*. Yet not to have resumed would have been an equally discriminating (though in that case inflationary) decision. Thus the government was forced to take sides — between economic interests and between generations — and subsequently to defend its choice in economic terms.

If Liverpool's ministry was the first to strive for a coherent theory of economic policy, it was perhaps the last to regard the industrial revolution as a malignant aberration, and to distinguish (albeit less blatantly than Sir Thomas Lethbridge

in 1822) between 'the *real* and the *false* people, describing
the former to consist of the manly yeomanry, and the latter
to be composed of a certain unfortunate portion of the population which inhabited great manufacturing towns.' After
1830 only the most eccentric seriously challenged or tried
to contain 'progress'. Economic growth continued to seem
socially and morally disruptive to many people, the source of
darkening gloom and satanic landscapes, but it was increasingly accepted as inevitable. The Victorians' ambition was no
longer to obliterate but to evangelize manufacturing industry;
as Carlyle said, to make Manchester organic that she might
bless and not afflict. This acceptance of growth may have
been symbolized by the so-called advent of middle-class
power in the 1830s, but it followed logically from policies
developed with quite different intentions under Lord Liverpool.

The measures of 1815-30 also had a strong and perhaps
deleterious effect in the long-run on economic policy. Free
trade reforms, which had been initiated to restrict indiscriminate growth and to stabilize rather than to expand the
economy, were followed in the second half of the nineteenth
century by national prosperity. The consequent myth that
equated free trade with power and plenty made it difficult
for twentieth-century governments to adapt economic
policy to new industrial competition, lack of confidence at
home, and outdated manufacturing and managerial tech-
niques. Politicians in the 1920s were often misled by the
superficial resemblance between their own times and the
1820s, and so dismissed those few who called for reflation
and deficit financing, public works, and monetary management to relieve the problem of unemployment as latter-day
Cobbetts, Attwoods, and John Sinclairs. Historians may
know that history never repeats itself, but there have always
been too many men of affairs who think that it does, or aim
to make it do so. And so it was by appealing to the stoicism
of Lord Liverpool's government one hundred years before
that 'orthodox' politicians and economists in the 1920s
helped to keep such cranks as Keynes at bay.

This book is substantially the same as my Oxford D. Phil.

thesis presented in spring 1973, and my greatest debt is to my supervisor, Angus Macintyre, for his stimulating advice, wit, and encouragement. I am grateful for the comments of my examiners, Michael Brock and Professor Norman Gash, and I have benefited more than I can adequately say from conversations with Trevor Burchell, Peter Conrad, Peter Dickson, Max Hartwell, Ross McKibbin, Colin Matthew, David Moss, William Thomas, Allen Warren, and Robert Robson. Tony Malcomson of Belfast, Piero Sraffa of Cambridge, and the late Sir Victor Mallet helped enormously in the search for manuscripts, and in this connection I should like to acknowledge with especial gratitude the kind help and brief friendship of the late Francis Needham. I am indebted to the Dean and Students of Christ Church, Oxford, where I was a Research Lecturer while most of this book was written, and I should mention the long-suffering help of the staffs of the New College, Christ Church, Codrington, Bodleian, and British Museum Libraries. For kind permission to quote from manuscript material I wish to thank the following: Earl Bathurst, Lady Mairi Bury (Castlereagh Papers), Lord Congleton (Parnell Papers), Dr. J. A. Cope, Major-General E. G. Goulburn, Sir Fergus Graham, Bt., the Earl of Harewood (Canning Papers), the Earl of Harrowby and the Trustees of the Harrowby Manuscripts Trust, Lord Hatherton, Lord Kenyon, Mr P. L. V. Mallet, Viscount Massereene, Viscount Sidmouth, His Grace the Duke of Wellington, and the Warden and Fellows of All Souls College, Oxford (Charles R. Vaughan Papers).

My greatest debt of all is to my wife, who has goaded and guided through every stage and is now word-perfect in *Corn, Cash, Commerce*.

Trinity College, A.J.B.H.
Cambridge.

CONTENTS

ABBREVIATIONS

A & P	Parliamentary Accounts and Papers
B. of E.	Bank of England
B.T.	Board of Trade
C.B.	Bank of England, Court of Directors Book
CP	Canning Papers, Harewood MSS.
CSC	House of Commons, Select Committee
C.T.	Bank of England, Committee of Treasury Minute Book
HHP	Holland House Papers
H. of C.	House of Commons
H. of L.	House of Lords
HP	Huskisson Papers
LP	Liverpool Papers
LSC	House of Lords, Select Committee
1 PD	First Series of Hansard's Parliamentary Debates
2 PD	Second Series of Hansard's Parliamentary Debates
3 PD	Third Series of Hansard's Parliamentary Debates

PART ONE

ADJUSTMENT TO PEACE, 1815-1819

THE CORN LAW OF 1815

Let the bread we eat be the produce of corn grown among ourselves, and I, for one, care not how cheap it is; the cheaper the better.
W. Huskisson, *A Letter on the Corn Laws, to one of his constituents, in 1814* (1827), 8-9.

The protectionist movement, 1813-15

'One of the most naked pieces of class legislation in English history',[1] a 'deliberate attempt to keep the price of corn, and therefore bread, artificially high',[2] 'a class measure passed to keep up rents',[3] a ruse 'to maintain prices by exploiting the political strength of the landed interest'[4] — the Corn Law of 1815 is still notorious. At the time it was bitterly resented by radicals, manufacturers, and the urban poor as a *pacte de famine* between Lord Liverpool's administration and the landed aristocracy. The latter welcomed the government's albeit grudging support as an official endorsement of the physiocratic view that Britain's prosperity was founded on agriculture and was independent of commerce. Liverpool, however, protested sincerely that the measure was calculated to benefit everyone; in appeasing those 'sabine tillers', the landed gentry, he did not altogether share their aspirations.

The previous Corn Law (1804)[5] had unaugurated a golden decade for most agriculturists. Though that law never operated, inflation having immediately dwarfed the prices at which it had imposed effective import duties, the wartime commercial blockade bestowed a natural protection on British and Irish corn. But what would happen when the war ended? Irish landlords, under Sir Henry Parnell, were the first to prophesy 'a malady of peace'. For like Baltic nations,

1. R. Blake, *The Conservative Party from Peel to Churchill* (1970), 15.
2. Ibid. 123.
3. D. G. Barnes, *A History of the English Corn Laws from 1600 to 1846* (1930), 287.
4. E. J. Hobsbawm and G. Rudé, *Captain Swing* (1969), 30.
5. See Table 1, below, p.6.

Ireland grew corn mainly for export, and her farmers feared that peace would terminate demand from troops in the Peninsula at the same time that it revived foreign competition in the British market.[6] In 1813, therefore, an "Irish job" of a Select Committee, engineered by Parnell, recommended that Parliament should impose very high import duties, abolish the preferential rates of duty allowed on corn from the North American colonies, and permit free exportation.[7]

Though Parnell and his witnesses, including the statistical authority, Edward Wakefield, all stressed Ireland's potential as a supplier of wheaten bread to England, Irish farmers themselves were mainly concerned about oats, a more extensive crop than wheat and a more important export.[8] And though in Dublin, Limerick, Cork, and Wexford, the merchants supported the agriculturists' campaign, Irish merchants and millers were privately less anxious to exclude imports than they were to remove the restrictions that prevented exports to lucrative markets in the New World. James Conolly, a Dublin corn merchant, thought that 'if anything could be done in our getting a preference in supplying the West India market, it would serve our mills essentially...But I think it would not only be very wrong but also very dangerous to Hint even at in the Corn Bill.'[9] He therefore opposed every claim for excessive import duties 'lest it should endanger the Bill altogether', and was delighted when in May 1814 the export clauses were withdrawn from the projected Corn Bill and the bounties and duties on export abolished separately.[10]

6. McDonnell to Conolly, 30 Nov. 1813, Foster /Massereene MSS. D562/15637; Dublin and Waterford Merchants' memorials, ibid. D562/15638-9; Foster to Sheffield, 5 Dec. 1813, ibid. D207/54/46.
7. CSC, *Report from the Select Committee appointed to Enquire into the Corn Trade of the United Kingdom*, 1813. Exportation was currently prohibited because prices were too high. Parnell also wished to protect food supplies by prohibiting distillation from corn when prices were high; and to encourage distillers to consume inferior grain, unfit for export, by prohibiting distillation from sugar when prices were low.
8. Conolly to Foster, 10 May 1814, Foster/Massereene MSS. D562/15678. In 1815 Ireland exported 598,000 qrs. of oats to Britain and only 190,000 qrs. of wheat and wheaten flour; in 1816 the figures were 684,000 and 122,000.
9. Loc.cit.
10. Conolly to Foster, 20 Dec. 1813, 11, 12 and 21 May 1814, ibid. D562/15646, 15679-81.

In 1814 the protectionist movement was dominated not by Irish but by Scottish landlords, who had been alarmed by the fall in price that followed the previous year's bumper harvest.[11] The proprietors of over-capitalized and infertile soils, as for example in East Lothian, claimed first that they *needed* protection owing to inferior resources, and then that they *deserved* it because of their heroic efforts to improve on nature. As in Ireland, they were likely to be most concerned about oats, but Scotland was different in the bitter way that the corn question divided town and countryside, producers and consumers. Of the first 120 petitions presented against the agriculturists' claims in 1814, 101 came from Scottish towns and burghs. This urban opposition was even more ferocious than in England, and was sometimes accounted for by the theory that whereas, under the English system of poor relief, wages could be expected to advance with the cost of subsistence, in Scotland they tended to fall as food became more expensive. For without relief, labourers had to work longer hours to maintain their living standards, and this in turn reduced the demand for labour and its price.[12]

At this time the English movement for protection was severly localized. Agitation was confined to the Fens, to the areas around Ely and Wisbech, and the nearby heavy clays and gravels. It was a region with much poor land ('farmed entirely by effort of capital'),[13] many insolvent country bankers and small farmers in arrears, facing eviction,[14] but it was also the scene of great wartime enclosures, reclamations, drainage and new cultivation — an object of national self-congratulation. When in February 1815 the ports shut to all grains except oats, frantic deputations were organized to save that 'staple article of the Fens'.[15] Elsewhere, during 1814, despite pockets of inferior land and protectionist enthusiasm, distress

11. See Table 2 below, pp. 7-8.
12. Milne and Lauderdale to LSC, *Reports from the Lords' Committees on the state of the Growth, Commerce and Consumption of Grain, 1814*, 50-1, 83-5.
13. Wakefield to CSC, *Report from the Select Committee on Petitions relating to the Corn Laws of this Kingdom*, 1814, 40.
14. Lord Ernle, *English Farming, Past and Present* (1936), 322-4; L. S. Pressnell, *Country Banking in the Industrial Revolution* (1956), 470-3; Maltby to Hardwicke, 4 Feb. 1815, Hardwicke MSS. 35700 ff. 312-13; Peppercorn to Whitbread, May 1814, Whitbread MSS.
15. Rayner to Hardwicke, 23 Feb. 1815, Hardwicke MSS. 35700 f. 350; Orton to Hardwicke, 1 Feb. 1815, ibid. f. 306; Linton to Hardwicke, 21 May 1814, ibid. ff. 189-91; Jackson to Hardwicke, 26 Feb. 1815, ibid. ff. 351-2.

TABLE 1

Legislation and proposed legislation on wheat to 1815

	Foreign wheat p.qr.	North American colonial wheat p.qr.
1773 Corn Law		
Export:	Prohibited at or above 44s. 5s. bounty under 44s.	
Import:	6d. duty at or above 48s. 17s. duty at 45s. to 47s. 22s. duty at and under 44s.	
1804 Corn Law		
Export:	prohibited above 54s. free at 49s. to 54s. 5s. bounty at or under 48s.	
Import:	7½d. duty at or above 66s. 3s. 1½d. duty at 63s. to 65s. 30s. 3¾d. duty under 63s.	7½d. duty at or above 56s. 3s. 1½d. duty at 53s. to 55s. 30s. 3¾d. duty under 53s.

This Act rarely operated until after the bumper harvest of 1813.

1806: Anglo-Irish corn trade made free

1813 Select Committee (Parnell's) proposals

Export:	prohibited above 90s. 2d. free at or below 90s. 2d.	
Import:	6d. duty above 135s. 2d. 2s. 6d. duty at 105s. 2d. to 135s. 2d. 24s. 3d. duty below 105s. 2d.	The preference on colonial grain to cease, and the same duties to apply

Price levels at which these duties would operate were to be reviewed annually, with reference to averages over the previous twenty years.

May 1814, Parnell's proposal

Import:	6d. duty above 87s. 2s. 6d. duty at 84s. to 87s. 24s. 3d. duty below 84s.	6d. duty above 77s. 2s. 6d. duty at 74s. to 77s. 24s. 3d. duty below 74s.

May 1814 Corn Bill (based on Huskisson's proposal)

Import:	1s. duty at or above 86s.	6d. duty at or above 86s.
	Duty to fall by 1s. for every 1s. rise in price	
	24s. duty at or below 64s.	12s. duty at or below 64s.

All corn to be admitted freely to warehouses.

1814: All bounties and restrictions on export repealed.

January 1815: Vansittart proposed a fixed 8s. duty on imports

1815 Corn Law

Import:	free at or above 80s. prohibited below 80s.	free at or above 67s. prohibited below 67s.

All corn to be admitted freely to warehouses

(Appropriate duties were fixed for rye, barley, and oats for each of the above proposals.)

TABLE 2

Corn prices 1812-30

	wheat		barley		oats	
1812	126	6	66	9	44	6
1813	109	9	58	6	38	6
1814	74	4	37	4	25	8
1815	65	7	30	3	23	7
1816	78	6	33	11	27	2
1817	96	11	49	4	32	5
1818	86	3	53	10	32	5
1819	74	6	45	9	28	2
1820	67	10	33	10	24	2
1821	56	1	26	0	19	6
1822	44	7	21	10	18	1
1823	53	4	31	6	22	11
1824	63	11	36	4	24	10
1825	68	6	40	0	25	8
1826	58	8	34	4	26	8
1827	58	6	37	7	28	2
1828	60	5	32	10	22	6
1829	66	3	32	6	22	9
1830	64	3	32	7	24	5

A. Annual average prices in *s. d.* of corn per Imperial quarter.
Source: B. R. Mitchell and P. Deane, *Abstract of British Historical Statistics,*
488-9.

	1812	1813	1814	1815	1816	1817	1818	1819	1820
Jan	105 9	119 10	78 2	62 1	52 10	104 1	84 10	79 3	64 0
Feb	105 2	120 0	77 4	63 2	55 6	101 10	84 10	80 0	64 10
Mar	112 5	121 9	77 3	67 3	55 4	102 4	84 8	79 1	69 0
Apr	125 5	120 10	75 8	70 1	60 2	103 3	89 0	75 10	69 4
May	132 6	117 10	69 7	70 4	73 7	105 4	87 5	72 3	70 0
June	133 10	117 10	69 10	69 2	74 11	112 8	83 7	68 10	69 10
July	144 6	116 3	68 4	67 10	74 0	102 4	86 6	74 3	70 0
Aug	152 3	112 6	73 8	68 10	82 1	86 5	81 3	75 0	72 5
Sept	136 6	100 1	78 6	63 7	85 11	78 8	81 9	71 7	67 10
Oct	113 7	93 11	75 5	57 9	90 10	77 5	81 10	66 10	58 9
Nov	121 6	86 2	73 5	56 6	98 10	80 4	82 5	67 6	57 6
Dec	121 0	74 11	70 4	55 7	103 7	84 0	80 8	66 3	54 6

	1821	1822	1823	1824	1825	1826	1827	1828	1829
Jan	54 0	48 8	40 4	59 8	66 5	60 3	53 6	50 0	72 3
Feb	53 4	48 6	40 8	65 10	66 0	59 3	53 6	50 6	70 3
Mar	53 10	46 0	47 10	65 6	67 6	55 7	55 8	51 9	65 2
Apr	53 2	44 7	50 8	64 10	67 3	59 8	56 2	54 8	68 0
May	51 10	46 4	59 4	63 1	68 9	58 9	57 0	55 3	67 5
June	51 8	43 10	61 4	62 9	68 6	57 0	58 11	54 9	68 5
July	51 0	43 1	59 6	60 2	68 0	56 7	59 6	54 0	64 7
Aug	55 0	41 10	58 10	57 10	67 9	56 9	57 11	59 2	64 4
Sept	62 3	39 8	53 10	55 4	66 7	55 6	55 0	58 1	62 1

Table 2 cont.

	1821	1822	1823	1824	1825	1826	1827	1828	1829
Oct	60 1	39 0	47 4	59 2	64 6	54 5	51 1	69 7	56 0
Nov	54 10	38 10	50 3	64 8	65 2	55 3	50 11	73 0	54 8
Dec	49 0	38 11	52 0	64 3	63 0	55 8	50 2	71 8	55 4

B. Monthly prices in *s. d.* of wheat per Winchester quarter.
Source: Tooke and Newmarch, *History of Prices*, ii, 390.

was never sufficiently general to ruin the tradesmen, and many country towns in these other corn-growing parts of England petitioned, along with the industrial north, against increased protection. Suffolk and Norfolk were enjoying full crops; Essex, Sussex, Gloucestershire, Wiltshire, and Devon were to remain fairly contented until the distress spread to mixed farms in 1816; in Somerset arable farmers were less discomforted than graziers; John Benett complained that Hunt was able to raise a clamour against the Bill in Wiltshire 'because this is a manufacturing county';[16] landlords in Surrey and Cheshire petitioned against higher protection; and substantial county meetings were summoned in Kent and Hampshire to contradict earlier, smaller petitions in its favour. With high over-all yields from the previous crop, distress was acute only in low-yield areas suffering from the internal competition of superior soils. By 1815 the English movement for protection had become rather more widespread. A mediocre harvest and renewed importation had led to a combination of low yields and low prices, and to more general suffering from external, that is foreign, competition.[17] But as a Canningite M.P., William Huskisson, observed, most English farmers still looked for succour to a renewal of the war rather than to a rigorous corn bill.[18]

For Parnell, protection was not 'merely to protect the farmer', but rested on the 'merits of one of two theories of political economy'.[19] All the other agricultural leaders were

16. Benett to Hardwicke, 20 Feb. 1815, ibid. 35700 ff. 342-3
17. In 1815 petitions purported to represent humble farmers or occupiers more frequently than in 1814, but this development may have simply been the result of artifice: 'Perhaps it would be better to confine the style of the Petition to Farmers only without including owners of Land.' Leworthy to Hardwicke, 24 June, 1815, ibid. 35700 ff. 301-2.
18. Huskisson to Canning, 27 Mar. 1815, CP 67.
19. 'The Substance of the Speeches of Sir Henry Parnell on the Corn Laws', *The Pamphleteer*, iv (1814), 136-7. Parnell was alienated from most of his protectionist allies. See Foster to Sheffield, 5 Dec. 1813, Foster/Massereene MSS. D207/54/46 and below, p. 20.

brazenly empirical. The attitude of Lord Sheffield, a past
President of the Board of Agriculture, who had recently 'got
rid of' all his Sussex tillage, was typical: 'I know nothing
of Ricardo, nor of Hume, nor of any of the other writers,
nor of their works.' [20] They had no understanding of the
theoretical opposition to protection, and little of the government's reasons for supporting it. Often marginal farmers
themselves, they could not appreciate Ricardo's criticism
that the Bill ignored the rent implications of marginal land.
And whereas the government justified protection by the need
to safeguard supplies of wheat, most of the agriculturists who
clamoured for support concentrated on oats. Their two main
arguments were subjective and inconsistent — that the natural
pre-eminence of agriculture entitled it to special, inequitable
treatment, and, conversely, that the protection already
granted to manufactures should equitably be extended to
agriculture. They insisted that wages were regulated less by
the cost of subsistence than by the demand for labour, the
greater part of that demand depending on agriculture; and
also that British farmers required nursing against the competition of lightly taxed 'continentals'. But their predilection
for high prices conflicted with their public declarations in
favour of expanding British production. The secretary of
the Board of Agriculture, Arthur Young, giving evidence to
a parliamentary committee, implied that the exclusion of
foreign corn would enhance production at home; privately,
however, he warned the Board's President, Lord Hardwicke,
that they must restrain applications for fresh enclosure.[21]
James Stuart-Wortley was aware that farmers on good land
were indifferent to higher protection because they stood to
gain more from the decultivation of poorer soils,[22] and
Benett attributed the hostility of tenants in Wiltshire to the
same motive:

20. Sheffield to Young, 5 Mar. 1815 and 20 Jan. 1814, Young MSS. 35132
ff. 336-7 and 7-9.
21. CSC, *Report on Petitions relating to the Corn Laws*, 1814, 86; Young to
Hardwicke, 7 Feb. 1815, Hardwicke MSS. 35700 ff. 318-19.
22. H. of C., 8 Mar. 1815, 1 PD, xxx. 56.

We have comparatively few small farms in Wiltshire, and our farmers as well as myself know, that the check to cultivation which must be occasioned by the ruin of the poor farmers in other counties, must at some time, not far distant, enable those men who can afford to hold their corn to obtain prices far above their wishes.[23]

Cynics observed that many agriculturists hoped for inadequate harvests, so long as they were not so slight as to open the ports, in order to maximize prices. In short, the farming interest was divided between those on poor soils who needed high prices in order to avoid decultivation, and those on good soils who connived at decultivation in order to keep up prices.

The Politics of Protection, 1814-15

Ministers held aloof from the protectionist movement for as long as possible. Liverpool and Castlereagh had persuaded Parnell not to press his claims in 1813 for fear of alienating the industrial north.[24] They were even less inclined to commit themselves after petitions had begun to flood in on either side of the question in 1814. So after parliament had proved unable to choose between Parnell's resolutions and a proposal by Huskisson for a graduated or sliding scale of duties at a lower, unprohibitive level, Liverpool reluctantly consented to the appointment of further select committees.[25] Unlike Parnell's, these committees inquired thoroughly and impartially into the recent history of agricultural practices and improvements, prices and costs. The Lords' Committee made no specific recommendation, despite the protectionism of its chairman, Lord Hardwicke, and the active canvasses of Lord Sheffield, Sir John Sinclair, and Lord Lauderdale.[26] The Commons' Committee, which included members with business, trade, and industrial interests, such as Patrick Milne (chairman), Samuel Scott, Kirkman Finlay, Henry Thornton, and Sir James Shaw, concluded that 80s. per quarter for wheat would remunerate the cultivators of average quality land, and added that cold clays and poorer

23. Benett to Hardwicke, 20 Feb. 1815, Hardwicke MSS. 35700 ff. 342-3; Barnes, op. cit. 144-5.
24. Parnell to Liverpool, 20 May 1814, LP 38257 ff. 312-14; Liverpool to Canning, 14 Oct. 1813, ibid. 38568 ff. 41-3.
25. Liverpool to Parnell, 21 May 1814, LP 38257 ff. 314-15.
26. Hardwicke MSS. 35700 passim.

soils, which contributed so much to the nation's food supply, would require a greater price.[27]

Liverpool still hesitated. Privately, Sheffield deplored his 'miserable apprehension of the possible loss of a little popularity among what Burke used to call the swinish multitude'. Sinclair warned him that benevolent neutrality was not enough. Parnell, whose main contact in official circles was the Chancellor of the Irish Exchequer, Vesey Fitzgerald, insisted that corn be made a 'cabinet question', otherwise it would founder beneath the violent prejudice of the manufacturers. Even Hardwicke, who attributed the price fall more to 'a depression of spirits among the farming Interest' than to 'the quantity imported', now for the first time demanded that the government take the question up itself.[28] Liverpool succumbed, possibly because he thought that by seizing the initiative, even at this late stage, he could moderate the protectionists' subversive demands. He may also have hoped to buy support for his financial plans. He had apparently been 'frightened out of the property tax'[29] by a series of commercial and agricultural demonstrations and by the embarrassing consequences of his fiscal *pourparlers* with provincial businessmen.[30] But he refused to jettison any more of the wartime taxes, and had therefore to contend 'for what will be a war expenditure in time of peace.'[31]

27. CSC, *Report on Petitions relating to the Corn Laws*, 1814, 4-5.
28. Sheffield to Hardwicke, 30 Nov. 1814, Hardwicke, MSS 35651 ff. 178-9; Sinclair to Sidmouth, 29 Jan. 1815, Sidmouth MSS. 152 (1815-16); Parnell to Hardwicke, 27 Jan. 1815, Hardwicke MSS. 35700 ff. 303-4; Hardwicke to Young, 6 Feb. 1815, Young MSS. 35132 ff. 310-12; Sheffield to Foster, 19 Jan. 1815, Foster/Massereene MSS. D207/54/15; Parnell to Vesey Fitzgerald, 2 June 1814, Fitzgerald MSS. 7831 pp. 113-14.
29. Huskisson to Canning, 14 Feb. 1815, CP 67.
30. *Morning Chronicle* and *Courier*, 12, 13, 20 and 24 Jan. 1815; Huskisson to Canning, 20 Jan. 1815, CP 67; Canning to Huskisson, 28 Feb. 1815, HP 38740 ff. 79-81; Liverpool to Canning, 28 Dec. 1814, CP 69; Bishop Tomline of Lincoln to Rose, 20 Jan. 1815, Rose MSS. 42773 ff. 101-2; Albemarle to Coke, 27 Dec. 1814, A. M. W. Stirling, *Coke of Norfolk and His Friends* (1912), 353.
Richard Hart Davis and John Gladstone had assured the government that the businessmen of Bristol and Liverpool would stomach one year's extension of the tax, but this roused energetic local dissent. For Lord Liverpool's correspondence with Davis, see LP 38260 ff. 331-2, 351-2, 356-7, 362-4, 373-4; and see S. G. Checkland, *The Gladstones. A Family Biography, 1764-1851* (1971), 75-6.
31. Liverpool to Castlereagh, 16 Jan. 1815, Wellington, *Supplementary Despatches, Correspondence, and Memoranda, 1797-1818* (1858-72), ix, 538-9.

Possibly he agreed to sponsor corn in order to win agricultural votes against a parliamentary opposition that would no
longer be restrained by wartime patriotism from assaults on
taxation.

Once Liverpool had decided to adopt the corn question,
he did his best to restrain rural demonstrations that could
only provoke a more vociferous response from the towns. He
also hoped, by carrying a measure through swiftly, to
forestall demagogues like Francis Burdett and James Shaw,
Lord Mayor of London, in their efforts 'to incite a clamour
amongst the people'.[32] At this point Huskisson became a
crucial figure in decision-making. After composing sections of
the Commons' Committee report,[33] he had taken office in
August 1814 as First Commissioner of Woods and Forests. In
February 1815 he was summoned to London for long, urgent
discussions with the Chancellor of the Exchequer, Nicholas
Vansittart, Vice-President of the Board of Trade, Frederick
Robinson, Earl Bathurst of the Colonial Office, and George
Rose, Secretary of the Treasury. It was here that Liverpool
and Huskisson forged a 'cordial' and lifelong alliance on
economic policy, and it was in deference to Huskisson's
sliding scale that Vansittart abandoned a far-sighted and
liberal scheme for 'an invariable protecting duty, operating
at high prices as well as low', of about 8s. per quarter. At
least this would have obviated the complex problem of computing a national average price for corn.[34]

A final decision on the proposed measure was left to two
'very full' inter-party meetings on 11 and 14 February, at
Fife House, the Prime Minister's London home.[35] Liverpool,
Huskisson, Vansittart, Bragge Bathurst, Charles Long, S. R.
Lushington, Charles Arbuthnot, George Rose, Long

32. Liverpool to Wellington, 28 Feb. 1815, ibid. ix. 582; Liverpool to Clancarty,
28 Feb. 1815, LP 38573 ff. 8-10; Simpson to Sidmouth, 4 Mar. 1815, Sidmouth
MSS. 152 (1815-16).
33. H. of C., 18 Feb. 1822, 2 PD, vi. 507.
34. Vansittart to Huskisson, 19 Jan. 1815, HP 38740 ff. 42-3. For this problem,
see below, p. 102.
35. *Courier* and *Morning Chronicle*, 13 and 15 Feb. 1815; *The Times*, 14 and 15
Feb. 1815. These were not cabinets as suggested in W. D. Jones, *'Prosperity'*
Robinson. The Life of Viscount Goderich, 1782-1859 (1967), 55. Professor
Jones endeavours to play down Huskisson's influence in 1815 in order to stress
Robinson's importance, but he also tries to saddle Huskisson with responsibility
for a 'reactionary' bill in order to strengthen Robinson's relative claims to be the
father of free trade.

Wellesley and Wellesley Pole represented government; Charles Callis Western, John Newport, Henry Bankes, Lords Lascelles and Lauderdale led the agriculturists. Liverpool began by explaining that the median of what the various committee witnesses had said would be a 'fair protecting price' was 84s. He then suggested that parliament should aim to secure rather less than this, to take account of the intervening decision not to renew the property tax. After a long discussion, 80s. was selected,[36] rather than 75s., but when Liverpool recommended the sliding scale of duties as the best way to achieve 80s., the agriculturists opted instead, under Western's guidance, for a 'contingent prohibition' — that is, a complete ban on imports while British wheat was below 80s., with duty-free importation at 80s. and above.[37] In return, the agriculturists had to stomach the government's determination to allow free warehousing at all times and to admit colonial wheat at only 67s. John Foster, an Irish leader with influence in ministerial circles, may have originated the idea of contingent prohibition.[38] Robinson, who was to handle the bill in parliament, also favoured it, wherefore with some misgivings Liverpool and Huskisson adopted it.[39] It was a novel device but a less radical departure from principle than is often supposed. All corn laws from 1773 to 1804 had imposed prohibitory duties at low prices and nominal duties at high, with just a very small mezzanine stage between the two. The new bill merely abandoned the mezzanine and substituted statutory for virtual prohibition at one time, and perfect freedom for minimal restraint at another. The abandonment of duties followed logically from the cessation of bounties — though for the sake of symmetry, exports should

36. 80s. p. qr. was roughly the average of the previous twenty years, and much less than most agriculturalists had demanded. Lower levels were stipulated for the other grains.
37. Huskisson to Wodehouse, 25 Jan. 1820, HP 38742 ff. 3-5.
38. MS memorandum, 'Amendment for Corn Bill, 6 June 1814', Foster/Massereene D562/9072 A-B; Conolly to Foster, 21 May 1814, ibid. D562/15681; Conolly to Foster, 6 Jan. 1814, Chilham MSS. T2519/4/1467. Barnes, op.cit. 130 and C. R. Fay, *The Corn Laws and Social England* (1932), 41, attribute this new device to a recommendation of the 1814 Commons' Committee, but in fact the report of that Committee merely opined (page 7) that even if the price at which foreign corn might be imported duty free were raised from 63s. to 80s., such corn would still be available when this country needed it.
39. Huskisson in H. of C., 18 Feb. 1822, 2 PD, vi, 507; Robinson in H. of C., 8 Mar. 1815, 1 PD, xxx, 73-4; B.T. 5/24, 52-3.

have been disallowed while corn was above a certain level.

The Fife House talks secured the support of all Irish M.P.s and 'almost all' the Whig gentry. Opposition leaders were indignant. The *Morning Chronicle* denounced the back-bench, back-stairs 'compact', Alexander Baring the 'sort of legislative committee' and George Tierney the 'unconstitutional kind of rehearsal'.[40] Baring led a vocal opposition of mainly business and radical members, but the bill nevertheless passed with huge majorities.[41] Ministers might not have persisted had they anticipated the extent of urban opposition outside parliament; once the mob had taken to violence and window-breaking, however, they resolved not to yield to clamour.

If the lamentable effects which resulted from the tumults that took place between the 12th and the 17th [of March], could have been fore-seen, it is probable that the question would not have been agitated; but after the discussions had proceeded for several days in the House of Commons, the very circumstance of those tumults, and unjust attacks on individuals, made it difficult to recede.[42]

So while popular disaffection may have influenced the government's future outlook, inclining them to refuse agricultural demands five years later, its immediate effect was to harden ministerial support for protection, and even to help reconcile George Rose, who had hitherto been a leading antagonist. By contrast, the corn question still divided the Whigs. Lauderdale was the bill's 'secret instigator and champion',[43] Newport, Coke, Western, Egremont, Ponsonby, and most of the Irish and squirearchical Whigs supported it. But several Whig peers, including Buckingham, King, and Carlisle, protested formally, while Brougham, Horner, Hamilton, Baring, the *Edinburgh* reviewers, and that 'implacable enemy' of corn bills,[44] Lord Grenville, all joined the radicals in denunciation. Whitbread 'stood alone' against the Bill 'even in the opposition county of

40. H. of C., 15 Feb. 1815, 1 PD, xxix 784, 787.
41. For the debates see Barnes, op.cit. 134-9 and W. Smart, *Economic Annals of the Nineteenth Century, 1801-20* (1910), 445-60. The mercantile and manufacturing opposition led by Baring argued that the proposed law would raise wages and so reduce exports. It was unable to lean extensively on the influential publicist Ricardo, who believed (just as gloomily) that profit margins rather than exports would narrow under pressure from wages. G.S.L. Tucker, *Progress and Profits in British Economic Thought, 1650-1850* (1960), 173-4.
42. Hardwicke to [?], n.d., Hardwicke MSS. 35700 ff. 374-5. See Coker to Sidmouth, 13 Mar. 1815 and Sidmouth to Coker, 15 Mar. 1815, Sidmouth MSS. 152 (1815-16).
43. Holland, *Further Memoirs of the Whig Party 1807-21* (1905), 215.
44. Grenville to Holland, 5 Jun. 1814, HHP 51531 provisional ff. 86-7; J. Clive, *Scotch Reviewers: the 'Edinburgh Review', 1802-15* (1957), 130-1.

Bedford',[45] and Tierney, lamenting the zeal with which 'the great body of our patriots' defied 'the voice of the people' and supported protection, predicted that corn would deal a 'finishing blow' to the party.[46] Not for the last time, Whig dissarray in parliament encouraged the ministry to bide the pelting of the storm without.

The administrative rationale of protection

The landed interest regarded the new Corn Law as a permanent (or at least long-term) endeavour to maintain prices; ministers related it specifically to the transition that had to be made from war to peace, and from a depreciated paper currency to a metallic standard. The influence of bullionism on the motives behind the Corn Law was obscured by the fact that the currency question was less controversial in 1814-15 than it had previously been. For despite an increase in note issues, the exchanges had improved while silver and gold had approximated to paper. This rather discredited the bullionist doctrine that an increased circulation invariably tended to depreciation.[47] It seemed that the Bank would soon be able to resume cash payments, suspended since 1797, and the matter was hardly raised in the corn debates. Huskisson and Parnell were unrepentant, however, and an ardent bullionism contributed to their protectionist theories.

Britain emerged from war with an excessive paper circulation and artificially high prices, the latter caused partly by the former and partly by the protection that the Continental System had afforded. Huskisson felt that, with the loss of military demands on the economy, Britain must retreat from depreciation and inflation, but should only do so gradually since a too rapid declension of demand might cause widespread stagnation. So long as paper remained below par, Parliament should emulate the effects of Napoleon's blockade in order to safeguard capitals invested in the war effort. This would stabilize economic relationships, both internally

45. *Courier*, 30 Jan. 1815.
46. Tierney to Holland, 27 Mar. 1815, HHP 51584 provisional ff. 54-5.
47. W. Jacob, *Considerations on the protection required by British agriculture, and on the influence of the price of corn on exportable productions* (1814), 191-3. Goderich in H. of L., 25 May 1827 2 PD, xvii. 991.

and externally, by slowing down the inevitable process of deflation. For while such artificial expedients continued as the Bank restriction, a huge national debt (about £860,000,000 in 1815) and wartime levels of taxation, it was essential to preserve the farmer's natural wartime protection if capital were not to quit corn for pasture or even leave agriculture altogether.[48] Not to protect corn now would be actively to discourage it. By tiding them over the transition, protection would give even the smallest farmers time to adjust leases and costs, while the government set about rectifying the condition of the circulation, the debt and taxation. Therefore, in 1815, despite his bullionist longings, Huskisson supported an extension of the restriction on cash payments, on condition that the Bank at once begin to curtail its issues in preparation for resumption.[49]

Vansittart openly defended the Corn Bill as a stepping-stone from artificiality to normalcy[50] (though, having obtained it, he was to be chary about taking the necessary steps). Huskisson never announced the Bill's transitional nature publicly, but in March 1815, after Napoleon had quit Elba and European war had broken out again, Huskisson confided to Canning that the sudden fall of prices during the brief wintry peace had been

a great inconvenience to all the active capital of the country — it is one of the difficulties which, in our artificial system, and with our debt, peace was sure to produce to a certain degree. Had peace continued, some management would have been necessary (as in the Corn Bill) to bring things gradually to their level, and to prices approximating to those of other countries.[51]

48. Huskisson in H. of C., 16 May and 6 June 1814, 1 PD, xxvii. 920-1 and 1095-6.
49. Horner was understandably afraid that the new Corn Law would disguise 'the magnitude of that evil', the Bank restriction. Horner to Malthus, 12 Feb. 1815, L. Horner, *Memoirs and Correspondence of Francis Horner* (1843), ii. 234. And Baring in H. of C., 27 Feb. 1815, 1 PD, xxix. 1077, warned that if the Corn Bill passed, Britain 'would never return to a money circulation'. Malthus thought that the time had become more ripe for agricultural protection since 1814, because the improved exchanges and fall in the price of gold had given the currency 'a fair prospect of permanence' at last. T. R. Malthus, *The Grounds of an Opinion on the Policy of restricting the Importation of Foreign Corn* (1815), 8.
50. H. of C., 17 May 1814, 1 PD, xxvii. 947-8.
51. Huskisson to Canning, 27 Mar. 1815, CP 67. Ministers considered the possibility of bringing "things" down gradually by adjusting the prohibition level every 5 or 7 years with reference to the movement of prices.

Agriculturists, had they read this, would have been dismayed by Huskisson's admission that the Corn Bill was an expedient, its uplifting effect on prices temporary. The Bill's opponents insisted that if importation was to be restricted until wheat at home reached 80s., then wheat would never fall below that level. Most agriculturists agreed and pointed to their outgoings in justification. Both sides were sceptical of the government's claim that 80s. would be a maximum price, and historians have been equally dismissive. Thus C. R. Fay condemned 1815 as 'the one and only serious breach in corn-law policy from beginning to end', traditional policy being to secure a 'just price' between grower and consumer. For D.C. Moore, 'the Corn Laws were predicated on the notion that rural prosperity could only be had on the basis of high arable prices. It was this which lay behind the Act of 1815.'[52] Now as ministers readily conceded, initially the Bill would keep prices above the level that they would fall to without it, but *only* until artificially high rents, costs, taxes, and currency had been corrected. Ultimately, grain need be just dear enough in scarce seasons to compensate farmers for paltry yields (up to a certain point where consumers would require access to foreign supplies), yet low enough in plentiful years to render surpluses competitive abroad, and to compensate producers for cheapness by extensive sales. As English prices gradually descended towards foreign levels, and as cultivation expanded, the second alternative would predominate. The long-term strategy of 1815 was that farmers' profits would accrue from large sales rather than from high prices.

Though radicals called their bluff and landlords took no notice, ministers were quite candid about this. Robinson, who claimed later that he had opposed any increase of protection and had only undertaken the Bill in Parliament to please Lord Liverpool, agreed that it might lift prices temporarily to 80s., but added that, by stimulating Anglo-Irish competition, it would eventually lower prices and rents.[53] Huskisson promised that it would restrict price fluctuations

52. Fay, op.cit., 35; D. C. Moore, 'The Corn Laws and High Farming', *Economic History Review*, 2nd Series, xviii (1965), 544-5. See also, for example, Ernle, op.cit. 255.
53. Jones, op.cit., 54-5; H. of C., 17 Feb. 1815, 1 PD, xxix. 800, 804.

to within 70s. and 80s. — recently they had veered between
55s. and 125s. — and that by keeping Britain independent of
foreign grain, it would prevent high prices. 'To protect the
small farmer', as this bill would do, 'at this moment, is
ultimately to protect the people.' Free imports, on the other
hand, might reduce corn for a year or two, but as small
farmers folded up and marginal land fell to waste, famine
prices would ensue. The only men to benefit would be those
who had profited already — 'overgrown farmers with large
capitals', able to withstand foreign competition and impatient
for the abandonment of other men's farms as guaranteeing
better prices.[54] For Liverpool too, 'the great object was
the interest of the consumer...The present measure...would...
render grain cheaper instead of dearer. The important point
to attain was a steady and moderate price.'[55] Wellesley Pole,
Charles Long, Harrowby, and other official spokesmen all
repeated that 80s. was to be a maximum.[56]

The fall of prices after 1815 does not prove these pro-
nouncements sincere. Country gentlemen like Western also
claimed that protection would reduce prices, yet only next
year they were to be found complaining that prices had not
climbed as expected. That ministers genuinely welcomed the
continued fall of grain, though they might have preferred it
to be less sudden, is proved by subsequent remarks made
privately. Thus in September 1815 Vansittart predicted that
rural distress due to low prices and short credit would 'admit
only of a gradual cure by a general settling down of the prices
of other articles in proportion to those of the produce of the
soil' (beginning with wages) and by exporting surplus grain to
Europe.[57] That winter the Bank's efforts to raise the currency
caused severe monetary pressure and several failures among
country banks and farmers; yet in the very month that food
prices, circulation, and credit were at their lowest (March

54. W. Huskisson, *A Letter on the Corn Laws, to one of his constituents, in 1814*
(1827), 13. W. R. Brock, *Lord Liverpool and Liberal Toryism, 1820 to 1827*
(1941), 219-20. H. of C., 3 Mar. 1815, 1 PD, xxix. 1241-2.
55. H. of L., 15 Mar. 1815, 1 PD, xxx, 181.
56. H. of C., 8 Mar., H. of L., 20 Mar. 1815, ibid. 63, 66-7, 261.
57. Vasnsittart to Castlereagh, 4 Sept. 1815, Vansittart MSS. 31231 ff. 344-57.
Londonderry, *Memoirs and Correspondence of Viscount Castlereagh* (1848-53),
3rd series, iii. 6.

1816), Huskisson explained with satisfaction to Canning that 'now...our prices and currency are restored to their natural value, and to somewhat like a level with the prices of other Countries.'[58] While Lord Sheffield and the landlords dreaded the effect of good harvests on prices, ministers were convinced that the consumers' salvation and the farmers' remuneration both lay in cheap abundance, in yield rather than price. A good crop, even at the existing low prices, as Huskisson said in August 1816, would quickly 'dissipate the general gloom' prevailing on the land.[59] Liverpool was satisfied in September 1816 'that the Prices of Corn are now as they ought to be, and higher than they need be'.[60] Even Sidmouth, who worried annually about deficient harvests, and who had thought at the time that a higher import threshold than 80s. was needed for the purpose of attracting capital to agriculture, did not wish to enhance prices. On the contrary, he told his close friend Sheffield in 1816 that the tenant farmers' only remedy lay in a reduction of rents and costs.[61] As Home Secretary, Sidmouth was responsible for the public peace, and he wanted prices to be steady and moderate, not in order to conserve merchants' and manufacturers' profits, but to keep consumers happy.[62]

The argument that high protection would lower prices was usually based on market factors — an extended home supply and inelastic demand. Parnell also contended, in defiance of the farmers (who generally considered 'high farming' and 'curious cultivation' prohibitively expensive) and also of Adam Smith (who had regarded agriculture as less susceptible than manufactures to economies of scale),[63] that increased investment in crops would raise productivity and lower unit

58. Huskisson to Canning, 13 Mar. 1816, CP 67.
59. Huskisson to Liverpool, 4 Aug. 1816, LP 38191 ff. 102-5.
60. Liverpool to Redesdale, 5 Sept. 1816, Redesdale MSS. D2002/C/23.
61. Sidmouth to Coker, 15 Mar. 1815, G. Pellew, *The Life and Correspondence of Henry Addington, 1st Viscount Sidmouth* (1847), iii, 127; Sidmouth to Sheffield, 21 Jan. 1816, Sidmouth MSS. 152M (1816-17).
62. Sidmouth did not consider whether restrictions on the corn trade would cause manufacturing unemployment; his complaint was simply that high food prices aggravated its dangers.
63. A. Smith, *An Inquiry into the Nature and Causes of the Wealth of Nations* (1776), edited by E. R. A. Seligman (1910), i, 6.

costs, so preparing the farmer for a gradual fall in price.[64]
Parnell is often described as an arch-villain who, 'for fear that
plenty should attain the poor', had instigated the whole
selfish campaign. Yet he had more in common with ministers
than with most other protectionist leaders. For instance, in
February 1814 he wrote to Sinclair (whom he had no cause
to deceive): 'I should hope that this plan for a free export
will lead to such an increased production that we may soon
be able to undersell the foreign farmers in foreign markets
and in time be quite safe without the protection of any law
whatever.'[65] Parnell's protectionism, like ministers', was
transitional, deflationary, and tending to 'increased production'. The last point touches the heart of government
motivation in 1815.

Fear of scarcity, of famine even, dominated official policy
on corn throughout the first half of the nineteenth century.
An administrative determination to ensure 'a sufficiency of
supply at *steady* and *moderate* prices' motivated successive
governments. For hunger had helped to topple feudalism
in France (where Huskisson had lived between 1783 and
1792) and had contributed to *la grande peur de quatre-vingt-
neuf.* Since then, a long war, with its formidable if largely
futile blockade, a precarious peace, a realization that in the
last fifty or sixty years Britain had become a net corn-
importing country, the dramatic growth of population as
highlighted by the first two censuses of 1801 and 1811, and
actual dearths in 1795, 1797, 1800/1, 1812 — in short, the
Revd. Thomas Malthus's terrifying spectre haunted the ministerial imagination. Faced with an eighteenth-century type
problème des subsistances, the government responded in the
legislative tradition of the 'maximum'. But since scarcity was
a past and prospective, not an actual, problem in 1815, and
the Corn Bill was preventive rather than remedial, ministers
were forced in debate to theorize about it in a way that hid
its essential pragmatism. There was theory to hand of course.
Adam Smith had exempted staple food and shipping from

64. D. C. Moore, 'Social Structure, Political Structure, and Public Opinion in
Mid-Victorian England', in R. Robson (ed.), *Ideas and Institutions of Victorian
Britain* (1967), 49-51 and n.
65. Parnell to Sinclair, 24 Feb. 1814, copy Young MSS. 35132 f.33.

the free trade imperative, on grounds of national security. Corn could be highly protected because it was, in Robinson's words, 'entirely contradistinguished from any other article of commerce'[66] — which was the reverse of the agriculturists' favourite contention that the Corn Law should be raised because many manufacturers were already sheltered by high tariffs.

But how could governments insure against famine? In 1815 Liverpool put his trust in autarchy, in a 'policy of rendering ourselves as independent as possible of foreign supply'.[67] Self-sufficiency based on 'a steady home supply' was for Huskisson 'the only safe foundation of steady and moderate prices'. External sources were unreliable, since all of Northern Europe, which was Britain's traditional area of supply, might suffer simultaneously from bad weather and poor harvests. In the scarcity of 1801, Europe had furnished a negligible one-fifteenth of the United Kingdom's total wheat consumption. Even if Europe *were* able to make good a deficit, there might be too few ships to transport all that was needed, or foreign governments might withhold supplies for political reasons. (Ministers did not share Ricardo's confidence in the power of free markets and reciprocal trading to prevent political interference.) Nevertheless, Liverpool's policy of independence was adopted neither for its own sake, nor because dependence would be strategically dangerous in wartime. The latter argument was occasionally put, but even Napoleon had been powerless to wield the starvation weapon effectively. The crux of the argument was that Britain could never *rely* on being able to import enough to remedy a deficiency, and that native corn would always have to supply the bulk of home consumption. Imports would be required from time to time, but should be discouraged in most years, lest English agriculture wilt under habitual competition, placing food supply in constant instead of merely occasional jeopardy. For 'If one quarter of the wheat land of the kingdom was thrown out of cultivation, no foreign supply could possibly make up the deficiency in the quantity of food.'[68]

66. **H. of L., 25 May 1846**, 3 PD, lxxxvi. 1086-7.
67. **H. of L., 15 Mar. 1815**, 1 PD, xxx. 181.
68. Liverpool in H. of L., 20 Mar. 1815, 1 PD, xxx. 262.

Historians miss the point when they condemn Liverpool for being afraid of a bogie, of foreign abundance that hardly existed, or when they defend him on the ground that such abundance did exist after all.[69] It was precisely because Europe could *not* feed England that English cultivation had to be protected and expanded. Such surplus as there was abroad would rarely suffice to fill a deficiency, but would be quite enough to drive down prices, especially since the home grower, never sure how large a foreign surplus would prove to be, was liable to rush his own corn on to losing markets in panic. Autarchy was not to succeed, but this particular argument for it held good until the 1880s, by which time Britain had become much more reliant on overseas sources and on regions with different climatic conditions.

But would not prohibition of imports in normal seasons discourage Continental agriculture and dry up an ultimate source of supply so essential in famine years? The Select Committees of 1814 denied this: habitual discouragement would not reduce the availability of European supplies, when England was *in extremis,* by so much as 'one single bushel'. European (and especially Polish) producers grew wheat solely for export; having few outlets for their surplus but the British market, and an occasional income being preferable to none at all, they would continue to raise wheat, however sporadic the demand in Britain might be. It would soon become clear that this was an arrogant and over-sanguine prediction.

Another assumption was that potentially Britain could feed herself in most years. Opponents like Baring and Grenville disputed this, but statistical crop surveys and catalogues of recent improvements encouraged ministers to hope that with a 'proper stimulus' the nation could, despite Malthus, be self-sufficient.[70] Reversion to the pre-1765 system of restraining imports should help to eliminate those price

69. See below, pp. 292-300.
70. See, for example, the county surveys or 'General Views' conducted under the aegis of the Board of Agriculture; Arthur Young's Norfolk-inspired propaganda; and John Sinclair's two reports, *An Account of the Systems of Husbandry adopted in the more Improved Districts of Scotland* (1809), and *General Report on the Agricultural State and Political Circumstances of Scotland* (1814).

fluctuations which, besides disrupting consumers, had deterred the improving farmer. As one of its members revealed, the
Lords' Committee inquired specifically into farmers' 'capacity to produce an increased supply by a more liberal application of capital, and by improvements in the manner of cultivation'.[71] The Commons' Committee reported that recent
exports of grain (including those from Ireland) had almost
balanced imports, and asserted that so long as no decultivation took place, the nation need never rely on foreign food
except in abnormally unfavourable seasons. An essential key
to this power of supply was Ireland, described by William
Elliot as a 'most fruitful and abundant granary for the
British empire' and by Parnell as potentially 'the granary,
not only of Great Britain, but of the south of Europe'.[72]
Her production had increased steadily since the Anglo-Irish
corn trade was freed in 1806, and Liverpool thought that 'it
was only necessary to permit capital to flow there, and that
there was then no limit to the quantity which might be
furnished from Ireland for the supply of this part of the
United Kingdom.'[73] In return, investment in her agriculture
might even 'civilize and improve' a miserable and lawless
country.

Clearly, whatever it might pretend later, the government
hoped not only to protect *existing* capital and cultivation,
but to take the process of investment and reclamation further
still. Not surprisingly, therefore, discussion centred on the
marginal lands (including most of Ireland), on which the
protectionist movement had originated. The Commons'
Committee reported that a very considerable proportion of

71. **Bridgewater to Ellman, n.d. [1814]**, F. P. Walesby, *Memoir of the late John
Ellman of Glynde, Sussex* (1847), lii.
72. H. of C., 3 Mar. 1815, 1 PD, xxix, 1230; Parnell, 'Substance of Speeches on
the Corn Laws', *The Pamphleteer*, 153.
73. H. of L., 15 Mar. 1815, 1 PD, xxx. 181. See Liverpool to Canning, 16 Feb.
1815, CP 69 and quoted in C. D. Yonge, *The Life and Administration of Robert
Banks, 2nd Earl of Liverpool* (1868), ii. 134-6 (misdated) and Wellington, *Supplementary Despatches*, ix. 564-5: 'if the measure should be adopted, I do not
despair of the United Kingdom being able to feed itself in the course of a few
years, except in very bad seasons. The deficiency of Great Britain may certainly
be made up from Ireland, if due encouragement is given to investing capital in
agriculture in that country.' See Sidmouth to Coker, 15 Mar. 1815, for his belief
in the prospect of 'an ample and independent supply' through capitalization.

wheat was raised on inferior soils, whose loss would greatly
diminish 'the general stock of national subsistence'. Most
witnesses were convinced that, without greater protection,
inferior and recently ploughed land must be abandoned, with
loss of food, capital, and − since poor soils required most
intensive cultivation − employment. The poor's rates would
escalate, especially as deconverted arable could not for several
years revert successfully to pasture. Huskisson believed
that lack of capital, combined with cheapness, had enervated
French society,[74] and though there was no shortage of
capital in England, protection was required (along with better
leasing arrangements and compensation for improvements) to
induce investment in 'high farming'. A highly capitalized
agriculture (leading to high yields, not high prices) would
help to reconcile lords and tenants over that 'grand agrarian
alchymy, high rent', since farmers 'with an adequate capital
for improved agriculture' could comfortably afford to pay
rents triple those of men without.[75] Capital investment could
also 'equalize' the value of good and bad soils, enabling
even the worst to bear a controlled and gradual deflation.[76]
But prices must be kept up in the interim, since it was commonly assumed that even if costs were to fall as rapidly as
prices were doing in 1814, farmers would be psychologically
deterred from improving their lands. 'Even when farmers, by
saving, acquire an increase of capital, they are very sparing in
the application of it to agriculture.'[77] Saving was not
spending, whereas profit-making was; inflation inspired whereas deflation deterred. Arthur Young agreed that cutting
expenses also meant cutting down on production, that 'the
moment the farmer economizes in consequence of the low
price of Corn, from that instant there is not a day that passes,
in which his farm will not suffer'. He uses less manure,
skimps his hoeing, ploughs less deeply: in short, 'It will be
miserably performed, it will not be performed with that

74. H. of C., 23 Feb. 1815, 1 PD, xxix. 1041.
75. CSC, *Report on Petitions relating to the Corn Laws, 1814,* 23.
76. See, for example, land agent Claridge's evidence, ibid. 19-26.
77. Question put to Wakefield, LSC, *Reports on the Growth, Commerce and Consumption of Grain,* 1814, 20.

spirit and energy which a man feels when he can get a price
for his crop...[then] a spirit, a vigour and energy runs through
his whole business...but languor and insufficiency whenever
the price affects him, so that he can have no profit.'[78]

Concern with capitalization and food supply led ministers
to affront the country gentlemen and allow foreign corn to
go on being warehoused duty-free at all times. The warehousing clause, so obnoxious to the gentry, was more than
merely a sop to merchants — 'to offset the impression...that
the change in the existing system was entirely for the benefit
of the landed interest'.[79] Huskisson inserted in the Commons'
Committee report of 1814 a promise that free bonding
would bring capital into the corn trade and make Britain a
deposit for foreign corn passing between northern and
southern Europe. It must 'have at all times a tendency to
keep the price more steady in the home market, and to
afford to the country a security, the best perhaps that, in
the present increased state of our population can be devised,
against the defects of a deficient harvest'.[80] In particular,
Canadian corn, which could only be shipped during the six
ice-free months of the year, should be hoarded for use in
emergency. It would be on hand when needed, yet would
not depress prices and discourage home production when the
harvest was good. Farmers insisted — and Wellington was still
insisting twelve years later — that the mere presence of such
supplies would depress the markets and damp activity.
Western continued to assure Parliament that the country had
no difficulty in feeding itself over a period of time, and that
the government should establish *greniers d'abondance* for
domestic corn only, in order to even out distribution between

78. CSC, *Report on Petitions relating to the Corn Laws*, 1814, 84. While Baring
reversed the argument by claiming that low prices stimulated producers to greater
effort, the Committees went to great lengths to confirm the opinion that *high*
prices were the spur to improvements (and not *vice-versa* as the Ricardian theory
of rent was to suggest). The Committees were also anxious for reassurance that
fear of imports, and not over-abundance at home, was the cause of falling prices
in 1814.
79. Barnes, op.cit. 130.
80. CSC, *Report on Petitions relating to the Corn Laws*, 1814, 8. See Smith, *The
Wealth of Nations*, ii. 40: 'the inhabitants of the country which, by means of
the carrying trade, becomes the magazine and storehouse for the supply of other
countries can very seldom be in want themselves.'

good and bad years, and to minimize the harvest factor on prices. But ministers, who shrank from the responsibility of such Jacobin rationing, maintained that only a free distribution could ensure steady prices, and that since there was always a danger of scarcity, foreign grain must go into the warehouses. So warehousing was 'part of a whole system', and without it the government would have pitched the import threshold below 80s. in 1815.[81] 'The public must learn a great moral lesson', declared Vansittart: 'they must be prepared to see, without dissatisfaction, great quantities of corn stowed in warehouses, and even shipped for exportation'.[82]

The Assize of Bread and the new 'moral economy'

The legislators of 1815 were influenced by Adam Smith's strictures against laws restraining regraters and forestallers. Internal free trade, with full facilities for 'capitalist' middlemen to pursue natural speculations, would adjust supply to demand and stabilize prices. The most important middlemen were millers and bakers, and the Assize of Bread Repeal Bill of 1815 was an important supplement to the Corn Law.[83]

Popular indignation against the Corn Bill was fed by the London Corporation's calculation that with wheat at 80s. the quartern loaf would cost 1s. 4d. Ministers believed that abolition of the Assize, thereby opening up the manufacturing and retailing functions, would make protection of the raw material compatible with a cheap loaf, would 'please all parties', and 'reconcile all interests'.[84] A Select Committee in April 1815, chaired by an independent supporter of the government, Frankland Lewis, and including Huskisson,

81. Jacob to Huskisson, 1 May 1821, HP 38742 ff. 210-23.
82. H. of C., 17 May 1814, 1 PD, xxvii, 947-8. See the evidence of Inglis, Ellis, Giles and Scott to CSC, *Report on Petitions relating to the Corn Laws*, 1814, 114-19 and of Solly to LSC, *Reports on the Growth, Commerce and Consumption of Grain*, 1814, 33-8. Ministers insisted that, without warehouses, corn would simply be bonded in Holland where it would be just as dangerous to farmers without benefiting consumers.
83. The Act of 1815 applied to London only; provincial assizes were not abolished until 1819. Smith, *The Wealth of Nations*, ii. 23-35; Horner to Malthus, 12 Feb. 1815, Horner, *Memoirs and Correspondence*, ii. 233; Whitbread in H. of C., 22 Feb. 1815, 1 PD, xxix. 995.
84. Playfair to Sidmouth, 16 Feb. 1815, Sidmouth MSS. 152 (1815-16).

Robinson, Rose, S. R. Lushington, and T. P. Courtenay, concurred in this assessment and recommended abolition of the Assize. In towns where Assizes were held, magistrates regulated the price or weight of loaves, and the baker's allowance per loaf. The usual practice in London was to vary the price according to the cost of the main ingredient, flour, as declared weekly by the bakers, allowing the latter a fixed 14s. 1d. per sack for their part in processing bread, irrespective of whether the price to the consumer was low or high. Lewis's Committee observed that bakers' returns were unreliable, that the Assize was likely to enhance prices artificially, and that 'more benefit is likely to result from the effects of a free competition in their trade, than can be expected to result from any regulations or restrictions under which they could possibly be placed.' For the Assize gave bakers an interest in high prices:

If 80 Quartern Loaves was the precise quantity of Bread they could at all times make from a sack of Flour, they would have no interest whatever in its general price, either one way or another; but the surplus Bread, whatever may be its amount which they can make above that quantity (and it is stated by various persons to average from two to four loaves) is to them a profit in kind, the value of which must necessarily increase with the price of Bread; and as the high price of Flour which occasions this increase is in no other respect disadvantageous to the Bakers, they have as far as it goes an obvious interest in the high price of Flour...[85]

Worse still, many of the regular, full-time bakers of London were in debt to millers, who had a less ambiguous interest in dear bread. Baking had appealed to men without capital, partly because it demanded little initial expenditure, but mainly because the Assize system protected such men from being undersold by bakers with the resources to pay cash for flour. What was needed was a class of competitive bakers that would be independent of the miller bosses; it was

85. CSC, *Report from the Committee on Laws relating to the Manufacture, Sale, and Assize of Bread*, 1815, 8. By leaving this crucial passage out of his quotation from the Report, Fay was misled into supposing that what upset the Committee was that the allowance system made bakers totally indifferent to prices; and he observed that whereas the 1774 Committee would have approved such indifference, a generation bred on Adam Smith found it unnatural, and looked to competition and enlightened self-interest to reduce prices. *The Corn Laws and Social England*, 47. In fact, the Committee's complaint was that under the allowance system, bakers were interested in pushing prices up, and it recommended repeal of the Assize, not out of free trade ideology, but to remedy this specific abuse.

expected that repeal of the Assize would weed out the more impecunious bakers, and attract into the trade men of substance, who could afford to sell loaves at competitive prices. Several bakers warned the Committee that repeal would allow the 'first men', the 'monied men', to 'get all the trade into their hands' by making a bigger loaf. Little men without capital or credit 'would all go to rack'. When the Committee wished to know whether the collapse of the small baker would 'be of advantage or disadvantage to the Public', one witness observed tartly: 'it would be a disadvantage to the man and his family.'[86]

So agriculture was to be capitalized by protection, baking by competition. Poor farmers would be cosseted, insolvent bakers sacrificed. Inflationary levels would be retained until the dust of war had settled, while a deflationary start was made with the unfortunate bakers. Perhaps this reflects their political impotence, and indicates that after all the government's policy was simply a concession to a selfish élite. On the other hand, bakers stood closest to the consumers, who had to be persuaded that protection was a boon. What cannot be maintained is that repeal of the Assize was part of the transition from a traditional to a dynamic or capitalist 'moral economy' — from an aggregate of local markets, where the problem facing policy-makers was how to distribute subsistence, to a national market in which it was necessary to provide the work and wages that would command subsistence.[87] In fact, middlemen were unfettered in order to expand the agricultural sector, which was still thought to provide the greatest opportunities for additional employment.

In the case of corn, Adam Smith had argued for international protection, internal freedom, free warehousing, and free exportation, commending the 1773 Corn Law in all respects except its bounty. The Corn Law of 1815 was like that of 1773 without the bounty. It was based mainly on Smith and also on a Malthusian concept of demand, on market (not subsistence) theories of wage and rent — and on physiocracy:

86. CSC, *Report on the Manufacture, Sale, and Assize of Bread*, 1815, 55, 96.
87. E. F. Genovese, 'The Many Faces of Moral Economy', *Past & Present*, lviii (1973), 161-8.

If no foreign corn had been imported, the nation would have saved sixty millions sterling. It might be said, that without this importation sixty millions worth of our manufactures would have remained unsold; but then it is not recollected what those sixty millions would have effected if they had been expended in the improvement of our agriculture; or what increased means of purchasing our manufactures they would have given to the agriculturists. If on being laid out at home they had produced the natural effects, then the country would have added to her means of independence, and have created a market of which no external relations could have deprived her.[88]

Castlereagh disparaged an international division of labour — which, as Smith himself had acknowledged, depended on foreign co-operation — arguing that the Corn Law had secured farmers against both foreign competition and 'domestic competition arising from the other modes of using capital', modes to which Britain might be more naturally fitted.[89] On the other hand, Huskisson, Parnell, and their fellow legislators followed a mainly empirical approach, and only really objected to 'the advocates for the theory of an *immediate* free trade'.[90] Their policy was over-sophisticated, attempting to bring down, slowly, prices, costs, and rents which had doubled in wartime, while maintaining the extended margin of cultivation. Even with reliable statistics of production and consumption, and with an industry more readily adaptable than farming to shifts in investment, the attempt would have been quixotic. They hoped to protect farmers by boosting yields, without giving any thought to the dangers of over-production. (Horner noted that, for the intended protection to operate, agriculturists would always have to produce just less than the domestic consumption).[91] And in guarding against the dangers of under-capitalization, they neglected those of excess investment.

88. Huskisson in H. of C., 5 May 1814, 1 PD, xxvii. 723-4. See Parnell, op.cit. 144-5, on the importance of domestic demand to the success of manufactures.
89. Smith, *The Wealth of Nations*, ii. 39.
90. Parnell, 'Substance of Speeches on the Corn Laws', *The Pamphleteer*, 140, 142.
91. Horner to Murray, 18 Jan. 1816, Horner, *Memoirs and Correspondence*, ii. 288.

As for the agriculturists, the Bill was never intended to do what they expected it to do, and their gratification hardly survived the year. After a handsome harvest in 1815, corn prices fell to a nadir in the following March — a 'disaster' that ministers, still blind to the dangers of over-production, obstinately blamed on delays in passing the Bill and on importations that had occurred in the interim. Throughout the kingdom, 1816 was one of the blackest years in agricultural history. The most appalling catalogue of distress, decultivation, arrears, and quittals still came from the Fenlands, where it found an outlet more in bloody riots and outrage than in respectable petitioning. But distress was now overtaking mixed and grass farms, and farmers who, having borrowed less in wartime or possessed of capital and credit, had tided themselves over the difficulties of 1814-15.[92] Hampshire, Sussex, Essex, Norfolk, and Wales were the new leaders of the petitioning movement in 1816. Occupiers of better-quality lands, lukewarm protectionists earlier, now joined the campaign. In Parliament, Western, Brougham, and an agricultural 'improver' from Cumberland — the Whig, John Christian Curwen — kept up a long and unrequited pressure for further protection, mainly in the form of reviving the export bounties (clashing here with Parnell and their Irish allies), abolishing the warehouses and imposing prohibitive duties on other produce besides corn.[93] The debate on agriculture was further reoriented in 1816 by renewed anxieties over the state of the currency.

92. Ernle, op.cit., chapter xv; Western and Brougham in H. of C., 7 Mar. and 9 Apr. 1816, 1 PD, xxxiii. 31-56, 1086-119; G. E. Fussell and M. Compton, 'Agricultural Adjustments after the Napoleonic Wars', *Economic Journal, History Supplement*, iii (1939), 184-204; A. J. Peacock, *Bread or Blood, a study of the agrarian riots in East Anglia in 1816* (1965), passim.
93. Here Western's logical inconsistency was not that he blamed distress on low prices while denying that his policy would raise them (Barnes, op.cit. 159), for he clearly implied that protection would so increase farmers' sales as to compensate them for low unit prices, but rather that while attributing low prices to overproduction, he demanded a policy which would have encouraged still greater production.

II

THE POLITICS OF CASH PAYMENTS

The transition from War to Peace had indeed been attended lately with
such a stagnation of internal trade, such a consequent check to circulation
and credit, such an interruption to all adventures, either in buildings, or
lands, in raw produce or manufactured goods, that all parties (the
annuitants excepted) were dissatisfied and uneasy.
Huskisson to Canning, 27 Mar. 1815, CP 67

Vansittart's 'expedients and ingenious devices'

Successful transition to peace depended on a return to specie
payments, suspended by Pitt in 1797 and due to be resumed
at par six months after a definitive peace treaty had been
signed. However, in February 1815, with gold fetching 89s.
per oz., parliament had postponed resumption for another
year. After Waterloo, gold fell steadily — being at a premium
over paper of less than one per cent by October 1816 — but
only at the cost of severe reductions in the Bank of England's
advances to government and commerce. Scarce money and
country bank failures exacerbated a depression caused by
loss of wartime demand, and affected the language of parliamentary debate. In 1815 agriculturists had been implacable
enemies of merchants and manufacturers; in 1816 a new
monetary theme united all three against classes rarely
mentioned in the previous year—creditors, fundholders, and
officials with incomes fixed while prices had been high. Now
that prices were falling, the country gentlemen and their
temporary allies besought the government to reduce salaries,
taxes, and public expenditure to 1792 levels, and also to quit
its wartime manoeuvres for bolstering stock. Western defined
his campaign for still more protection to agriculture as
essentially 'a drive at the sinking fund', which was keeping
stocks artificially high. Deflationary periods naturally frus-
trate men whose wealth lies in real property, and on this
occasion many landowners, having borrowed or mortgaged in
a depreciated currency (which had itself encouraged loans

and mortgages), now faced having to repay their creditors at par. Landlords feared that, notwithstanding the spread of strict settlements, estates could be 'permanently absorbed by the stockholder'.[1] Deflation would transfer property from 'the holders of land...to the holders of money, from those, in fact, who paid taxes to those who received them'.[2]

This unholy alliance of town and country 'tax payers', though it was to recur in the 1820s, only survived long enough to defeat the property tax, an achievement that grievously disrupted the transition to peace. The tax had not lapsed as planned because of the Hundred Days and renewal of war with France, and in 1816, ministers proposed a two-year extension at half-rate (1s. in the pound). They completely underestimated public hostility to the tax, but even after this had become apparent, Liverpool declined to abandon it graciously, telling a deputation that its repeal 'should be the act of the House of Commons, and...the Government should have nothing to reproach itself with'.[3] A score of counties met to denounce the iniquitous and inquisitive impost, and almost 400 petitions were presented. 'Those taxes are best which pervade consumption', wrote Lord Sheffield, since a 'crampt' property owner might, by private thrift, evade them; whereas assessed taxes, which 'principally answer *ad captandum vulgus*', would hamper a landlords' efforts to maintain the public display that local deference depended on.[4] Merchants and financiers staged protests in the City, and were also prominent at some of the county meetings.[5] Brougham characterized the commotion as a triumph of whig propaganda and organization, but it seems more likely that the campaign was spontaneous and that the Opposition, in agreement for once, simply exploited it. With the Irish ministerialists abstaining in division, and supported by one-half of Dr. Austin Mitchell's 'waverer' M.P.s and by

1. Frankland Lewis in H. of C., 28 Mar. 1816, 1 PD, xxxiii. 701.
2. Western in H. of C., 28 Mar. 1816, ibid. 668.
3. Liverpool's memorandum on Bank advances, HP 38741 ff. 270-7.
4. Sheffield to Sidmouth, 19 Jan. 1816, Sidmouth MSS. 152M (1816-17); Sheffield to Colchester, 19 May 1819, *The Diary and Correspondence of Charles Abbot, Lord Colchester*, edited by Charles, Lord Colchester (1861), iii. 77.
5. As, for example, in Kent. Young to Liverpool, 15 Mar. 1816, LP 38262 ff. 315-16.

one-third of his 'government fringe', the Whigs triumphed (238-201).[6] Ministers promptly surrendered the war malt duties as well. Castlereagh intimated that this would help to reconcile the 'people' to the governing classes' selfish abolition of the property tax; and since the latter would force the government to borrow money anyway, the loss of another £2,000,000 seemed immaterial.[7]

The loss of about £18,000,000 of revenue over two years (1816-17) afforded ministers an excuse (possibly genuine) to delay resumption. Castlereagh announced that postponement 'would go a great way towards remedying the inconveniences which the country would otherwise feel by the rejection of the property tax'. Though ministers would have preferred to redeem public debt and abstain from further loans, thereby affording 'indirect' but material relief, 'Parliament had preferred the direct relief. It would in consequence become necessary to borrow money for the public service, and the extension of the bank restriction act would afford greater facilities for doing so.'[8] Accordingly, resumption was postponed for two years more, and Vansittart's reign of expedients carried over into peacetime.

Vansittart's so-called 'system' as Chancellor of the Exchequer depended on raising money in the City to see him through the year, and his financial policy was geared to keeping the market favourable for loans. In particular, he abused the sinking fund, directing its commissioners to buy stock four times a week with some of the money borrowed from the loan contractors. He argued that these regular purchases were necessary to prevent 'stock-jobbers' from

6. A. Mitchell, *The Whigs in Opposition, 1815-30* (1967), 92-7. See A. Hope-Jones, *Income Tax in the Napoleonic Wars* (1939), 111-25; B. E. V. Sabine, *A History of Income Tax* (1966), 42-6; Smart, *Economic Annals of the Nineteenth Century, 1801-20,* 466-70; F. Shebab, *Progressive Taxation. A Study in the Development of the Progressive Principle in the British Income Tax* (1953), 60-9; A. W. Acworth, *Financial Reconstruction in England, 1815-22* (1925), 27-37; *Annual Register* (1816).
7. H of C., 20 Mar. 1816, 1 PD, xxxiii. 461.
8. H. of C., 9 Apr. 1816, ibid. 1127. See Vansittart to Governor and Deputy of B. of E., 1 May 1816, C.B., Ma 47-8 on the financial adjustments necessary as a result of the property tax repeal.

cornering the market and exploiting those who had to sell;
but his detractors understandably regarded them as crude
devices to keep the market favourable until such time as he
might need to sell exchequer bills at short notice to meet
some pressing need. If, despite such 'management', he were
unable to arrange an advantageous loan, or if he needed
short-term accomodation, or if the circulation became
inadequate for internal needs, the Chancellor would apply to
the Bank of England for an addition to the unfunded or
floating debt.[9] In 1816 for example, he secured an advance
of £9,000,000 in exchequer bills in order to provide for the
year with 'as little pressure as possible upon the money
market'.[10] In 1817 he again 'made good' a deficit, estimated
at over £15,000,000, by augmenting the floating debt,[11]
though critics urged him to suspend a useless sinking fund
that was almost large enough to eliminate that deficit. By
such mysterious 'expedients and ingenious devices' did the
Chancellor succeed in 'balancing' his budgets without making
drastic inroads into patronage and other public spending.[12]
He was sanguine that by keeping up the 3½ per cents, he
would soon be able to reduce the 5 per cents to 4, and that
such gradual debt redemption would slowly make straight
the way for cash payments. But in practice the strategy
entailed a hand-to-mouth passivity, exemplified by Liverpool's belief that 'the restoration of public credit, the rise

9. Acworth, op. cit. 38-54; Smart, op. cit. 476-81, 559-62; J. H. Clapham, *The
Bank of England* (1944), ii. 64; Vansittart in H. of C., 13 May 1819, 1 PD, xl.
354.
10. Liverpool and Vansittart to Governor and Deputy of B. of E., 16 Jan. 1816,
LP 38262 ff. 252-3; C.B., La 222-4. Initially the Bank agreed to advance £6,000,000
at 4 per cent; then, after the property tax defeat, it agreed to lend another
£3,000,000 at 3 per cent, in return for permission to add £2,910,000 to its capital
of Bank stock, and on condition that during the advance its notes might be
received in payment of revenue. Vansittart to Governor and Deputy of B. of E.,
1 May 1816, C.B., Ma 47-9. Vansittart borrowed £2,500,000 on top of this in
1816 by renewing that amount of exchequer bills.
11. Which included the issue of another nine millions of exchequer bills.
12. For an indication of the government's awareness that retrenchment might
accentuate unemployment and add to the peace-time loss of demand in the economy, see Canning on demobilization in H. of C., 29 Jan. 1817, 1 PD, xxxv.
125-6. The whig-instituted but government-controlled Finance Committee of
1817 led, however, to some genuine retrenchments.

of the funds, and the consequent fall of the interest of money, will afford more relief to the existing distresses of the country, than any other measure of relief which could be adopted.'[13]

By 1818 Vansittart's system was under fire. Pascoe Grenfell, a London merchant, and David Ricardo, a new M.P., were deriding his use of the sinking fund to redeem old debt by creating new. The device had been quite successful in 1817 when the 3 per cents stood at 69 and there was only £40,000,000 of unfunded debt; but in 1818, with the 3s at 78 and £55,000,000 of debt, it involved buying stock in the dearest market while selling in the cheapest. Moreover, the increase of the floating debt, dangerous in itself, precluded interest reduction on the main debt. Huskisson was therefore able to convert the prime minister to the view that there should be either an *efficient* sinking fund, based on actual surplus revenue, or none at all. Furthermore, Vansittart's system required the goodwill and co-operation of the Bank and City financiers, such as Rothschild, Baring, John Irving, Hart Davis, and Goldsmid. For a time the Bank generously allowed the Treasury advances on loans, and purchased exchequer bills or similar government securities at only 3-4 per cent, when it might have earned 5 per cent by discounting mercantile bills of limited duration and more subject to control. Its complaisance struck Whigs and Radicals as proof of an 'ominous and dangerous confederacy', and even Arthur Young despised an administration that was 'in all money matters little better than a Committee of the Bank.'[14] But the Court of Directors was growing impatient. In April 1818 it reproached ministers with their failure to defend the Bank in parliament against Mackintosh's motion inquiring into the extent of forgery.[15] Then in May and July the Court declined to renew any more exchequer bills until the government had repaid £6,000,000 of its advances from the Bank.[16]

13. Liverpool to Canning, 13 Feb. 1816, CP 69, draft in LP 38568 ff. 56-9; Yonge, *Life and Administration of Lord Liverpool*, ii. 253-5.
14. Grenville in H. of L., 21 May 1819, 1 PD, xl. 653; C. Bowdler, *On the punishment of death, in the case of forgery; its injustice and impolicy demonstrated*, 3rd edition (1819), 45-7; Young's diary, 17 Feb. 1816, in M. Betham-Edwards, *The Autobiography of Arthur Young* (1898), 465-6.
15. C.B., Oa 15-19; H. of C., 21 Apr. 1818, 1 PD, xxxviii. 272-84.
16. C.B., Oa 47-8, 101-6.

Similar rebuffs culminated in a bitter showdown in April 1819, when the directors refused to participate in preparations for resumption unless ministers repaid £10,000,000.[17] Worse still, the directors threatened to sabotage the other half of Vansittart's system, which mainly revolved around Nathan Meyer Rothschild. George Harrison, Secretary to the Treasury and its chief contact with the City, reported in alarm that, according to the director Samuel Thornton, the Bank mean to be less generous in future in accommodating *'our* agent' (Rothschild):

Its effect upon our concerns and upon the Stocks may be very considerable — for such a proceeding would drive him in all probability to become a Seller of his Stock...and would inevitably affect the Funds more or less...We could not with justice or propriety be pressing him to extend his accommodations to us, when the Bank refused to accommodate him by Discounts — as he would then be driven to become a Seller to a larger extent to enable him to meet our Wants.[18]

Another threat to the Rothschild alliance came from Huskisson, by now the least dispensable member of the 'little Committee' that settled economic business.[19] Early in 1818 Hart Davis advised Vansittart privately that he might raise £6,000,000 towards his deficit with a 3½ per cent fund, and Rothschild offered up to £15,000,000 for funding exchequer bills. This elicited a trenchant memorandum from Huskisson in which he argued that the Treasury should not still be 'at the Mercy of the Money Market' after three years of peace. He warned of how evil speculators, confident that Vansittart was about to announce another large loan or funding, were selling out in order to drive stock prices down below 80. To defeat these 'sordid' machinations, Huskisson made three suggestions: first, a 'conditional funding' — whereby 3 per cent exchequer bills would be fundable at 80 but not below; second, a loan of just £6,000,000 (which

---

17. *The Times,* 24-27 Apr. 1819; Liverpool in H. of L., 26 Feb. 1822, 2 PD, vi. 713-15; C.T., 22 July and 5 Aug. 1818.

18. Harrison to Vansittart, 1 Oct. 1818, LP 38273 ff. 246-7. See J. R. Torrance, 'Sir George Harrison and the growth of bureaucracy in the early nineteenth century', *English Historical Review,* lxxxiii (1968), 56-8.

19. *The Correspondence of Charles Arbuthnot,* edited by A. Aspinall (1941), 19 n.2.

should be readily forthcoming, since speculators had sold more than that amount 'to create the late depression') for repayment of the contentious Bank advances; and finally, a fresh issue of exchequer bills to meet any further needs. Such a scheme might prevent the funds from rising much above 80 (as they had been doing artificially under Vansittart), but it would keep them steady thereabouts and cool the 'inordinate spirit of gambling'. At 80, many holders would fund outstanding exchequer bills, thereby diminishing the unfunded debt. The state would have to pay a little extra, but 'I consider the getting rid of the excess of the Unfunded debt as so important with a view to a steady high price of the Funds, and the consequent reduction of the fives, as well as to our political ease, and *independence of the money market,* that I should not grudge a small sacrifice for the more speedy attainment of this object.[20] The City responded contumaciously. A 'little' stockbroker warned Liverpool that the capitalists — 'the Jew interest alias Mr. Rothschild' — meant to defeat Huskisson's obnoxious plan, and 'force' government on to the market on their own 'capricious' terms: 'My Lord beware of them, they are your great enemies in finance, ward off a Loan or funding and you'll obtain any terms, do either of a Loan or funding and you are their Victim.'[21]

Towards the resumption of cash payments

Meanwhile Huskisson, eloquently seconded by Canning, was crusading for cash payments. Some historians have regarded bullionism as a theorem whose success in 1819 was to be 'wrested from a reluctant Cabinet' by triumphant Whigs.[22] But there was a stronger and more practical strain, pushing up from the administrative ranks of the tory party. As a youth, in Paris, Huskisson had resigned from 'the Club of 1789' over the Constituent Assembly's decision to issue

20. Huskisson's 'Memorandum: Proposal for meeting the financial demands of the year, 22 Mar. 1818', HP 38741 ff. 202-8; Vansittart to Huskisson, 25 Mar. 1818, ibid. ff. 197-200. E. Halévy, *A History of the English People in the Nineteenth Century: Vol. 2, The Liberal Awakening, 1815-30,* translated by E. I. Watkin, second (revised) edition (1949), 37-8.
21. Anon to Liverpool, 16 and 25 Apr. 1818, LP 38271 ff. 173, 247-8.
22. Halévy, op. cit. 54.

assignats. Later, as vice-chairman of the 1810 Committee,
he had helped Horner to draft the Bullion Report — along
with Parnell and Henry Thornton, the banker — and had
published his celebrated *Question Concerning the Depreciation
of Our Currency* — 'which the monied men of the City will
never forgive him.'[23] Its 'visionary' theories were attacked
by Vansittart's former private secretary, John Charles Herries,
who wrote anonymously and on behalf of 'practical man'.[24]
Opposition Tories accused the Bullion Committee of neglecting internal requirements just when the Continental System
was throwing England back on her own internal resources.
'How small, comparatively, is the external question, and how
absurd would it be for us to suffer our immense transactions
at home to be deranged, by attempting to conform them to
all the violent fluctuations which the enemy's lawless power
can give to the continental exchanges, and, through them, to
the price of bullion.'[25] Encouraged by Castlereagh, with his
'ideal standard' and 'sense of value', and also by backroom
intimates like Herries, Francis D'Ivernois, Jasper Atkinson,
and Henry Beeke, Vansittart won this first battle against the
bullionists. But he earned undying ridicule for his third
resolution of 1811, declaring that promissory notes were
equivalent to coin in public estimation. It was, in truth, as
innocuous (and as wilfully misconstrued) a statement as
Harold Wilson's allusion in 1967 to the pound in one's pocket.
Vansittart simply meant that for *practical* purposes in *internal*
transactions, gold and paper were to be regarded as officially
equipollent. But it seemed to imply an ideological commit-

23. Mallet, MS. Diary, 20 Jan. 1823, iv. 122. But in 1816, Huskisson admitted
that only the continuation of the Bank restriction in 1811 had made Britain's
final glorious efforts against Napoleon possible, and explained that in opposing
its continuation then he had failed to anticipate Wellington's successes.
24. As Commissary-in-chief (until 1817 when he became Auditor of the Civil
List), Herries defended the Bank restriction because it encouraged individuals to
bring into Britain some of the capital which her government was required to pay
out in foreign subsidies. J. C. Herries, *A Review of the Controversy respecting the
High Price of Bullion, and the State of Our Currency* (1811), 43-4, 79-85 and
passim. See F. W. Fetter, 'The Politics of the Bullion Report', *Economica*, new
series, xxvi (1959), 109-11; F. W. Fetter, *Development of British Monetary
Orthodoxy, 1797-1875* (1965), 46.
25. Castlereagh in H. of C., 7 May 1811, 1 PD, xix. 1008.

ment to anti-bullionism, a suspicion strengthened after 1815 by Vansittart's unenthusiastic attitude to cash payments.

In a memorandum of October 1816, Huskisson pleaded for a swift, 'spontaneous' resumption while the exchanges were high, in order, at that time, to *extend* a diminished circulation.[26] In 1817 the Bank did redeem a few of its older notes, and half-heartedly attempted to reduce its issues; but the following year brought poor exchanges and capital efflux due to foreign loans and a bad harvest, and the restriction was prolonged once again (until July 1819). Huskisson recorded his dismay,[27] and then in February 1819 delivered a sustained criticism of Vansittart's financial mysteries. This memorandum called for an early resumption (to be effected by dear money and deflation) — a reduction of funded and unfunded debt (enabling the Bank to collect gold without contracting its mercantile discounts) — a 'financial effort' in the form of new taxes — an end to deficit budgets and sham sinking funds — a return as it were to 'simplicity and truth'.[28] Lord Liverpool was persuaded; already, in August 1818, he had apprised a reluctant Sidmouth that cash payments could hardly be put off beyond another year.[29]

Though many Whigs were anti-bullionist, most of the sincerest bullionists were Whig, creating an impression of 'quasi-coïncidence entre le "parti bullioniste" et l'opposition whig et radicale.'[30] Theirs was an ethical bullionism and Horner, who died of consumption in 1817, almost a sort of martyr. Fox had castigated Pitt's restriction, and paper money symbolized Tory war. Tierney — no political economist — spoke without irony of the Bullion Report as 'his creed', Grenville of the '*sacred* standard of metallic value'

26. 'Memorandum on 1816 Distress, 29 Nov. 1816', HP 38760 ff. 116-24; Huskisson to Castlereagh, 27 Jan. 1817, HP 38741 ff. 91-2.
27. 'Rough draft on coin and currency to Lord Liverpool, 12 July 1818', HP 38741 ff. 242-52.
28. Yonge, op. cit. ii. 382-4.
29. Liverpool to Sidmouth, 6 Aug. 1818, LP 38273 ff. 14-20. Liverpool had himself inherited sound bullionist instincts from his father, the first earl. Charles, Lord Liverpool, *A Treatise on the Coins of the Realm, in a Letter to the King* (1805), 218-29.
30. F. Crouzet, *L'économie britannique et le blocus continental, 1806-13* (1958) ii. 554.

and the 'sacrilege that the Bank should ever suspend its payments'.[31] Most Whigs were still repelled by the idea of devaluation, which might have enabled Britain to resume without disrupting business and trade. Yet for all their moralizing, the Whigs hoped to exploit the nation's dilemma for party advantage. Grey admitted to Holland what he denied in public — that it would be impossible 'to resume cash payments, without encountering a degree of distress, which no Administration can encounter'. He anticipated Liverpool's overthrow on currency, but envisaged a 'middle administration' intervening and the depression passing over before the Whigs came to power.[32] More immediately, Grey selected the Bank restriction as the best focus for opposition in the 1819 session.[33] His party had been strengthened slightly in the recent elections, and was to score several victories in the new parliament on such issues as the Windsor Establishment and Criminal Law — individually not significant enough to 'involve the fate of an Administration',[34] but, taken together, making the Tories' retention of office seem, even to Liverpool, 'a *positive* evil'.[35] Ministers were anxious to save their faces on the cardinal issue of the session, but being divided, were baffled and embarrassed when Tierney gave notice to move for a committee of inquiry. Huskisson wrote home: 'For this as for many other scrapes, they may thank the genius of old Mouldy [Vansittart]. L[iverpool] is in one of his grand fidgetts. Yesterday he said if Tierney were to beat us, it would be fatal.'[36]

At first the prime minister tried to postpone discussion by

31. H. of C., 2 Feb. 1819, 1 PD, xxxix. 215; H. of L., 21 May 1819, 1 PD, xl. 654-5. 651.
32. Grey to Holland, 13 Dec. 1818, HHP 51545 ff. 215-16.
33. Holland to Creevey, 19 Jan. 1819, H. Maxwell, *The Creevey Papers* (1903), i. 292.
34. Wilbraham to Colchester, 24 Feb. 1819, Colchester, *Diary and Correspondence*, iii. 71.
35. Liverpool to Eldon, 10 May 1819, H. Twiss, *The Public and Private Life of Lord Chancellor Eldon* (1844), ii. 329. There were rumours of the government's imminent collapse throughout the session. For its political apprehensions, see Arbuthnot to Hertford, 15 Jan. 1819, Hertford MSS. 3261 ff. 44-5.
36. Huskisson to his wife, 23 Jan. 1819, HP 39949 ff.37-40; C. R. Fay, *Huskisson and His Age* (1951), 196-7.

extending the restriction for one more year, but at Fife
House on 15 January the Bank objected that even this
indulgence would not enable them to prepare sufficiently.
Piqued by its intransigence, ministers 'abandoned' the
Bank;[37] then, in order to recover the parliamentary initiative, they occupied Tierney's 'vantage ground'[38] by counter-
proposing 'a little snug SECRET Committee',[39] whose
members they themselves could virtually nominate. This ruse
succeeded. Tierney scored many debating-points in the
February discussions, but ministers made the running
without committing themselves on the substantive issues,
and without revealing their differences. Huskisson avoided
using

arguments which were better left in the background, until we have
more fully ascertained whether we are likely to agree. I mean by *we*
the men in office; for they cannot expect Canning and myself to
recede from our principles upon the subject of Restriction...

Van. was therefore *commanded* not to speak upon the principles of
the question, and on that condition we [Canning and Huskisson]
observed the same course...He kept his promise.

Canning made a very clever speech, in which enough was said without touching upon any difference of opinion, to guard us against the
insinuation of anything being given up on our side.[40]

In selecting committees for both Houses, ministers included
'a large sprinkling of Opposition'. The Lords' Committee
included Grenville, Lansdowne, Lauderdale and King, to
show 'that it is not intended as an ex parte inquiry'.[41] Seven
of the twenty-one commoners chosen were in opposition,
while Tierney, Lamb, Bankes, Mackintosh, Littleton, Newport,
Lewis, Grenfell, and Horner's friend, Abercromby, had all
spoken or voted since 1815 in favour of a precipitate resump-

37. Liverpool in H. of L., 21 Jan. 1819, 1 PD, xxxix. 31-2; C. T., 20 Jan. 1819;
CSC, *Second Report of the Secret Committee on the Expediency of the Bank
resuming Cash Payments*, 1819, 25.
38. Thomas Grenville to Lord Grenville, 26 Jan. 1819, *Historical Manuscripts
Commission Report on the Manuscripts of J. B. Fortescue preserved at Dropmore*
(1892-1927), x. 444; Ward to Copleston, June 1819, *Letters of the Earl of Dudley
to the Bishop of Llandaff* (1840), 222; Canning, MS. Diary, 25 Jan. 1819, CP 29
D 1.
39. *Morning Chronicle*, 26 Jan. 1819.
40. Huskisson to his wife, 3 Feb. 1819, HP 39949 ff. 58-61; Fay, *Huskisson and
His Age*, 198-9.
41. Liverpool to Grenville, 26 and 30 Jan. 1819 and Grenville to Liverpool,
27 Jan. 1819, LP 38275 ff. 126-7, 133-4, 167-8.

tion. Peel was made chairman, and unctuously announced his impartiality. He has been described as an 'umpire', summoned by the nation to decide the issue,[42] but though a convenient 'front man' for the government, it was remarked at the time that he 'knows little about it',[43] and, to Herries's frustration, 'leans so much, besides, upon Huskisson'.[44] The Lords' chairman was Lord President Harrowby, who was 'louder than anybody in saying that he shall regard the resumption of cash payments whenever it may happen as the consummation of certain ruin to the country'.[45]

Huskisson, Canning, and Frankland Lewis immediately seized the initiative in their Committee, while 'Poor Vansittart sits silent and dejected at seeing all his opinions over turned'.[46] He took refuge from humiliation in slumber — 'Mr. Irving was one of Mr. Vansittart's own witnesses, and during his Examination he fell asleep'.[47] Tierney threw in party gibes, and Castlereagh asked strangely evasive questions. Both Committees began with Bank witnesses — Dorrien, Pole, Harman, Haldimand, Ward, and Samuel Thornton. All except Harman acknowledged the connection (which the directors John Whitmore and John Pearse had denied in 1810) between the amount of circulation, the price of bullion and the state of the exchanges; but they were invariably gloomy about prospects of resuming in 1820 owing to foreign loans, overseas investment of British capital and Bank advances to government. Only William Haldimand, the most optimistic, made a favourable impression.[48] Other witnesses included

42. Halévy, op.cit. 52-3. See Stanhope, *Conversations with the Duke of Wellington 1831-51* (1888), 289; Peel to Lloyd, n.d., Peel MSS. 40342, C. S. Parker, *Sir Robert Peel from his private correspondence* (1891-9), i. 291-4.
43. Mallet, MS. Diary, 13 Feb. 1819, quoted in P. Sraffa, *The Works and Correspondence of David Ricardo* (1951-5), v. 352 et seq. John Louis Mallet was Secretary of the Audit Office, a friend of Ricardo and a founder member of the Political Economy Club.
44. Herries, MS. Memoranda, 27 Apr. 1819, Herries MSS. 57445 f.12.
45. Thomas Grenville to Lord Grenville, 28 Jan. 1819, *Historical Manuscripts Commission, Fortescue,* x. 445.
46. Mallet, MS. Diary, in Sraffa. op. cit. v. 354.
47. Littleton, MS. Journal, 26 Feb. 1819, Hatherton MSS. D260/M/F/5/26/2/ 199-201.
48. Littleton, MS. Journal, 8 and 11 Feb. 1819, 5 Mar. 1819, ibid. 193, 195, 213-14; Peel to Lloyd, n.d., Peel MSS. 40342, Parker, op.cit. i. 294-5; Mallet, MS. Diary, in Sraffa, op.cit. v. 353; Buckingham and Chandos, *Memoirs of the Court of England during the Regency, 1811-20* (1856), ii. 326.

London and country bankers, bill and bullion brokers, and general merchants,[49] almost all of whom doubted whether trade and industry could survive the initial loss of currency and credit that cash payments would entail; they seemed to E. J. Littleton, a country gentleman, virtually to deny the possibility of ever resuming. The discussions proceeded fairly aimlessly, however, until after Alexander Baring's return from Paris, where he had been negotiating foreign loans. His several long and detailed interrogations greatly impressed.[50] He had refused to sign the 1810 Committee Report and now, while avowing impeccably orthodox theories of bullion and exchange, he counselled in practice a longer postponement of cash payments than even previous witnesses had done — perhaps four or five years:

Every one agrees that it is knocking the thing on the head, and that such an extension of time is tantamount to doing nothing...Narrower means of credits, a closer system of discounts, a return to a sound currency in this great commercial country, could not fail affecting all Europe for a time; and it is *for a time*, and for that *very time*, that Baring wants facilities of every kind.[51]

Thereafter, cross-examination concentrated on technicalities — mainly Ricardo's plan for bullion payments as recommended by Baring; and also, in the case of the Lords' Committee, Lauderdale's 'crotchet' that it was the Mint regulations, not depreciated paper, that had depressed the exchanges, and that there should be a silver standard instead of a gold standard.

The bent of all this discussion was practical — *when* and *how*, rather than *whether*, to resume. Doctrinal truth, as promulgated in 1810, was taken for granted, and anti-bullionists were ignored. There was simply no point in dragging along Thomas Attwood, the leading theoretical heretic, to advise on implementing a policy he abhorred in principle.

49. e.g. Lewis Loyd, Matthias Attwood, Hudson Gurney (country bankers); William Masterman, James Hammett (London bankers); John Irving, John Gladstone (merchants).
50. Liverpool in H. of L., 21 May 1819; Vansittart in H. of C., 24 May 1819, 1 PD, xl. 621, 739; Bankes to Colchester, 24 Feb. 1819, Colchester, *Diary and Correspondence*, iii. 70.
51. Mallet, MS. Diary, 2 and 6 Mar. 1819, Sraffa, op.cit. v, 352n.; viii. 18n. Apart from Ricardo, Thomas Tooke was the only witness to think that resumption was immediately possible.

Thomas Smith, propagandist of the 'abstract pound' and devaluation, was heard (at his own request) 'politely' but 'impatiently', and was 'cut short in the exposition of my theory'.[52] Matthias Attwood was confined to practicalities, and Hudson Gurney not allowed to elaborate his unorthodox monetary views.[53] Although Peel claimed to have reached a decision according to the evidence, most of that evidence, like his reading — Huskisson, Ricardo, McCulloch, Copleston — was one-sided.[54]

Interim Reports having been presented on 5 April, all crucial decisions were left to the ministerial members of the two Committees, in conclave with Grenville, who was slowly abandoning the Whigs for an elder statesman's role. Huskisson pressed for an immediate resumption, confident that the exchanges would improve as a result, while a faction around Harrowby insisted that the exchanges should be corrected first. No doubt they hoped thereby to secure perpetual suspension, and stalled by suggesting a physical limitation of Bank issues to correct the exchanges.[55] Canning recorded this conflict telegraphically in his diary:

1 April...Meeting at Liverpool's about Bullion. A strange proposal for *limiting* the amount of Bank Issue, to try experiment. What experiment? This is *nobody's* principle. This will never do. Harr[by] & Bath[t] at the bottom of it...

2 April...Dined with Huskisson, Binning & Arbuthnot. Talked of Bullion for the purpose of impressing A.[btht] with the necessity of a Report on *right principles*, & thro' him Liverpool...

3 April...Meeting at Liverpools about Bullion. Quite a new proposal. That of Thursday [1st April] given up. *All* agreed. Van & Casgh & Bath & Har — *all*. Is this a consequence of the talk last night?...[56]

This 'agreement' of 3 April was a compromise, requiring the

52. T. Smith, *An Address to Robert Peel, late Chairman to the Committee on the Currency* (1819), 6.

53. Gurney, MS. Diary, 26 Feb. 1819, quoted in Fetter, *Development of British Monetary Orthodoxy*, 86n.

54. W. Huskisson, *The Question Concerning the Depreciation of Our Currency* (1810); D. Ricardo, *Proposals for an Economical and Secure Currency* (1816); J. R. McCulloch's review of the above in *Edinburgh Review*, xxxi (1818), 53-80; [E. Copleston], *A Letter to Robert Peel on the pernicious effects of a variable standard of value* (1819).

55. Apparently by ordering the Bank to curtail its issues without its having to resume.

56. Canning, MS. Diary, CP 29 D 1.

Bank to commence payment of its notes in gold bars very shortly, but postponing actual *cash* payments until mid-1823. Huskisson and Canning were happier with this than their adversaries, as a series of acrimonious Committee meetings in the second half of April revealed.

All the first men were agreed, including Lord Wellington. — Lord Castlereagh and Vansittart lagged behind: Ned Cooke, Lord Castlereagh's right-hand man, was at the very time writing the most alarming pamphlets.[57] Lord Harrowby and Lord Bathurst were dragged into the measure, but Lord Liverpool, Lords Grenville, Wellington and Lansdowne, Peel and Canning being agreed, no paper administration could be formed, and the reluctant multitude were obliged to yield.[58]

Most non-ministerial members of the Committees acquiesced in the decision; only Lauderdale, Tierney and the director Manning dissented. Peel wrote some 'right principles' into the Commons' Report, Harrowby more reluctantly adorned the Lords' Report,[59] and these bullionist professions helped to camouflage the fact that the final consummation was to be delayed longer than had seemed politically possible in February. Predictably Herries welcomed the recommendations while repudiating the principles laid down, and Lansdowne hoped that Parliament would unequivocally declare its belief in specie payments '*before* the expediency of further delay is stated'.[60]

Whigs and radicals contended that, for the sake of trade, resumption must be accompanied by tax relief,[61] ministers that taxation must first be *augmented* to make good the loss of advances from an unco-operative Bank. Thus, one year before, Liverpool had used the impossibility of increasing

57. E. Cooke, *The Real Cause of the High Price of Gold Bullion* (1819); E. Cooke, *Address to the Public on the Plan proposed to the Commons Committee on the Bank* (1819).

58. Mallet, MS. Diary, n.d., in Sraffa, op.cit. v. 365-6. For Harrowby's distaste, see Harrowby to Aberdeen, 1 May 1819, Harrowby MSS. 1st series, XV. ff. 66-9; Aberdeen MSS. 43230 f. 327.

59. In drafting the report of the Lords' Committee, Harrowby attempted — in deference to the majority — to be, in his own eyes, 'as *unprincipled* as possible': ibid.

60. Herries, MS. Memoranda, 1 May 1819, Herries MSS. 57445 f. 13; Lansdowne to Harrowby, 16 May 1819, Harrowby MSS. 1st series, XV, ff. 213-4.

61. Lauderdale to Holland, 12 Feb. 1822, HHP 51692 ff. 69-70; Lansdowne in H. of L., 4 May 1821, 2 PD, v. 498-500.

taxes at that time as an excuse for extending the restriction.[62] Now, Herries's advice to revive the property tax being impracticable, the civil servants William Hill and Charles Long recommended ten per cent duties on excise and customs. Huskisson objected 'that the Money could not be raised',[63] and convinced Liverpool instead that a revival of the war malt duties and a few minor tariffs, such as an additional 6d. per lb. on the imporatation of foreign raw wool, would bring in £3,000,000. On 27 April, Huskisson enjoined Vansittart, now almost a cypher, to meet his deficit by appropriating all but £2,000,000 of the sinking fund, rather than by floating further loans as proposed by Herries, the friend of Rothschild. This was an important episode in Huskisson's lifelong rivalry with Herries, who observed bitterly that Huskisson and Canning were playing 'an under-game... about Lord Liverpool'.[64] The Prince Regent objected to the additional taxes, as did certain important ministers (notably Eldon, who wished to stave everything off for two years more), but Liverpool warned them that 'a strong and decisive effort can alone redeem our character and credit'.[65] On 8 May the cabinet adopted Huskisson's financial proposals,[66] which required Vansittart to resolve in Parliament (7 June) that henceforward a genuine surplus of £5,000,000 would be provided for debt redemption. This was the momentous decision of 1819, one which made it possible to implement the Reports on cash payments. Wellington felt that the 'resolution to put our finances on a solid basis or to resign' (if beaten) had made an honest man of him again.[67]

The Commons debates on cash payments were curiously unreal. Several members had prophesied disaster when suddenly Ricardo, 'the phenomenon of that night',[68] trans-

62. Liverpool to Sidmouth, 6 Aug. 1818, LP 38273 ff. 14-20.
63. Arbuthnot to Herries, n.d. [circa 30 Apr. 1819], Herries MSS. Herries, MS. Memoranda, 23 Apr. 1819, 57445 f. 10.
64. Herries, MS. Memoranda, 27 Apr. 1819, f.12.
65. Liverpool to Eldon, 10 May 1819, Twiss, Life of Lord Chancellor Eldon, ii. 329; Liverpool to Prince Regent, 9 May 1819 and Prince Regent to Liverpool, 10 May 1819, LP 38264 ff. 85-7 and 38190 ff. 28-30.
66. Canning, MS. Diary, 8 and 10 May 1819, CP 29 D 1.
67. Littleton, MS. Journal, 22 May 1819, 248.
68. Mallet, MS. Diary, in Sraffa, op.cit. v. 17.

formed the situation. He was wildly cheered throughout, perhaps because he said authoritatively things that his apprehensive audience was only too relieved to hear: 'The difficulty was only that of raising the currency 3 per cent in value...He had no doubt that if they were cautious they might arrive at cash payments without giving out one guinea in gold...He was quite astonished that such an alarm prevailed at a reduction of perhaps one million in four years.'[69] At once the alarm dissipated and wild bullionist enthusiasm succeeded to doubt and discord: 'It was quite wonderful to observe how members' minds changed as the debate proceeded — at its commencement the numbers of those who were inclined to oppose the resolutions either from ignorance or apprehension were considerable, but every speech made seemed to gain the confidence of the House in the plan.'[70] On 25 May to everyone's amazement, amid turmoil and 'great confusion', Canning called for unanimity 'to show the public that the House was in earnest in its attempts to restore the ancient standard', and the resolutions were passed 'without a dissentient voice'. Individuals raged but found no support and were 'at last...persuaded to be quiet'.[71] Holland was 'bothered' by the postponement of actual *specie* payments, but realized the futility of opposition. Denison and Moore failed in attempts to organize a lobby for devaluing the standard, and Ellice could not even find anyone to second such a proposal. Hudson Gurney, Heygate, Cripps, Manning, and Peel's father were silenced by an extraordinary fervour which gripped the Commons. Matthias Attwood left the debate rather than appear to acquiesce.[72] It was much the

---

69. H. of C., 24 May 1819, 1 PD, xl. 743-6. Ricardo did not oppose devaluation on theoretical grounds, and would have welcomed it had the premium on gold been 25 per cent and not 5 per cent in 1819. See below pp. 93-4. Baring retrospectively concurred, CSC, *Three Reports of the Committee on the State of Agriculture and of the Causes and Extent of the Distress which presses thereon*, 1836, 478.

70. Littleton, MS. Journal, 24 and 25 May 1819, 248.

71. R. I. and S. Wilberforce, *The Life of William Wilberforce* (1839), v. 27.

72. T. Doubleday, *The Politcal Life of Sir Robert Peel* (1856), i. 218; A. Alison, *Lives of Lord Castlereagh and Sir Charles Stewart* (1861), iii. 83-8; T. Tooke and W. Newmarch, *A History of Prices and of the state of the circulation from 1792 to 1856* (1838-57), edited by T. E. Gregory (1928), ii. 65-6; J. H. Barrow, *Mirror of Parliament*, xvii. 1775-6; Canning, MS. Diary, 25 May 1819, CP 29 D 1.

same outside — a simulated unanimity, as if to obscure
doubts and difficulties, prevailed. The funds fell, apprehension
suffused trade and industry, and yet there was, as Sir John
Sinclair found to his cost, a 'delirium' in favour of gold that
branded dissenters as public enemies.[73] 'Notwithstanding
that extraordinary unanimity, everybody seems to differ.'[74]
What was the cause of this transient but contagious euphoria?
Perhaps, as in 1914, the decision finally to do that which
had been repeatedly staved off brought on hysterical relief.
At last the Napoleonic wars were to be liquidated. Apprehension of the consequences was deliberately stifled and
doubters were vilified. In 1819 Englishmen embraced gold,
seduced by its moral force as a symbol of truth and stability,
of immutability and impartiality, like swimmers leaping into
the cleanness of fixed parities. 'Canning says, "it is the greatest wonder that he has witnessed in the political world".'[75]

The Bullion Plan and the Bank

The decision to resume was, for Ricardo, a 'triumph of
science, and truth, over prejudice, and error';[76] for the
country gentlemen, an act of intuitive morality; for Huskisson,
a victory over Vansittart and Herries; and for the government
generally, a tactical blow against City and Bank in a constitutional battle for power and responsibility. This last interpretation revolves around the technicalities of resumption.
Specifically the Cash Payments Act stipulated that as from
1 February 1820 the Bank would be liable to pay its notes in
gold bullion, assayed and stamped, and in amounts of not less
than 60oz., at 81s. per oz. (roughly the then market price);
likewise from 1 October 1820 at 79s. 6d.; and from 1 May
1821 at the mint price of 77s. 10½d. Payments in cash (coin)
were to be resumed between 1 May 1822 and 1 May 1823.[77]

73. J. Sinclair, *Memoirs of the Life and Works of Sir John Sinclair* (1837), ii.
299.
74. Sheffield to Colchester, 19 May 1819, Colchester, *Diary and Correspondence*,
iii. 76-7.
75. Ward to Copleston, June 1819, *Letters of Earl Dudley to the Bishop of
Llandaff*, 222.
76. Ricardo to Trower, 28 May 1819, Sraffa, op.cit. viii. 31.
77. The Bank might anticipate this timetable but was not allowed to procrasti-
nate; nor, having once accelerated, might it slow the process down again.

Laws against melting and exporting coin were repealed. Meanwhile the government was directed to repay £10,000,000 of its advances from the Bank.

This graduated reduction from market to mint price enabled the Bank to make immediate redemption of its notes, and despite allegations that it would set a precedent for future devaluations and encourage speculations in bullion, the scale was a sensible means of cushioning the effects of resumption. Historians have, however, been more interested in the novel Bullion or Ingot Plan. The idea of ingot or bullion payments, deriving immediately from Ricardo's *Proposals* of 1816, was 'rescued...from oblivion' by McCulloch in the *Edinburgh* and by Baring, Swinton Holland, and Ricardo himself in their evidence to the Committees.[78] They envisaged it as a *permanent* device, and in recommending it to Parliament, the Committees stressed its permanent, technical benefits, the most important being that at a time when money was scarce, 'there cannot, while this Plan is acted on, be any demand for Gold for the purposes of internal circulation.'[79] Also, the minimum convertibility limit of 60oz. should prevent runs on the Bank, since it was mainly small note-holders, with least to lose, who indulged in panics of that sort. Some historians find surprising the adoption of a plan that very few witnesses had approved, and stress the influence of Baring and Ricardo.[80] But in fact, the Plan's permanent economic advantages were not what decided the Committees. A little-noted passage in the Commons' Report explained that the Committee did 'not express any preference for the system of Bullion payments over that of payments in Specie abstractedly; nor are they prepared to recommend

---

78. See above, p. 44 n. 54. See also D. Ricardo, *The High Price of Bullion, a proof of depreciation of bank notes* (1810), appendix, Sraffa, op. cit. iii. 123-7; Ricardo to McCulloch, 7 Apr. 1819, ibid. viii. 20. See J. Bonar, 'Ricardo's Ingot Plan', *Economic Journal*, xxxiii (1923), 281-304. See LSC, *Reports from the Lords on the State of the Bank of England, with reference to the Expediency of the Resumption of Cash Payments at the period now fixed by law, &c.*, 1819, 427 (appendix G. 4), for a more elaborately graduated scale of ingot payments, devised by Haldimand and Lord King. Mallet, MS. Diary, Sraffa, op. cit. v. 353.
79. CSC, *Second Report on the Expediency of resuming Cash Payments*, 1819, 15; J. Viner, *Studies in the Theory of International Trade* (1937), 179-80.
80. e.g., Fetter, *Development of British Monetary Orthodoxy*, 92.

them as a permanent substitute'. The point was simply that
Parliament had already, three times before, requested the
Bank to prepare for resumption at its own discretion, and the
Bank had not complied. Therefore, in postponing cash payments again, it would be prudent 'to devise some additional
security' (such as the Ingot Plan) that this time preparations
would actually be made.[81] Merely naming a date would give
the public no such security, but the Ingot Plan should *force*
the Bank gradually to contract its issues.[82]

Some such mechanism was the only alternative to a
'positive obligation' or 'statutory mandate' on the Bank
— which most witnesses had agreed would be unwise. But
if the Plan was basically just a mechanism to coerce an
unwilling Bank, then its essential feature was the graduated
scale, which made it possible to begin immediately.[83] Bullion
payments were incidental, but temporarily necessary because
payments in coin could not be combined with a graduated
scale, unless the coin underwent 'successive variations in its
circulating value'.[84] The Bank's fierce objections amazed
Ricardo and McCulloch, since technically bullion payments
were 'an immense advantage' to it compared with specie
payments;[85] but what the directors resented was rather the
threat posed by the scale to their monetary independence —

81. CSC, *Second Report on the Expediency of resuming Cash Payments*, 1819,
16-17. Parnell in H. of C., 25 May 1819, 1 PD, xl. 758. Huskisson, however, may
have preferred with Ricardo to adopt the Ingot Plan permanently, because of its
economical use of gold. H. of C., 11 June 1822, 2 PD, vii. 906; 'Rough draft on
coin and currency', July 1818, HP 38741 ff. 242-52.
82. LSC, *Second Report on the Expediency of the Resumption of Cash Payments*,
1819, 17.
83. Thus Tooke opposed ingot payments in principle because he would have
preferred to eliminate paper money at once, but he accepted the Ingot Plan for
the sake of the scale, anything less than which might be ineffectual to ensure that
resumption actually took place as promised. Ibid. 179-80. Conversely, the Bank
was willing to make ingot payments, but without the scale and at the market
price. Ibid., appendix A,8.
84. Ibid. 17.
85. McCulloch to Ricardo, 18 Apr. 1819 and Ricardo to McCulloch, 8 May 1819,
Sraffa, op.cit. vii. 23-8. Ricardo soon learned to appreciate the mandatory advantages of the scale, however: Ricardo to Trower, 25 Sept. 1819, ibid. viii. 79.
The other 'plans' that the Committees seriously considered (including Harrowby's, see above p. 44) would have forced the Bank to reduce issues mechanically
with the rise of gold or fall in exchange rates, or would have removed discretion
from the Bank in some other way.

the implied slur on their good faith — the resort to compulsion in order to prevent their alleged profiteering in inconvertible paper.[86]

Even if the Committees could have been certain that on this occasion the Bank would genuinely prepare for resumption, they might still have adopted the graduated scale in order to prove the point to businessmen, and force *them* to anticipate by 'limiting their acceptances'. A Committee member wondered whether, if they took 'merely the same precautions...that have been already taken by a declaration of the opinion of Parliament...the public would not still calculate upon some circumstances intervening which would again render it necessary to postpone the resumption...and hold out an inducement to the public, to postpone at the same time those measures of precaution which...are necessary in order to prepare the public for that resumption.'[87] By operating immediately, the graduated scale would serve as an earnest to the public.

As it happened, however, the Committees were far from certain about the Bank's sincerity, and their suspicions were enhanced by an injudicious paper from the directors. When on 24 March the Lords' Committee examined Ricardo, they showed no interest in his Ingot Plan, beyond a few desultory inquiries as to its economic advantages. Then on 25 March the directors replied to a questionnaire from the Commons' Committee with a contentious paper in which, deprecating an early resumption, they could not 'refrain from adverting to an opinion, strongly insisted on by some, that the bank has only to reduce its issues to obtain a favourable turn in the exchanges, and a consequent influx of the precious metals; the Court conceives it to be its duty to declare, that it is unable to discover any solid foundation for such a sentiment.'[88] In context this was less a denial of exchange theory than a reasonable reminder that it had not yet been conclusively demonstrated.[89] However, it had a catalytic effect

87. CSC, *Reports on the Expediency of resuming Cash Payments*, 1819, 220.
88. Ibid. 262-4.
89. J. K. Horsefield, 'The Bankers and the Bullionists in 1819', *Journal of Political Economy*, lvii (1949), 442-8.

on the Lords' Committee,[90] which on the following day
(26 March) recalled Ricardo. This time the tone of inter-
rogation was quite different. Seventy or eighty questions
concentrated in detail on the Ingot Plan and its graduated
scale, and probed the possibility of its application, as though
their Lordships had already determined to implement it. For
it was no longer possible to believe, with Baring,[91] that the
Bank's neglect during 1816-19 to make proper preparations
for resumption by drawing in its paper, was due to an
'ignorance' and 'folly' of which its directors must now be
ashamed. Here was written evidence that Threadneedle Street
still offered asylum to unrepentant heretics. Ricardo was
asked:

Is it not also a great Advantage of such a Plan, that nearly the whole
Progress of its Operation, and that of our Currency as connected with it,
would thus be brought successively under the View of Parliament,
instead of its being left to the Discretion of the Bank, until the Arrival
of the Time ultimately fixed for Payment in Cash or Bullion at the Mint
Price, without any such Gradation?...Do you not think, that the longer
the Time allowed the Bank for the Payment of their Notes in Cash or
Bullion, at the Mint Price, the more necessary the graduated Scale
would be, as a security to the Parliament, and to the Public for the
Accomplishment of this ultimate Object? &c., &c...[92]

Wellesley Pole, Master of the Mint, announced in Parliament
that he would have rejected the Ingot Plan but for the Bank
directors' contentious paper. And Peel declared that he could
not trust the directors to obey a mere parliamentary directive
to resume at a given date, adding slyly that it would be unfair
'to give to them a discretion as to a plan which they themselves conceived was neither founded in truth nor sanctioned
by experience', or to ask them 'to act on a principle which
they thought untenable'.[93]

90. Despite Clapham's view that the committees ignored the paper, *The Bank of
England*, ii. 70.
91. 'I should hope that the Opinion will now become perfectly established, that
the Price of Bullion and Rates of Exchange are governed by the Amount of the
Paper Currency.' LSC, *Reports on the Expediency of the Resumption of Cash
Payments*, 1819, 136-7.
92. Ibid. 197-8, 201.
93. H. of C., 24 May 1819, 1 PD, xl. 684-5, 714. This motivation clearly resembles
Horner's in 1810 when, alarmed by the directors' adherence to 'real bills'
blasphemy, he decided to press for *total and immediate* resumption in order to
combat it. Huskisson, *The Question Concerning the Depreciation of Our Currency*,
xv-xvii.

A gratuitous protest by the Bank directors on 20 May merely strengthened the government's argument against them. They demanded repayment of most of the exchequer bills advanced to government, and justly observed that the Ingot Plan 'seems to take away from the Bank any thing like a discretionary consideration of the necessities and distresses of the commercial world'. Then, in warning of the dangers of resumption, they rashly added that they felt themselves 'obliged, by the new situation in which they have been placed by the Restriction Act of 1797, to bear in mind, not less their duties to the establishment over which they preside, than their duties to the community at large, whose interest in a pecuniary and commercial relation, have in a great degree been confided to their discretion.'[94] So the directors considered themselves above Parliament as well as above the laws of political economy! This was what Huskisson had mainly objected to in the Bank restriction — that it vested power in an irresponsible company of merchants. Peel pronounced that 'the moment has arrived, when the nature of the relations existing between the government and the Bank should be changed.' Most speakers took up this point. The director Manning, for example, protested against the Ingot Plan as 'fettering the Bank', while his colleague Pearse claimed that it was Vansittart's negligence and abdication of responsibility which had 'forced' the directors to behave as 'a species of legislators interfering with the commerce of the country'.[95] When the relations between Bank and Treasury were further formalized, (and Vansittart's system further undermined) by the Bank Advances Bill of 1819, defining and limiting future Bank advances to the government and subjecting them to parliamentary scrutiny, Vansittart commented ironically that it would 'fetter government'.[96]

Just for observing that cash payments might involve some hardship, the directors were pilloried for wishing to 'erect themselves into legislators'.[97] The charge was fantastical.

94. H. of L., 21 May 1819, 1 PD, xl. 601-4.
95. H. of C., 24 and 25 May 1819, 1 PD, xl. 688, 741, 778.
96. H. of C., 16 and 25 June 1819, 1 PD, xl. 1192-4, 1373.
97. Samuel Turner, *A Letter to Peel with reference to the expediency of resumption*, second edition (1819), 36.

After all, ministers had often urged the *public interest* when they craved advances that the directors begrudged. At one moment they denied that the directors had any right to discretion over issues — at the next they argued that they were 'like any other trading corporation, and must manage their own affairs'.[98] The directors were similarly inconsistent in complaining that the Ingot Plan, like their advances to government, deprived them of discretionary control over the circulation, since at other times they deprecated all such discretion, and claimed merely to discount all bills representing 'sound' business, and to use their 'own liquidity position as a barometer giving guidance concerning the entire economy'.[99] But however unreal all these debating-points, they certainly demonstrate the rancour that now obtained between government and Bank, and the total rupture of their close wartime relations. Perhaps the directors wished to move into the private discount market. Possibly ministers wished to detach themselves from an object of contemporary odium.[100] Maybe, when faced by Tierney's February motion, they decided to lead a movement that they could no longer restrain, and, in order to appear consistent, cynically blamed the Bank for all previous failures to resume, 'instead of fairly…acknowledging that their own dangerous system of keeping sixty millions of unfunded debt floating in the market'. was a contributory if not 'the true, sole and single cause of the Bank's inability to pay in cash tomorrow'.[101] Tierney's

98. Stapleton's memorandum (quoting Canning), 27 Dec. 1825, A. G. Stapleton, *George Canning and His Times* (1859), 227-8.
99. S. G. Checkland, *The Rise of Industrial Society in England, 1815-85* (1964), 194.
100. There was an intense clamour against the Bank, partly because it was widely believed that the 1808 arrangement allowed it to exploit the public financially, but mainly because of capital commitals for forgery. The latter was a highly emotive issue, which bullionists — and especially Whigs — inevitably and correctly exploited. But Ferrer's 'impression', *Development of British Monetary Orthodoxy* 71-3, 285, that Parliament adopted resumption, 'in spite of the impressive economic arguments against it', because of the pressure of public opinion on the forgery issue, surely goes too far. At any rate, forgery was not germane to the administrative tory or Huskissonian approach, which was decisive in 1819. Incidentally, Peel was no repriever in forgery cases. See Acworth, *Financial Reconstruction in England*, 95-9.
101. *Morning Chronicle*, 4 Feb. 1819.

parliamentary philippics, however subjective, nicely illustrate the shifting alliances and accusations. On 2 February he still regarded the directors as knaves, controlling 'the movement of wires behind the curtain', and ministers as fools for allowing themselves to be manipulated. By 24 May these derogatory terms had been reversed: 'If stupidity were not the right word, as applied to the directors' — implying that it was — 'guilt was undoubtedly the right word, as applied to the ministers.' Despite this, 'the shepherd was to be put into the stocks, while the wolf was to be allowed to prey upon the flock.'[102]

Perhaps the government's recent failure to control country banks made it seem all the more necessary to shackle the Bank of England. Huskisson, who had long regarded country banks as dangerous, wanted to compel them to give security for their issues, and also wished to see joint-stock banking legalized.[103] When in April 1818, however, Vansittart had tried to establish control by making private banks deposit government securities to the amount of their small note circulation, he had felt the political strength of the country bank interest — or, as sceptics put it, of the 'insolvent bankers' lobby under Sir William Elford — and had had to withdraw his proposal ignominiously.[104] Despite several subsequent bank failures, legislation could not be attempted so soon after that capitulation. Besides, it was generally believed, and Ricardo encouraged the notion, that country banks would endanger the credit system only so long as cash payments remained suspended. In that situation, they formed a sort of superstructure resting on the Bank of England, their issues virtually controlled by the Bank, since their proprietors generally gauged their liquidity positions by the size of their London balances. Under convertibility, however, private bank issues would be controlled directly by movements in the foreign exchanges, just like those of the Bank of England,

---

102. H. of C., 24 May 1819, 1 PD, xl. 729-30.
103. e.g., 'Memorandum on 1816 Distress', HP 38760 ff. 116-24.
104. Beeke to Bexley, 13 Sept. 1826, Vansittart MSS. 31232 ff. 360-2; Pressnell, *Country Banking in the Industrial Revolution*, 473-7; LP 38271 ff. 237-9, 250-2, 257-60, 271-2, 280.

and legislative control would therefore be unnecessary.[105]
At all events, the 1819 Committees largely avoided the
problem of the country banks.

The social implications of bullionism

W. R. Brock characterized resumption as the 'virtual abandonment of the agriculturalists by the Government and its
conscious seeking after commercial support'. S. G. Checkland
maintains that the landed interest had to 'stomach the return
to gold, in spite of its deflationary effects, because the commercial and industrial groups insisted that if British trade
was to revive, the currency must return to its pre-war footing'.
For Asa Briggs, resumption inaugurated an alliance between
orthodox political economy, the City and the cotton trade.[106]
Many other historians have agreed that in 1819 the Government 'sacrificed the landed interest to the money power'.[107]
These judgements may have been influenced by later nineteenth-century balance of payments theory, which prescribed
export booms to correct low exchange rates. But in fact
resumption did not signify a conscious policy for expanding
exports. Agricultural hostility to 'Peel's Bill' (as it misleadingly
became known) was *ex post facto*. Merchants and cotton
manufacturers bitterly opposed the Cash Payments Bill,
though they may have been encouraged to adopt an orthodox
'free trade' attitude as the subsequent deflation rendered
their goods universally more competitive, and as they strove
to compensate abroad for the loss of home demand that
accompanied deflation. In 1819, however, merchants, manufacturers, bankers, bullion brokers, financiers — businessmen
of all kinds — were as overwhelmingly hostile to resumption
as they had been in 1811. They all dreaded the pressure of
monetary stringency, but very few could see the ultimate
commercial benefits of deflation and a 'sound' currency.[108]
   Birmingham's opposition was the most sophisticated and

105. E. Wood, *English Theories of Central Banking Control 1819-58* (1939), 33;
Ricardo to CSC, *Reports on the Expediency of resuming Cash Payments*, 1819,
142.
106. Brock, *Lord Liverpool and Liberal Toryism*, 182; Checkland, op.cit. 178;
A. Briggs, *The Age of Improvement, 1783-1867* (1959), 205.
107. W. Cooke Taylor, *Life and Times of Sir Robert Peel* (1846-51), i. 100-1.
108. On 1811, see Crouzet, op.cit. ii. 552-8; *The Correspondence of Sir John
Sinclair, with reminiscences* (1831), i. 110-14.

doctrinaire,[109] but in 1819 the great exporting centres were just as antagonistic. Hart Davis sponsored a strong Bristol lobby of over seventy businessmen and tradesmen, urging the 'utter impracticability' of an early resumption. From 400 to 500 merchants, bankers, and traders signed a City of London petition under the aegis of John Irving and the elder Peel. James Cropper remonstrated on Liverpool's behalf, while Leeds, Halifax, and Bradford also petitioned for a continuance of the Bank restriction.[110] Even Manchester, with whom cash payments became peculiarly associated, and whose ideological reputation was to rest on gold and free trade, demurred in 1819. Some 147 Manchester merchants, bankers, and tradesmen,[111] in a memorial to Lord Liverpool, prayed that resumption be deferred until the exchanges had righted themselves and the foreign loan operations had been completed. It would be fatal to resume while foreign loans were embarrassing the money market and depriving commerce of funds. Furthermore, resumption with gold at a premium would lead to its exportation; loss of specie would force the Bank to discount fewer bills of exchange; and Lancashire would suffer especially because no local notes circulated there.[112] But the most significant reason for delaying resumption was 'upon account of the rise of the British Exchange with Foreign Countries (that will take place when the Bank of England Notes are convertible into Specie) enhancing the prices of all our Manufactures, and other

109. S. G. Checkland, 'The Birmingham Economists, 1815-50', *Economic History Review*, second series, i (1948), 1-19; A. Briggs, 'Thomas Attwood and the Economic Background of the Birmingham Political Union', *Cambridge Historical Journal*, ix (1948), 190-216.
110. S. G. Checkland, 'The Lancashire Bill System and its Liverpool Protagonists, 1810-27', *Economica*, new series, xxi (1954), 129-42. Arbuthnot to Huskisson, 3 Sept. 1818, HP 38741 ff. 253-4; Hart Davis to Vansittart, 24 Nov. 1818, LP 38274 ff. 187-91; Hart Davis to Liverpool, 19 Dec. 1818, ibid., ff. 333-6. See *Cowdroy's Manchester Gazette*, 22 May 1819, for the personal financial difficulties that may have prompted Davis to interfere.
111. Including many of the most respectable: Birley, Hornby, W. J. Loyd, Ashton, Heywood, Houldsworth, &c.
112. T. S. Ashton, 'The Bill of Exchange and Private Banks in Lancashire, 1790-1830', *Economic History Review*, xv (1945), reprinted in T. S. Ashton and R. S. Sayers, *Papers in English Monetary History* (1953), 37-49; L. H. Grindon, *Manchester Banks and Bankers* (1878), 102-8; A Prentice, *Historical Sketches and Personal Recollections of Manchester, 1792-1832* (1851), 218-24; A. Redford, *Manchester Merchants and Foreign Trade 1794-1858* (1934), 158-63.

exported Merchandize — to Foreign Consumers, and thereby lessening their Consumption and favouring the products of our rivals.'[113] In other words, Manchester feared that, at least in the short term, cash would render cotton *less* competitive. Logically, of course, merchants should have pressed for a return to gold at a lower parity,[114] thereby securing stable exchanges without enhancing them, and thereby making exports more competitive. But since the idea of devaluation was ethically repugnant, they asked instead for a postponement, at least until such time as, the exchanges being at par, resumption would not initially raise them against British exports.

Similarly, for all Tierney's and Cobbett's taunts that the 'Muckworm', or 'Change-Alley people', manipulated governments at will,[115] the fact remains that the decision to commence resumption in 1819 went as much against the financiers' advice as against that of the merchants.[116] Radicals mixed incongruously with merchants, manufacturers, and bankers at the City of London Tavern in May to protest against the Committees' Reports.[117] Stocks came tumbling as the recommendations passed the Commons. Consols, already low at $71\frac{3}{8}$ on 24 May, fell a further ten per cent during the following week. There was panic in the City — 'consternation' in paperless Manchester — Bath, Bristol, and the West were 'completely astounded, not knowing what to do...Bank of England paper would not pass'. In Derbyshire, 'everything is completely suspended...country banks decline advancing money to persons of the first credit."[118] Behind the scenes, Rothschild worked into the autumn to try to reverse the decision, but his power was waning with Vansittart's. In 1819, far from the 'monied power' ruling the day,

113. Manchester memorial, 5 Jan. 1819, LP 38275 ff. 19-21.
114. As the Liverpool petition of March 1821 did. Baring later referred to the 'moral feeling' that stymied devaluation in 1819. CSC, *Reports on the State of Agriculture*, 1836, 478.
115. e.g., W. Cobbett, *Political Register*, 4 Sept. 1819.
116. e.g., Bartley to Liverpool, 6 and 28 May 1818, LP 38271 ff. 317-18; 38272 ff. 38-9; Haig to Liverpool, 1 June 1818, ibid., ff. 54-6; Rowcroft to Liverpool, 29 Apr. 1819, LP 38276 ff. 272-5; Turner to Grenville, 27 Mar. 1819, ibid., ff. 96-100.
117. *The Times*, 19 May 1819.
118. Sheffield to Colchester, 19 May 1819, Colchester, *Diary and Correspondence*, iii. 76-7; *New Times*, 24 May 1819.

the government broke loose from the stranglehold of the bankers.

Bullionists, it is fair to say, assuming the neutrality of money, took too little account of the effect their plans might have on the economy.[119] Because low exchanges coincided with only a slight premium on gold in 1819, doubts about resumption centred on the dangers of inadequate circulation and rising exchanges against exports; the possibility of price deflation and rising money values against debtors was virtually ignored. Therefore, when apprehension was felt, it was for trade, not for agriculture.[120] For their part, country gentlemen strongly supported gold in 1819, except for an occasional maverick like John Sinclair. The Agricultural Association, a rural pressure group in pursuit of higher protecting duties, specifically absolved 'dear money' from contributing to the darkening gloom that was descending on agriculture.[121]

Agricultural bullionism was not a case of economic self-interest. In strictly material terms, the possessors of landed property might well have wished to retain a system that had inflated the value of their prime asset while it depreciated the value of money. (It would not take many years of gold to remind them of their wartime advantages.) But apart from its considerable moral force, gold represented social stability, paper the industrial revolution and social dislocation. The anticipated advantage of a reign of gold over the paper interregnum was that it would freeze social relations and economic inequalities, cut down on *nouveaux* adventurers and their fictitious capitals, on men who had been able to make easy fortunes out of the restriction, but lacked the propensity, traditional in England, to make their wealth respectable by buying landed property. As Littleton surmised, 'Merchants and manufacturers, & those whose business it is to make their fortunes by a few years of speculation always require large discount and think the larger the circulating

119. E. V. Morgan, *The Theory and Practice of Central Banking, 1797-1913* (1943), 49-50, discusses the growing divergence between 'real' and 'monetary' economics.
120. As Peel admitted in H. of C., 18 Feb. 1822, 2 PD, vi. 493.
121. See below, pp. 101 and 132-5.

medium the letter for them.'[122] Convertibility would combat
the challenge of manufacturing, commercial and financial
wealth, which had thrived on monetary instability and easy
credit; it might even moderate the expansion of manufacturing
industry and encourage a movement back to the land. A
Victorian popular economist claimed that as a small child
during the restriction, she had relished the prospect, much
canvassed, of a national bankruptcy, because she 'could not
help thinking that there would be something very amusing in
having no money, and every body being brought to a state of
barter; and all, *except landowners,* having to begin the world
again, and start fair.'[123] In this sense, resumption was a
victory — pyrrhic as it turned out — of landed conservatism
against the 'Wen', the monied oligarchy, old Rothschild and
the Jews. The irony of 1819 is that the one class that had
economic cause to reject gold was, at the time and through
considerations of status and social stability, its most
enthusiastic champion.

The particularist interpretation of cash payments, as a
policy by and for exporters and finance houses, anachronisti-
cally ascribes to 1819 the motives that prompted Britain's
next return to gold in 1925. Then, to be sure, bullionists did
consider above all the stability of the exchanges, the international value of the pound, the exporter's desire for low
prices and a secure currency, and the place of London as a
financial centre and source of invisible earnings. In so doing
they neglected the state of the internal economy. But when
bullionist statesmen sought a stable exchange rate in 1819,
they were thinking precisely of the domestic economy and of
the need to eliminate abhorrent fluctuations, which disrupted
all economic contracts, and which, as Baring said, even undermined 'the moral state of the community at large'. The
object of resumption was not to "force" additional exports,
but rather to vet and prune them; not to create fortunes but
to *deflate* the arrogant speculator; not to encourage industry
at agriculture's expense, but to stimulate what was best in
both, while discarding what was unprofitable and unproductive, 'speculative' and unsound. Bullionists and anti-

122. Littleton, MS. Journal, 26 Feb. 1819, Hatherton MSS. D260/M/F/5/26/2/
199-201.
123. H. Martineau, *Introduction to the History of the Peace. From 1800 to 1815*
(1851), cclxiv (my italics).

bullionists agreed that periodic excitements succeeded by depression (1815-16, 1818-19) were mainly caused by 'those who traded, not upon their capital',[124] by little men who had 'speculated rashly' and now wished only 'to keep up the circulation as full as possible, that they might fatten and flourish upon that fulness.'[125] On the assumption that demand was relatively inelastic, depressions were the result of speculation and over-stocking. However, bullionists went further and claimed that such evils were only likely to occur if the currency were depreciated, and that resumption would prevent them. For Peel, the link between rash commercial speculation and an over-issue of paper 'was a fact not to be disputed'. He announced subsequently that though manufactures and trade had been active in 1819, they had been 'unsound' because conducted in an insecure currency. Similarly, Liverpool attributed 'periodical revulsions' to 'a system by which fictitious capitals might be...created and extended'.[126]

A more extraordinary assumption by the bullionists was that speculators made up a distinct class, which could be isolated from the mass of fair traders, a cancerous limb that could be excised without danger to the main body of merchants. Bullionists resented the easy credit facilities by which small men could aspire to a quick greatness without prior accumulation of capital, and were apprehensive that the collapse of bubble enterprises might threaten the security of even established commercial empires. In the past, Castlereagh had gaily assured Parliament that 'the sagacity of the lender will keep the borrower within bounds', and that 'though individuals may suffer [from over-trading], the nation will be benefited.'[127] Bullionists were not convinced, but most surprisingly they did suppose that convertibility, deflation, and dearer credit would leave genuine enterprise untouched while it killed off 'improvident and unreasonable

124. Frankland Lewis in H. of C., 2 Feb. 1819, 1 PD, xxxix. 239.
125. Tierney, ibid. 217.
126. Peel in H. of C., 24 May 1819, 1 PD, xl. 683 and 18 Feb. 1822, 2 PD, vi. 492; Liverpool in H. of L., 26 May 1820, 2 PD, i. 583.
127. Tierney, H. of C., 17 Feb. 1826, 2 PD, xiv. 550-1, sarcastically compared speculation to rebellion, since both needed to succeed before they were deemed legitimate. 'When a man did not succeed, he was nicknamed an overtrader...[but] when success followed the speculator, then he became the sagacious and adventurous British merchant.'

speculations'.[128] Steadier foreign exchanges would somehow
eliminate the stock-jobber; dear money would discourage the
use of continuation stock and accommodation paper; deflation
would 'improve the quality; but diminish the quantity of
commerce', as a bullionist Bank director, William Ward, put
it.[129] Ministers mistakenly dismissed all petitions against cash
payments as coming from speculators and debtors, who could
not bear the light of convertibility and justly faced ruin. But
neither they nor anyone else explained just how a metallic
standard could successfully discriminate between worthy and
speculative transactions, and thus impersonally select the
'real bills' from the dross.

So resumption was a deflationary policy — and as such
the culmination of the transition to peace — but it was not
specifically an export policy. Bullionists did not plan to
correct depressed exchanges by improving the balance of
trade so much as by improving the balance of investment.
Excess paper issues had boosted the funds, but had also
lowered interest rates and, since investors prefer to lend where
it is most profitable to lend, capital had left the country.
Bullionists therefore looked to deflation and high interest
rates to bring about a reflux and even some domestic investment of foreign money.[130] Rothschild had reluctantly to
admit that the restriction had greatly favoured the foreign
loan contractors, and that dearer money at home would
counter the 'growing passion' for investment in foreign
securities.[131] Fifty years later, investment booms in foreign
enterprises were to be approved as bringing Britain ample
returns in trade and hidden assets (including power), but
investment after Waterloo was merely for personal profit in
continental stocks. In his memorandum of July 1818,[132]

128. CSC, *Reports on the Expediency of resuming Cash Payments*, 1819, 221.
Gladstone sensibly objected (ibid. 113-14) that so-called 'excessive speculation'
was *inseparable* from the best interests of trade, for it grows out of prosperity;
we never have such speculation in bad times, but we always have abundance
of it in good'. See also Samuel Gurney and Ebenezer Gilchrist, ibid. 175 and 217.
Thomas Attwood defended 'speculation', along with 'inconvertibility', pointing
out that a mere drop in business confidence could render a hitherto 'sound'
transaction 'speculative'.
129. Ibid. 76.
130. Wood, *English Theories of Central Banking Control*, 105-6.
131. CSC, *Reports on the Expediency of resuming Cash Payments*, 1819, 157-63.
132. Huskisson, 'Rough draft on coin and currency', 1818, HP 38741 ff. 242-52.

Huskisson predicted that Britain had only to adopt an inviolable standard of value, and to repeal 'those universally exploded laws' forbidding free trade in bullion, and then 'the extent of our commercial dealings and operations of exchange, which make this Country the Emporium not only of Europe but of America north and south,...would make London the chief Bullion Market of the World.' If only London could become 'the *Settling House* of the money transactions of the world', all trade would be secure, steady and efficient. This motive was to be resumed in the commercial reforms of the 1820s, which were also geared, less to expanding British exports artificially than to attracting foreign goods and capital into British warehouses and funds — to making England the world's 'mart and banker' rather than its workshop.

Finally, while it may be impossible to interpret the policy of cash payments consistently in social or particularist terms — as a victory for trade, say, or established wealth — there is a more cogent case for regarding it as an act of retrospective justice to all creditor elements in the economy, the victims of inflation. Obviously, legislation could never undo all the disruption caused by war, and whether Parliament resumed at the old par or allowed the currency to go on depreciating, individual injustices were bound to occur. A creditor of 1800 might, because of the depreciation, be a debtor in 1819, and consequently be twice legally robbed. Anti-bullionists such as Torrens would have preferred to continue the restriction because any unavoidable injustice would in that case be at the expense of the 'drones' of society — the *rentiers*, mortgagees, annuitants, landlords, classes which spent only on their own pleasures and whose sufferings would be confined to themselves. Depreciation would effect a redistribution of wealth in favour of the productive classes — manufacturers, merchants, farmers.[133] But the bullionists, consistently with their desire to stabilize rather than simply augment activity, ignored the needs of the economy as a whole. Resumption and forced appreciation were desirable because they would

133. R. Torrens, *A comparative estimate of the effects which a continuance and a removal of the restriction upon cash payments are respectively calculated to produce, &c.* (1819), 52-69.

benefit those gentlemen-drones who had suffered most from the suspension. They had suffered, that it is to say, in relation to people beneath them who could exploit cheap money for careers of adventure: landlords complained of farmers who had become used to living like gentlemen, just as established merchants fulminated against gamblers.

Some anti-bullionists attempted to demonstrate that creditor classes had not in fact suffered, that fundholders, for example, had gained out of the war. The Committees countered by citing the elaborate calculations of Robert Mushet, a clerk at the Mint, who computed that, *in toto*, fundholders had lost £72,704 by lending money to the state in currency that subsequently depreciated.[134] Moreover, in so far as contemporaries ever tried to distinguish vertically between the contractual status of agriculture and commerce — and on the whole they preferred to draw the line horizontally between the established and the aspirant within each sector — then it was to proclaim that the merchants, 'whose incomes rise and fall with the price of commodities', had in fact done best out of the war, and that resumption would benefit the agriculturists most.[135] There was a widespread opinion that landlords had fared worst since 1797, due to declining real values of nominal payments previously stipulated, though in fact many had been able to increase their rents more than commensurately. An agriculturist, Lord King, welcomed cash payments as moving back the clock: 'By putting an end to the restriction, an alteration in the employment of capital, and the distribution of wealth must be produced in an opposite direction to that which the depreciation of the currency had produced'[136] — that is, wealth would revert to the land. Here the motive of 'equitable adjustment', disguised in legitimacy but as tangible as Cobbet's, coincided with the instinctive enthusiasm of the landed interest for a symbol of tradition and stability against

134. R. Mushet, *A Series of Tables, exhibiting the gain and loss to the fundholder, arising from the fluctuations in the value of the currency, from 1800 to 1821,* second edition (1821).
135. Haldimand to LSC, *Reports on the Expediency of the Resumption of Cash Payments,* 1819, 48-50.
136. H. of L., 21 May 1819, 1 PD, xl. 640.

improvement and industrialization. However, too much weight cannot be placed on this redistributive argument, for in 1819 few people anticipated the extent to which money would appreciate. Most pundits followed Ricardo in believing that it would be ten per cent at most, or hardly more than the existing premium on gold. The danger seemed to be that commerce would lack facilities; the threat to debtors and vendors (such as agriculturists) was seriously underrated.

The decision to resume cash payments was hardly an intellectual achievement — that belonged to 1810.[137] In 1819 a few academic bullionists like Huskisson persuaded cabinet and Parliament to adopt a gold standard on largely administrative grounds. Huskisson achieved this by his 'under-game' for Liverpool's ear, and in so doing he established himself as the government's chief economic counsellor at the expense of the Vansittart-Herries faction, which still enjoyed the remote patronage of Castlereagh. At the same time the government, while covering its retreat from anti-bullionism with full-scale parliamentary inquiries, threw over the Bank and the bankers, and determined henceforward to direct the economy itself. Nevertheless, ministers relished responsibility as little as servitude, and so, rather than assert a continuous control over the economy, they took refuge in gold as an automatic regulator and stabilizer. An impersonal system of this kind appealed far more than Ricardo's proposed National Bank or Attwood's managed currency. The gold standard would render the Bank of England 'the great steam engine of the state, to keep the channel of the circulation always pressing full'; and convertibility would be 'the regulator and index of the Engine, by which the extent of its operations and the sufficiency of the supply would be determined and ascertained'.[138]

Thomas Attwood protested that, on the contrary, bul-

---

137. Though Fetter, 'The Politics of the Bullion Report', 99-120, and 'The Bullion Report Re-examined', *Quarterly Journal of Economics*, lvi (1942), 655-65, reprinted in *Papers in English Monetary History*, 66-75, has demonstrated that Ricardo's personal influence on the preparation of the Bullion Report was less considerable than it was once thought to be.

138. Huskisson, 'Rough draft on coin and currency', 1818.

lionism would *prevent* the circulation from 'pressing full'.
It seemed absurd to him that Parliament should force the
'practical currency, under which all the transactions, and all
the establishments and engagements of the present generation
have been formed', to adapt themselves to the arbitrary
'legal or theoretical parts of our monetary system', instead
of the other way about.[139] Tory ministers were less satisfied
about the validity of the present generation's transactions,[140]
however, and they were perhaps misled by recent experience
into exaggerating the dangers of over-issue while neglecting
those of unnatural deflation. Their timing was unfortunate
too, in that they launched a programme of deflation and
dear money just when commercial and agricultural depression
invited an expansionary policy. It was not their fault that the
Bank decided to rush resumption through quickly, so
rendering it more abrasive than it need have been.[141] Besides,
the decision to resume could not have been postponed any
longer — the effort had to be made at once or not at all.
Opposition to resumption was often expressed in terms of
procrastination, but in reality everyone knew that this would
mean indefinite suspension. Liverpool congratulated himself
that the decisions to resume and to increase taxes were the
final two steps back to normality. As he wrote in the autumn
of 1820, 'Now that the circulation is settled on a fixed
foundation, and that the annual loans are beginning to be no
longer wanted, the Country appears, for the first time, to be
settling itself into a state of peace.'[142]

139. T. Attwood, *A Letter to the Earl of Liverpool on the Reports of the Committees of the two Houses of Parliament, on the questions of the Bank Restriction
Act* (1819), 14-15 and *passim*. Heygate in H. of C., 25 May 1819, 1 PD, xl. 750-6.
140. Liverpool claimed, moreover, that despite increases in the amounts of
business, commerce, manufacturing, cultivation, taxation and public debt that
had taken place since 1797, it was not necessary to provide more money than had
sufficed then because that money now circulated much more rapidly, and was
used more economically, than before the wars. H. of L., 21 May 1819, 1 PD, xl.
622-4.
141. See below pp. 89-91. Herries would have liked to accompany resumption with
counter-cyclical tax cuts; in the same way Ricardo urged the Bank to *sell* and not
buy gold.
142. Liverpool to Huskisson, 29 Sept. 1820, HP. 38742 ff. 26-7.

PART TWO

ADJUSTMENT TO THE GOLD STANDARD
1819 – 1822

III

DEPRESSION AND DISCONTENT

Nothing can be more annoying than the levity with which some persons...treat the present state of the country, fancying that its distress will correct the mischief, and that things will find their proper level. Perhaps some of these wise people might as well talk of the advantage of re-organising by returning to a state of nature. But we are in a very artificial state...
Sheffield to Sidmouth, 19 Jan. 1816, Sidmouth MSS. 152M (1816-17)

Paralytic Toryism and the 'over-production men'

A short boom in 1817-18 was followed by serious economic depression. The domestic price index fell from a modest peak in April 1818 to a severe trough in September 1822. In these four and a half years, wheat plummeted from 90s. per quarter to 39.7s. Non-agricultural prices fell similarly, but recovered more quickly. The import price index declined to March 1821, and remained low until the autumn of 1824, while the volume of exports was well down in 1819 and did not pick up until after 1820.[1] Economic crisis was accompanied by social and political tension. Manufacturing unemployment in 1819-20 occasioned radical disaffection in the towns, while deepening agricultural distress led to movements within the landed classes for constitutional and policy changes in favour of agriculture.

This crisis gave rise to a series of contentious debates, in which ministers were reluctantly forced to declare a coherent strategy of sorts. They had simply marked time on economic policies since 1815, proposing little and conceding much.[2] Their supporters sighed for 'a daring Minister' to revitalize them;[3] Whigs complained that they were 'shifting the odium of strong measures from their shoulders to those of the opposition',[4] neutrals considered them 'so completely

1. A. D. Gayer, W. W. Rostow, and A. J. Schwartz, *The Growth and Fluctuation of the British Economy, 1790-1850* (1953), i. 140-7.
2. Huskisson to Canning, 11 Aug. 1822, HP 38743 ff. 192-5.
3. Redesdale to Colchester, 4 Jan. 1820, Colchester, *Diary and Correspondence,* iii. 107-8.
4. Holland to Grey, 22 May 1820, HHP 51546 ff. 55-6.

paralyzed, that they dare do nothing, and it becomes a
Government of Committees of the House of Commons'.[5] By
1820, however, the argument that distress was entirely due to
the transition from war to peace was beginning to sound
platitudinous, and ministers felt compelled to admit that
there might be less fatalistic causes. If the Tory government
became more assertive in the 1820s, this was due less to
changes in personnel than to the parliamentary imperative,
in times of crisis, for ministers to defend and clarify their
policies. In the same way, their opponents were forced to
rationalize their dissent in theoretical terms.

   The economic policy of the 1820s, which was to harden
into Gladstone's *pax Britannica* and Niemeyer's 'Treasury
View', appealed to Ricardian political economy for justification, but was pragmatically rather than theoretically
motivated. Official sanction helped the Ricardian tradition
to 'defeat' Malthusianism so rapidly — and against academic
odds — after Waterloo, and establish itself as orthodox.[6] And
if, in the 1930s, when politicians were frustrated by their
own helplessness in the face of unemployment, the fact that
Keynes's *General Theory* 'purveyed what might be called an
activist philosophy sealed its success',[7] so — conversely —
Ricardianism appealed to Liverpool's government because it
justified passivity and inaction. Economic radicalism, on the
other hand, based on Malthusian fears of underconsumption
and concern with aggregate demand, found coherent and
forceful political expression for the first time. Webb Hall,
Thomas Attwood, and William Cobbett, who in normal
times might well have been dismissed as cranks and agitators,
became for a while the leaders of powerful movements of
opinion.

   Academic attempts to develop a counter-classical theory of
underconsumptionism never matured,[8] but at the less
sophisticated level of pamphlets and parliamentary debate,
conflict between 'orthodox' Ricardianism and radical under-

5. Fremantle to Buckingham, 9 Feb. 1819, Buckingham and Chandos, *Memoirs
of the Court of England during the Regency*, ii. 301.
6. S. G. Checkland, 'The Propagation of Ricardian Economics in England',
Economica, new series, xvi (1949), 40-52.
7. D. Winch, *Economics and Policy* (1969), 177.
8. B. A. Corry, *Money Saving and Investment in English Economics, 1800-50*
(1962), 109.

consumptionism dominated discussion of the distress. It was evident to everyone that an excess of supply over demand was a major cause of the fall in price of many articles and products: manufacturing goods, agricultural produce, shipping, urban and rural labour — all were in surplus. Wartime inflation and the 1817-18 boom had encouraged production, while peace and the collapse of that boom had reduced demand. Most people agreed that over-production and under-consumption had both operated to some degree, but most also felt obliged to isolate one or the other as the real, the original cause of distress.[9] Repeatedly throughout the debates of 1820-2, the Whig peers Lansdowne, Lauderdale, Grey, and King alleged an internal failure of consumption, largely due to cash payments coupled with crippling taxation. The fact that agriculture and the Midlands iron trade remained depressed until 1822, while exports recovered, seemed to confirm that the trouble was basically a 'want of demand' at home, an 'inability to consume'.[10] Denying this, Liverpool and Harrowby paraded a panoply of excise statistics, showing that the consumption of articles like tea and malt had increased, and maintained that wartime prices and capitalization had engendered over-production.[11] Brougham reminded the Commons, however, that improved excise figures had to be set off against the still greater rise in population, while Dugdale of Birmingham, dismissing all such statistics as a 'fallacious criterion' of prosperity, insisted that there had been 'a most material diminution of the consumption' of necessaries in the Midlands.[12] Ricardo alone broke with the party line, defending the government opposite, and prescribing disinvestment as the only cure for a bloated

9. Ricardo was uncertain as to which was the original cause (H. of C., 7 Mar. 1821, 2 PD, iv. 1158), but his writings dismiss the possibility of Malthus' "general glut" due to a failure of demand. In attributing distress to marginal production, Ricardo assumed that demand would automatically increase to meet it. R. L. Meek. 'The Decline of Ricardian Economics in England', *Economica,* new series, xvii (1950), 43-62 and reprinted in *Economics and Ideology and Other Essays* (1967), 51-74.
10. H. of L., 5 and 21 Feb. 1821, 26 Feb. and 25 June 1822, 2 PD, iv. 356-60, 824-36; vi. 721; vii. 1323.
11. H. of L., 26 May 1820, 26 Feb. 1822, 2 PD, i. 568-70; vi. 698-701; Harrison to Liverpool, 19 Sept. and 30 Nov. 1820, LP 38287 ff. 233-4; 38288 ff. 221-4.
12. H. of C., 8 Feb. 1821, 2 PD, iv. 523-4; see Gladstone in H. of C., 9 Feb. 1821 2 PD, iv. 572-3.

iron industry. Finally, that "noble refrigerator", Lord Castlereagh, admitting that distress existed superficially, reassured
Parliament that increased consumption, which showed
through the excise figures, revealed a basic prosperity that
entirely absolved ministers from intervening. 'Consumption,
both as to the comforts and even the luxuries of life, is
advancing, not only with rapidity, but with a universality of
distribution which clearly shows that the principle of prosperity subsists...it requires only an animating cause to produce
its full and natural effects.'[13] Needless to say, he thought
that this animation should come, not from the government,
but from individuals reacting spontaneously to market forces.

All this had little to do with economic analysis. It was a
political struggle between government and opposition to
place and evade censure and responsibility. Ministers and
their supporters rallied to the thesis of over-supply as a way
of exonerating themselves from blame for a failing economy
(since in a sense an over-productive economy might be said
to be doing *too* well) and of excusing themselves from the
need to take action to correct it. Distress was not confined
to Britain, but was the universal consequence of speculative
over-trading during the war and Bank restriction. The only
cure would be the passive administration of dear money,
deflation, and the winnowing out of inefficient or otherwise
unsound producers — a step (albeit unintentional) towards
an international division of labour based on comparative
advantage. Huskisson believed that if only the country,
without violating public credit, 'disentangled itself from
those branches of trade which, instead of promoting, impeded
its interests', it would emerge from the crisis purged but all the
more powerful.[14] Having resumed cash payments, ministers
felt they need take no further measures. Meanwhile political
opponents, and everyone that was suffering from the
depression, stressed under consumption and failures on the
demand side, often dating them from 1819, not the peace.
'The evil was not [in Landsdowne's opinion] to be remedied
by taking lands out of cultivation, but by raising the con-

13. H. of C., 15 Feb. 1822, 2 PD, vi. 360.
14. H. of C., 21 Mar. 1821, 2 PD, iv. 1398.

sumption so as to make the produce and the demand meet each other.'[15] This diagnosis led to diverse proposals — either more or less protection (to stimulate respectively domestic or foreign demand); tax cuts or occasionally new taxes; cheaper money; either public lending and spending, or public saving and parsimony. No doubt this diversity prevented underconsumptionism from becoming a political force, but what all the proposals had in common was that they involved direct action by government. Whigs wanted ministers to commit themselves; distressed interests needed relief. The cabinet excused itself on the grounds that all interests were interdependent, and that policies of sectional relief would, by damaging other classes, ultimately harm everyone.

The Whigs had a point in condemning the government's abnegation of responsibility, but they themselves tempered altruism with ambition, half welcoming distress as antiministerial propaganda and being chary of succeeding to power before it had subsided. Grey had pressed cash payments in 1819, cynically aware that it would damage trade and shake the Ministry.[16] He criticized ministerial inactivity in Parliament, while privately admitting that relief was impossible — that the 'embarrassment and confusion' caused by cash payments was incapable of speedy solution — that any positive measures would be inexpedient. It was well that his party was in the wilderness still, since

The embarrassment of our finances, and the distress of the Mercantile Interests is so great, so little capable of any immediate relief, and indeed so likely to increase in spite of all that can be done to repair them, that a system of wise and moderate policy has not a fair chance. It will not give employment to the manufacturers or bread to those who are starving...All measures of gradual improvement would be exposed to the clamour which the radicals would be ready and eager to excite against them of delusion, and there is too much reason to apprehend that even if we were in power, with a *carte blanche* for our conduct, we should be able to do little to appease the growing discontent of the people. This would lead to flat despair...[17]

'The great advantage of our present situation', he wrote elsewhere, 'is that it relieves [us] from all responsibility for

15. H. of L., 26 Feb. 1822, 2 PD, vi. 721.
16. See above, p. 39.
17. Grey to Holland, 24 Oct. 1819, HHP 51546 ff. 12-14.

the measures, which the times require'.[18] Whigs should stick
to general principles, 'proposing nothing' specific, while
attacking what ministers put forward. This was Grey's
answer to the government's delegation of responsibility to
select committees and commissioners.

The government's (and especially the Prime Minister's)
reluctance to interfere with the economy in the face of
widespread demands that it should do so has sometimes been
interpreted as evidence of a *laissez-faire* commitment, and a
pointer towards the age of free trade. But it was not yet an
intellectual ideal so much as a political tactic of doing
nothing, and indicated an unwillingness to interfere with
established restrictions on trade, rather than an active desire
to release trade from such trammels. When Liverpool said that
'things would find their own level if allowed to remain free',
he meant, of course, if parliament abstained from interfering
with prevailing restrictions, not if those restrictions were
swiftly removed. By 'their own level' he meant that interests
would adjust to the prevailing *status quo*, rather than to
a complete international division of labour. The crucial
premise was that the crisis was temporary and that, left to
itself, the system would automatically recover, provided only
that certain conditions were observed, notably that public
credit and confidence were maintained and capitalists
induced to invest in appropriate enterprises. Confidence
required convertibility, without which any apparent recovery
would be speculative and artificial, and it required also that
opposition spokesmen should not, in modern idiom, 'rock
the boat'. When the funds wavered in the aftermath of Peterloo, Liverpool assured Vansittart that 'if we are quiet all will
come right'.[19] Attempts by government to mend matters
could only unsettle and deter investors. Presumably Liverpool,
Castlereagh, Huskisson, and Vansittart came to believe this
utterly after repeating it so often. 'Government or Parliament
never meddle with these matters at all but they do harm
more or less.' Mortals must wait patiently 'till Trade comes

18. Grey to Holland, 23 Apr. 1820, Grey MSS., quoted in Mitchell, *The Whigs
in Opposition*, 141.
19. Liverpool to Vansittart, 31 Oct. 1819, LP 38574 ff. 144-7; Yonge, *Life and
Administration of Lord Liverpool*, ii. 416-17.

round and the Population can find Employment in a natural way'.[20] 'The truth is that the thing must be left to set itself right', through cheapness and increasing demand, through loss of profits and diminishing production.[21] Peel dismissed all interference as 'quackery', and insisted that only by bleeding the economy of its excesses could governments bring about a revival.[22] Ministers sought recovery through disinvestment, rather than through Say's Law of marginal supply creating demand.

Conversely, everyone who craved positive action of whatever sort argued that, left to itself, the crisis would not pass, that the economy was not self regulating. A disgruntled agriculturist complained that 'he had heard much of the political economy of the chancellor of the exchequer and that of the gentlemen near him, who so often said, that those things would right themselves but he wished to know from these economists by what process such things could be righted, or the equilibrium so much desired could be restored?...the fact was, that in the midst of plenty the country was suffering all the inconveniences of want'.[23] 'I should concur with you', wrote another, 'in thinking that any interference on the part of Government was altogether undesirable (except in a trifling degree on acc^t. of local distress) but I much fear we cannot hope for any return of such sort of prosperity on account of the extensive use of machinery and the contemplated increased use of it.' Machinery had displaced human labour and rendered the present crisis much more serious and less self-correcting than previous depressions. Moreover, the twenty years' war and consequent monopoly of supplying the world had led to the employment of such a vast proportion of the population in manufactures, 'that the supply does but continually overstock a glutted market, and the Poors' Rates unhappily make it even yet the interest of speculators to increase that glut'.[24]

20. Liverpool to Kenyon, 18 Dec. 1819, Kenyon MSS. draft in LP 38281 ff. 347-9.
21. Liverpool in H. of L., 26 Feb. 1822, 2 PD, vi. 710.
22. Peel to Goulburn, 31 July 1826, Goulburn MSS. II/16.
23. Lockhart in H. of C., 3 Apr. 1821, 2 PD, v. 14.
24. Kenyon to Liverpool, 20 Dec. 1819, LP 38281 ff. 363-6; see the motto at the beginning of this chapter.

There were two main groups of activists. For free traders, the only way to move the economy out of crisis was to demolish the barriers (corn and usury laws being the greatest) to trade, investment, and the free distribution of resources, and to open up new channels of foreign commerce. Supply would create its own demand only so long as distribution was free. Faced by the protectionist demands of the agriculturists, Ricardo, Coke, and the free-trade wing of the Whigs found themselves siding with ministers, who endorsed the doctrine of over-production in agriculture;[25] but they were quick to perceive how preposterous was a ministerial position that held both production and population to be in surplus. As Coke put it,

Lord Liverpool attributes the low prices to an excess of cultivation; Lord Sidmouth attributes the distress among the manufacturers [unemployment] to an excess of population. These two questions of produce and population are of the very highest order in political economy. They are great powers, and, as such, it has been the business of all the celebrated statesmen and lawgivers of ancient and modern times to increase their amount...[But] if the abundant produce of these realms be incapable of [?assuming] a direction by which it can find its way to the mouths of our abundant population, then has Lord Liverpool rightly condemned us to be punished for our industry, and then is Lord Sidmouth wiser than all the great sages of antiquity, wiser than Providence itself, which had commanded us to increase and multiply.[26]

Coke's search for a 'more consoling and a more rational result' centred around the distribution of resources. The free play of 'capitalism' would carry surplus food to the surplus mouths. With the manufacturing recovery of 1821, ministers were to drop 'over-population' and concentrate on 'over-cultivation' as the cause of continuing agricultural distress. This was to make their position more logical and place them more firmly alongside the free trade Ricardian school. Meanwhile, ministers relied upon Malthusian population theory to

25. William Cobbett, *Rural Rides* (1930), i. 79, caustically described Ricardo and his temporary allies in government as 'the Oracle and the over-production men'.
26. Coke to Eyres, 27 Jan. 1821, Stirling, *Coke of Norfolk and His Friends,* 456-8. Sinclair's son and biographer also exposed this paradox: 'The bullionists spoke of over population as coexisting with over production, thus preposterously maintaining that there was too much food and clothing in the country, and at the same time too many people to be fed and clothed; they were never able to perceive that the actual root of the evil was deficiency in the means of *distri bution.' Life and Works of Sir John Sinclair,* ii. 310-11.

refute Malthus on gluts.

Against the free traders were the underconsumptionist activists, for whom the need was to create, not simply redistribute, resources, and for whom the basic fear was that of Malthus, that demand might not keep pace with marginal production. The Whig leader Lauderdale, formerly Citizen Maitland, came the nearest to presenting a coherent radical policy of underconsumption. As early as 1804 Lauderdale had presciently warned that when peace returned, the ministers of the day should beware lest 'abstraction of demand' cause such a price collapse 'as to discourage reproduction'. Also, 'they must be cautious not to mistake, for the effects of abundance, *that which in reality may be only the effect of failure of demand*'.[27] Though the Napoleonic war had prejudicially shifted the ownership of wealth into new hands, it had nevertheless created additional prosperity by consuming all of the revenue and much capital for year after year. 'It was the check given to expenditure' at the end of the war that had 'produced the sensation of calamity.'[28] Where Ricardians would have said that wartime wealth had been unreal and the post-war slump largely an inevitable reaction, Lauderdale proposed that it was the slump which was an artificial 'sensation', and that the wartime prosperity had been genuine.[29] Lauderdale rejected the government's assumption that all that was necessary was to provide the conditions for capital investment, and the rest would follow. There was, he told Lord Holland, 'no notion so false' or so 'fatal' as the popular fallacy 'that Capital is the prime mover which can create or extend every branch of industry'. Capital was assuredly necessary for the satisfaction of consumer demand, but, 'it is these demands that are the prime movers in putting every branch of Industry into action, and at the present moment the only relief that can be administered to the country is that which creates an increased Demand for commodity.' The apparent revival of

27. Lauderdale, *Inquiry into the Nature and Origin of Public Wealth, and into the Means and Causes of its Increase* (1804), 263-4 .
28. Lauderdale to Holland, n.d. [?1821], HHP 51692 ff. 58-65.
29. And whereas Ricardo thought that the economic recovery of 1821 was valid because it was based on gold, Lauderdale argued that it was false because based on cheapness.

manufactures in 1821 was based upon fictitious demand —
that is to say, upon speculative *consignments* of goods manufactured at very low wages, and sent to foreign markets in the
mere hope of their finding a sale (as distinct from true
demand when goods were produced on *commission*). The
crisis was not yet over, and would eventually terminate in
glut and revulsion — 'the sure effect of setting any branch of
Industry into Motion by Capital instead of using capital for
the purpose of facilitating the supply of that produce of our
Industry for which the consumers indicate a demand'.[30] The
only ways to raise demand and to create prosperity were by
the silver standard, public spending and — more feasibly —
tax reductions to liberate private spending and enhance the
yield of the remaining taxes. The accumulation and hoarding
of capital would swiftly put an end to all production — 'On
the other hand a country cannot consume too much.'[31]

Thus whereas ministers hoped to escape from the depression
merely by keeping up the funds, and claimed that once
manufactures began to revive, agricultural improvement would
follow, their opponents demanded positive measures of relief.
Lauderdale and many other Whigs, and increasingly the
agriculturists, pressed for tax reductions and other more
direct methods of creating demand, such as cheaper money.
This conflict underlay all the economic debates of 1819-22,
especially those on taxation, the sinking fund, and monetary
policy. The more radical position took some time to develop.
When the wisdom of bullionism or the prospects of tax relief
were debated in 1820-1, it was generally in terms of social
justice — how to alleviate the sufferings of the distressed, to
reduce their production costs and the burden of their debts.

30. Lauderdale to Holland, n.d., HHP 51692 ff. 58-65. But Liverpool in H. of L.,
15 Mar. 1815, 1 PD, xxx. 183, maintained that capital, credit and fuel were
more essential to the success of manufacturing industry than the 'secondary
consideration' of cheap labour.
31. M. Paglin, *Malthus and Lauderdale, the anti-Ricardian Tradition* (1961);
F. A. Fetter, 'Lauderdale's Oversaving Theory' , *American Economic Review*,
xxxv (1945), 263-83; M. A. Corry, 'The Theory of the Economic Effects of
Government Expenditure in English Classical Political Economy', *Economica*,
new series, xxv (1958), 34-48; R. L. Meek, 'Physiocracy and the Early Theories of
Under-Consumption', ibid, xviii (1951), 229-69; A. V. Cole, 'Lord Lauderdale and
his "Inquiry"', *Scottish Journal of Political Economy*, iii (1956), 115-25; J. A.
Schumpeter, *History of Economic Analysis* (1954), 487-8, 623-6, 656.

But by 1822 there was a much more widespread under-consumptionist awareness behind the activists' demands; discussions of taxation concentrated as much on the level of demand as on mere retrenchment, and monetary debates analysed the nature, reality, and creation of wealth, instead of concentrating on how to adjust debts to a new standard.

As this underconsumptionist attack developed in 1822 ministers were compelled to discard the philosophy of passive neutrality, and to approach the Ricardian, free-trade altern-ative. Like their clerical counsellor, Edward Copleston, they came to appreciate (from Ricardo) that they must first remove 'obstacles' if Britain's 'capitalist' economy was to obtain 'that principle of self-correction which the analogy of nature teaches us is the universal law of her consti-tution'.[32]

The economics of law and order

As an historian has commented, economic policy in the pre-police age was mainly a matter of law and order.[33] The shadow of the French Revolution lowered over politics. At the Home Office, Sidmouth was forever inquiring anxiously about the forthcoming crops and the prospects of employ-ment. He believed that 'instincts for disaffection' were fundamentally economic, though they might have to be manipulated by incorrigible demagogues before bursting into revolt.[34] Ministers dreaded a coincidence of dear bread and urban unemployment for social reasons, but did not yet reflect that the one evil might cause the other. Sidmouth also thought that shorter working hours would usefully spread available employment over a greater number of persons.[35] Agriculturists claimed that since they employed more hands than the manufacturers, their importance was paramount, but after 1815 ministers snubbed their demands. For it was not a rural *jacquerie* that they feared, but riots in Lancashire, urban Cheshire, the West Riding and south-west Scotland.

32. E. Copleston, *A Letter to Robert Peel* (1819), 37.
33. L. Brown, *The Board of Trade and the Free-Trade Movement 1830-42*(1958), 4-5.
34. Sidmouth to Exmouth, 21 Sept. 1817, Sidmouth MSS. 152M (1816-17).
35. Sidmouth to Charles Bathurst, 11 Aug. 1816, ibid.

Historians have frequently dismissed the constant post-war rumours of sedition as fantasy, concocted as likely as not by Sidmouth's own *agents provocateurs* to justify repression. But recently, writers of quite different ideological persuasions have confirmed the reality of the social menace.[36] Justified or not, ministers' alarms were genuine; so was their reluctance — humanitarian or merely prudent — to exercise legislative repression. Manufacturing distress posed this dilemma for ministers: ought they to cut indirect taxation to gratify the lower classes, and seek to forestall disaffection by economic concession? Or should they cut direct taxation, even though it meant raising tariffs on the working man's diet, in order to please the governing classes, and secure their support for repression? In the anxious months after Peterloo, ministers were inclined to think that Lancashire was amenable to concession, and that 'preventive measures may even now prove effectual', but that in the famine-threatened west of Scotland 'the Evil is in a more advanced state and will not be stopped without bloodshed.'[37] Most of them took a complex view of sedition, unlike some recent historians.[38] Canning thought the combination of disaffection and distress merely an 'unlucky coincidence at an embarrassing time',[39] and Liverpool explained to Grenville:

Tho' it cannot be denied that the great increase of our manufacturing population, the dependence of a great part of that population on Foreign Demand, and the refinements in Machinery (which enable manufacturers to perform that work in weeks which formerly occupied months and which leads consequently to extravagant wages at one time and to low and inadequate ones at another), have recently subjected and must in the nature of things subject this Country to evils with which in the same degree we were formerly unacquainted, yet all these circumstances would not have accounted for the present state of the Public Mind in certain parts of the Country if the events of the French Revolution had not directed the attention of the lower Orders of the Community and those immediately above them to Political Considerations, had not shaken all respect for established authority and antient

36. E. P. Thompson, *The Making of the English Working Class* (1963), 603-710; R. Walmsley, *Peterloo: The Case Reopened* (1969), *passim*.
37. Liverpool to Grenville, 14 Nov. 1819, LP 38381 ff. 1-9; Hamilton to Liverpool, 6 Dec. 1819, ibid. ff. 225-6.
38. e.g. W. W. Rostow, *British Economy of the Nineteenth Century* (1948), 125 and *passim*.
39. Canning to Huskisson, 14 Aug. 1819, HP 38741 ff. 312-17.

Institutions and had not familiarized mankind with a system of organization which has been justly represented to be as ingenious and
appropriate to its purpose as any Invention in Mechanics.[40]
In other words, disorder was caused not by economic mismanagement but by political events beyond Liverpool's
control. Therefore political 'repression' came before economic
concession, but was extremely mild — setting loyal declarations in motion to counter Whig and Radical meetings;
activating a loyal press to shout down licentious publications,
the chief carriers of revolutionary fever; encouraging sheriffs
to refuse county meetings and dismissing Fitzwilliam from
his lieutenancy; and introducing the notorious but hardly
barbaric Six Acts. George Harrison arranged with the Bank
directors, Harman and John Whitmore, for about fifty of the
City's 'wealth and respectability' to declare support for
the Constitution, and fifteen hundred signed this declaration
in three days.[41] Very possibly these precautions contributed
to the creeping apathy of the Whigs' campaign.[42] Many
country gentlemen, and the Duke of York, wanted ministers
to go further, and to 'put down discontent by force'.[43] But
Liverpool flatly refused to augment the standing army — first,
because he did not have the money; second, because political
friends would suppose that ministers were 'availing ourselves
of the present circumstances to tread back our steps on the
subject of the Army Establishment';[44] finally, because it
would smack of centralism. 'We must have an army in peace
to protect the Metropolis, including as it does, the King, the
Parliament and the Bank. We must have a regular force
likewise for the protection of our Dock Yards, and other
great public depots — but the Property of the Country must
be taught to protect itself.'[45] By setting a 'tide' going for
loyalty, by condoning the Manchester magistrates in order to
encourage the others,[46] by congratulating Tories who were

40. Liverpool to Grenville, 14 Nov. 1819.
41. *Courier*, 2, 4 and 5 Oct. 1819; Harrison to Liverpool, 1 Oct. 1819, LP 38280
ff. 69-78; Reid to Harrison, 6 Oct. 1818, ibid. ff. 108-9.
42. Brock, *Lord Liverpool and Liberal Toryism*, 111-19.
43. Lethbridge to Liverpool, 1 Nov. 1819, LP 38280 ff. 274-5.
44. Liverpool to Arbuthnot, 20 Oct. 1819, ibid. ff. 250-1.
45. Liverpool to John Beckett (Under-Secretary of the Home Office), 25 Oct.
1819, ibid. ff. 205-6.
46. Liverpool to Canning, 10 Nov. 1819, LP 38568 ff. 72-4.

organizing volunteer forces locally, ministers avoided direct
action. Wellington, back in England, had no wish to use the
army as a political weapon. He welcomed local effort (which
did not merely rely on governments as 'a sort of commutation
for what they paid to it') because it must conduce to a
'national character'.[47]

One obvious economic concession would have been progressive taxation. The property tax was held to be merely in
abeyance. George Harrison had long desired its reimposition
as a financial expedient, but in the 1819 crisis he argued for
it on social grounds, as did Lord Kenyon and other staunch
Tories. Harrison considered that it would

arrest the progress of those sentiments which if not arrested, must
inevitably overturn the constitution and government...A *modified*
Property Tax upon the Income of all *realized* Capital only to such an
extent or percentage as might enable a Reduction of other Taxes to
a corresponding amount, which may bear hardly or inconveniently
upon the Income of labour. — Such a measure would be the best
practical Refutation of the Calumnies of the Demagogues against the
Rich.[48]

Direct taxation was reluctantly rejected, however, because
just then votes were needed for the delicate divisions on the
Six Acts. Thus the need to push 'repression' through parliament thwarted policies of concession.

More pertinent was the question of public assistance to
languishing manufacturers like the weavers of Kilmarnock,
Ardrossan, and Lanark. There had been a precedent for this
in 1817 when, moved by the distress around Birmingham,
ministers had agreed to issue £500,000 of exchequer bills,
on security of parish rates, to commissioners for instigating
public works and encouraging the fisheries; and a further

47. E. Phipps, *Memoirs of the Political and Literary Life of Robert Plumer Ward*
(1850), ii. 43. See Wellington, *Despatches, Correspondence and Memoranda,
1819-31* (1867-78), iii. 385-92 for correspondence between Wellington and Peel
on the question of whether distribution of food to starving Irish peasants should
be administered locally or centrally.
48. Harrison to Liverpool, 1 Oct. 1819. The Cabinet did consider introducing a
small income tax at this time. See Bute and Dumfries to Liverpool, 20 Nov. 1819,
LP 38281 ff. 79-80; Ricardo to Trower, 12 Nov. 1819, Sraffa, *Works and Correspondence of David Ricardo*, viii. 135.

£250,000 to the Lord Lieutenant of Ireland for advances out of the consolidated fund.[49] In 1819 there were many applications for short-term loans to help launch public works and state-aided emigration. Liverpool never supposed that planned emigration was susceptible of more than 'gradual accomplishment'. He agreed to assist the Glasgow Dock scheme, but reminded one Scotch adviser that the government had no disposable funds for poor relief, that 'the People of England provide for their Poor by local Assessments', and that they could not also be expected as rate-payers to look after the paupers of countries where no such imposition existed.[50] Initial self-help was the only foundation for any state assistance.

Besides, Liverpool was convinced that such assistance could be of little 'permanent value'; it could merely 'relieve temporary distress till Trade comes round, and the Population can find Employment in a natural way'.[51] This attitude became clearer during the next period of industrial stagnation, rioting, and loom-breaking, in 1826. Many Tories took Mrs. Arbuthnot's line that if the populace behaved itself it could not be in want, and that if it rioted it forfeited all sympathy. Liverpool was less callous, but felt that short-term aid to workers in redundant occupations would but impede beneficial redeployment. 'Is not the *London Silk Manufacture* on the Decline, and must not those engaged in it seek employment elsewhere?' he asked Peel.[52] Again, 'there is no prospect of the Hand-Looms ever being able to compete again with the Power-Looms. This must throw an immense population out of employment, and be the cause of appalling distress till the individuals interested shall have been dispersed

49. M. W. Flinn, 'The Poor Employment Act of 1817', *Economic History Review* second series, xiv (1961), 82-92. Ministers included safeguards to prevent the grant being used in the countryside, and as they had just previously rejected Vansittart's scheme for advances to agriculturists, an Exchequer Loan Plan to mortgage landed estates, the favouritism shown to the towns was evident. Vansittart 'consoled' the landed interest by asserting that it was 'to such an extent identified with the state, that he could not conceive any circumstance by which it could be so far separated from its prosperity or difficulties as to receive relief from any sum which parliament could wisely advance to it'. H. of C., 28 Apr. 1817, 1PD, xxxvi. 29. C.B., Ma 202-3.
50. Liverpool to Hamilton, 8 and 14 Dec. 1819, LP 38281 ff. 251-2, 289-91.
51. Liverpool to Kenyon, 18 Dec. 1819, ibid. ff. 347-9.
52. Liverpool to Peel, 29 Mar. 1826, Peel MSS. 40305 f. 168.

and engaged in other Pursuits.'[53] On the other hand, under
Herries's co-ordination, much was done for Lancashire where,
unlike Spitalfields, silk could be stimulated into a self-
generating recovery. It was calculated that here, less than
£50,000 could be used to employ 4,000 labourers and
thereby feed 20,000 "souls" for sixteen weeks.[54] But where
unsound industries were already on the decline, humanitarian
relief could only prolong and exacerbate the misery.

Where basically prosperous areas like Lancashire were
concerned, the familiar argument against public works and
other schemes to stimulate employment was that they
merely diverted resources from a more profitable private
sector. For Peel, direct relief would 'slacken the exertions of
the Master Manufacturers'.[55] His predecessor at the Home
Office had also deprecated individual and parliamentary
charity because, although it might afford temporary relief,
ultimately it would prevent workers from providing for
themselves 'through the medicine of labour'.[56] In this
context, Charles Grant made a revealing distinction when,
having succeeded Peel as Chief Secretary, he urged Liverpool
to grant moneys to Ireland for 'the promotion of public
interests'. Grant conceded that in England government
interference could only raise false hopes and benefit nobody;
but the present condition of Ireland should be compared
with that of an England long past.

Nobody can doubt that one hundred and twenty years ago a prodigious
stimulus was afforded to that national industry and prosperity of
England by the direct interposition of Government in a multitude of
ways, which would be disapproved by our modern political œconomists,
and which were perhaps adopted on false principles. I take the present
state of Ireland to be in some material respects similar.[57]

This must mean that in an economy that had taken off into
capitalism and self-sustained growth, economic effort by the
government merely diverted funds from the more important

53. Liverpool to Herries, 24 Jan. 1827, Herries MSS.
54. For the emigration committees, soup kitchens, clothing stores, McAdam
roadworks, turnpike trusts, manufacturers' relief committees and other relief
work undertaken in 1826, see D. Bythell, *The Handloom Weavers, a study in the
English Cotton Industry during the Industrial Revolution* (1969), 157-8, 240-2;
H.J.M. Johnston, *British Emigration Policy, 1815-30: 'Shovelling out Paupers'*
(1972), 100-4. Liverpool to Herries, 9 and 17 Aug., 27 Oct. 1826, Herries MSS.
55. Peel to Littleton, 31 July 1826, Hatherton MSS. D260/M/F/5/27/3/45.
56. Sidmouth to Talbot, 31 Oct. 1816, Sidmouth MSS. 152M (1816-17).
57. Grant to Liverpool, 28 Dec. 1819, LP 38282 ff. 43-8.

private sector. In England public aid would only disturb an enlightened self-interest that was operating successfully. But in pre-capitalist Ireland (as in seventeenth-century England), where the propensity to invest privately was so much lower, and often non-existent, public investment and other forms of interference were needed in order to get the economy moving. Ministers preferred to see the 1819 crisis as a temporary, cyclical reaction, which would heal of its own accord, and Grant was reminding them that in Ireland this was not the case, and that there deflationary depression did not (as in England) contain the seeds of its own recovery.

The diversionary objection continued to apply to Ireland, despite Grant's pleading, though in an unusual way. Vansittart objected to the large amounts spent on Ireland in the past ('and I am afraid generally upon mere jobs'),[58] and agreed with Grant that though government interference could divert wealth (often unjustly by damaging those already in possession of business resources), it was in no sense empowered to stimulate activity, multiply business, accelerate growth or create riches. Even if in Ireland there was no profit-oriented, super-productive private sector, from which funds could be diverted by state enterprize, the state could not manufacture *real* wealth. This had to come from somewhere. Representatives of Scottish fishermen were quick to point out that aid for Irish fisheries could only succeed at the expense of their own livelihoods, which had been established after great outlay of capital.[59] Grant himself conceded that governments could not 'create funds where a whole nation is in want', but could merely divert resources: 'something may be done towards equalizing the pressure.'[60]

Thus the government could offer nothing but palliatives

58. Vansittart to Liverpool, 30 Dec. 1819, ibid. ff. 74-5.
59. S. W. Grant and James Loch to Marquis of Stafford, 14 Feb. 1820, LP 38283, ff. 67-8. Many argued that it was only fair to go on protecting such interests as had invested capital on the assumption that they would remain protected, although governments frequently warned that tariffs no more bound the future than a Bank Restriction did. Theorists like John Stuart Mill, who argued that protection was justified in the case of infant industries, until they were in a position to withstand and benefit from blasts of healthy competition, overlooked the fact that it was precisely those industries which, having been sheltered from infancy, asserted a claim to permanent protection.
60. Grant to Liverpool, 28 Dec. 1819.

and social justice, and these 'on the ground of humanity'
or 'with reference to political disturbances'.[61] It had no
economic strategy of relief. Castlereagh, 'of hole-digging
memory',[62] recommended that the poor should be put to
making and filling holes all day — a task sufficiently less
eligible than normal employment to force redundant workers
on to the market. Ministers rejected outright the ideas of
Lauderdale, Malthus, James Cropper,[63] and the Attwoods for
increasing production by direct action, rather than for merely
redistributing it. When they did suggest spending, it was with
a much more modest intention, such as Huskisson's recommendation that the government should take shares in the
Arun and Portsmouth Canal at a time when it was difficult to
raise funds privately. 'The case is simply this — that the
advance of a comparatively *small* sum by Govt. for a work in
which it is admitted that the state has a material interest, is
necessary at this moment to enable individuals to lay out a
much *larger* sum of their own in the same work, and without
any other inducement than the probable benefit they expect
to derive from the speculation.'[64] For their part, Whigs
were especially chary of public spending because state
activity implied irresponsible power and additional patronage.
Brougham opposed taxation on the ground that it might
encourage profligacy and waste on 'visionary schemes' for
aiding the distressed classes. Relief should come from the
private sector, not from the state.[65] So on the rare occasions
that public spending was approved, it was merely as an anodyne. Ministers could not be expected to appreciate the
'multiplier' effect of government expenditure on the level of
aggregate demand, but still it is ironic that when they did
recommend such expenditure it was in order to *slow the
economy down*. Public works could be useful, not to stimulate
production, but as part of the Tory government's conven-
tional practice of overcoming a crisis — defined as a crisis of

61. Ibid.
62. Cobbett, *Rural Rides* i. 117.
63. Cropper to Canning, 10 Apr. 1817, Liverpool Parliamentary Office MSS.
2/59. Cropper opposed emigration schemes on the grounds that depopulation
would reduce demand. For a discussion of Cropper's grasp of the 'multiplier', see
Fay, *Huskisson and His Age*, 251-4.
64. Huskisson to [? Liverpool], n.d. [1815-16], LP 38191 ff. 99-101.
65. H. of C., 11 Feb. 1822, 2 PD, vi. 258-9.

over-production — by judicious *dis*investment. In 1817, for example, Grant demanded government aid to provide labour on public works, but not to set up new factories or extend agriculture, since this would lead to over-production. Nine years later Liverpool explained to Herries that 'The advantage of all these Measures of Employment of the Poor are that they act *doubly* — They give bread to those who want it, for work; and they withdraw them from Manufactures, by which there is less probability of the Manufactures themselves being precipitately forced, and the general distress thereby prolonged.'[66]

The struggle over resumption

Despite their determination not to interfere with the economy, ministers had to face the possibility that a decision of theirs, which they had tried to disguise as a return to some *status quo ante bellum*, was intensifying post-war distress. Opponents of the Cash Payments Act attributed to it all the political and economic difficulties of autumn 1819. Rothschild, for example, followed Vansittart into the countryside to warn of approaching financial collapse: 'His panacea as usual is a continuance of the Bank Restriction'[67] — but if Vansittart was also hoping to wriggle out of resumption, Liverpool never wavered. Not to resume for fear of diminishing the circulation too much would be tantamount to sanctioning a 'perpetual restriction'. 'Let us therefore determine to stand upon our present system, and let no one entertain a doubt that this is our determination.'[68]

The directors of the Bank had not forgiven ministers for the humiliating Ingot Plan, and an unidentifiable minority group, 'partly from pique, partly from timidity, and partly from ill will',[69] had been trying meanwhile to disrupt it. When, in June 1819, a pliant Committee of Treasury (Dorrien, Pole, Thornton, Whitmore, Pearse, and Langley) proposed that the Court should comply with Liverpool's request for advances on a loan, provided that the Bank might retain

66. Liverpool to Herries, 17 Aug. 1826, Herries MSS.
67. Vansittart to Liverpool, 28 Oct. 1819, LP 38280 ff. 240-2.
68. Liverpool to Vansittart, 31 Oct. 1819, LP 38574 ff. 144-7, Yonge, op.cit. ii. 416-17.
69. Vansittart to Liverpool, 28 Oct. 1819, LP 38280 ff. 240-2.

£5,000,000 of the instalment in payment of outstanding government debt, the Court of Directors flatly refused any advance whatever. Shortly afterwards it rejected a Committee of Treasury recommendation for advances to the Stock Exchange.[70] Inevitably, such nonco-operation hampered Vansittart's efforts to repay government debt to the Bank.[71] Yet in October the Court formally demanded reimbursement in order that, without expanding its note issues, it might accumulate bullion in preparation for the demands expected in February 1820, 'in pursuance of a Plan which this Court, after a calm and dispassionate consideration...continue to view with unabated solicitude'. The directors also threatened not to make good deficiencies in the consolidated fund, nor to accommodate the 'commercial world'.[72] At this point, Vansittart opened negotiations with the three most influential directors — Harman, Thornton, and Haldimand — for a 'distinct understanding with the Bank'. He did not offer to postpone resumption, as cynics supposed,[73] but did agree to repay £5,000,000, either in silver bullion or by raiding the sinking fund, before the following April.[74] By November Huskisson was confident that 'all the difficulties with the Bank are adjusted.'[75]

Yet a minority of directors continued to wrangle. Most of their propositions and protestations were defeated in the Court, but they successfully moved resolutions in January 1820, declaring that it was unfair to expect the directors to carry out the Ingot Plan, until they had placed 'a much larger comparative amount of their notes in circulation under their more immediate control'.[76] This implied cutting down on 'uncontrollable securities', and discounting privately instead. They reproached the Chancellor with having increased deficiency bills to an extent that cancelled the reduction of

70. C. T., 13, 15-17; C.B., Pa 65-6; Liverpool to Governor and Deputy of B. of E., 29 July 1819, LP 38278 f. 350; Governor and Deputy of B. of E. to Liverpool, 29 July 1819, ibid. f. 351; C.B., Pa 105-7.
71. Vansittart in H. of C., 30 Nov. 1819, 1 PD, xli. 514.
72. C.B., Pa 155-8.
73. Ricardo to Trower, 12 Nov. 1819, Sraffa, op.cit. viii. 134-5.
74. C.B., Pa 173-7; Liverpool and Vansittart to Governor and Deputy of B. of E., 13 Nov. 1819, LP 38280 ff. 245-6.
75. Huskisson to his wife, 2 Nov. 1819, HP 38741 ff. 318-33.
76. C.B. Pa 208-11.

exchequer bills, and thus enhanced the government's indebt-
edness. The recurring cry of the recalcitrant directors was for
'discretion' over note issues. They railed against the declared
aim of shackling the Bank, and possibly hoped to escape
from the straitjacket of the Ingot Plan by thwarting
Vansittart's attempts to perform the government's side of the
bargain.[77]

Certainly it was not long before the Bank managed to
throw over the Ingot Plan. Between June 1819 and February
1821 it greatly reduced its public balances, commercial
discounts and — to a lesser extent — note issue. With country
bank circulation also declining, gold reached par by March
1820. Thereafter the Bank was able to buy gold (at a loss,
as Huskisson had directed)[78] and by February 1821 it
held £11,900,000 in bullion.[79] Then, quite suddenly, the
directors craved permission to anticipate Peel's Act — that is,
to abandon the Ingot Plan, withdraw small notes almost
immediately and pay in cash from 1 May 1821, a year earlier
than the enabling date and two years before the compulsory
period stipulated in 1819. Since ministers had no particular
affection for the Ingot Plan, except as a corollary of the
graduated scale and a means to coerce the Bank, they gladly
agreed to jettison the use of ingots now that the Bank was
prepared to resume at once.

Clapham remarked that there was no point in continuing
with gold bars because there had been no demand for them,
but this does not explain the decision, which certainly
originated with the Bank.[80] The ostensible motive, which
Fetter endorses, was to forestall forgery by substituting coin
for small Bank notes. Announcing the decision to the Court
of Proprietors of the Bank, Pole explained that a Forgery

77. C.B., Qa 63-9, 114-16, 236-8.
78. Though Huskisson had recommended that the circulation be reduced *gradually*
and *without* any contraction of mercantile discounts. Viner, *Studies in the
Theory of International Trade*, 183.
79. Clapham, *The Bank of England*, ii. 69, 75.
80. Pole to the Court Proprietors of B. of E., 22 Mar. 1821, *Courier*, 23. Mar.
1821; Clapham, *The Bank of England*, ii. 73; C.T., 13, 174; C.B., Qa 244-5.
Fetter, *Development of British Monetary Orthodoxy*, 97 and n.6, suggests that
the Bank did not instigate this move, but his citation (C.B., Qa 312-3) refers not
to this decision to bring resumption forward, but to the defeat of a motion
(probably Ward's) for adopting the Ingot Plan permanently.

Commission had tried and failed to design a note that would not be susceptible to counterfeit, and he gave this failure as the 'principal object of the alteration'. It is, however, a dubious argument. More people had been charged with illegal coining than with forgery in previous years.[81] Besides, so long as *any* notes remained in circulation, 'whether they formed one-half or two-thirds of the circulation, facilities and temptations to forgery would still exist'.[82] And as Ricardo complained, the directors had for a decade defied the forgery argument in opposing all plans for metallic payments 'which did not leave the uncontrolled power of increasing or diminishing the amount of currency in their hands'.[83] Significantly, when Vincent Stuckey told the Court of Proprietors that, were it not for the forgery problem, it would be unwise to abandon the Ingot Plan, he met with cries of 'No', 'No'. Evidently there were other reasons, which were not elaborated in public and which remain obscure. The forgery issue seems to have been used to cloak the obvious division within the Court. Possibly the Bank wished no more than to escape from the inhibiting programme for cash payments laid down in 1819. Having been forcibly prevented from slowing down resumption, did it, as Huskisson suspected, exercise a spiteful discretion in the only way left open to it — which was, undue haste?

The *Ricardo* plan will at all times be effectual to prevent a depreciation of the currency from excess; but with respect to the opposite evil, an inconvenient contraction of it, it places the country too much in the hands of the Bank. From ignorance or perversity they appear to me to be now affording a strong practical proof of the extent to which that evil may be carried.[84]

More deviously, the Bank might even have reckoned to discredit convertibility altogether, by bungling resumption. Ricardo, who had hoped that his Ingot Plan would be

81. Payne to the Court of Proprietors, 22 Mar. 1821, *Courier*, 23 Mar. 1821. Lansdowne calculated that there had been 1,581 convictions for forgery and 3,191 for coining in the previous twenty years, H. of L., 4 May 1821, 2 PD, v. 497; Huskisson in H. of C., 29 Apr. 1822, 2 PD, vii. 206-7; Acworth, *Financial Reconstruction in England, 1815-22*, 95-9, 105.

82. Baring in H. of C., 19 Mar. 1821, 2 PD, iv. 1317, 1326-8; Ricardo in H. of C., 19 Mar. 1821, ibid. 1331-2.

83. Ricardo, *On Protection to Agriculture* (1822), Sraffa, op.cit. iv. 225-6.

84. Huskisson to Copleston, n.d. [1822], HP 38761 ff. 77-89.

continued indefinitely once its role in oiling the transition to gold became clear, expostulated that

the Bank had strong prejudices against the plan and immediately com-menced purchasing bullion and coining money, and were absolutely forced to come to the legislature for permission, last year, to pay in specie, as they had accumulated a large quantity of coin. After they had been foolish enough to do so, it became a matter of indifference whether parliament agreed to their request or refused it.[85]

But whether ignorant or perverse, the premature resumption of cash exacerbated the difficulties of restoring a metallic standard.[86] The Bank need not have so curtailed its discounts, and by forcing gold into a premium over paper, it created an unnecessary drain on the world's gold supplies and exaggerated pressures on liquidity. This outraged the bullionists — Tooke, Huskisson, and especially Ricardo, who was 'held responsible for the consequences' of actions not his own. He had promised that resumption would appreciate the currency merely to the extent of the narrow difference between paper and gold in 1819; but by *buying* gold (instead of selling, as he repeatedly urged), the directors were forcing gold to appreciate as well, and rendering 'the revulsion as oppressive as possible...They are indeed a very ignorant set'.[87]

Mismanagement of resumption soon led to criticism of bullionist principles. Whereas, in 1819, merchants had over-whelmingly opposed cash payments, subsequent deflation, domestic stagnation and the revival of exports prompted a new polarization between those that depended on internal markets and those that did not. Cotton, having resisted resumption, did well out of it — while the landed interest, its protagonists, suffered. Inevitably their attitudes changed. More consistently, Birmingham and the Midlands, and the iron industry generally, spearheaded opposition. The only significant foreign demand for Birmingham hardware and

85. Ricardo to McCulloch, 3 Jan. 1822, Sraffa, op.cit. ix. 140-1.
86. For the particular difficulties caused in 'paper-less' Manchester, see Clapham, op.cit. ii. 73; Grindon, *Manchester Banks and Bankers*, 101-10; *Cowdroy's Manchester Gazette*, 12 May 1821.
87. Ricardo to Malthus, 9 July 1821; Ricardo to Trower, 11 Dec. 1821, 5 Mar. 1822; Ricardo to McCulloch, 23 Mar. 1821; Sraffa, op.cit., ix. 15, 122-3, 176; viii. 360.

Sheffield cutlery was in the United States, which was the
branch of foreign trade most seriously impaired in 1819-20.[88]
A local committee disclosed in 1820 that consumption of
malt, beer, and other necessaries in the Birmingham district
had declined by one-third to one-half. Roused by Thomas
Attwood, the City notables petitioned Parliament in May and
August, inaugurating a series of discussions on the effects of
Peel's Bill on internal demand. Pointing to the uncanny
similarity in the price movements of different commodities,
Lansdowne, Baring, Ellice, Heygate, and Irving stressed the
monetary causes of depression in the iron and corn trades.[89]

In 1821 Baring and Matthias Attwood chose to attack
resumption obliquely by suggesting a bimetallic solution.
Whichever of gold or silver happened to be cheapest at any
time would regulate the standard. Initially, 'the present pound
sterling, which was somewhat too high, [would be]
relaxed.'[90] However, bimetallism probably split the anti-
bullionist lobby more than it attracted waverers, and with
Ricardo's support ministers easily defeated a motion for
inquiry on 9 April (141-27). They were successful again
(194-30) in June 1822, when Western and Matthias Attwood
moved for a committee to consider devaluing the standard
and adjusting dividends, debts, contracts, salaries, and taxes
'equitably'.[91] The latter protested that because Parliament had
denied depreciation in Vansittart's 1811 resolution, people

88. Gayer, Rostow and Schwartz, op.cit. i. 126-8, 145, 151-3; T. S. Ashton,
Iron and Steel in the Industrial Revolution (1924); Calthorpe to Liverpool, 19
Dec. 1820, LP 38288 ff. 317-18.
89. When in 1822 Western blamed resumption for the fall in prices, the Inspector
General of Imports and Exports (William Irving) pointed out that cotton and
refined sugar (which 'constitute a full moiety of our exports') had fallen much
more than other commodities, and that they must therefore have been affected
by special factors, such as new machinery in Lancashire and over-production in
the West Indies. Irving to Huskisson, 9 July 1822, HP 38743 ff. 171-2.
90. Baring in H. of C., 8 Feb. 1821, 2 PD, iv. 535. Calthorpe (who personified
the links between agriculture and industry in the Midlands), Bennet (a Radical
bitterly antagonistic to *rentiers*), Gascoyne of Liverpool, Gurney, Irving, Heygate,
and Whitmore divided with Baring.
91. Western in H. of C., 11 June 1822, 2 PD, vii. 877-96, summarized in W.
Smart, *Economic Annals of the Nineteenth Century, 1821-30* (1917), 96-7,
cited corn as the surest long-term standard of value. Western secured rather more
agricultural support than Baring had in 1821. See Matthias Attwood in H. of C.,
12 June 1822, 2 PD, vii. 965-1009 and C. C. Western, *Address to the Landowners
of the United Empire* (1822).

had neglected to take precautions against a post-resumption appreciation. Ministers retorted that 1811's had been no blanket denial, merely a resolve to act *as though* money was not depreciated; and that in the same way, they must now act as though there had been no appreciation. Huskisson, Peel, and Londonderry genuinely deplored the idea of devaluation, as dealing a 'death blow' to public credit, contractual confidence and social relations generally, while they poured administrative ridicule on 'adjustment'. Finally, Huskisson sealed the triumph of cash payments by carrying an amendment pledging Parliament not to alter the standard. His coup effectively precluded future devaluation, however unpopular 77s. 10½d. might become at times. For this landslide vote could be appealed to as a declaration to subsequent creditors that the standard was secure, and that they might lend in the certainty that they would never be legally defrauded.[92]

Ricardo held that the amount of appreciation caused by resumption *could* not be more than 5 per cent, roughly the 1819 premium on gold, and that any fall of prices beyond 5 per cent must be due to an enhancement of the standard itself, or to non-monetary factors such as good harvests. Measuring by the price fall, however, Baring calculated the *real* appreciation since 1819 to be as much as 40-50 per cent. Baring's explanation was that in 1819, the *real* premium on gold had greatly exceeded the 5 per cent difference between bullion and paper, because country bank and other credit had then been so distended. Ellice agreed that the premium from which they were now attempting to reduce gold was more like 30 per cent than five, and accused bullionists of ignoring the preliminary appreciation of 1817, which, following an issue of coins by the Bank, had been obscured by a temporary second depreciation in 1818.[93]

Ricardo and Huskisson disagreed significantly here. Ricardo persisted in the view that the premium on gold had only been 5 per cent in 1819, but conceded that *if* it had been 25 per

92. Huskisson in H. of C., 11 June 1822, 2 PD, vii. 897-925; *The Speeches of William Huskisson*, edited by J. Wright (1831), ii. 129-66; Smart, op.cit. 97-8.
93. H. of C., 22 Feb. 1821, 2 PD, iv. 895-90.

cent or more, as Baring and Ellice alleged, he would have
agreed to sacrifice the old par, which it was simply not worth
doing for the sake of 5 or 6 per cent.[94] Huskisson, however,
while acknowledging — as Ricardo would not — that cash
payments were responsible for much suffering, maintained
that to alter the standard by legal means, *whatever* the
justification, would be an egregious fraud against creditors,
public and private. He explained to Copleston, who had
submitted an anti-Ricardian pamphlet to him, that 'depreciation' signified a debasement of paper currency and
its departure from 'the standard of the gold coin which it
purported to represent'. It was illegitimate and unjust, first
to creditors and later to debtors:

It is only in this sense of the word depreciation that Mr. Ricardo's
position is, I conceive, correct. But if he carries his doctrine to the
length of maintaining that the difference between paper and gold is to
be taken as the measure of the fall of prices occasioned by our return to
a metallic currency, I certainly differ with him in a very material degree.
I have always thought and maintained [especially in the 1819 and 1821
Committees] that the permanent fall would be far more considerable.[95]

Consequently, whereas Ricardo considered the circulation
sufficiently extended to meet internal needs[96] and opposed
any lowering of interest rates, for example, Huskisson
maintained that currency and credit must adjust to domestic
as well as external factors. He reminded Copleston that 'to
make money as cheap as is consistent with that [antient]
standard ought to be our peculiar endeavour, and this is all
that we can honestly do.' He declared publicly that a
diminution (as distinct from depreciation) in the value of
money harmed nobody individually and benefited the
community. The economy had lately begun to recover
because such 'diminution was gradually effected and extended
in all the various modes of verbal, book and circulating
credits'.[97] As depreciation had not been the sole cause of
price rises during the restriction, so it was not 'the measure

94. H. of C., 22 Feb. 1821, 2 PD, iv. 895-90.
95. Huskisson's MS.comments on Copleston, HP 38761 ff. 77-89. E. Copleston,
*Address to Members of the House of Commons on the Necessity of Reforming
our Financial System* (1822).
96. H. of C., 29 Apr. 1822, 2 PD, vii. 200.
97. Huskisson in H. of C., 15 Feb. 1822, 2 PD, vi. 428-32. See below p. 161.

of the fall of prices since 1819'.[98] Huskisson therefore
defended the standard more rigidly than Ricardo, for the
sake of justice, public credit, and honest government, but was
wisely more flexible on interest rates.

As merchants, Baring and Ellice condemned cash payments
for having caused appreciation, which benefited the 'monied
class', while Matthias Attwood, a banker, attacked them for
causing deflation, which benefited commerce. They all agreed
that resumption was forcing the currency into a mould that
had 'no connection with the present state of the country',
and 'attempting to bring the existing state of things round to
the standard of value', instead of adjusting the latter to
reality. Baring knew instinctively that 'the habits, and
feelings, and prejudices of the community' could not be
expected to adapt mechanically or overnight to *de facto*
alterations of the standard.[99] Ricardo's detractors saw only a
system-mongering theoretician, whose feet never touched
the groundwork of facts,[100] and denounced resumption as
a dangerous academic exercise. Moreover, whereas ministers
thought with Ricardo in terms of how income was *distributed*
among the various classes of the community, the anti-
bullionists aspired actually to *increase* productive capacity
and aggregate demand. Diagnosing distress as an under-
production of currency, they could have no sympathy with
the government's desire to cut commodity production. Their
ambition was rather to maintain in circulation sufficient
money to keep the labouring classes fully employed at
customary wages and, if necessary, to stimulate production

98. Halévy, *The Liberal Awakening*, 116, has pointed out the paradox that anti-
bullionists, having denied the fact of depreciation during the Bank restriction,
now argued that resumption had led to appreciation and that it should be neg-
ated; whereas bullionists, having condemned restriction on the grounds of depreciation, now just as irrationally denied that resumption had led to much appreciation. Ricardo would probably have retorted that in 1819 gold was climbing to
par anyway, which made that year a good time for resumption.
99. H. of C., 9 Apr. 1821, 2 PD, v. 96.
100. Though other detractors saw him in the role of Stock Exchange bear, and
advising government in his own (deflationary) interests. Schumpeter, *History of
Economic Analysis*, 470-3, has effectively demolished this accusation. Ricardo
claimed that he depended mostly on his rentals at this time, and also that he was
'not answerable for the effect which the present measure might have upon particular classes'. H. of C., 9 Apr. 1821, 2 PD, v. 137.

by public works.[101] Under perpetual restriction, the circulation would accommodate to internal prices, debts, and
taxes, rather than be squeezed into correspondence with the
exchanges and international monetary equilibrium. Thomas
Attwood would have gone on depreciating until full employment was achieved. To bullionists, however, depreciation was
a drug that relieved symptoms but could not cure. Sooner or
later the economy would have to exist without its artificial
stimulation. If depreciation were really the secret of prosperity, it would have to be a 'constantly progressive depreciation'. The saga of John Law convinced Huskisson that
'You must either retrace your steps, or the bubble must
burst at last.'[102]

What basically was in dispute during the monetary debates
of 1821-2 was the validity of Britain's wartime prosperity.
It was felt essential to 'ascertain how much of [this visionary
wealth] is shadowy and ideal, and how much of sterling
worth'.[103] Assuming that money was a 'veil' and that they
could not create wealth by juggling with the currency,
ministers asserted that the apparent prosperity of wartime
had been artificial, 'fictitious', 'drunken prosperity',
which was bound eventually to end in a revulsion. 'Profit
from depreciation became confounded with the legitimate
return of capital, and, in too many instances, the ancient
spirit of the British tenantry degenerated into dashing
speculation, and consequent extravagance.'[104] Resumption
had been the 'manly' policy, ensuring that the current
revival would be sound, and that profits, though smaller,
would be genuine. Against this, anti-bullionists and monetary
reformers held that fortunes made during the restriction had
been legitimate — and that the subsequent distress was
artificial. Burdett attributed the coincidence of material
wealth and poverty entirely to monetary policies, and Lauderdale and Matthias Attwood dismissed the late export revival
as bogus. Nor was Western 'amongst those who thought that,

101. J. M. Keynes, *The General Theory of Employment Interest and Money*
(1936), 4 and n; Baring in H. of C., 9 Apr. 1821, 2 PD, v. 96.
102. H. of C., 11 June 1822, 2 PD, vii. 900-1.
103. Copleston, *A Letter to Robert Peel on a variable standard of value*, 83.
104. Huskisson in H. of C., 11 June 1822, 2 PD, vii. 918.

during the restriction of cash payments this country had acquired merely a fictitious prosperity'.[105] In short, the iron industry's wartime success could be considered genuine because based on demand, or false because the demand was unnatural; whereas the progress of cottons in 1822 could be thought delusive because based on unnatural cheapness, or real because it was taking place in a metallic currency.

Despite the heat generated by the combatants on the currency question, most M.P.s reacted with 'torpid indifference'.[106] The frighted enthusiasm of 1819 had died away, and the bitter bewilderment of 1826 had not yet set in. Huskisson's amendment took advantage of this lull to secure a currency settlement that was to continue, without substantial alteration, until the First World War (despite, ironically, Huskisson's own later attempts to substitute bimetallism). Henceforward malcontents had to concentrate on reforms in banking practice only. But though ministers had presented a united front, an unrepentant 'paper faction' in the cabinet had been silently gloating over the bullionists' discomfiture. Writing to Bathurst in December 1821, Harrowby alluded to low prices in words rather like those Melbourne was to use about 'the d—d fools' and Ireland: 'You and I believe that the general diminution of all circulating medium, paper here and gold elsewhere, is at the bottom of all this, but we are fools and the wise enjoy their triumph and their ruin.'[107]

105. Ibid. 884.
106. Brougham in H. of C., 12 June 1822, ibid. 1025.
107. Harrowby to Bathurst, 22 Dec. 1821, *Historical Manuscripts Commission Report on the Manuscripts of Earl Bathurst preserved at Cirencester Park* (1923), 527.

IV

THE NEW AGRICULTURAL POLICY,1821

She stood in tears amid the alien corn
John Keats, 'Ode to a Nightingale' (March 1819)

George Webb Hall and militant protection

All British agriculturists, but especially arable farmers, suffered dramatically during 1819-23. Foreign wheat and oats flowed in until February 1819 and helped to make a wretched spring. Farmers, already troubled by this alien corn, had soon to bear the brunt of their own outrageous fortune. After one of the finest harvests in living memory, wheat fell from 72s. 5d. in August 1820 to 51s. in July. Unfortunately this bounty was selective. Gloucestershire, Herefordshire, Worcestershire, Cheshire, and North Wales raised record crops, which lowered the price of corn nationally, while Sussex, Essex, Norfolk, Suffolk, and Kent suffered very low yields, which together with low prices caused terrible distress. Indications of a short crop in 1821 boosted prices a little, but only forced farmers prematurely on to the market, to prevent the ports opening to continental accumulations. And as it happened, late summer sun saved the harvest and further depressed the market. 1822 was the worst year of all with holders of old wheat having to sell at a loss.[1] With the situation little better for wool and the lesser grains, agriculturists united in a prolonged political campaign. It is possible to isolate three distinct objects: more protection; retrenchment and tax relief; cheaper money. All three implied a rejection of the government's diagnosis of over-production, being predicated on a decline in the demand for domestic agricultural produce. Those who ascribed this decline mainly to foreign competition demanded increased protection; those who blamed personal

1. T. Tooke and W. Newmarch, *A History of Prices and of the state of the circulation from 1792 to 1856*, edited by T. E. Gregory (1928), ii. 79-85; Ernle, *English Farming Past and Present*, 316-31; L. P. Adams, *Agricultural Depression and Farm Relief in England, 1813-52* (1932), 87-120.

taxation looked to tax relief and economical reform; those who stigmatized cash payments demanded monetary relief. The protectionists mainly operated outside Parliament and were most active and influential in 1820-1, declining thereafter. They were aggressively rural, contrasting the vulnerability of farmers to foreign competition with the tariff walls that shielded manufacturers. On the other hand, the economical and currency movements, which reached their climax in 1822, were mainly parliamentary affairs in which country gentlemen and men of business co-operated against the government.

In January 1819, at Henderson's Hotel in Westminster, a Gloucestershire landlord, George Webb Hall (whom Sinclair branded 'a species of "Hunt" in agriculture'), and John Ellman junior formed a Central Agricultural Association from among several existing local societies, and proceeded to organize agriculturists into a force for combating merchant pressure groups, like those that had attacked the Orders in Council. They lobbied the Board of Trade directly, corresponded with local associations through Evan's & Ruffy's *Farmers' Journal*, which they distributed freely round the countryside, and collated petitions for presentation by their parliamentary contacts — Western, Dundas, Fane, Holme Sumner, Curteis, and Dickinson. All this activity was counter-productive, since ministers took the identical format of many hundred petitions to indicate a lack of spontaneity on the part of the farmers, but it did anticipate the methods of Chandos in the 1830s and of the Anti-League.[2] Webb Hall's ambition was to possess the Board of Agriculture, for use as a political weapon in fostering agricultural interests, and a counterweight to the pernicious sympathies of the Board of Trade. He even managed to succeed Arthur Young as secretary to the former Board in 1820, but his intrigues only provoked ministers to

2. D. Spring and T. L. Crosby, 'George Webb Hall and the Agricultural Association', *Journal of British Studies*, ii (1962), 115-31; D. Spring, 'Lord Chandos and the Farmers, 1818-46', *Huntington Library Quarterly*, xxxiii (1969-70), 257-81; *Farmers' Magazine* (Nov. 1821). Webb Hall was tactically mistaken in supposing that 'If various petitions offer contending allegations and…a different prayer, nothing effectual can be expected': *Farmers' Journal* (Feb. 1816), 51.

abolish it, as a concession to retrenchment, in 1822.[3]

By 1820 the Agricultural Association contained some fifty affiliated local organizations, and delegates were sent to the Central Association from twenty counties. The movement was concentrated in the south of England — 30 out of 73 delegates represented four counties only — Essex, Sussex, Suffolk, and Gloucestershire. Most of the active members were large tenant farmers, or else small encumbered landlords, squires unable to bear arrears of rent, landowning solicitors and millers, gentlemen graziers and land agents. Thus the Warwickshire Agricultural Association craved Parliament's protection, before cultivation should have passed out of their own hands as tenants, and into those of the proprietors.[4] Members commonly styled themselves 'yeomen': 'We are *neither notables* nor *Radicals,* but we are UNQUESTION— ABLY the most numerous class of inhabitants in the kingdom...and the largest employers.'[5]

The protectionist movement was more concerned with wool than corn. The graziers had first begun to organize the countryside in 1816, with the aim of securing greater duties on the importation of foreign raw wool. They were mostly merino men, having invested large sums in a breed that was declining rapidly in value, owing to the preference of manufacturers for German fine wool. Webb Hall in Gloucestershire, both Ellmans in Sussex, Western, Burrell, Lord Somerville, Holme Sumner, and Sinclair had all gambled on the success of merino, and so had the movement's aristocratic patron, Lord Sheffield, whose annual Wool Fair at Lewes, like Somerville's Cattle Show, was often the scene of protectionist activity.[6] In 1819 they secured their duty, but Webb Hall had to spend the following year defending this boon against

3. R. Mitchison, 'The Old Board of Agriculture (1793-1822)', *English Historical Review*, lxxiv (1959), 41-69.
4. Minutes of meeting in Warwickshire, Dec. 1821, Foster/Massereene MSS. D562/8302A.
5. *The Origins and Proceedings of the Agricultural Associations in Great Britain, in which their claims to protection against foreign produce, duty free, are fully and ably set forth* (1820), 17-22.
6. Growers of coarse wool, less seriously affected by the return of peace, were more concerned to achieve freedom of export than duties on import.

outraged Yorkshire weavers.[7] Corn was a secondary consideration,[8] but here too their impulse was entirely protectionist. The Central Association demanded export bounties
and massive import duties of 40s. p. qr. on foreign wheat,
26s. 6d. on oats, peas, and beans, and 33 per cent *ad val.* on
other produce. It supported this claim with its usual animus
against highly protected manufactures, and with physiocratic
arguments as to the supremacy of *internal* demand; moreover, if agricultural production and employment were to
decline, 'CHEAP BREAD will, at no very distant period,
become NO BREAD, and starvation must ensue.'[9] Partly,
no doubt, for tactical reasons, the Association refused to
be side-tracked into alternative theories of distress, such as
currency and taxation. Adverting to suspicions that cash
payments were a contributory factor, the Central Committee
insisted that 'the principal if not the only cause of the distresses of the agricultural part of the community, and consequently of all classes, is the liability to competition from
foreign agriculture not subject to the same burdens.'[10] In
1821 the Association attacked quantity theory and embraced
'real bills' in an anti-Attwood manifesto attributing the
contraction of the circulation not to preparations for resumption, but to 'an actual, positive, and *bona fide* declension in
the gross returns of agricultural produce'.[11] As for *taxation,*
Webb Hall declared that agriculturists would readily pay their
taxes, if only they were protected.[12] Possibly not all the rank
and file agreed. It was suggested that some only supported
protecting duties for the sake of increasing public revenue
and enabling the government to cut taxes. But in these years
Webb Hall's bid to rule the countryside went uncontested,
and so it was with protection that Liverpool's government
had first to deal.

7. Webb Hall to Liverpool, 19 Dec. 1819 and 20 Jan. 1820, LP 38281 ff. 358-60,
38282 ff. 238-45.
8. As is clear, for example, from Coke to Eyres, 27 Jan. 1821, Stirling, *Coke of
Norfolk and HIs Friends,* 456-8.
9. *Origins and Proceedings of the Agricultural Associations,* 10-16.
10. Ibid. 25-37.
11. *The Times,* 6 Dec. 1821; Sheffield's report at Lewes in 1820, George Chalmers
MSS. 22902 ff. 295-8.
12. See also Eyres to Coke, 19 Jan. 1821, Stirling, op.cit. 455-6, on the impossibility of affording relief by tax reduction.

The Agricultural Committees of 1820 and 1821

The government welcomed low prices because they 'enable the Labourer and workmen to subsist upon lower wages',[13] and it cast a cold eye on the landed interest in its agony. 'The labouring parts of the community have had least reason to complain'[14] – and this mattered far more than any pecuniary pressure on the landed classes. When country gentlemen demanded that the 1815 law be made 'effective for the purposes for which it had been passed',[15] ministers retorted that they had never intended or claimed that it would help to keep prices above 80s. After the agriculturists under Holme Sumner had carried a motion (150-101) against government, on 30 May 1820, for the appointment of a select committee of inquiry, the cabinet seized on a suggestion of Sir Robert Wilson, an anti-protectionist Whig, and on the following day moved an instruction limiting the competence of the committee to a technicality – the method of computing the average of corn prices in the twelve maritime districts. The petitioners had hardly mentioned this issue, and Robinson himself had previously dismissed it with the observation that frauds would operate in both directions and cancel each other out. The government's intervention was clearly a cynical ruse to thwart the protectionists, justified by the 'perilous situation' with respect to public feeling in the towns, and it succeeded. 'This night the agriculturists were beat all to pieces [251-108] – ministers and most of the opposition voting together.... So, no corn bill this year.'[16]

Thus emasculated, Holme Sumner's Committee represents a technical interlude in the debate on the corn laws. After hearing twenty-five witnesses (the receiver and four local inspectors of corn returns, landlords, farmers, millers, factors, and merchants), it found that 'the greatest neglect and inattention has universally prevailed' in the system of computing the average price of wheat.[17] Apart from confusion

13. Liverpool to Calthorpe, 20 Dec. 1820, LP 38288 ff. 329-30.
14. Huskisson in H. of C., 11 June 1822, 2 PD, vii. 913-4.
15. Gooch in H. of C., 30 May 1820, 2 PD, i. 640.
16. J. C. Hobhouse, MS. Diary, 31 May 1820, Hobhouse MSS. 56541.
17. CSC, *Report from the Select Committee on Petitions complaining of Agricultural Distress*, 1820, 5.

over the proper standard measure, there had been a tendency not to return the sales of inferior quality grains so that, as agriculturists alleged, the computed price was likely to turn out higher than the actual average price. Robinson and Wallace had in fact been engaged in desultory attempts to check such malpractices, and had been combated by the self-interest of bakers and millers, who 'may have an interest in making the price (particularly in towns where an Assize of Bread is set) appear high'.[18] Moreover, merchants and factors often felt 'the same inducements to open the ports and warehouses'. It was generally agreed that if prices were in the upper seventies just before harvest time, and if few stocks remained in the country, dealers could open the ports by paying a little extra for a small purchase of corn. After the crop had been gathered in, farmers could often retaliate by rushing corn to market to keep the price below 80s. Successful or not, such practices clearly prevented an even distribution of supply. Smith's model, whereby crops would be rationed and prices steadied by the the small farmers marketing first and the more opulent waiting awhile for slightly higher prices, was dislocated by the need for all of them to dash to market to counter the machinations of merchants. This 'dreadful system of gambling',[19] which so embittered relations between merchants and farmers, was blamed on the Corn Law of 1815. 'In the early periods of the corn laws, the import price was fixed so much above the remunerating market price, that an occasion for such struggles, and consequent perpetual speculations, could rarely occur; nor was the difference between the British and Continental price at that time so considerable, as to excite so much interest as now exists.'[20] To prevent frauds in future, the Committee recommended several administrative reforms, the most important being that henceforth the 139 towns in the 12 districts should return to the Central Receiver the sum total of sales and monies paid, 'thus dividing only once to find the aggregate average price'. It would replace a system that had computed the national average from the sum of the district averages, and whereby a few

18. Ibid. 6; B.T. 5/28, 375, 390-4.
19. Wodehouse in H. of C., 31 May 1820, 2 PD, i. 715.
20. CSC, *Report on Petitions complaining of Agricultural Distress*, 1820, 7.

'purchases made at only a trifling sacrifice' in unpopulous districts could disproportionately affect the aggregate average. The Committee also recommended including sales of Irish corn in the returns. In 1821 these proposals passed with little controversy,[21] but could not prevent the protectionist campaign from spreading. Ministers were therefore forced to concede another Committee, this time one that would investigate all aspects of agricultural distress.

The 1821 Committee has generally been regarded as a protectionist body, which was bamboozled by Ricardo and Huskisson into presenting a free trade report. In fact, it was only just weighted in favour of the Association, being 'a perfect *Babel*', where according to Ricardo, 'not two men agreed.'[22] On past record, sixteen of its members might be expected to support increased protection, twelve (including ministers) to oppose, with two neutral. There were three Irishmen implicated in the existing Corn Law — Parnell, Foster, and Dennis Browne. The two last were arch-protectionists, demanding a permanent 56s. duty on wheat, or else permanent prohibition to be suspended in dearths![23] Then came several protectionist squires — ministerialists like Gooch the Chairman, Holme Sumner, Lethbridge, Knatchbull, Wodehouse, Bucknall Estcourt, Hunter Blair — and Whigs like Western, Rowley, and finally Curwen, who desired a fixed 40s. duty. All these still aspired 'to render this country independent of a foreign supply' and derided the 'visionary project of feeding the country by the sale of its manufactures'. Naturally they defended marginal lands, as helping to ensure that the ports need 'never again be opened'.[24] But Tremayne, Calthorpe, Watkin Williams Wynn, two Canningites Littleton and Sturges Bourne, Bankes, Althorp and Stuart Wortley all

21. Except that pertaining to Irish grain, see below p. 106; B.T. 5/29, 18-23, 381-4; Fay, *The Corn Laws and Social England*, 64-7; C. R. Fay, 'Price Control and the Corn Averages under the Corn Laws', *Economic Journal, History Supplement,* i (1926), 149-54.
22. Mallet, MS. Diary, 7 May 1821, quoted in Sraffa, *Works and Correspondence of David Ricardo,* v. xxv.
23. Foster's paper on corn, 18 Apr. 1821, Foster/Massereene MSS. D562/8300; Foster to Conolly, 7 Sept. 1820, ibid. D562/15916.
24. Western in H. of C., 30 May 1820, 7 Mar. and 5 Apr. 1821, 2 PD, i. 651; iv. 1154; v. 44. Wodehouse to Huskisson, 20 Jan. 1820, HP 38742 ff. 1-2. Brougham was on circuit and did not attend the Committee.

preferred to relieve agriculture by public retrenchment than by protection. Then there were five businessmen, of whom two — Ricardo and Baring — were committed free-traders.[25] For government, Castlereagh (now Marquis of Londonderry) could not attend until after the recess, and Robinson was feeling characteristically lethargic, so Huskisson was unwillingly 'induced...by circumstances...to take the labouring oar'.[26]

With representatives of the Agricultural Association thronging at its doors to brief witnesses, the Committee interrogated forty-two persons, including Association leaders (Harvey, Lousley, both Ellmans, and Webb Hall) and farmers from all over the country. The pattern of these interviews was consistent — protestations of distress from the farmers, followed by theoretical interrogations in which Ricardo and Huskisson sadistically exposed 'their ignorance of the first principles'.[27] This reached its climax when Webb Hall came face to face with Ricardo — 'flippant pertness, opposed to abstract and even visionary subtilty'.[28] The most important witnesses were the merchants Solly, Tooke, and David Hodgson, and an observant traveller, William Jacob, all of whom proffered information on the state of British and European markets. Jacob peppered Huskisson with facts and figures in private, while Tooke appeared before the Committee on five separate occasions, and it was only by putting leading questions to him that Ricardo 'got sound opinions to appear on our minutes'.[29]

Some agricultural members, like Curwen, disgruntled by the dominance of Huskisson and Ricardo, ceased to attend long before the decisive discussions began on 7 May. At first it seemed that Londonderry was going to help agriculture, for

---

25. The others were Brydges, Irving and a protectionist, Calvert.
26. Huskisson to Liverpool, 12 May 1822, HP 38743 ff. 148-51, quoted in L. Melville, *The Huskisson Papers* (1931), 137-9.
27. Ricardo to Trower, 21 Apr. 1821, Sraffa, op.cit. viii. 369-70. They so baffled James Conolly, for example, that when he was asked whether it was to the consumer's advantage that corn should be cheap, he replied: 'I should imagine so, though the conviction of my mind is, that it would not.'
28. Jacob to Huskisson, 16 May 1821, HP 38742 ff. 227-42.
29. Ricardo to McCulloch, 25 Apr. 1821, Sraffa, op.cit. viii. 373-4. See below, pp. 292-300, for Jacob's influence.

he pretended to approve the principle of Foster's extremist proposals, objecting only to his 'quantum of remedy'.[30] But then on 17 May, to the protectionists' dismay, he suggested a do-nothing report, containing 'no plan of alteration', but 'all bottomed on report of the evidence only'. Worse still, he insisted on rescinding a concession recommended by the 1820 Committee — the inclusion of Irish corn in the returns for the national average, which Irishmen had promised themselves would 'operate nearly as a prohibition'. Londonderry objected that this inclusion 'would be raising the protection to 88s.' and Robinson, with his usual pliancy, 'said that it could be left out'.[31] The words 'Great Britain' were duly substituted for 'Great Britain and Ireland' in the act of 1821.[32] Dennis Browne complained that Londonderry, though sympathetic, had 'adopted too much of the System of the Philosophers at the Head of which are Ricardo and Huskisson'.[33] Poor Browne, recently so enthusiastic, was petulantly moved to 'wish this Committee had never existed'.[34]

Finally Huskisson proposed twenty-two resolutions,[35] including a prospective recommendation for a permanently free (which is to say, open) trade in corn, with a moderate

30. Browne to Foster, 12 May 1821, Foster/Massereene MSS. D562/15993.
31. Browne to Foster, 18 May 1821, ibid. D562/15995.
32. 1 & 2 Geo. IV c.87. In 1820 Huskisson had admitted privately that the inclusion of Irish corn might raise the general average price by 5s. to 8s. and that it was 'perhaps the only relief which can now be attempted with any hope of success'. Huskisson to Wodehouse, 25 Jan. 1820, HP 38742 ff. 3-5. But when Burrell suggested this in Parliament, Castlereagh had objected ('There were two ways of raising the protecting price on imported grain; namely, either by increasing the scale of prices at which it might be imported, or by altering the mode of striking the averages'), and had threatened to reduce the prohibition level from 80s. to 72s. if Irish corn were included in the averages. H. of C., 31 May 1820, 2 PD, i. 725-6. Moreover, a MS. list of instructions to the 1820 Committee included the question, 'What reduction below 80s. p. qr. would it be necessary to make in the price at which the importation of foreign wheat should be permitted in order to continue the same degree of protection to Agriculture as is now given by that Price, under the existing laws, in the event of its being found expedient to regulate future importations by the average of Great Britain, or by the average of the United Kingdom?' HP 38742 ff. 14-15. See Conolly to Oriel, 15 Apr. 1825, Foster/Massereene MSS. D562/16318.
33. Browne to Foster, 18 May 1821, ibid. D562/15995.
34. Browne to Foster, 9 June 1821, ibid. D562/16007.
35. HP 38761 ff. 1-4.

fixed duty, which could be suspended in dearths. They were carried against the protectionists by ten votes to six, and Huskisson incorporated them into a draft report.[36] This document then had to be defended against 'the prejudices and passions of the country gentlemen', and Huskisson and Ricardo were forced to include some verbal concessions, which damaged its coherence as free trade propaganda. For example, they were forced to define 'countervailing' duties as charges that 'countervail the differences of expense' in corn production between Britain and the Continent.[37] Even so, Althorp was rumoured to be the only member for a large agricultural constituency to sign the Report, and most were outraged. The Chairman, Gooch, assailed it as a 'piece of mystification...worse than useless'.[38] Certainly, it killed any hopes of increased protection. Henceforth, every initiative for changes in the corn law was to come from its urban opponents, whom the Report encouraged, while agriculturists had to fight to keep what they already possessed. Huskisson foresaw this when he remarked to Ricardo that the country gentlemen had gone into the Committee as plaintiffs, and had emerged as defendants.[39] Meanwhile, for the 'official' or 'administrative' Tories, this long and masterly document settled future corn law strategy — an ever-open and progressively freer corn trade, and increasing reliance on imported food.

It was not a statement of immediate policy. Huskisson recognized that the extraordinary glut abroad, which had accumulated partly because of Britain's prohibitive system, could not be removed at once without immediate danger to agriculture. But once that glut had evaporated, parliament

---

36. This report was apparently adopted by 11 votes to 8, *Hampshire Telegraph and Sussex Chronicle*, 2 July 1821.

37. Ricardo defined 'countervailing' duties not as compensating for the lower production costs of foreign competitiors, but as neutralizing any special burthens imposed on one sector only of the community, such as, in this case, tythes and the agricultural horse tax. His 'countervailing' duties would thus restore a natural internal distribution of capital — whereas the agriculturists defined such duties so as to create an unnatural international distribution. D. Ricardo, *On Protection to Agriculture* (1822), sections 3 and 7, Sraffa, op.cit. iv. 216-19, 243-4; H. of C., 7 Mar. 1821 and 3 Apr. 1822, 2 PD, iv. 1156 and vi. 1447.

38. H. of C., 18 Feb. 1822, 2 PD, vi. 463.

39. Ricardo to Trower, 22 Aug. 1821, Sraffa, op. cit. ix. 37.

should implement a policy of free trade with a fixed duty. Like Peel over bullionism in 1819, Huskisson blandly assumed that the truths of free (open) trade were 'universally acknowledged'. For him agriculture's great problem was overproduction. This was the case with all the distressed industries, but agriculture was different because Say's Law did not apply — that is, an excess supply could not by lowering prices increase demand, because demand for basic necessities was inelastic. Market forces could not operate to restore price equilibrium automatically.[40] Also, since prices did not affect demand, they became extremely sensitive to variations in supply, which accounted for the immense fluctuations since 1815. The contingent prohibition device — complete freedom followed by rigid prohibition — merely accentuated these fluctuations.[41] Finally, the Report praised resumption, exalted warehousing, and defended taxation. It looked for relief to the reduction of interest rates that would result from 'the cessation of public loans' and the formation of 'large accumulations of capital'.[42]

Here was no mere agricultural document but a forward statement of over-all monetary, fiscal and financial policy. Nor was it Huskisson's alone. Liverpool and Londonderry successfully dissembled their 'real opinion'[43] by pretending to be still the farmer's friends, and slyly saddled a non-cabinet minister with the brunt of unpopularity just as they had

40. In the eighteenth century mercantilist and physiocratic economists had usually agreed that agricultural (but not industrial) expansion would lead to an increase of population to consume its increasing production — in other words, that what later came to be regarded as 'Say's Law' did operate in agriculture, while over-production or gluts were likely to occur in manufactures. With the development of classical economics these positions reversed: agriculture was now thought liable to glut, while in manufactures 'Say's Law' was expected to operate and marginal supply to create demand.
41. The situation would have been less unfavourable if British prices, though low, had not still been so far above European levels as to obliterate all hope of exporting a domestic surplus.
42. CSC, *Report from the Select Committee to whom the Several Petitions complaining of the depressed state of the Agriculture of the United Kingdom were referred.* 1821, 26-7.
43. Mallet, MS. Diary, 10 May 1821, Sraffa, op.cit. v. xxv. For agriculturists' tributes to Londonderry's supposed consideration towards them, see Curwen in H. of C., 18 Feb. 1822, 2 PD, vi. 469 and Knatchbull to a West Kent Agricultural Meeting, 13 Dec. 1821, *The Times*, 20 Dec. 1821.

thrown responsibility for resumption on to Peel in 1819. In fact leading ministers were agreed on the policy, though some were less enthusiastic than Huskisson. One exception was Wellington's toady, Arbuthnot, who assured Huskisson that farmers deserved high prices, and that on them depended the prosperity of all other classes.[44] This view was rapidly being superseded, and the Agricultural Report of 1821 marked the beginning of its end.

Free trade and food supply

The 1821 Report laid down a programme of prospective corn law reduction and repeal. Thus the important break in official thought on agricultural protection between 1815 and 1846 occurred before 1821. This early, dramatic and little-noticed reversal of policy cannot be satisfactorily explained in structural or ideological terms — as an attempt to make Britain the workshop of the world or in response to a 'liberal awakening'. The basic aims of 1815 did not change, though the method by which they were to be fulfilled changed radically.

The paramount aim of safeguarding food supplies still pertained. Ministers emphatically rejected the arguments of those who inferred from the domestic glut that supply was no longer a problem. Unlike many agriculturists, they had welcomed the recent and widespread abundance ('a subject of general joy'),[45] and in 1819 had even thought that a limited importation would be 'rather an advantage in the present manufacturing and commercial state of this Country'.[46] Huskisson's Report cited *Wealth of Nations* and Burke's *Thoughts and Details on Scarcity* to argue that good crops and bad crops often occurred in consecutive cycles of

---

44. Arbuthnot to Huskisson, n.d. [20 Oct. 1820], HP 39948 ff. 50-1. The Opposition was as divided as it had been in 1815: Tierney, Ellice, Hobhouse, Burdett, and Wilson supported ministers — Grey, Brougham, Curwen, Smith, and Lambton the landed gentry.
45. Sidmouth to Liverpool, 30 July 1820, LP 38574 ff. 208-9.
46. Huskisson to Liverpool, 26 Aug. 1819, LP 38191 ff. 117-20. On 19 Sept. 1817 Huskisson had told Liverpool that he would regard a limited importation of corn as 'a great benefit', ibid. ff. 106-8.

two to three years. A poor run in the future could augur
terrible famine. But though ministers still feared for supply,
they no longer considered autarchy to be essential to it; on
the contrary, they now feared that autarchy might be fatal
to supply in years of scarcity. In 1820 Huskisson said merely
that Britain 'should not be dependent *to too great an extent*
on foreign countries for the necessaries of life';[47] his Report
that she should never be 'too habitually or extensively
dependent'. This was a very modest ambition compared with
the passionate fervour with which Huskisson as much as anyone had appealed for self-sufficiency in 1815. Browne
revealed that the government now considered protection a
positive danger to subsistence when he reported home that he
had at least secured one useful concession for Ireland: 'Lord
Londonderry [said] that there would be no objection to
raising the importing rate of Oats, Peas and Beans which could
not be considered as Articles of prime necessity.'[48] Liverpool,
Huskisson, Catlereagh, and Robinson never acknowledged a
change of heart on autarchy, but their motives can be surmised.

   In the first place they had lost their former faith in the
potential capacity of a protected and capitalized home
agriculture to feed the country. Though recent crops had
been full, this was only at the cost of great distress and
bankruptcy, which obviously threatened *future* production.
More particularly, the 1815 strategy had depended on
Ireland's contribution. In 1816 heavy summer rainfall
damaged the wheat and oats in Ireland and caused the first
great failure of the potato, the staple food of most Irish peasants. This not only presaged famine there, but threatened to
cut off vital supplies to the industrial north of England.[49]
The crisis reached a height just before the next harvest, in
June 1817, when armed attacks on Irish food transports and
vendors forced the government to intervene directly by
providing public subscriptions and soup kitchens.[50] At the

47. H. of C., 30 May 1820, 2 PD, i. 678 (my italics).
48. Browne to Foster, 18 May 1821, Foster / Masserrene MSS. D562/15995.
49. Sidmouth to Sheffield, 4 Nov. 1816, Sidmouth MSS. 152M (1816-17).
50. N. Gash, *Mr Secretary Peel. The Life of Sir Robert Peel to 1830* (1961),
219-26; R. Shipkey, 'Problems in Alcoholic Production and Controls in Early
Nineteenth-Century Ireland', *Historical Journal*, xvi (1973), 300-1.

time, ministers made light of the implications of this episode for autarchy, bravely maintaining that famine was 'partial and local', that over-all 'there was...a sufficiency of food'. Like the French Physiocrats they insisted that if only distribution were free, if only Ireland could develop roads, capital, credit, and a rapid circulation, 'the surplus of one district might supply the deficiency of others.'[51] As it was, government must intervene to deploy resources. Despite discouraging reports from the Liverpool merchants and crop-spotters, James Cropper and David Hodgson, Huskisson continued to maintain that the two islands were self-sufficient.[52] Fortunately, by 1821 Irish exports to England had revived, but the lesson was not forgotten. Huskisson warned readers of his Report that the risk of seasonal fluctuations in the harvest 'must increase in proportion as the produce of Ireland (the part of the United Kingdom of which the climate is the most fickle) may become a more extended part of our general supply. It must, therefore, be manifest, that the evil of a failing crop would be aggravated as our dependence upon Ireland increased'.[53] Thus the first potato blight of 1816/17 led to the first reconsideration of the protective Corn Law, just as the Great Famine, which finally dispelled the illusion of an Irish granary, was to occasion its final abolition.[54] Huskisson later emphasized colonial (mainly Canadian) preference to provide dependable granaries and captive markets to compensate for the failure of the Irish dream of 1815.

Having discussed Ireland, Huskisson's Report noted that 'It may, also, be a question, whether the produce of the poorer soils in England is not more likely to be affected by

51. Vansittart in H. of C., 5 Mar. 1817, 1 PD. xxxv, 891; Liverpool in H. of L., 14 Mar. 1817, ibid. 1079-80; Peel to Sidmouth, 21 July 1817, Parker, *Sir Robert Peel*, i. 244-5. See R. C. Cobb, *The Police and the People. French Popular Protest 1789-1820* (1970), 269-78.
52. Huskisson to Liverpool, 19 Sept. 1817, LP 38191 ff. 106-8; Cropper to Huskisson, 16 Sept. 1817 and 18 Aug. 1818, HP 38741 ff. 119-20, 256-8.
53. CSC, *Report on Petitions complaining of the depressed state of Agriculture*, 1821, 11.
54. In H. of C., 31 Mar. 1828, 2 PD, xviii. 1404-5, Peel recommended the decultivation of some English wheatlands in favour of pasture, dairy farming and manufacturing, yet he still looked to Ireland's 'great fertility, great powers of production, and vast capabilities of improvement'.

ungenial seasons.' This awareness that agricultural distress
was due, not to importation or the fear of it, but to over-
production at home, further undermined the strategy of
1815. The 1814 Committees had expressly denied that
over-production had caused distress then, or that it had even
existed, but there had not been any corn imports since
February 1819, so that the present low prices must be caused
by domestic glut. It followed that the partial distress must be
due to internal and not foreign competition, and governments
could do nothing about this since 'protection cannot be
taken further than monopoly'. The intention in 1815 had
been to remunerate farmers by high yields, not high prices.
By 1821 it was obvious that, though prices were fairly
uniform, some farmers had higher yields than others — that
agriculture was not a monolithic interest — and that farmers
on inferior soils or without capital could not survive the
blasts of internal rivalry, even with protection against the
foreigner. Thus by 1820 Huskisson was admitting that the
real cause of distress was that the crops were scanty in some
areas and abundant in others, and that this partial abundance
kept down prices even where yields were slight. On bad lands
therefore, 'a scanty produce is aggravating the pressure of
inadequate prices'.[55] The only remedies were rent reduction
and the complete abandonment of unfit or hopelessly
encumbered estates. Decultivation, however, contradicted the
1815 policy of expansion. Then, pressure for a Corn Law had
come mainly from marginal and recently cultivated soils,
and ministers had hoped that increased protection for agriculture would 'extend the present scale of its exertions and
produce'.[56] So when in 1820 they said that agriculture was
not in a 'natural state', that the 1815 Law had been devised
merely to protect capital *already* invested during the last
heady years of war, and in order simply to prevent a
revulsion of landed property, they were tacitly reversing
their former policy of pushing the margin of cultivation
higher still. Liverpool announced that even if the bill had
been rejected in 1815, he would not now have supported

55. Huskisson to Wodehouse, 25 Jan. 1820, HP 38742 ff. 3-5.
56. CSC, *Report on Petitions relating to the Corn Laws*, 1814, 8.

higher protection because 'the principal cause of [agricultural] distress was the quantity of Land that was brought under the Plough in the last years of the war'.[57] Castlereagh had for some time spoken contemptuously of soils that had been forced into 'an unnatural fertility, which was of course followed by a proportionate barrenness'.[58] Robinson declared pitilessly that 'it was not by any act of the legislature that [unfit] land had been called into cultivation, and it was not therefore to be expected that by any act of the legislature it should be continued in cultivation'.[59] Ministers now wanted disinvestment as well as deflation.

Agriculturists were dismayed. Just as debtors often claimed that Vansittart's 1811 resolution had encouraged them to go on borrowing in what it officially pronounced to be an undepreciated currency, so, more reasonably, agriculturists — including many who had borrowed to invest and were now in debt — claimed that the 1815 Corn Law and ministers' attendant panegyrics about an independent food supply, had encouraged them to go on investing and expanding. If the 1815 Bill had been designed solely to tide agriculturists over a period of adjustment, surely this should have been made clear. Brougham urged cogently that Parliament had a moral responsibility towards agriculturists, who instead of spending wartime profits on consumption had invested in tillage to safeguard food supply. Besides, the successful cultivation of huge tracts of 'rudeness and desolation' was a national trophy and a proud example of technological triumph over nature.[60] The government's attitude called in doubt the comfortable doctrine of enlightened self-interest, and with it the thirst for improvement that was transforming the landscape. The Duke of Bedford was only one of many landowners to be baffled by Liverpool's condemnation of over-production and excess. 'What then, in such a case, became of the industry, skill, and talent of the agriculturist? These virtues became a mischief instead of a good, and thus my hon. friend Mr. Coke is the most mischievous person in

57. Liverpool to Kenyon, 18 Dec. 1819, Kenyon MSS., draft in LP 38281 ff. 347-9.
58. H. of C., 9 Apr. 1816, 1 PD, xxxiii. 1124.
59. H. of C., 30 May 1820, 2 PD, i. 643.
60. Aberdeen to Vansittart, 29 May 1821, Vansittart MSS. 31232 ff. 274-5.

the world.'[61]

Thus ministers abandoned autarchy because they no longer believed it to be possible. Meanwhile, they became increasingly confident of Europe's ability to supply Britain habitually, *if the corn law were reduced*,[62] and conversely, much less confident of her ability to supply Britain at all, even in direst need, if the Corn Law were *not* reduced. In 1819 the government set about compiling systematic information about foreign agriculture. The burden of most private and consular reports was that the good crops of 1818 and 1819 had created cheapness and abundance everywhere, and especially 'in most places whence we are accustomed to derive our supplies.'[63] Admittedly, William Jacob told the 1821 Committee that, despite this glut, the whole world could not feed Britain for more than three weeks, and that even habitual importation by Britain would not extend Continental cultivation to a significant extent. And Tooke, who as a mercantile opponent of corn laws wished to play down the competitiveness of foreign corn before a committee of agriculturists, was equally pessimistic about a European granary. But the interesting point is that their interrogators utterly disagreed with them. They asked William Jacob: 'If this country allows a free importation of grains, and if, in consequence, a part of the labour and capital employed in the manufactures, such as they are of the countries you have mentioned, were employed on the land, and the manufactures imported, would not the quantity of corn for exportation be very greatly increased?' And they put it to Tooke that, 'If the ports of this kingdom were opened for the free importation of corn, might you not import from Russia and other places in the

61. Bedford at the Holkham Sheep Shearing, 2 July 1821, *The Times*, 10 July 1821.
62. In *On Protection to Agriculture* (1822), Sraffa, op.cit. iv. 265, Ricardo wrote that dependence on foreign food would not be dangerous because 'if our demand was constant and uniform,...a considerable quantity of corn must be grown abroad expressly for our market.' See Harvey to Gooch, 11 Mar. 1822, Foster/Massereene MSS. D562/8312.
63. Hodgson to [?], 28 Aug. 1819, LP 38279 ff. 179-82; Mellish to Castlereagh, 1820, HP 38742 f. 16; Huskisson to Liverpool, 31 Aug. 1819, LP 38191 ff. 121-2; B.T. 5/29, 47; A & P, *Prices of corn, grain, and other agricultural products, at British residencies abroad*, 1821.

North of Europe to an indefinite extent, whatever the price in this market may be?'[64] On the other hand, ministers increasingly feared that, with Continental agriculture so depressed, the source of emergency supply in scarce years would dry up altogether if British acceptance of it remained intermittent and unreliable, or as Huskisson said, if 'the demand is unusual'.[65] They were losing confidence in the emphatic assurance of the 1814 Commons' Committee that European supplies would always be available, however sporadic the demand. For it was already becoming clear that, rather than cultivate for an uncertain market, Continental powers might try to emulate British industrialization. Again, the chief danger in this possibility was not that it would interfere with Britain's manufactures, but that it would diminish her emergency food reserves.[66]

Thus there had been large importations in 1818, when they had turned out to be not really necessary, but in the autumn of 1816, when a poor crop rendered them essential, importers were unable to obtain much foreign corn owing to the prior needs of Southern Germany, Austria, and especially France, where an import bounty had been imposed. In this

64. Other questions put to Jacob included: would not 'a constant trade' with Europe increase European arable farming? 'Under the supposition that the ports were always open here, would not there be a certain supply always to this country?' 'If there existed a constant foreign demand for the agricultural produce of Russia, could not that immense country greatly increase its exports of grain?' As the questioners are not identified, it is just possible that in this case they were agriculturists apprehensive of foreign competition; but internal evidence, and especially Jacob's replies, makes it fairly certain that they were in fact free-traders optimistic about the availability of foreign food. This distinction is important with reference to the conclusions presented below, pp. 292-300, on the origins of free trade in corn: that free trade did not derive from Jacob's (albeit mistaken) view that foreign agriculture was unable to compete with British — as has been suggested — but from a rejection of Jacob's view and from confidence in the ability of overseas farmers to supply Britain's food requirements.
65. H. of C., 29 Apr. 1822, 2 PD, vii. 209.
66. CSC, *Report on Petitions complaining of the depressed state of Agriculture,* 1821, 12, pointed out the danger that foreigners might exclude British manufactures in retaliation against the Corn Laws, but its main fear was that manufactures were a feeble bargaining weapon in any 'conflict of retaliatory exclusion', since Germans could manage without clothes more easily than Britons could without food: 'Prohibition must yield to the wants of the people.' Besides, under the existing system, the ports might not open after a bad harvest until 13 November, which would be after the Baltic had iced over for the winter, making navigation impossible.

way Europe's climatic unity prevented special treatment of an offshore island.

Apart from these questions of supply, monetary factors indicated a need to switch from intermittent to regular importation. Ministers believed that resumption would restrict credit facilities to genuinely worthwhile ventures, and discourage over-speculation. This should ensure that, henceforward, corn would only be imported to answer the genuine needs of food supply, and not for speculative profit. In January 1820 Huskisson explained to Wodehouse:

I do not apprehend that we shall ever again witness such monstrous (and to the Parties embarked in them) ruinous speculations as those which filled this country with foreign corn last year. If the speculators are not cured of the inclination, at any rate they will no longer find the facilities which were then afforded them, to force an export of several millions of British manufactures, beyond the amount for which there was any real demand abroad, in order to force an import in payment of several millions of foreign Corn for which there was no real want at home.[67]

More importantly, though cash payments would diminish speculation, they would render any speculation that did occur so much the more dangerous. The restoration of a standard and a stable currency made it more than ever necessary to put an end to the irregularities caused by contingent prohibition. A lengthy period of prohibition, followed by sudden heavy importation, could upset the delicate monetary balance. The 1821 Report warned that

inasmuch as reciprocity of demand is the foundation of all means of payment, a large and sudden influx of corn might, under these circumstances, create a temporary derangement of the course of exchange, the effects of which (after the resumption of cash payments) might lead to a drain of specie from the Bank, the consequent contraction of its circulation, a panic amongst the country banks – all aggravating the distress of a public dearth.

It was essential to avoid any 'sudden revulsion in the foreign exchanges' for fear of damaging circulating credit and business confidence at home and abroad. Such stability was far more important to Huskisson than exports *per se,* and indeed exports were chiefly useful as a guarantee of stability. Once, contemplating the prospect of corn imports, he had written

67. Huskisson to Wodehouse, 25 Jan. 1820, HP 38742 ff. 3-5.

to Liverpool that 'the demand for our goods abroad may create a fund to pay for it' and so 'I do not apprehend any great effect upon our Foreign Exchanges.'[68] This aspect of Huskisson's policy may suggest that, in 1845, one of the motives impelling Peel towards corn law repeal was a desire to buttress the strict fiduciary system of 1844. At least, Peel presumably connected the liquidity crisis of 1839 with the extraordinarily large imports of corn in that year.[69]

Thus the move away from protection since 1815 was not the consequence of an ideological conversion to free trade, nor of a political appeal to new industrial or commercial classes, but was an adjustment to altered conditions of supply. Freer trade was now considered the safest way of ensuring food supplies, which, despite temporary glut, still seemed the overriding problem. It was a pragmatic development, which had one theoretical aspect that must now be examined.

Diminishing returns

Briefly the law of diminishing returns states that if extra doses of a variable factor (say capital or labour) are applied to a fixed dose of another factor (land), then each extra dose will increase the total production or marginal yield (say of corn) by progressively smaller amounts. Edward West, Malthus and Ricardo formulated this law simultaneously in January 1815 — a coincidence that can be explained by their common impulse to resolve a controversy current in the previous year's debates, although Malthus forged the theory to defend the Corn Bill and Ricardo to attack it.[70] It came

68. Huskisson to Liverpool, 26 Aug. 1819, LP 38191 ff. 117-20.
69. See J. C. Hobhouse, Lord Broughton, *Recollections of a Long Life,* edited by Lady Dorchester (1909-11), v. 221-13: 'At our cabinet to-day [10 Aug. 1839] Rice brought before us the state of the Bank of England, and told us that, if we had a bad harvest, we should be obliged to have recourse to a Bank Restriction Act.'
70. E. West, *Essay on the Application of Capital to Land* (1815); T. R. Malthus, *An Inquiry into the Nature and Progress of Rent, and the Principles by which it is Regulated* (1815); D. Ricardo, *An Essay on the Influence of a Low Price of Corn on the Profits of Stock* (1815). R. Torrens, *Essay on the External Corn Trade* (1815) also promulgated diminishing returns as they applied to inferior land, but not as to marginal capitalization. See W. C. Mitchell, *Types of Economic Theory, from mercantilism to institutionalism* (1967-9), i. 283 *et seq.;* E. Cannan, *A History of the Theories of Production and Distribution in English Political Economy from 1776 to 1848* (1893), 147-82.

too late to affect the legislation, but in 1817 it was stated definitively in Ricardo's *Principles of Political Economy and Taxation* (in the famous chapter on rent) and was confidently affirmed by McCulloch in 1818.[71] The Ricardian theory of diminishing returns and rent did not rest on empirical observation, but was logically essential to the labour theory of value. If the value of a commodity was to be convincingly defined by the amount of labour expended in its production — a postulate to which Ricardo was committed — then rent must be eliminated as a factor in value. This recondite theoretical requirement led Ricardo to define the price of corn as the cost of growing it on that portion of land to which most capital was applied in its cultivation. This land, which was only notionally cultivated,[72] would yield no rent. The rent of any other (intramarginal) portion of corn-growing land was thus defined as the difference between the capital cost of growing corn on that land and the cost of growing it on the land that yielded no rent. Thus rent was dependent on price, instead of being a factor of price as had been generally supposed. Ricardo's theory of diminishing returns was applied in practice mainly to the differential fertility of land,[73] since inferior soils would need to have more capital (and labour) expended on them in order to raise a given unit of production. The diminishing effects of successive applications of equal doses of capital or labour to the same soil was hardly emphasized. But theoretically, diminishing returns applied to marginal investment as much as to marginal land;[74] indeed, it was because the latter required extra capital (or labour) that it cost more to cultivate.

71. J. R. McCulloch, 'Ricardo's Political Economy', *Edinburgh Review*, xxx (1818), 59-87 and 'Taxation and the Corn Laws', ibid. xxxiii (1820), 155-87; D. P. O'Brien, *J. R. McCulloch, A Study in Classical Economics* (1970), 395-401.
72. This was a point that led to much misunderstanding, wilful or naïve. Many opponents of diminishing returns theory objected that there was no such thing in practice as land that yielded no rent — which may have been true but was beside the point.
73. Schumpeter, *History of Economic Analysis*, 675.

There were frequent allusions to diminishing returns theory in Parliament from 1820 onwards,[75] and it permeated almost every other page of Huskisson's Report. One passage contrasting farms with manufactories (where economies of scale were practicable) was unambiguous:

The price of corn, taken for any series of years, is necessarily regulated by the expense of production upon the lands which, at that price, make no return beyond the charge of raising it, together with the ordinary profit of the capital employed upon those lands...If the demand for corn were doubled it would force into cultivation poorer lands, requiring a larger capital to raise the same quantity of produce; the price of that produce would determine the price of the whole, or those poorer lands could not be maintained in cultivation.[76]

The obvious deduction was that if Britain, in attempting to feed her own population, extended tillage to ever worse land, costs would rise and the import protection price would need to be increased *indefinitely*, bringing extra and unnecessary profits to the better-quality soils.[77]

Agricultural witnesses were naturally hostile to a theory that threatened to explode all their arguments. For example, in question after question, Ricardo tried to make the senior Ellman admit that as population growth necessitated recourse to poorer land, the price of corn must rise. 'Certainly not. I have never yet been given to understand that an increased produce can tend to increase the price; an increased produce

74. This point was often missed in debate. For example, Brougham and Matthias Attwood argued that the theory failed because farmers did not necessarily cultivate the best land first and would not necessarily abandon land in order of merit either. Such considerations as locality, transport and proprietary rights often induced farmers to cultivate poor land when better was available. H.of C., 30 May 1820, 2 PD, i. 688 and 7 May 1822, 2 PD, vii. 378-82. For the same objection made later by Carey, Mease and McCulloch, see O'Brien, op.cit. 399. Ricardo had to explain in H. of C., 7 May 1822, 2 PD, vii. 394 that the order in which lands came to be cultivated was irrelevant, that population pressure might lead farmers 'to employ on land previously cultivated a second portion of capital which did not produce as much as the first'; then a third and so on; and that 'it was manifestly by the return on the last portion of capital applied, that the cost of production was determined.'

75. Huskisson and Robinson, especially, used diminishing returns theory to attack proposals for extending cultivation.

76. CSC, *Report on Petitions complaining of the depressed state of Agriculture*, 1821, 24.

77. Ibid. 10.

will diminish the price.' Here Ellman, like other farmers, defended marginal land and refuted diminishing returns theory by asserting a market theory of wages. Ricardo's postulated rise of population would increase the supply of labour, and the consequent reduction of wages would counter the effect of poorer soils on the production cost of corn.[78] Ricardo therefore harangued Ellman on the market theory of wages and argued for the subsistence theory instead. His relentless, remorseless logic soon had Ellman floundering, but the farmer held consistently to a supply and demand determinant of corn prices against Ricardo's cost theory:

The farmer has it not in his power to charge what he thinks proper, or what will remunerate him for the expense of the article he produces; he is subject to other circumstances [i.e. market factors] ; he is different from a common manufacturer who calculates all his expenses in producing an article, and charges accordingly for that article.

Similarly, when it came to wages:

As human labour is a marketable article, like everything else, the super-abundance from an increase of population will have a tendency to reduce the price of that labour, for which reason I think much of the poorer lands of this country might be brought into cultivation, which now remain a positive waste, and the labourers be employed under proper protection.[79]

Here the agriculturists' market explanation of prices and wages clashed with Ricardo's subsistence theories. In so far as Peel's chosen justification for his conversion in the 1840s to a repeal of the Corn Laws was genuine – that is the 'many concurring proofs that the wages of labour do not vary with the price of corn'[80] – he was adopting the same market theory of wages that the agriculturists had used to justify protection in 1821. The difference was, of course, that the latter saw the main opportunities for economic growth and the employment of a rising population in the marginal parts of the agricultural sector, and argued that the effect of dear bread on real wages would be offset by the increased demand for agricultural labour; whereas by the 1840s, it was evident that only the towns could accommodate expansion, and that

78. Ibid. 57.
79. Ibid. 57-8. Curwen offered a similar analysis, ibid. 63-6.
80. *Memoirs by Sir Robert Peel*, edited by Earl Stanhope (1856-7), ii. 102.

dear bread was interfering with manufacturing exports and economic growth.

Ellman's fumbling objections to diminishing returns theory were more lucidly articulated by the young Nassau Senior in a critical but complimentary review of the Agricultural Report. Senior concurred in Ricardo's view that marginal capitalization in agriculture (as distinct from manufactures) yielded diminishing returns, and that rent was a consequence and not a concomitant of price. But he disagreed that the cost of cultivating the most expensive land governed the price of all corn. He attributed the price of raw produce wholly to supply and demand; as demand rose with population, agriculture became more profitable, and at the point when to invest in even poor land became more profitable than to invest in manufactures (in which production costs were much less variable between different producers), so capital would switch to agriculture and to marginal land:

To say that it is the price of this last portion of corn, which governs that of the remainder, is to mistake the effect for the cause. The price of other corn does not rise because the last portion has been produced at a greater expense, but the last portion is produced, because the proportion of demand to supply has previously occasioned such a rise in the price of the corn already produced, that additonal capital laid out in producing additional corn, at a greater proportionate expense, will return the average profit of capital. Corn does not become dear because a portion is raised at a great expense, but a portion is raised at a great expense because corn has already become dear.[81]

The doctrine of rent and diminishing returns in agriculture could explain the government's move away from autarchy and protection in 1821. In the first place, it endorsed Malthus's fears of famine, by showing that agricultural improvements could not after all enable food supply to keep pace with the growth of population. By showing 'remuneration' to be a relative concept, it highlighted the internal competition between good and bad lands (which ministers had underestimated in 1815) and explained the selectivity of distress in

81. 'Report – on the State of Agriculture', *Quarterly Review*, xxv (1821), 467-77. For similar views see J. Wheatley, *A Plan to Relieve the Country from its difficulties* (1821) and Tooke to CSC, *Report on Petitions complaining of the depressed state of Agriculture*, 1821, 287. For a later physiocratic view of rent, see Edward Edwards, 'On Agriculture and Rent', *Quarterly Review*, xxvi (1827), 391-437.

1820-2. And whereas, in 1815, the government had planned a gradual reduction of corn prices, as reclamation and investment increased the supply of produce in the market, diminishing returns theory predicted that additional cultivation and over-capitalization would, on the contrary, *enhance* prices. The way to reduce price was in fact by decultivation and disinvestment. Finally, in 1815 rent had been held to be price-determining, and prices had had to be bolstered awhile against a sudden drop, until leases began to fall in and rents could be revised; but if rents were price-determined, as Ricardo maintained, it would be expedient to let prices fall more rapidly and leave rents to adjust automatically.[82]

But was the theory of rent and diminishing returns a *cause* of the change in policy? Or was it simply a convenient theory enabling ministers to justify a change founded solely on a realization that dependence on Continental food was more reliable than autarchy? No conclusive answer is possible. In 1815 ministers had employed protectionist theory, defensively and even apologetically, to sanction a policy that was basically pragmatic and administrative. If it could be demonstrated that the breakdown of protectionist theory over diminishing returns, and its supersession by free trade philosophy, was a decisive cause of the policy change, this would be a fascinating example of how ideas, initially employed in a supporting role for debating purposes, could on occasions subsequently take over, twist, and dictate legislative changes.

Later on, Parnell attributed his change of heart on corn in part to the Ricardian theory of rent.[83] But then Parnell was particularly vulnerable to its charms, for he alone had explicitly argued in 1815 that increased investment in agriculture would lower unit production costs. Ministers had simply prophesied that increased amounts of food supply would lower the price because of market factors, a prediction which was cracked but not totally shattered by diminishing returns theory. However, there are indications that Liverpool failed to realize that diminishing returns applied with equal

---

82. Harvey was asked: since rent was 'regulated by the price...may not a low price of corn be more beneficial to the farmer than a high price?' CSC, *Report on Petitions complaining of the depressed state of Agriculture*, 1821, 37.
83. H. of C., 9 Mar. 1827, 2 PD, xvi, 1102 and see below, p. 292n.

force to capital-intensive production as to marginal land.
Refusing one landlord's demand for an Enclosure Act to help
in reclaiming wastes, he commented that if only, in wartime,
'one half of the Capital had been employed in improving the
cultivation of the old Lands which was made use of in forcing
new Lands into cultivation, the produce of the Country
would have been considerably greater, and the distress that
was felt to so great a degree would scarcely have existed.'[84]
Thus Liverpool wanted decultivation but not disinvestment.
It seems that while he appreciated the need to abandon poor
soils (which raised prices and produced little food) in favour
of foreign supplies, he was still anxious to squeeze as much
food as he could out of Britain's respectable lands. What
about Huskisson? His Report clearly recognized the dual
application of diminishing returns. It pointed out that since
the price of all corn was regulated by the amount of capital
needed to raise it on land not able to afford any rent, it
could not also be affected by increases in taxation:

The price of corn, therefore, might fall in a country, notwithstanding
additional taxation, if the quantity required for the consumption of
that country could be raised, either by the cultivation of more fertile
and productive soils, or *by the application of a diminished capital to
the same soil*, in consequence of increased skill or improvements in
husbandry.[85]

However, though diminishing returns theory pervades the
Report, there is nothing of it in Huskisson's original resolutions. These made only one reference to marginal lands,
and this (the 21st) in fact declared that they must be kept up.
Of those passages in the Report that Ricardo condemned,[86]
this one alone was Huskisson's own, and not inserted as a
concession to the agriculturists. It referred to the difficulties
that the most expensive soils at present in cultivation would
have in competing with the more fertile areas. Huskisson

84. Liverpool to Kenyon, 18 Dec. 1819, Kenyon MSS. Kenyon disagreed, mainly
because supplies of such ingredients as manure were limited. Kenyon to Liverpool,
20 Dec. 1819, LP 38281 ff. 363-6.
85. CSC, *Report on Petitions complaining of the depressed state of Agriculture*,
1821, 21.
86. Ricardo to McCulloch, 8 July 1821, Sraffa, op.cit. ix. 7-8. See also Ricardo,
On Protection to Agriculture, ibid. iv. 245: 'After shewing the evils resulting from
prematurely taking poor lands into cultivation, [the Report] countenances a
system, which, at all sacrifices, is to keep them in tillage.'

suggested that the proposed fixed duty on foreign corn should be such

as would not aggravate to the occupiers of such soils the difficulty of that competition. The general question, how far the forced cultivation of some of these inferior lands may have been expedient or advantageous for the public interest, is one upon which it is unnecessary to offer a positive opinion...However...within the limits of the existing competition at home, the exertions of industry and the investment of capital on agriculture, ought to be protected against any revulsion, but that the protection ought not to go any further; and that if protected to that extent, the growth of our population, the accumulation of our internal wealth affording increased means of employment to that population and consequently increased means of purchasing all those articles of consumption and enjoyment, which must be derived from the soil of this country, will continue to give, as they have given during the last ten years, the most effectual stimulus and encouragement to the progressive improvement of our agriculture, and to the consequent value of the landed property of the kingdom.

Clearly, then, Huskisson did not accept the logical consequences of diminishing returns theory and an international division of labour. Though Ricardo joyfully observed that 'there were very few points on which Mr Huskisson and I differed', and that the minister was 'for establishing the trade on the most free and liberal foundation',[87] he in fact divined what to Huskisson, if not to himself, was a vital distinction: 'The difference between him [Huskisson] and me is this, he would uphold agriculture permanently up to its present height — I would reduce it gradually to the level at which it would have been if the trade had been free.'[88] This is essential. No more than on currency was Huskisson Ricardo's fool. Huskisson was an administrator with a talent for utilizing abstract concepts of political economy. Like Liverpool, he was anxious to clear the government of blame for having caused distress, and of responsibility for curing it — to justify, in other words, a policy of negation. Caught between the activists — the agricultural protectionists on the

87. Ricardo to Trower, 22 Aug. 1821, Sraffa, op. cit. ix. 37; Ricardo to McCulloch, 18 June 1821, ibid. viii. 390.
88. Ricardo to McCulloch, 8 July 1821, This was an essential (because practical) distinction to Huskisson, whereas Ricardo was so delighted to find that they were agreed in principle that this practical difference seemed inconsequential. Huskisson warned in H. of C., 8 May 1822, 2 PD, vii. 445, that capital was more likely to be destroyed by monopoly than by importation.

one hand, who wanted to force the cultivation of more lands, and on the other the free traders, who wanted to decultivate all lands already under the plough except those that could compete internationally — Huskisson and Liverpool offered a do-nothing conservatism. They would bury dead farmers but pledge the safety of those still in business.

Ministers insisted that the crisis would right itself; agriculturists and underconsumptionists on the one side, and free traders on the other, insisted that Parliament must act. Agriculturists like Webb Hall, Kenyon, and Western defended the extension of cultivation to waste lands on the grounds that it would create opportunities for employing the redundant population of the towns, and enable Britain to feed herself without imports. This was a 'back to the land' solution to the urban problem. Ricardo, however, did his best to discredit marginal land, and proposed decultivation, free trade, and an international division of labour — in other words, an intensification of the industrial revolution to solve the unemployment of the countryside. One looked to internal demand, the other to foreign. For agriculturists, who wanted an agricultural solution to unemployment, it would be wicked folly to give up the marginal lands, since, as Jacob pointed out, it was these 'which made use of the most labour at a time when the main symptom of distress was want of employment'. For Ricardo, labour spent on such land was wasted opportunity. The agriculturists' solution was not so much expansionist as social — they wished to employ the poor for humanitarian and prudential reasons — whereas free traders smelt potential growth, and wanted to abolish unemployment in order not to waste resources.[89]

In this struggle between an agriculturally based and an industrialized economy, ministers would have preferred to remain aloof and neutral. For their own purposes, they wished to retain grain farming in its present state, while sanctioning decultivations which had occurred naturally and withholding all encouragement to arable expansionists. But they were

89. 'I am not contented with a little prosperity if I can obtain a great deal for my country.' Ricardo to McCulloch, 23 Mar. 1821, Sraffa, op. cit. viii. 359.

obliged to side with Ricardo over the corn law for administrative reasons — food supply and steady prices — and this clearly militated against the agriculturalists' vision of extending cultivation. Thus, in order to defend the new corn law policy, Huskisson had to forget physiocracy and argue in terms of an economy geared to manufacturing exports, external demand, and international equilibrium. As in 1819 on resumption, Ricardo had offered a convenient and optimistic solatium, and ministers had swallowed gratefully. Reduction of the corn law would stimulate employment in the towns, free trade would safeguard supply by keeping Continental farmers in business, and British manufacturers would benefit. Ironically, the philosophy was emerging *(malgré lui)* of an industrial nation that would sell its wares in return for food from rural countries, although Huskisson and Liverpool did not wish to take the process too far. The important point is that this changeover to an export philosophy was not the cause of the *volte-face* on corn law policy, but a result of it.

V

THE POLITICS OF
AGRICULTURAL RELIEF, 1821–22

The issue of the four millions is...a beam of sunshine, precluding a
terrible storm inviting the ignorant and unwary abroad, for the purpose
of drenching them to the very skins. The storm is sure to *burst*, as soon
as ever the Public are fully *abroad*, rejoicing in their imagined prosperity,
as in 1814 and 1818, and then they will be struck to the Earth, *in
thousands* as in 1815, and 1819, and Lord Liverpool will coolly attribute their ruin and frustration to *"speculation"* and *"over-trading"*
and other chimeras more baseless than the winds.
Thomas Attwood to Davenport, 2 Apr. 1822, Davenport MSS.,
Attwood ff. 5-8.

The rural flight from high protection

Huskisson had confined the discussions of the 1821
Committee to protection, which was the most vulnerable
of the landlords' claims, by quashing attempts to involve
currency and taxation.[1] But once agriculturists began to
blame under consumption for their distress, they aspired to
remedy it by cheaper money and tax relief. Remnants of
protectionism lingered in 1822,[2] but no longer met with the
old response in the countryside. For example, at Stow-
market agriculturists forced Lord Huntingfield to recant his
arguments for high duties; at Lewes they threw out Ellman's
protectionist resolutions in favour of an amendment for
reconsidering cash payments; while in Devon they shouted
down a supporter of Webb Hall. Gooch turned his back on
corn laws, Holme Sumner, who had 'once thought with
Mr. Webbe Hall, that we had to fear every thing from the
opening of the foreign ports', no longer believed that 'the
cause of our present distress lay in that competition'; and

1. Althorp at the Holkham Sheep Shearing, 2 July 1821, *The Times*, 10 July
1821; Curwen in H. of C., 14 June 1821, 2 PD, v. 1185; C. M. Wakefield, *Life
of Thomas Attwood* (1885), 82.
2. Newcastle to Londonderry, 24 Mar. 1822, Castlereagh MSS. XXXVII,
mmcxvi-mmcxx; Oriel to Skeffington, 18 Aug. 1822, Chilham MSS. T2519/4/
2014.

Wodehouse declared, amid cheers, that Peel's Act was the root of all their ills, and that corn duties or 'laying the world under an interdict' were false policy.[3] Only four out of thirty-four nostrums, devised by country gentlemen and communicated to Londonderry early in 1822, requested more stringent restrictions.[4] Webb Hall, whose extremism and 'bustling, precipitate, and inconsiderate activity' were everywhere blamed for the government's refusal to legislate in 1821,[5] lost most of his following. This flight from high protection was apparent at Westminster. Charles Wynn, who had thought the 1815 Law 'foolish and unjust',[6] perceived that 'upon corn...the eyes of the public [i.e. landed classes] are beginning to open'; Ricardo detected 'a decided improvement in the public mind', while Wallace saw that the gentry had 'abandoned much hope from new Corn Bills' and were 'likely to direct their attack upon our Taxation'.[7] When faithful Lethbridge moved the protectionist programme in the Commons in May 1822, it was annihilated (243-24).

Agricultural protection would have sustained agriculturists at the expense of the rest, whereas economical and currency reforms stood to benefit all productive interests equally. Is it not then paradoxical that the gentry should have pursued the partisan solution in 1820, when distress was common to all interests, only to turn from it to general measures just as the industrial and commercial distress was lifting and agriculture sinking deeper into depression? Perhaps it was simply a tactical response to the government's intransigence over protection. But more fundamentally, ultra-protectionism depended on the existence of a *general* crisis rather than a mere farming depression. Kenyon, Sinclair, Webb Hall, and

---

3. *The Times,* 6 Dec. 1821; 7, 22, 23 and 31 Jan., 4 and 5 Feb. 1822. *Courier,* 14 Jan. 1822.
4. Castlereagh MSS. XXXVII, mmcii-mmclxiii, *passim.*
5. *Farmers' Magazine* (1821), 485-6; *Farmers' Journal* (1822), 98; *The Times,* 23 Jan. 4 and 5 Feb. 1822.
6. Wynn to Southey, 15 Jan. 1817, G. Evans, 'Charles Watkin Williams Wynn, 1775-1850', University of North Wales unpublished dissertation (1934), 109.
7. Wynn to Buckingham, 23 Jan. 1822, Buckingham and Chandos, *Memoirs of the Court of George IV, 1820-30* (1859), i. 276; Ricardo to Trower, 25 Jan. 1822, Sraffa, *Works and Correspondence of David Ricardo.* ix. 151-3; Wallace to Oriel, 21 Jan. 1822. Foster / Massereene MSS. D562/16104.

Jacob had different views, but they all looked beyond protection and high prices to the fertilization of wastes,[8] as
providing not only food but permanent employment for the
manufacturing labourers made idle in the industrial depression
of 1819-20. High protection would help to reverse the
industrial revolution, to bring back migrants to the rural
womb (where compared with the towns "all was peace, and
innocence, and bliss") and to re-create communities of
yeomen farmers and artisans. The crude antagonism between
élites — squirearchy and urbanocracy — represented conflict
between a pre-industrial, localized, paternalist myth and a
centralized, competitive, industrial vision of the future. And
obviously, physiocracy, as a 'back to the land' solution to the
urban problem, became less compelling once the urban
problem began to recede. As commerce recovered and
farmers languished, a manufacturing solution to the rural
problem — Ricardo's decultivation no less — appeared more
persuasive.

So the movement of agriculturists away from high protection in 1821-22 marked a silent retreat from rigorous
physiocracy as a remedy for the problem of urban unemployment. A similar process took place in the 1840s and 1850s,
by which time high protectionism was dead, agriculturists
being unable even to keep what they already had. Many who
were protectionists in this retentive sense ceased to be so in
the early fifties. The assumption behind their defence of the
Corn Law had been — no longer to excise the great wen —
but to preserve the existing balance and to prevent further
industrialization. The 1850s' industrial boom, the Great
Exhibition with its monuments to a manufacturing civil-
ization, and the 1851 census (showing that for the first time
a *majority* of the population was urban) seemed to prove,
however, that the industrial revolution would go ahead willy-
nilly. The former protectionist pronounced the Corn Laws
dead and damned in 1852, and in that year the Iron Duke
foresaw that Greater London would engulf the Home
Counties. Hitherto physiocrats like Disraeli, O'Connor,

8. Protection was frequently associated with demands for a national enclosure
act.

Sadler, Oastler, and O'Brien had half-accepted cholera and typhoid as evils likely to drive working men back to agriculture and the arms of the aristocracy. Once the struggle against industrialization was seen to be lost, however, the preservation of social peace and the need to reconstitute the tory-democratic alliance on an urban basis required that town dwelling be made tolerable. In this way the spirited opponent of the 1848 Public Health Act became the protagonist of *sanitas*.

While manufactures and agriculture were simultaneously depressed, as in 1819-20, the foreigner had appeared to be their common enemy, and this provoked demands for an external remedy, adjusting Britain's relations with the world. Joint suffering only emphasized sectoral strife, however, since farmers demanded a higher Corn Law to give them a monopoly against the foreigner while mill owners wanted Corn Law reduction to open up access to overseas markets. This conflict was distorted by the selective revival of manufactures after 1820. Cheap food, the bane of the farmers, helped exports to recover in 1821, yet manufacturing for the home market remained as depressed as ever.[9] The common fate of corn and iron 'proved the union of the two interests',[10] and prompted agriculturists to unite with Birmingham in stressing internal under consumption rather than foreign competition. In debate a new polarity, between the importance of internal and external sources of demand, was imposed on the previous dialectic as to whether agriculture or manufacture was the ultimate basis of a nation's wealth. Agricultural witnesses to the 1821 Committee frequently predicted that cheap food would cause rural unemployment and so damage manufacturers by slashing the spending power of their chief customers: 'From the great proportion of the produce of every country which is consumed at home, some idea may be formed of the greater portion of wealth, that is created by internal production and

9. See above p. 91.
10. Western in H. of C., 8 Feb. 1821, 2 PD, iv. 535. Ricardo observed that foreign commerce ruptured the identity of interest between agriculture and manufactures, H. of C., 30 May 1820, 2 PD, i. 674; Maxwell in H. of C., 31 May 1820, ibid. 711.

consumption, than by an external commerce.'[11] Ricardo retorted as often that redundant farm labourers could flock to the towns, and that cheap food and corn imports would stimulate a foreign demand for (and investment in) British manufactures, greater than ever agriculturists could have provided:

Must we not pay for [foreign corn] in money or in manufactures? — [Orton]: It would not matter how we paid for it; I believe we have generally paid for it in money.
We must pay for it in something? — Yes.
Can that something be obtained without labour? — I am not competent to answer that question.
If the people of England employed less labour on their land, would they not have the means of employing more in manufactures? — That I would very much doubt; the agriculturist and his labourers would be capable of purchasing, if he was remunerated for his labour, a great deal of manufactured goods of the country.[12]

Thus the conflict between manufactures and agriculture was now being expressed, not in terms of the internal distribution of capital between the two (as affected by the Corn Law), so much as in terms of external commercial equilibrium against internal equilibrium and, as it were, full employment.

Once agriculturists began to see low prices as the result of internal underconsumption, the obvious scapegoats were taxation, which cut into consumer spending, and Peel's Act, which, by curtailing the circulation, contributed directly to deflation and stifled demand. Given this analysis, two types of action were possible: either to replenish the consumption function by vigorous methods; or, less heroically, to enable producers to accommodate to an unhappy situation by more immediate and humane methods than the government's formula for weeding out marginal producers. Cobbett's equitable adjustment of wartime debts and contracts, or modest amounts of tax relief that might be recouped from savings in public expenditure, were examples of the second type — ways of helping straitened country gentlemen to adapt to deflation and external equilibrium by cutting down

11. Jacob to CSC, *Report on Petitions complaining of the depressed state of Agriculture*, 1821, 371.
12. Ibid. 134; Jacob, ibid. 373: 'The consumption of that part of the community which depends on agriculture, is the largest and if their means of purchasing are limited..., then consumption of manufactures must be lessened.'

costs. They were measures of social justice, affecting the internal distribution of resources, rather than adjustments of the balance between internal and external activity or attempts to increase resources and demand. On the other hand, there were proposals for reverting to an inflationary situation, such as repealing cash payments, lowering the standard, or large tax reductions going beyond what might be saved by retrenchments, and involving the annihilation of the sinking fund and repudiation of public and private debts. These more extreme suggestions were not defended on grounds of social justice — indeed many of their advocates conceded that they might frequently entail grave injustice for individuals — but as necessary crisis measures to release consumer spending, increase internal demand and set the economy to rights.[13] Now in debate, this distinction between curative and merely anodyne proposals was often confused. By and large, however, in so far as country gentlemen embraced tax and currency reforms at all in 1821, it was mainly for the less exalted purpose of immediate relief and accommodation. They only moved towards an underconsumptionist position gradually, from 1822, and in the wake of individual Whigs and Radicals.

Corn and currency

Ministers had consistently based agricultural policy on the monetary situation, and had moreover tended to play the financiers and a landed parliament off against each other. Harrison reminded Liverpool in 1820 that owing to 'ill humour amongst the landed Interests', it was essential to 'put the monied Interest in the City in good Humour' by boosting the funds.[14] That is, loans would be needed if taxes were withheld. Country gentlemen had not made the connection hitherto, but in 1821 they began to consider monetary causes of distress and to toy with monetary remedies — taxation of funded wealth, reduction of interest on the

13. This distinction clarifies the position of Cobbett, who recommended equitable adjustment and Corn Law repeal as measures of alleviation that would enable farmers to adjust to a deflationary gold standard, but who bitterly repudiated Attwood and the paper inflationists.
14. Harrison to Liverpool, 30 Nov. 1820, LP 38288 ff. 221-4.

national debt, equitable adjustment of all debts and contracts, enhancement of the circulation, devaluation of the standard, bimetallism and Bank restriction. The old debating theme — 'farmer versus fundholder' — reappeared in force. It was 'a conflict of which they had already seen some symptoms between the landed and funded proprietor, as to the share which each should bear in the general calamity.'[15] Should landlords become the 'ascripti glebæ, or the mere serfs' of the fundholders?[16] Hitherto Cobbett's had been almost a lone voice, but now, suddenly, his arguments were taken up like ready-tailored garments, and worn all over the countryside.

John Sinclair, whose following had until now been chiefly mercantile, exhorted agriculturists in this direction. His economic ideas were based on national independence and internal stability, which would require protection, autarchy, and the centralized issue of promissory notes. He had consistently opposed the bullionists and resumption, and had indefatigably harangued paper-sympathizers in, and connected with, the government — such as Castlereagh, Vansittart, and George Chalmers. He opposed Webb Hall from the first, maintaining that dear money, not competition, was the originating difficulty,[17] but linked the corn and currency issues with an argument deriving from Thomas Attwood and Henry James. Resumption would put a premium on corn imports by raising the exchanges and rendering a fixed duty commensurately less formidable to speculative importers. Consequently the exchanges must be righted by additional circulation *before* the ports next opened to corn, even at a duty. 'If a new Corn Bill had passed without the question of *Exchange* being adverted to', he reflected in 1822, 'nothing could have saved the British farmer, *from* total ruin.'[18]

15. Ellice in H. of C., 9 Apr. 1821, 2 PD, v. 142-3.
16. Lockhart in H. of C., 3 Apr. 1821, ibid. 13.
17. J. Sinclair, *On the Means of Arresting the Progress of National Calamity* (1817); J. Sinclair, *Thoughts on Paper Circulation* (1819); Sinclair to Liverpool, 6 Apr. 1817, 27 Oct . 1819 and 22 Apr. 1820, LP 38265 ff. 324-7; 38280 ff. 230-9; 38284 ff. 180-1; Sinclair to George Chalmers, 15 Mar. 1820, Chalmers MSS. 22902 ff. 274-7; *Life and Works of Sir John Sinclair*, ii. 325; R. Mitchison, *Agricultural Sir John* (1962), 238-48.
18. Sinclair to Oriel, 4 Feb. 1822, Foster/Massereene MSS. D207/13/1; J. Sinclair, 'Means to Remedy Distress' and 'Effects of Cash Payments on Exchange Rates and Corn Prices', *Farmers' Magazine* (1822), 22-47, 82-5.

When Baring, Ellice, and Matthias Attwood raised the currency question in Parliament in 1821,[19] they forsook underconsumptionism for arguments about social justice and the rights of industrious classes over the 'drones'. There was little verbal support, but silent among Baring's meagre lobby of twenty-seven were Calthorpe, Western, Lethbridge, and Wodehouse. Here was an invitation for Thomas Attwood to court the countryside. He was already conducting a public correspondence with Western and Webb Hall in the *Farmers' Journal*, whose editors observed — 'Mr. Attwood...is all *cash*, ... Mr. Webb Hall ... all corn.'[20] The former dashed expectantly to London for two four-hour sessions with the 1821 Agricultural Committee, denouncing resumption as socially dangerous and unjust rather than as economically restrictive. He claimed to have made a great impression and to have quite 'mortified' Ricardo and Huskisson with his infallibility, but they for their part thought him perfectly silly. The chasm of comprehension separating Ricardian orthodoxy, based on international equilibrium, from Attwood's economic radicalism (which subordinated the foreign exchanges to domestic considerations), is superbly caricatured in the following dialogue on the central question of the Bullionist controversy — whether monetary policy should have reference to the state of the foreign exchanges. The interrogator is presumably Ricardo, and Attwood is presumably being disingenuous:

Would not the exchanges be affected quite as soon by such an alteration in the standard, as .the prices of all commodities in the country? — I am not intimately acquainted with the theory of the exchanges.
Is not the theory of the exchanges absolutely necessary to the full understanding this subject? — Certainly not.
Without knowing the theory of the exchanges, is it possible for you to judge of the bounty that would be given on the exportation of British commodities, to which you have alluded? — Yes.

19. See above pp. 92-6. Matthias had intrigued with Vansittart in 1818 to agitate against resumption. M. Attwood to Brogden, 12 Jan. 1818, Castlereagh MSS. XXXIV, mclxxxvi.
20. *Farmers' Journal* (1820), 61.

How do you judge of that bounty, without knowing at what rate of exchanges the payments for the goods must be made? &c., &c.[21]

Attwood may have succeeded in convincing the chairman, Gooch, that resumption had been 'intended to operate a total transfer of the landed rental of the kingdom into the hands of the fundholders', but he realized that whereas the country gentlemen on the Committee were 'dull as beetles', Huskisson and Ricardo were 'sharp as *needles* and as active as bees'.[22] Huskisson refused to let the Committee hear Attwood's henchmen, Rooke, James, and Cruttwell, and included in his Report a veritable pæan to convertibility. It was probably this incident, rather than events of 1825/6,[23] that turned Attwood from loyal Tory to parliamentary reformer. He held the country gentry responsible for the return to gold in 1819, and had flattered himself that he had only to disabuse *them* of bullionism for that Act to be repealed. The government's ability to overrule them in their own Committee, just when they were coming round to currency-mongering in place of high corn laws, convinced Attwood that agricultural influence needed strengthening by a parliamentary reform. For if Peel's Act were not soon repealed, 'The *Sword* will be the only arbitrator that will remain. To that stern arbitrator the landowners must appeal, or they must drop into the workhouse as the dried leaves of autumn to the ground.'[24]

The campaign for tax relief, 1820-1

Protection was entirely compatible with cheap money and reflation, whereas tax relief aimed rather to help sufferers adjust to deflation. After Baring's first defeat on currency

21. CSC, *Report on Petitions complaining of the depressed state of Agriculture*, 1821, 258-9. Ricardo to Trower, 21 Apr. 1821, Sraffa, op.cit.viii. 370. This "exchange" parodies John Smith's bland confession to the CSC, *Reports on the Expediency of resuming Cash Payments*, 1819, 226: 'I do not understand the subject of exchanges.'
22. Attwood to his wife, 11 and 13 Apr. 1821, Wakefield, op. cit. 81-2.
23. A. Briggs, 'Thomas Attwood and the Economic Background of the Birmingham Political Union', *Cambridge Historical Journal*, ix (1948), 209, has suggested that Attwood's failure to convert ministers to currency reform in 1826 was a crucial turning-point. See below, p. 217. I have benefited much from discussion with Dr. D. J. Moss on this point.
24. Attwood to Davenport, 9 June 1822, Davenport MSS., Attwood ff. 21-34.

(19 March 1821), Ellice admonished the gentry that, having thus rejected 'depreciation', they might 'bid adieu' to high remunerating prices and should 'bend their attention entirely to the reduction of expenses' instead.[25]

Demands for tax reductions traditionally derived from radical movements against governments bottomed not on opinion but on venality and corruption. 'Ministers would never begin the long promised work of retrenchment, until the House refused them some of the taxes.'[26] This had nothing to do with theories of consumption or prices. Ricardo, for example, did not attribute distress to taxation and ostentatiously said so, yet he demanded tax cuts as a political manoeuvre against Tory ministers — 'To keep them peaceable you must keep them poor.'[27] The coincidence of political crisis and economic distress made 1820 a particularly dangerous year for government, since independent members could be tempted to vote away taxes for both political and personal reasons. The 1818 and 1820 Elections had involved only slight losses numerically, but had deprived the government of some of its 'steadiest props'. New members might be unduly influenced by hustings opinion, while economic privation could cause political disaffection. Huskisson explained to Arbuthnot in March 1820 that 'the spirit which is spreading through the country, even in the agricultural districts...is a soreness on every subject connected with expense, a clamour for economy, a feeling growing out of the present straitened circumstances of the Yeomanry contrasted with the ease which they enjoyed during the war.' This soreness threatened to debilitate the whiter corpuscles of the countryside, and enable tumescent radicalism to spread from the 'Bubble of the towns' to the normally healthy tissues of rural society. It was therefore necessary 'To do something to secure the affection and more cordial good will of some great class in the state. To bid for the lower classes or the manufacturing population [by parliamentary reform presumably] is out of the question.

25. H. of C., 21 Mar. and 9 Apr. 1821, 2 PD, iv. 1390; v. 141.
26. Monck in H. of C., 5 Mar. 1821, 2 PD, iv. 1080.
27. Ricardo to Trower, 25 Mar. 1822, Sraffa, op. cit. ix. 180.

Duty and policy would equally forbid it. But the yeomanry are still within your reach, and to them in my opinion we must look.'[28] To this end Liverpool with difficulty persuaded the King to forego any addition to his Civil List. It was a political gesture only and, having made it, ministers refused to translate any saving into tax reduction, preferring to apply the less immediate but more 'valuable relief' of public debt redemption.[29]

Inevitably, the Opposition chose taxation and retrenchment as less divisive topics than protection for their 1821 campaign.[30] After Curwen and Maberly had failed with motions to repeal the husbandry horse tax and to halve the house and window duties, Western carried (149—125) a motion against the extra malt duty imposed in 1819.[31] A judicious threat to resign if the 1819 'system' were disturbed in this way enabled Castlereagh to reverse the decision (242—144) a fortnight later,[32] which showed the Whigs that while the gentry might revolt to change measures, they had no desire to replace the present men. But at least the agriculturists were shifting ground. They had begun the session as protectionists exclusively; Holme Sumner even attributed distress partly to tax *remission* since the war, Gooch and Wodehouse denied that taxes hit agriculture especially, and Knatchbull condemned fiscal reductions as inimical to public credit.[33] Hardly any Tory squires supported Maberly and Curwen in March and April. A high price was still 'the remedy most in vogue' among agriculturists.[34] Perhaps Huskis-

28. Huskisson to Arbuthnot, 24 Mar. 1820, HP 38742 ff. 6—9.
29. Robinson in H. of C., 7 Mar. 1821, 2 PD, iv. 1144-6; Twiss, *Life of Lord Chancellor Eldon*, ii. 363; S. Walpole, *A History of England from the Conclusion of the Great War in 1815* (1878-86), ii. 4-5; Buckingham and Chandos, *Memoirs of the Court of George IV*, i. 18.
30. For details, see Walpole, op.cit. ii. 28-9; Smart, *Economic Annals of the Nineteenth Century, 1821-30*, 35-42; Mitchell, *The Whigs in Opposition*, 160.
31. Canning to his wife, 23 Mar. 1821, CP 26 ff. 154—9.
32. Although the vote against the tax was numerically similar on 21 Mar. and 3 Apr., about one-third of those who divided on one occasion did not do so on the other. Only five persons reversed their votes in favour of ministers following the resignation threat; yet the original government vote was doubled on 3 Apr., showing how placemen and gentry rallied after the threat.
33. H. of C., 7 Mar. 1821, 2 PD, iv. 1143, 1152.
34. Ellice in H. of C., 21 Mar. 1821, 2 PD, iv. 1389.

son's behaviour in Committee goaded them towards alternative remedies. But whatever the reason, on 14 June Gooch suddenly warned his fellow landlords that there was no longer any hope of increasing their means, and that they must look instead to reducing costs and outlays.[35] On the same occasion Curwen secured 141 votes against the agricultural horse tax, including sufficient of the gentry's to induce ministers to surrender it.

Independent support strengthened the Opposition's fiscal campaign, which was overshadowed nevertheless by the anti-patronage movement of the Radicals — Joseph Hume, Thomas Creevey and Henry Grey Bennet. The 'Mountain', as they were known, proceeded to 'obstruct and puzzle the examination of the annual estimates to an extent and with a degree of perseverance which is without example'.[36] The Whigs' attitude to this was equivocal and their support guarded. Tierney and several others voted against Creevey's resolution condemning Lord Fife's dismissal from the Bedchamber for his vote against the malt tax. Whigs resented the loss of initiative to Hume, whose 'maxims of reform' were anyway 'unpalatable to all official expectants as well as to all men in office'.[37] Lauderdale realized that sound government required 'means of influence', and Tavistock did not wish 'to see that House assume the functions of the executive government'.[38] It was the existing government that Whigs wished to cripple, not future administrations. The country gentlemen, however, did not even wish to cripple Liverpool's, and only toyed with retrenchment to blackmail ministers into granting relief. Gooch attacked Hume's motion of 27 June, calling for a reduction of £4,000,000 expenditure, because of its 'tone of censure against ministers'.[39] Thus a curious polarity marked the division lists of 1821. Tory

35. 2 PD, v. 1186.
36. Bankes to Colchester, 9 Apr. 1821, Colchester, *Diary and Correspondence,* iii. 216-7; Walpole, op.cit. ii. 35-8; Mitchell, op.cit. 160-1; *Annual Register (1820)* and *(1821);* T. Creevey, *Remarks upon the Last Session of Parliament by a near observer* (1822), 59.
37. Mallet, MS.Diary, 6 Mar. 1822, iv. 31. The Whigs became more extreme on this point as their hopes of forming their own administration dwindled.
38. Lauderdale to Holland, n.d., HHP 51692 ff. 21-3; H. of C., 27 June 1821, 2 PD, v. 1418.
39. 2 PD, v. 1422.

gentlemen voted for keeping up places and armies and against the taxes needed to pay for them; while Ricardo and Baring's section of the Whigs supported Liverpool's stand for "public credit"against tax reduction, yet defied him over retrenchments, which they hoped would enable taxes to be lowered without detriment to public credit. Meanwhile, country gentlemen were moving towards a fiscal (as well as a currency) solution, simply as a means of immediate relief, and without appreciating its underconsumptionist implications, or even sharing the political motives of Hume, its instigator.

As before, ministers conceded a considerable amount to retrenchment in 1821,[40] but not to tax reduction, against which they proclaimed the sacred obligation to maintain public credit and its symbol, the sinking fund — an obligation all the greater because Britain was struggling to restore her currency.[41] Their stock argument was that since taxation could hardly *cause* low prices, tax concessions could not relieve agricultural distress. Since concessions were usually demanded on the ground of alleviation, the argument was irrelevant; and to the extent that underconsumptionist theory underlay the opposition to taxation, it could be retorted that fiscal relief might stimulate demand and raise prices.[42] But so long as tax relief remained the hand-maiden of radical retrenchment, its underconsumptionist possibilities were dormant. The main cause of demand failures being the transition to peace, a logical remedy would have been to revive government spending, for example on public works. Now many Whigs thought with ministers that this would only *lower* aggregate demand by detracting from private spending, and blamed government prodigality in the past for piling up a burdensome debt. Lansdowne 'attributed our present pressure to the circumstance of our living so long on the capital of the country, and our being obliged now to confine

40. Though they sacrificed more humble public officers, rarely the mighty. H. of C., 1 June 1821, 2 PD, v. 1073-98; Liverpool to George IV, 27 July 1821, LP 38289 ff. 282-6, A. Aspinall, *The Letters of King George IV, 1812-30* (1938), ii. 449-51.
41. Castlereagh and Peel in H. of C., 21 Mar. and 18 June 1821, 2 PD, iv. 1399-1400; v. 1204. A very few Radicals hinted that public credit might be expendable, e.g. Folkestone in H. of C., 21 Mar. 1821, 2 PD, iv. 1395-6.
42. Though ministers might well have replied, with Tooke, that in the case of corn, demand was inelastic and therefore fairly independent of spending power.

ourselves to its revenue'.[43] But even those Whigs who did
press a consumptionist solution had to oppose public works,
because these would have clashed with the parellel and parent
movement for retrenchment. The appointment of commissioners to supervise public schemes could only augment the
Tory government's power. This is why those writers who
almost or actually recommended public spending to offset
failing demand — notably Malthus, Lauderdale, Thomas
Chalmers, and Spence — found, except in Matthias Attwood,
so little parliamentary response.[44] With public works taboo,
opposition spokesmen who wished to press a demand policy
were compelled to think in terms of liberating *private*
spending. The latter could only be achieved by less taxation,
whereas public spending would have required more. Thus the
anti-patronage movement, though politically motivated,
affected the direction of economic pressure groups. The
possibility of urging tax-cuts in order deliberately to liberate
private spending (as distinct from mere relief or preconditions
of retrenchment) only got under way after the end of the
1821 session.

Underconsumptionism and the Whigs

The Whigs, being divided on corn laws, were delighted to
observe the gentry turning away from high protection. It
was clear after the 1821 session that the independents would
never vote them into office as a moderate party. Therefore
they began to seek support beyond the pale of the constitution and, by a modicum of parliamentary reform, to
change a system that they could not exploit.[45] At the same
time, the need to win over the gentry and to assert themselves
against the 'Mountain' encouraged many to adopt a more
radical economic programme. Whigs were still regarded as

43. H. of L., 5 Feb 1821, 2 PD, iv. 359.
44. T. R. Malthus, *Principles of Political Economy considered with a view to
their practical application* (1820), second edition (1836), 420 et seq., 320 et seq.
But see P. Sraffa, 'Malthus on Public Works', *Economic Journal*, lxv (1955),
543-4; B. A. Corry, 'The Theory of the Economic Effects of Government
Expenditure in English Classical Political Economy', *Economica*, new series, xxv
(1958), 40; R. D. C. Black, *Economic Thought and the Irish Question, 1817-70*
(1960), 159-202 and passim.
45. Mitchell, op.cit. 166-8; Mallet, MS.Diary, 1 Mar. 1822, iv. 29-30; F. Bamford
and Wellington, *The Journal of Mrs Arbuthnot 1820-30* (1950), i. 160.

arch-champions of bullionism and public credit, who had led
ministers to church by a halter in 1819. They had hitherto
sought to abolish only as many taxes as could be spared by
dismantling the Tory spoils system. But privately, individual
Whigs were beginning to contemplate a solution involving
repudiation of the national debt, either by gross tax
reductions or modification of the currency. In 1820 even
that instinctive bullionist, Lord Holland, who had demanded
an *immediate* restoration of cash payments and 'national
honour' the year before, was 'satisfied that the crisis requires
some very strong decisive measures and especially these two
— Bankruptcy without the name of it — and the name of
reform with as little real alteration as possible'. Only a
'bankruptcy avowed or disguised' could relieve distress and
conciliate the disaffected. Grey did not demur, though he
warned Holland not to say so much in public.[46]

Late in 1821 the Whigs shed some of their caution in a
bid for the hearts of the gentry. Many of them — Grey,
Lansdowne, even Tierney — were coming to see that mere
curtailment of patronage was not enough to make substantial
tax reductions possible. The sinking fund, and taxes supporting it, must be abandoned. Lauderdale was the most
passionate opponent of 'a device which...must...invade
private property, one hundred times more than all the thefts,
acts of swindling, of House breaking, robberies, forgeries'.[47]
In future, tax relief should be no mere appendage of retrenchment, but should be pressed with the conscious intention of
releasing private spending and raising internal demand.
Lansdowne saw that 'the inability to consume was continued
by severe taxation,' and recommended cuts 'to increase and
secure consumption.'[48] Lauderdale saw several advantages in
removing £5,000,000 of taxes: direct relief; savings in revenue
collection costs; increased proceeds from the taxes remaining;
the release of capital at present needed to offset commodity
taxes, thereby creating 'a source of additional demand for

46. Holland to Grey, 20 Apr. and 22 May 1820, HHP 51546 ff. 45-8, 55-6; Grey
to Holland, 23 Apr. 1820, Grey MSS., quoted in Mitchell, op.cit. 141.
47. Lauderdale to Page, 14 Nov. 1821, Bodleian MSS., Eng. lett., b.3 ff. 50-3.
48. H. of L., 26 Feb. 1822, 2 PD, vi. 721. Only Curwen has said this publicly in
1821, H. of C., 5 Apr. 1821, 2 PD, v. 42-6.

labour and of increase of wealth'; and finally, the 'multiplier' effect of private consumption:

The sum which was devoted to accumulation making no Call or Demand for Labour will be expended in Consumeable commodity...In enriching each Person who shares the benefit it enables him to have a demand for an additional quantity of commodity, and that again creates in those who supply it also an additional demand for Commodity. Besides it is quite ridiculous to suppose that a demand for five millions of Commodities will only raise these commodities five millions. According to Davenant and every man who has treated on the subject the value of the commodities undergoes a much greater rise — for example he calculates that extra demand for one-tenth will raise the price three-tenths which will add very much to the efficacy of the measure in giving relief.[49]

Meanwhile other Whigs, Erskine, Robert Heron, and the Whiggish young Radical, James Graham, vied with Stanhope, an "ultra tory", in prophesying that unless the 1819 settlement was revised, or interest on the debt reduced, society would disintegrate in pauperism or explode in revolution.[50] Western best illustrates the shift of opinion (of both Whigs and agriculturists). Early in 1821 he had still been the apostle of protection, autarchy, and marginal cultivation. But in July, following his public indoctrination by Attwood, and immediately after serving on the Agricultural Committee, he decided that tax reductions were the only means of relief obtainable. By 1822 convertibility was the culprit — not importation (he even conceded that subsistence needs might sometimes justify imports). The measure of 1819 had suddenly become 'almost the sole cause of the evil', 'the greatest calamity the public had endured in modern times', 'one of the most impolitic, and mischievous measures that ever was adopted in this or any other country.'[51]

It was with these radical economic ideas that landed Whigs attempted to wrest control of the countryside from Webb

---

49. Lauderdale to Holland, 2 Mar. 1822, HHP 51692 ff. 76-80; H. of L., 25 June 1822, 2 PD, vii. 1323. See the 'Tudela' letters in *The Times*, 10 Jan. 1822 et seq.
50. *Life and Works of Sir John Sinclair*, ii. 314-6; *Correspondence of Sir John Sinclair*, i. 126-9; Stanhope to Kenyon, 22 May 1822, Kenyon MSS.; R. Heron, *Notes printed but not published* (1850), 134-6. Heron had used almost identically apocalyptic language about 1816, ibid. 73-4.
51. H. of C., 1, 3 and 29 Apr., 8 May and 11 June 1822, 2 PD, vi. 1405, 1444-5; vii. 199, 429-30, 877-96 (especially 878).

Hall, and of Parliament from the 'Mountain'. The attempt was first co-ordinated early in July 1821 at Coke's Sheep Shearing at Holkham. This xenophobic, merino-baiting affair was a breeding-ground of rural Whiggery, a counter-weight to Sheffield's Toryish Wool Fair at Lewes. On this occasion the proceedings were less convivial than usual. Coke, Albemarle, Erskine, Althorp, Nugent, Bedford, Hume, Western, and Benett all demanded severe tax reductions, and Burdett was cheered wildly as he recommended reduction of interest on the National Debt.[52] These themes were taken up by Russell in his published letters to the yeomanry of Hunts,[53] in which he condemned the forced appreciation of 1819 and the current 'fashion' for political economy, whose exponents 'care not for the difference between an agricultural and manufacturing population, in all that concerns morals, order, national strength, and national tranquillity. Wealth is the only object of their speculation.' Russell perceived that ministers had taken up political economy because it sanctioned their inertia, and also that in the Agricultural Report Huskisson intended — 'with many sugared words' — to 'lay the foundation for subverting the principle of the corn bill altogether, and introducing foreign corn at all times into the market'. Parliament should defy him, and attempt to stimulate demand at home by abolishing the sinking fund and removing taxes on salt, leather, candles, soap, and malt. The evil consequence of ministers having borrowed to redeem debt was that 'money, instead of being expended with profusion, has been collected and accumulated, in the hands of capitalists or monied men.' This had produced 'artificial distress' in agriculture, since instead of lending the capital to landlords at low rates, as ministers promised in the 1821 Report, the financiers were investing it at 7 or 8 per cent abroad. Ultimately the land's only recourse was to increase county representation by a reform of Parliament.

The Whigs stirred up more spontaneous enthusiasm than they had bargained for. They strove to stem extremism, yet

52. *The Times*, 10 and 14 July 1821; *Farmers' Magazine* (1821), 380-1.
53. *The Times*, 18 and 22 Jan. 1822; Halevy, *The Liberal Awakening*, 115; H. of C., 21 Feb. 1822, 2 PD, vi. 571-7.

to retain their hold over rural opinion by keeping abreast of
its excesses. For the agricultural movement spread 'like wild
fire' in 1822.[54] At the first great county meeting, in Norfolk
on 12 January, the liberals Albemarle and Suffield kept
control, warded off 'Cobbettism', defeated a motion in
favour of going off gold, and confined the resolutions to the
subjects of parliamentary reform and immense tax
reductions.[55] But elsewhere Cobbett and the 'resurrection-
men' intervened, the former often in person, to challenge
Whig domination. In Kent and Sussex, Cobbett moved
proposals calling for reduction of interest on the Debt and
for milching the fundholders. The Whig grandees — Darnley,
Cowper, Jersey, Thanet, Sondes — begged the meetings to be
content with retrenchment, but Cobbett triumphed with
immense majorities.[56] Ricardian orthodoxies were howled
down in Surrey.[57] There were two meetings in Rutland, one
thinly attended on retrenchment, and a much more popular
assembly for reform.[58] In all about eighteen counties met,
many of which prayed for parliamentary reform and for
monetary re-adjustments.[59] What alarmed many persons
(including the Whigs) was a new impetus from below. Mallet
discerned a new class of agitator — millers, small farmers,
graziers that had done well out of the war, mere 'overgrown
yeomen' — 'these are the men who almost everywhere stand
up for Parliamentary reform and Radical opinions, in
opposition to the old gentry.' Fraser has noted the new
'democracy' alive in the counties.[60] In Hertfordshire, humble
men disputed with the Whigs, Sebright and Lamb, over
whether M.P.s were delegates or representatives. Gooch met
with 'tumultuous disapprobation' and motions of censure in
Suffolk,[61] while Wodehouse was 'bearded' and 'catechised'

54. E. Hughes, *Studies in Administration and Finance, 1558-1825* (1934), 492.
55. *The Times,* and *Courier,* 14 Jan. 1822.
56. Cobbett, *Rural Rides,* i. 52-72; *The Times,* 7 Jan. 1822; *Annual Register*
(1822), 10.
57. *The Times,* 19 Feb. 1822; Ricardo to Trower, 20 Feb. 1822, Sraffa, op. cit.
ix. 165-7.
58. Heron, op.cit. 134.
59. Mitchell, op.cit. 162.
60. P. Fraser, 'Public Petitioning and Parliament before 1832', *History,* xlvi
(1961), 205-7.
61. *The Times,* 2 Feb and 31 Jan. 1822.

in Norfolk by one Palmer of Yarmouth: 'One reason of the distress suffered in the country was, that for the last 20 years, the Country Gentlemen had, instead of dispensing blessings to the tenants on their estates, been dancing attendance at levees, and playing the part of sycophants at Court. [Loud cheers].'[62]

Alarmed by this social threat in the countryside, the Whigs attempted to reunite the various strata of landed society by showing that they faced common enemies in fundholders and placemen. The Ricardian theory of rent was useful in covering over the fissures that had often opened between landlord and tenant in the days of high protection. Rent, announced Lord Dacre in Hertfordshire, was mere residue, and so 'It was, not now a question between the owner and occupier of land, which should derive a particular share of the profit; but whether there should be a transfer of the whole land of England altogether into other hands.'[63]

The squires' revolt

Whereas ministers grounded bullionism on the need to prevent national bankruptcy, which the events of 1789 had shown to be a precursor of revolution and dislocation, many Whig leaders considered that bullionism was in itself institutionalizing confiscation and, by transferring property from landlords to fundholders, threatening conflagration. But all their extra-parliamentary initiative did the Whigs little good politically. They approached the 1822 session dispiritedly. Brooks's was empty — they were leaderless in the Commons — and, from Northumberland, Grey proffered only supine epistolary advice.[64] Brougham's opening philippic, for tax reductions equal to the amount of currency appreciation and at the expense of the sinking fund,[65] was obviously more of a bid to wrest the initiative from Hume, who had already moved on the sinking fund, than a serious attack on ministerial

62. *Courier*, 14 Jan. 1822; *Manchester Guardian*, 1 June 1822.
63. *The Times*, 2 Feb. 1822.
64. *The Times*, 29 Jan. 1822; Russell, *Memoirs, Journal, and Correspondence of Thomas Moore* (1853), iii. 280; *Letters of Earl Dudley to the Bishop of Llandaff*, 308; Mitchell, op. cit. 162-3; Cockburn, *Letters chiefly connected with the Affairs of Scotland to T. F. Kennedy, M.P., 1818-52* (1874), 40-1.
65. H. of C., 11 Feb. 1822, 2 PD, vi. 220-59; Smart, op. cit. 59-61.

policies. It was an exciting harangue but, as economic theory, a 'standing dish' of solecisms[66] ('worthy of a drunken mob in Palace-yard').[67] As usual, vivid insights were interspersed with *naïveté*. He justified Whig support for the landlords' selfish movement against taxes, by tracing the desire for taxation to large capitalists, who could afford to pay, and who would benefit from the mulcting of the small competitor. He hinted broadly at devaluation and confiscation of the funds and, like most Whigs, disparaged voguish economists, who spoke in 'honeyed accents' about supply and demand, transfers and decultivation, when what they actually referred to was 'the breaking up of all endearing connexions...the destruction of all local attachment, the tearing up by the roots of that fabric of society'. Brougham was able to muster 108 votes (against 212), including those of several Tory waverers and borough members, but the influential gentry — Gooch, Lethbridge, Knatchbull, Holme Sumner, and Wodehouse — were loyal to Londonderry, while even Tierney, who was increasingly hesitant about tax concessions, abstained.[68] Possibly Ricardo, though he voted with Brougham, deterred potential supporters by denying that taxation was the cause of agricultural distress, for which he was cheered throughout on the government benches. His abstract theories afforded 'a good handle to the enemies of economy and retrenchment'.[69]

The opening skirmishes of 11 and 15 February revealed the Whigs' desperation. They hoped to bribe the gentry with tax reductions, but the limits of feasible retrenchment having been reached, fiscal concession would have to be at the expense of the fundholders. This seemed unscrupulous opportunism:

The result therefore was that the ostensible leader of the opposition [Brougham], was ready to fall in with the popular cry, and to make

66. Ricardo to Trower, 20 Feb. 1822, Ricardo to McCulloch, 19 Feb. 1822, Sraffa, op.cit. ix. 163-7.
67. Huskisson in H. of C., 15 Feb. 1822, 2 PD, vi. 439.
68. Maxwell, *The Creevey Papers*, ii. 33-4; Brougham to Grey, 16 Feb. 1822, *The Life and Times of Henry, Lord Brougham* (1871), ii. 439-40.
69. Whishaw to Smith, 16 and 26 Feb. 1822, Seymour, *The "Pope" of Holland House—selections from the correspondence of John Whishaw, 1813-40* (1906), 243-4; Mallet, MS. Diary, 20 Feb. 1822, iv. 25.

any sacrifice, even a sacrifice of public faith, to those men who had for twenty years voted away millions after millions, without scruple or enquiry. A large and meritorious part of the community, the fund-holders, who might as yet have considered the leading members of Opposition as men of enlightened and liberal principles, found them at once ready to prey upon the Public creditor, with a view of favouring that Class of the community (namely the Landed Gentry) who have alone the power of bringing them into office. The fundholders also perceived that their real friends were the Ministers, who notwith-standing the difficulties of their situation, made a decided and firm stand for maintaining the public credit of the country.[70]

The strategy was to succeed in 1830, but made no parlia-mentary headway in 1822, which belonged once more to radical retrenchment. The 'Mountain' conducted an even more pedantically heroic campaign: 'It almost destroyed us; we divided on every item of every estimate; we were glued to these seats. The evening sun went down upon us in this hostile array; and when he arose in the morning, he arose upon our undiminished ranks. If ever Opposition despised hunger and thirst, and watchfulness for conscience sake',[71] it was that pertinacious band of twenty-five or thirty 'during those never-ending sessions.' Most Whigs were now openly hostile to the *louche* Hume and combative Bennet.[72] Several ostentatiously walked out of Hume's divisions, and after some spectacular successes, support for retrenchment fell away. But the 'Boodle Cabinet', as Huskisson called the independents' London club, was entirely behind Hume. 'Boodles not Brookes will be the head quarters of faction this Session', lamented one despondent Whig.[73] All observers agreed that the squirearchy was in uproar and crying out for relief.[74] Calcraft won many gentlemen for repealing the salt duties,[75] and Gooch, Knatchbull, and Lethbridge were among the 182 who succeeded in axeing two junior lords of the Admiralty.

70. Mallet, MS. Diary, 20 Feb. 1822, iv. 24.
71. Hobhouse in H. of C., 27 Apr. 1826, 2 PD, xv. 692.
72. See, for example, Heron, op.cit. 133.
73. Lansdowne to Holland, 21 Jan. 1822, HHP 51687 ff. 1-3.
74. Liverpool to Vansittart, 11 Dec. 1821, Vansittart MSS. 31232 ff. 288-9; Liverpool to Harrowby, 19 Dec. 1821, Harrowby MSS. 1st. series, XV ff. 253-4; *Journal of Mrs Arbuthnot*, i. 145-7.
75. Hughes, op. cit. 495-507; Smart, op. cit. 73-5.

This rebellion of independents against the administration
— Boodles 'acting in concert...and without consultation'[76]
— disconcerted ministers. They knocked ten per cent off
official salaries, and directed that all departments should
revert as far as possible to the 1797 situation in respect of
complement and emoluments. Then, after a considerable
struggle with the King's baser nature, they persuaded him to
surrender £30,000 of his Civil List.[77] Next, they cynically
attempted to excite alarm for a 'King in danger'. On 8 March
Arbuthnot sent a Treasury Letter to all potential friends,
pleading with them to 'aid in stemming the torrent of such
dangerous innovation' as was threatening all sanctions of
law and order.[78] Robinson, applying a theory of checks and
balances, cited the 'growth of public opinion' as a 'valid
ground for adding to the influence of the Crown'.[79] The ruse
worked with Stuart Wortley and Holme Sumner (who
described the Postmastership-General as a useless and costly
office that had yet to be preserved for the sake of the Crown's
legitimate influence),[80] but not with Gooch, Fane and Wodehouse, Knatchbull and Lethbridge. And though Canning's
witty eloquence saved the Board of Control from Creevey,
forty of the country gentlemen who had voted with ministers
on the Postmastership in March, rebelled in April, enabling
Normanby to abolish it. Such volatility in divisions disturbed
Mallet — 'People get into irregular modes of voting; and all
security is at an end.'[81] 'The Country may be said to be
governed by about fifty independent Members who turn the
scale. Those men are essentially Tory: but when in no fear of

76. Wellington to Buckingham, 6 Mar. 1822, Buckingham and Chandos, op.cit.
i. 292.
77. ' "I cannot as a Gentleman make my Servts pay ten per cent and not make a
similar sacrifice myself." We all applauded.'   Wellington to Mrs. Arbuthnot,
10 Mar. 1822, Wellington MSS., Arbuthnot 106.
78. H. of C., 15 Mar. 1822, 2 PD, vi. 1173-8. See Mallet, MS. Diary, 16 Mar.
1822, iv. 34-6; Fremantle to Buckingham, 11 Mar. 1822, Buckingham and
Chandos, op. cit. i. 295-8.
79. Hughes, op. cit. 505. Hughes points out that when forced to retrench,
ministers preferred — for the sake of maintaining patronage — to lessen several
taxes, thereby keeping up staff to collect them, rather than abolish any one of
them.
80. H. of C., 13 Mar. 1822, 2 PD, vi. 1091-5.
81. Mallet, MS. Diary, 14 May 1822, iv. 65-6.

popular encroachments, they are not disposed to arbitrary rule: they partake of the wild spirit and enlightened opinion [of] the age, altho' they are unwilling to allow them their due influence.'[82]

'They are stripping the Crown naked', expostulated Eldon. But as in 1821 a resignation threat 'brought the country gentlemen to their senses'.[83] On 10 May Arbuthnot let it be known, through the 'official people', that the next defeat would be the last.[84] Thus admonished, the country gentlemen conferred and agreed to finish their sport. Soon afterwards the Radicals suffered huge defeats on the Swiss Mission and the Civil List, only Lethbridge and a handful of gentry supporting. But though it died abruptly, the country revolt had been alarming enough to compel Liverpool's government to make agriculturists some concessions at last.

The Corn Law of 1822

There were indications of an indifferent harvest during spring 1821, and ministers calculated that if they could only spin the Agricultural Committee's proceedings out until the end of the session, prices would have recovered naturally by the time Parliament next met. When the crops turned out unexpectedly full, ministers — though delighted from the point of view of subsistence — had to start looking round for the 'largest tub' that could be thrown to a blubbering country whale.[85] They determined to stake everything on the financial settlement of 1819, to 'stand or fall' with the sinking fund,[86] and met Hume's attacks with appeals to 'public faith', which they believed was essential for effecting the only type of relief open to the landed interest — 'the facility of borrowing money at a moderate rate of interest.'[87] 'A real relief to the landed interest must be produced, if they will have patience to wait for it, by the increased circulation

82. Ibid. 14 Mar. 1822, iv. 34.
83. Eldon to Lady Bankes, n.d. and 16 May 1822, Twiss, op. cit. ii. 450-1.
84. *Journal of Mrs Arbuthnot*, i. 162-3.
85. Peel to Goulburn, 31 Jan. 1822, Goulburn MSS. II/14, quoted in Gash, *Mr. Secretary Peel*, 300-1.
86. Huskisson to Canning, 8 Feb. 1822, CP 67; *Journal of Mrs Arbuthnot*, i. 140.
87. Vansittart in H. of C., 5 Feb. 1822, 2 PD, vi. 74.

and greater facility of accommodation arising out of a clear sinking fund and the accumulation of moneyed and commercial wealth.'[88] They spoke, that is, as though the fortunes of agriculture depended on commerce, a viewpoint quite alien to physiocrats like Webb Hall. The gentry, however, no longer content with advice to rest and be hopeful, clamoured for tangible concessions. Throughout January 1822 the cabinet, with Baring in attendance, discussed four types of relief — tax remission, loans, cheaper money (all of which were made possible by a £5,000,000 surplus) and increased protection. It eventually resolved, at the beginning of February, to combine financial, monetary, and limited fiscal relief in a single package, but to withhold higher protection or substantial tax reductions.[89] This decision was justified in a cabinet memorandum,[90] which deprecated any legislative attempts to increase prices, and suggested lending money to tenants to enable them to withstand cheapness until a gradual reduction of wages, rates, and taxes should give them 'the ultimate capacity of thriving under low prices.' Meanwhile an open corn trade would boost commerce, improve the revenue, and allow tax remission to be 'distinctly held out as a consequence, and not a concomitant' of the policy. A commercial boom would enable farmers to make deflationary adjustments to cash payments.

So from the outset, the reappointment of the Agricultural Committee on 18 February 1822 was little more than a sop to the gentry. Its brief was to evolve a better but not a more stringent corn law, which could be applied *after* the ports next opened. Its composition was similar to that of 1821, the main difference being that Huskisson refused to attend, ostensibly because Tory squires had dealt him 'a little pelting'.[91] His loss to Ricardo was partly mitigated by the inclusion of a zealous free-trader, William Wolryche Whitmore, who was in correspondence with Huskisson, and whose

88. Vansittart to Liverpool, 20 Dec. 1821, Yonge, *Life and Administration of Lord Liverpool,* iii. 164-5.
89. Charles Wynn to Buckingham, 28 and 30 Jan. 1822, Buckingham and Chandos, op. cit. i. 279-80, 283.
90. Castlereagh MSS., XXXVII, mmlxxiii.
91. Grenville to Buckingham, 20 Feb. 1822, Buckingham and Chandos, op. cit. i. 288.

current pamphlet was considerably influenced by him. It reiterated diminishing returns theory, diagnosed over-production, denied that taxation, importation, or even Peel's Bill were important causes of distress; denied that domestic consumption had fallen; argued that poorer soils should be abandoned; and contended that 'the only safe and effectual remedy...is by again reverting to that situation in which we are naturally placed, namely, that of a *constantly* importing country of corn, by giving up that most pernicious and absurd attempt to preserve to the home grower the monopoly of the home market.'[92]

The Committee did not call witnesses, but at once set about discussing practical relief, and a joint report was concocted by Gooch and Henry Bankes, without interference from ministers.[93] It was accepted unanimously, though Ricardo, who found the agriculturists determined to yield nothing resembling 'diminished protection' (even though they were less eager to augment it than before), objected to the document on principle, and Western opposed the resolutions as harmful to agriculture.[94] No doubt it gave some satisfaction to agriculturists after their treatment of the previous year. As even Ricardo agreed that the ports should not open at once to cheap European accumulations, it was decided that no new law should operate until the ports opened naturally at 80s. The Committee recommended that thereafter there should be an open trade below 70s., and above 70s. a fixed countervailing duty — countervailing, that is, in Webb Hall's rather than Ricardo's sense, for it was to 'compensate to the British grower the difference of expense at which his corn can be raised and brought to market, together

92. W. W. Whitmore, *A Letter on the Present State and Future Prospects of Agriculture addressed to the agriculturists of the county of Salop* (1822), 49 and *passim*. Ricardo to Trower, 5 Mar. 1822, Sraffa, op. cit. ix. 176-7.
93. Londonderry was not the chairman of the 1822 Committee, nor the author of its Report, as suggested in Sraffa, op. cit. ix. 180n. and Smart, op. cit. 75.
94. Ricardo to Trower, 25 Mar. 1822, Sraffa, op. cit. ix. 180; Ricardo in H. of C., 3 Apr. 1822, 2 PD, vi. 1446-8.

with the fair rate of profit upon the capital employed, compared with the expense of production, and other charges attending corn grown and imported from abroad.'[95]

When on 29 April Londonderry introduced to Parliament a scheme based on the Report, several counter-resolutions were proposed. Lethbridge failed abysmally (243-24) with the Webb Hall solution, a 40s. fixed duty.[96] Benett's 24s. duty, balanced by an 18s. drawback or bounty, was negatived without division, and Althorp's fixed 18s. duty was beaten 201-24.[97] The eclectic Curwen suggested a quantitative limit to importation — say 400,000 qrs. at 10s. for six weeks when the price reached 80s. — but sensibly did not press it.[98] More significantly, Ricardo and Huskisson proposed compromise plans, which were similar to the official scheme and which Londonderry was prepared to accept instead of it.[99] (Liverpool assured Huskisson that he need not resign over this independent stand.)[100] The main point of principle on which the Huskisson and Ricardo plans differed from Londonderry's was that they would have left trade always open — though subject to duty — even under 70s. (this was often referred to as a 'free' trade). Londonderry objected that agricultural 'feelings' and European glut forbade any such experiment

95. CSC, *First Report from the Select Committee to inquire into allegations of Petitions complaining of the distressed state of Agriculture*, 1822, 8. The eventual proposal was that with wheat at 70-80s., a duty of 17s. per quarter should operate for three months, and 12s. thereafter; at 80-84s., a 10s. duty followed by 5s. after three months; at and above 85s., a duty of only 1s. Colonial preference was included by imposing the same duties, but at the lower 'turning-points' of 67s. and 71s. Appropriate scales and rates were devised for the other grains. The Committee submitted a second report on the subject of warehousing abuses.

96. Curteis, Dennis Browne, and Fane supported a 40s. duty.

97. Western, Curwen, Brougham, Bankes, H.G. Bennet, and Knatchbull supported 18s.

98. Wellington had suggested this in cabinet. *Journal of Mrs Arbuthnot*, i. 139-40; Wellington to Lady Shelley, 14 Oct. 1821, *The Diary of Frances, Lady Shelley, 1818-73*, edited by R. Edgcumbe (1912-13), ii. 111.

99. Huskisson proposed 15s. duty at 80s. or below, 5s. at 80-85s., 1s. above that; he did not press it. Ricardo proposed a fixed 20s. duty to operate as soon as prices reached 70s., this duty to decrease by 1s. per annum until it came to rest at 10s., and to be balanced by a 7s. bounty on exports; this plan was defeated by 218-25 — whereupon Londonderry's proposals were adopted, 218-36.

100. Huskisson to Liverpool, 12 May 1822, HP 38743 ff. 148-51, quoted in Melville, *The Huskisson Papers*, 137-9; Liverpool to Huskisson, 13 May 1822, HP 38743 f. 152.

with 'sound principles', and that they must wait until 'the world had returned to its natural state.'

Our safest course is, not to take our protection exclusively in import price as at present, or exclusively in duty, as these gentlemen [Huskisson and Ricardo] recommend; but to combine the operation of both principles in a due degree, so that a regulated intercourse may take place, subject, however, to prohibitions whenever that intercourse shall tend to lower the price beyond that point which is consistent with a reasonably remunerating price to the home grower.[101]

There were also significant differences between Ricardo's plan and the other two. Both Londonderry and Huskisson omitted the export bounty and followed the *principle* of a sliding scale, the very low duty operating as the price increased. Ricardo contended that his fixed duty would give more relief to the farmer, who needed compensation most when prices rose owing to a poor harvest — which was precisely when Londonderry and Huskisson would deprive him of protection. 'The short harvest ought to be compensated by high prices.'[102]

All three plans made provision for releasing corn already bonded on to the market *before* the price rose to 80s. and foreign corn was allowed in.[103] This might prevent the ports from opening, and 'secure the farmer from being placed in competition with the holders of foreign corn in bond and in foreign countries at the same time; he would first have to cope with the former, and if the price should afterwards rise, he would then compete with the latter'.[104] Some agriculturalists wanted to eliminate the 'formidable mass' of bonded corn altogether, by subjecting corn intended for warehouses to the same restrictions as corn entered for immediate consumption. The Report repudiated this in favour of giving an option to the owners of foreign grain to remove their corn at 70s., thereby giving them 'some control conjointly with all the dealers in British corn' over the market; and, more important,

101. Londonderry in H. of C., 7 May and 29 Apr. 1822, 2PD, vii. 400 and 188.
102. Ricardo in H. of C., 3 and 29 Apr. 1822, 2 PD, vi. 1447; vii. 200-1.
103. The proprietor was to have the option of entering such corn at 70s. under Londonderry's and Huskisson's resolutions, and at 60s. under Ricardo's, on payment of duty; or of entering it duty-free at 80s. as entitled by the 1815 Law under which he had warehoused it.
104. Ricardo in H. of C., 7 May 1822, 2 PD, vii. 420.

the interest of the proprietors of this grain will be brought strictly into
unison with that of the British agriculturist, and into direct hostility
to that of all other importers of foreign grain; so that every endeavour
will be resorted to, on their part, to advance the price to 70s that they
may liberate their own stock; but to keep it below 80s that they may
exclude all foreign competitors. The equitable claim which the holders
of the grain, already deposited...appear to possess, will thus be beneficially preserved to them, and the danger of an immense influx of
foreign produce will be mitigated and deferred, if not wholly
prevented.[105]

Several expedients for peripheral and temporary relief
were canvassed. Bankes proposed to the Committee, and
Baring to the cabinet, that the government should spend one
million exchequer bills on buying up grain to store in national
granaries until the markets rose. By doling it out in scarcities,
governments could both protect consumers and safeguard
producers against abundance. Ministers objected that interference in the market would be a dangerous precedent, and
would simply inhibit the speculations of middlemen, who
would feel incapable of competing with the state. They also
rejected initially John Irving's suggestion that government
should lend £1,000,000 cheaply to holders of corn for
deposit in warehouses, 'so that they might not be forced to
come into the market simultaneously, and under the disadvantage of excessive competition'.[106] It was claimed that
this would not constitute interference, but merely encourage
enlightened self-interest to work properly in a period of
abnormality due to glut. Huskisson disliked it, but recognised
that since

this country *would* place itself in the situation of having no free intercourse with other nations in the trade in corn, and still continued

105. CSC, *First Report on Petitions complaining of the distressed state of Agriculture,* 1822, 7-8. Merchant holders of foreign grain in Liverpool, Newcastle,
Hull, Bristol, &c. petitioned to complain that post-Resumption deflation had
augmented the prohibition price for corn imports, and prayed that their
merchandise be treated preferentially to fresh importations. Baring suggested
that when corn prices reached the importation level, bonded corn should be
admitted immediately, but that no fresh imports should be allowed to enter
until a fixed period (say three months) had elapsed after the opening. This would
prevent a sudden glut of imports from taking advantage of an unsustained price-
rise. Castlereagh MSS., XXXVII, mmlxxx.
106. CSC, *First Report on Petitions complaining of the distressed state of Agriculture,* 1822, 3-4; Ricardo to Trower, 5 Mar. 1822, Sraffa, op.cit. ix. 176.

liable to the fluctuation of seasons, it followed of course, that a wise permanent system would be to try if possible to hoard the surplus of a year of plenty to meet the possible exigency of an unfavourable harvest.[107]

He preferred to ration supplies by awarding an equivalent to the former bounty as an incentive to holders to hoard corn. Monthly allowances might contradict sound principles, but would avoid direct interference: 'it would not amount to a premium to force speculation, [but] would nevertheless cover the expenses of warehousing, and the interest of money and thus tempt individuals to make speculations in grain'.[108] This was too mild for the agriculturalists, and Londonderry agreed to implement Irving's plan on the grounds that if farmers thought it would help them, it might bolster confidence and actually *do* so. Brougham complained that the really desperate farmers did not possess the grain to deposit as security, and Huskisson warned that artificial price rises would merely induce wealthy farmers (who had hitherto held aloof from glutted markets) to sell, making the poor farmer's situation worse than ever. Against such powerful debaters, the country gentlemen 'wd not father their own offspring',[109] and so to their chagrin Londonderry suddenly abandoned the Irving plan.

It will be evident from all these suggestions that what preoccupied Parliament in 1822 was not so much corn imports, as the breakdown of the market mechanism whereby in theory prices should have been kept reasonably steady, and corn supplies rationed throughout the year, through the spontaneous activity of middlemen and dealers.[110] It is equally clear that the Agricultural Committee rejected the diagnosis of over-production, with all its sinister implications, for the less drastic explanation that farmers had had to force a supply on the market in order to meet rents Its short- and long-term remedies were geared chiefly to ensuring that, in future, foreign supplies *'fed'* rather than *'inundated'* the market.

107. H. of C., 29 Apr. 1822, 2 PD, vii. 208.
108. Londonderry in H. of C., 6 May 1822, 2 PD, vii. 358.
109. *Journal of Mrs Arbuthnot*, i. 161-2. Apart from anything else, ministers feared that loans to farmers might inhibit necessary rent reductions.
110. E. P. Thompson, 'The Moral Economy of the English Crowd in the Eighteenth Century', *Past & Present*, 1 (1971), 89-94.

The government approved neither of the Agricultural Report nor of the new Law, which was simply a minor political concession to the landed interest. Londonderry was alleged to have 'taken no part' in the Committee's proceedings,[111] and Phillimore, a Grenvillite free-trader, was not too perturbed by the document because he was certain that 'Londonderry does not mean to act in conformity with the spirit in which it is drawn up.'[112] Ministers were confident that the markets would soon right themselves automatically as an inevitable consequence of cyclical depression. A few concessions might even instil confidence into the market and hasten that event. Almost certainly, leading ministers already intended to alter the Act before it became operative. What else can Canning have meant when in March 1827 he referred to the clause by which the 1822 Corn Law was not to operate until the price had risen to 80s. as 'an outwork, as it were, to prevent the body of the law from being ever approached'?[113] The concessions granted in 1822 can hardly be used to undermine the interpretation placed on the policy of 1821, that it represented a shift by the government towards free trade in corn. The 'great object' was still 'the substituting a more extended commerce in grain instead of a monopoly, and then prospectively the removal of restrictions'.[114]

Financial and monetary palliatives

There remained the possibility of relief through public loans, monetary relaxation, and tax reduction. The surplus revenue might be lent on deposit of grain to tide farmers over until the markets revived naturally. Bathurst suggested lending to landlords for the redemption of mortgages, but apart from

111. Newcastle to Londonderry, 24 Mar. 1822, Castlereagh MSS. XXXVII, mmcxvi.
112. Phillimore to Buckingham, 25 Apr. 1822, Buckingham and Chandos, op. cit. i. 319.
113. H. of C., 1 Mar. 1827, 2 PD, xvi. 767.
114. Londonderry in H. of C., 7 May 1822, 2 PD, vii. 401. Individual cabinet ministers wanted to step up protection – none more so than Westmorland, who argued for an increase in the 80s. wheat prohibition level. Nevertheless, Ricardo was correct to feel that his only enthusiastic parliamentary allies on the question of free trade sat muzzled on the 'ministerial bench'; Ricardo to Trower, 20 May 1822, Sraffa, op. cit. ix. 198.

the practical difficulties of establishing legal titles and of isolating mortgages that had been contracted during the depreciation, Vansittart feared that it would require such an issue of exchequer bills as would 'entirely overset our plans for restoring a Metallic Currency'. No comparable favour had been shown to annuitants and stockholders during the war, and it would be invidious to vote 'an immense Boon at the Public Expense...exclusively to the Landed Proprietors comprising a great majority of both Houses'.[115] He preferred to advance four millions of exchequer bills to landlords via country bankers, whose local knowledge would equip them to recognize 'real bills', but the governors of the Bank and a group of City financiers met the suggestion with derision, since it was security — not money — that was scarce. So the cabinet decided instead to advance the four millions of exchequer bills at 3 per cent to parishes on security of rates.[116]

Besides enabling embarrassed cultivators to survive the crisis, this advance enhanced the circulation and lowered interest rates. Ministers also considered more direct methods of monetary relief. Their excuse for requesting a Bank advance at this time was 'not the convenience of the Public Service,'[117] as usual, but 'the relief which the Public might expect to derive from an increase of the general Circulation.'[118] They then requested the Bank to lower its discount rate to 4 per cent. The directors refused outright at first, whereupon ministers turned their attention to methods of increasing the circulation via the floating debt. When the £4,000,000 loan was announced, Huskisson declared that a much better method of relieving the scarcity of money

115. Vansittart to Liverpool, 21 Jan. 1822, copy in Castlereagh MSS. XXXVII, mmlxxxvii; *Journal of Mrs Arbuthnot*, i. 139-40.
116. Mallet, MS. Diary, 5 Feb. 1822, iv. 21; *The Times,* 5 Feb. 1822. By April ministers had abandoned the idea of loans to parishes, in favour of lending money to individuals needing relief and of public works in Ireland.
117. i.e. the government's own pecuniary needs.
118. Liverpool and Vansittart to Governor and Deputy of B. of E., 27 Feb. 1822, LP 38290 ff. 309-10; Vansittart to Liverpool, 20 Dec. 1821, Yonge, op.cit. iii. 164-5. Henry Beeke, an academic and Vansittart's economic mentor, was warning his friend against 'any sort of recurrence to a forced Circulation'. Beeke to Vansittart, 9 Oct. 1821, Vansittart MSS., 31232 ff. 282-5.

(which stemmed from the Bank's insistence on being repaid
£10,000,000)[119] would have been for the Bank to expand its
discounts. It could have kept control over its own issues and
generated fresh demands for credit:

Why this should not be done or why [the Bank] should prefer lending
to government at three per cent was to him inconceivable...Discount
was their prior duty...Privileges were given [it] in the expectation that
the Bank, by keeping their rate of discount rather under the market
rate, would tend to lower the latter, and to make the loans of money
cheaper here than in other parts of the world...[Otherwise] the tables
will be turned against us; commerce will find cheaper accommodation
elsewhere.[120]

Liverpool and some of the gentry also complained of the
Bank's reluctance to discount freely, while the exchanges
were favourable, so as to relieve the shortage of money.[121]
One director M.P. (Manning) replied that lower interest rates
would 'force British capital into foreign funds', another
(Pearse) that interest rates must be governed by the price of
funds — and not vice versa. But at last, on 22 June, the
directors yielded and proposed to lower Bank rate to 4 per
cent.[122] Throughout the controversy, ministers criticized the
Bank for eschewing discretionary control over its banking
function, i.e. to counteract movements of the business cycle,
while still denying it discretion over issue, which should
adjust automatically to the exchanges. This ambiguous
attitude to a *central* but *private* bank was to result in Peel's
separation of the currency and banking departments in 1844.

Huskisson's insistence that the Bank ought always to keep
its rate of discount below the market rate applied only to
moments of scarce money, as did his comment that it should

119. See above, p. 49.
120. H. of C., 15 Feb. 1822, 2 PD, vi. 434-5. Ricardo, however, thought that
the Bank rate should be kept in line with the market rate, and asserted —
against Huskisson — that cheap interest rates indicated low profits and 'advancement to a stationary state'. Ricardo, *On Protection to Agriculture* (1822), Sraffa,
op. cit. iv. 233-5.
121. e.g. H. of L. 26 Feb. 1822, 2 PD, vi. 713-16.
122. Viner, *Studies in the Theory of International Trade*, 181-2, n. 19. At least
one director, William Ward, favoured adjustments of discount rate. W. Ward,
On Monetary Derangements, in a letter addressed to the proprietors of Bank stock
(1840), 12-13, 37.

'make money as cheap as is consistent with the [antient] standard'.[123] In 1819 he had wished to abolish the Usury Laws and increase rates in order to attract money into the English funds. By 1822, however, money was too dear, so that — as Liverpool said — any measure would suffice 'which will have the effect of getting these 4,000,000£ into general circulation' and so 'extend and quicken the general circulation'.[124] This was a tacit and belated recognition that the crisis was one which, left to itself, the country might not surmount after all. The government must act to set the machine in motion again. 'What is most urgent is, to stop the progress of depression. — That once effected, speculation, which is now in a manner dormant, will revive, and it is in this view, more than by its actual amount, that this operation of the Bank seems to hold out a prospect of reviving confidence and hope.'[125] A touch of cheap money would give the economy a fillip; speculation, the enemy in 1819, was to be encouraged again.[126]

Meanwhile, there was growing concern over the extent to which country banks were adding to the stringency by accumulating gold and reducing their circulations of paper, in preparation for the scheduled expiry of small notes (under £5) in May 1823.[127] On 4 April, without any warning or consultation, Vansittart and Liverpool informed the Bank of their intention to extend the life of these notes until 1833, in order to relieve the scarcity of money felt especially in agricultural districts.[128] Ministers also desired to relax the Bank's Charter, in return for extending it by ten years, so as to end the restriction on the maximum number of partners (six) allowed to engage in a private bank, outside a 65-mile

123. Huskisson to Copleston, 1822, HP 38761 ff. 77-89.
124. H. of L., 26 Feb. 1822, 2 PD, vi. 715-16.
125. Huskisson in H. of C., 15 Feb. 1822, 2 PD, vi. 434.
126. See Attwood to Davenport, 2 Apr. 1822, above, p. 127, for condemnation of this policy.
127. e.g. Harrowby in H. of L., 26 Feb. and Londonderry in H. of C., 29 Apr. 1822, 2 PD, vi. 745; vii. 158-60. Ricardo to Trower, 5 Mar. 1822, Sraffa, op. cit. ix. 176. Babbington to Harrowby, 2 Mar. 1822, Harrowby MSS. 1st series, XIV ff. 46-7. Vansittart to Littleton, 1 Apr. 1822, Hatherton MSS. D260/M/F/5/27/1/79.
128. LP 38290 f. 354.

radius of London. 'What an increase of security it must afford to the public', announced Londonderry, 'when so many individuals combine in the responsibility of a banking concern, and render themselves liable to be sued by their legal representative.'[129] This additional security could counteract any tendency of the small note extension to feed wild-cat speculation. Unfortunately, however, such was the opposition amongst country bankers and others, that after long negotiations the government suddenly backed down on the question of relaxing the Bank's monopoly.[130] The country was thus left with the extension of small notes, and without the means of making those notes more reliable.

The extension of small notes has often been regarded as a last-ditch effort by the 'paper' faction in the cabinet to defeat, or at least emasculate, the legislation of 1819. Cobbett, for example, damned 'the SMALL-NOTE BILL' as 'that last brilliant effort of the joint mind of VAN and CASTLE-REAGH', and as a dishonest, ineffectual 'respite' from the rigours of Peel's Act. [131] Archibald Alison praised the bill as Londonderry's personal inspiration and 'to all practical purposes a repeal of the Act of 1819, save when a general demand for gold sent all the notes in the kingdom to the Bank for payment'.[132] 'The object of the Ministers', wrote Thomas Attwood, 'is to *fritter away* this famous Bill [1819] so as greatly to neutralize its operation'.[133]

This interpretation is altogether too dramatic. In fact the suggestion for the extension of small notes originated with Huskisson (in 1818 and in the Bank Committee of 1819),[134] whereas it was the so-called '*cheap* money' man, Vansittart, who had been most anxious to curb country bank issues in 1818. Huskisson initiated the move in 1822 and Londonderry and Liverpool approved it, whereas Vansittart later

129. H. of C., 29 Apr. 1822, 2 PD, vii. 161-2.
130. Clapham, *The Bank of England*, ii. 88; J. H. Clapham, *An Economic History of Modern Britain. The Early Railway Age, 1820-50* (1926), revised edition (1964), 271.
131. Cobbett, *Rural Rides*, 11 Nov. 1825, i. 327.
132. Alison, *Lives of Lord Castlereagh and Sir Charles Stewart*, iii. 172-5.
133. Attwood to Davenport, 27 Apr. 1822, Davenport MSS., Attwood ff. 17-20.
134. Huskisson to Liverpool, 12 July 1818, LP 38191 ff. 115-16; Huskisson's 4 Feb. 1819 memorandum, Yonge, op. cit. ii. 382-4. Ricardo had recommended that the Bank of England should retain only its small notes.

complained that it was 'much against my inclination that the prohibition of the issue of notes under £5 was suspended beyond the period of two years from the resumption of cash payments'.[135] It was Huskisson's measure, and replying to Western he denied that it would depreciate private notes, since convertibility alone was proof against depreciation.[136] The small note measure was a method of alleviating deflation, of restoring confidence in a period of crisis and of bolstering agriculture, without infringing the foundation of bullionism, which was convertibility. It was not a return to the 'war level', as Attwood hopefully supposed, but a temporary expedient in a crisis, and probably a substitute for cheaper credit (which the Bank refused).

But though only an expedient, this measure does reveal the danger of arguing, as some have done, from the saga of 1819, that Huskisson was (with Ricardo) a dear money deflationist and Vansittart the opposite. The essential distinction was rather between bullionist and anti-bullionist; and just because in 1819 — the year of bullionism's greatest trial — to be a bullionist was to be a deflationist, it must not be supposed that the two went necessarily together. Huskisson distinguished between depreciation and diminution in the value of money,[137] and in a depression he was anxious to promote the latter. So in 1822 he argued against Ricardo for a reduction of Bank rate and credit control, and against Vansittart for a continuation of small notes. The gold standard man of 1819 was, in the context of 1822, a counter-cyclical inflationist.

Finally there was the possibility of direct financial relief. In January 1822 ministers had their £5,000,000 surplus to dispose of, and Charles Wynn and some others in the cabinet favoured tax reduction as the most 'comprehensible' and gratifying of concessions. But most ministers discounted this as a humiliating surrender to parliamentary pressure. There was, anyway, the problem of which tax to select; the window

135. Bexley's memorandum, 11 Jan. 1826, LP 38371 ff. 83-93, Yonge, op. cit. iii. 358-61.
136. H. of C., 29 Apr. 1822, 2 PD, vii. 206.
137. As, of course, did Ricardo. See T. E. Gregory's introduction to Tooke and Newmarch, *A History of Prices,* i. 37.

tax was the most eligible but its repeal would have benefited
the towns more than agriculture.[138] So, on proposing the
official plan of relief on 15 February, Londonderry included
only a meagre amount of remission — £1,400,000 — by
deducting 8s. p. qr. from the malt duty. The entire surplus
was to be applied instead to debt reduction, by converting the
five per cents to four (which would save the £1,400,000 p.a.
devoted to malt tax reduction), in order to boost the funds,
cheapen credit, and secure a £5,000,000 sinking fund as
recommended by Parliament in 1819. The details were
modified later, but the government stuck rigidly to these
principles.[139]

In pressing for tax cuts, the opposition obviously had to
attack the ministers' sinking fund. Hume, Lauderdale, Russell,
Brougham, Parnell, Grey, Landsdowne, Ellice, and even
Tierney (a former enthusiast) attacked that fund in 1822,
partly on the utilitarian grounds that it was a complicated
and ineffectual piece of financial machinery, partly because
it took circulating capital out of men's pockets. It encouraged
investment and loans abroad, pandered to the monied men,
operated a 'perpetual transfer of capital'. 'The object of all
this was, to raise the price of stock, and to reduce the rate of
interest, without reflecting that a useless accumulation of
capital, so drained from the productive industry of this
[country], must, when the desired effect was produced, be
transferred to other countries for investment.'[140] For their
part ministers defended (and exaggerated) their own virtuous
attachment to the sinking fund and public credit with
astonishing fervour. It was of course a demonstration of
political virtue, a means of attaching themselves to the Pitt
tradition as pilots weathering the self-interested 'storm'
that was 'blowing from the country', and of exploiting Whig
equivocations on public credit to brand them as Foxites and
anti-patriots. Here they were able to exploit the public
mentality concerning the sinking fund — 'the majority of

138. Charles Wynn to Buckingham, 30 Jan. 1822, Buckingham and Chandos, op.
cit. i. 282-3.
139. For the budget, the reduction of the Navy five per cents, Vansittart's Dead
Weight Annuity Scheme, &c., see Smart, op. cit. 80-91.
140. Ellice in H. of C., 6 May 1822, 2 PD, vii. 350.

mankind...have never connected it, in their imaginations, with anything that is not praiseworthy...they are habituated to a train of thought...'.[141] Moreover the fund was useful to governments in case of any sudden emergency requiring expenditure, like war (which was why Ricardo objected to it). 'Without some resource of this kind, therefore, a nation did not give itself elbow-room, nor prepare for any of those exigencies which were of perpetual recurrence'.[142] This hardly explains the extravagance of their language, which exceeded even the encomiums heaped on gold in 1819. Londonderry associated a nation's ability to pay its debts with 'manliness', and apostrophized 'that religious respect for public credit, which is the foundation of national honour, and without which no nation can be, or ought to be prosperous'.[143] In defending the sinking fund, he conceived that he was upholding 'a sacred cause...treading on sacred ground'. Even an invasion would not constitute just cause to violate the national debt. Rebuking Russell, he declared 'the right of the public creditor to the interest of the debt as sacred as that of the duke of Bedford to the manors to which he was legally entitled'.[144]

Such hyperbole arouses suspicion. No doubt Londonderry talked so strongly in order to mask the extent to which he was prepared to deviate from Mr. Pitt's sacred principles. Initially, he proposed to deprive the sinking fund of its 'vital power of *compound interest*', which turned Grenville (hitherto its champion) against the fund. And, though Huskisson denied it, Ricardo interpreted the legislation of 1822 as a virtual abandonment of the sinking fund.[145] No doubt also Londonderry hoped to conceal uncomfortable differences inside the ministry. How far dissent was carried is uncertain, but Canning told Huskisson in October that he

141. Lauderdale to Page, 4 June 1822, Bodleian MSS., Eng. Lett., b.3 ff. 42-3.
142. Liverpool in H. of L., 4 May 1821, 2 PD, v. 507.
143. H. of C., 15 Feb. 1822, 2 PD, vi. 361, 374.
144. H. of C., 14 June 1822, 2 PD, vii. 1080-2. See Huskisson in H. of C., 15 Feb. 1822, 2 PD, vi. 442.
145. Bankes to Colchester, 26 Feb. 1822, *Diary and Correspondence*, iii. 248; Lord Grenville to Buckingham, 17 Feb. 1822, Buckingham and Chandos, op.cit. i. 286-7; Ricardo in H. of C., 29 Apr. 1822, 2 PD, vii. 200.

felt inclined to quit England, and to take up the Governor-
Generalship of India, because the Prime Minister was 'still
upon the old ground of the Sinking Fund and the pledge of
1819 — which doctrine is absolute nonsense in the present
state of things; — which is against my conviction; — which
cannot stand; and of which I will not fight the battle'.
Huskisson had helped to secure the pledge of 1819, but
now agreed that 'to have the Resolution and not the surplus'
was embarrassing.[146] Both had violently opposed Vansittart's
violation of the fund in 1813,[147] but now wanted to rummage
in it for greater immediate relief to the public.

But whatever their private doubts and differences, ministers
were anxious to keep up a pretence of the inviolability of the
sinking fund. For its purpose by this time was psychological,
as Mallet recognized when he chastised its Whig opponents:
'the sinking fund...is a popular piece of machinery, not
without a considerable moral influence, although it may be
worse than useless as part of a financial scheme.'[148] Huskisson conceded, even in Parliament, that the only *real* sinking
fund would be a surplus of revenue, yet that it was essential
to maintain the existing sham, if only because it was,
symbolically, the 'monument of our greatness and our
strength.'[149] Certainly the sinking fund's role in boosting the
funds was more important than any debt it might redeem.
Whereas Whigs recommended tax relief and personal
consumption as the key to recovery from a depression,
ministers insisted on a healthy stock market.[150] They still
contended that the economy was potentially self-regulating,
and that direct interference was unnecessary. The vital precondition of a self-correcting *laissez-faire* mechanism was
public confidence in the economy, and the sinking fund was
the outward and visible sign of public credit and trust. With it,

146. Canning to Huskisson, 9 Oct. 1822, HP 38743 ff. 235-9; Huskisson to
Canning, 11 Oct. 1822, ibid. ff. 242-4; Canning to Liverpool, 22 Nov. 1822,
21 Jan. and 5 Mar. 1823, CP 70.
147. E. L. Hargreaves, *The National Debt* (1930), 126-30.
148. Mallet, MS.Diary, 23 Feb. 1822, iv. 27.
149. H. of C., 15 Feb. 1822, 2 PD, vi. 442-4.
150. Russell countered with the view that the funds were more likely to be
boosted by commercial prosperity than by financial machinery.

Londonderry promised that public credit would shortly 'restore everything to a satisfactory state'.

The ministerial changes of 1822

The hypothesis that Liverpool's administration experienced a dramatic 'liberal awakening' in 1822 has been based partly on changes in personnel. Yet in economic affairs, the consequences of the change were a new constructiveness and energy, rendered possible by the possession of a revenue surplus and by improvements in the government's political situation, rather than any significant liberalization of policy or radical substitution of the men most responsible for economic decisions.

Behind the intrigue for place in 1821-2 lay the need to evict Vansittart and admit Canning.[151] Canning was politically 'weary', having discovered the poverty of 'first speaking' as an instrument of personal advancement, and sick to death of throwing his talents at Liverpool's service while playing 'second fiddle' to the Tories.[152] Yet the ministry badly needed what Croker called his 'gift of the gab', and despite the King's hostility, he was appointed Foreign Secretary on Londonderry's death. Vansittart was technically competent ('indefatigable at his pen' — 'made to be actuary to an Insurance Office'),[153] but, an inept and tactless debater who frequently had to be gagged, he was too blandly pliant over policy to win respect. True, 'L[iverpool]. *still likes* Van. better than any thing that could be put in his room',[154] but even Liverpool had to agree that Vansittart was 'abused, ridiculed and deserted by everybody', especially at the Bank

---

151. Brock, *Lord Liverpool and Liberal Toryism,* 120-71; A. Aspinall, 'Canning's return to office in September 1822', *English Historical Review,* lxxviii (1963), 531-45.

152. Canning to his wife, 3 Apr. 1821, CP 26 ff. 167-75, quoted in W. Hinde, *George Canning* (1973), 307; Canning to Liverpool, 10 Jan. 1822, LP 38568 ff. 112-14. Huskisson was equally frustrated by having to bear the odium of decision-making in return for 'empty compliments' — Huskisson to Liverpool, 11 Jan. 1822 and Huskisson to Canning, 14 Nov. 1821, HP 38743 ff. 117-20 and 13-14 — and was infuriated by Charles Wynn's prior promotion to the cabinet and to the Board of Control.

153. Mallet, MS. Diary, 20 Jan. 1823 and 1 May 1822, iv. 121-2, 59-60.

154. Canning to Huskisson, 3 Oct. 1822, HP 38743 ff. 217-20.

and in the City. Londonderry had done his best to protect
him in Parliament, and after Londonderry had gone, the
Chancellor's 'devoted friends and adherents', Hill and Herries,
agreed that he should move.[155] Canning felt strongly about
this. 'I think poor V.'s euthanasia an incalculable *publick
Advantage*'.[156] At one point, when it seemed that, by coveting
the Board of Control, Huskisson might thwart plans afoot
for Vansittart to replace Wynn there, Canning lectured his
friend:

The getting Van. out of the Exchequer is so great an object, for the
Publick, for the House of Commons, and for the Government, that if it
were to be ever known or suspected that that object had been frustrated
by your adherence to the succession to W[ynn] instead of that to
Robinson [Board of Trade], the best friends of government and of our
own friends too (Littleton for example) would never forgive you.[157]

Eventually, however, Bragge Bathurst was induced to resign
and Vansittart was able to succeed him, amicably enough, as
Chancellor of the Duchy of Lancaster, and to be raised to the
peerage as Lord Bexley.

'Every body expected that [Huskisson] would be Van's
successor',[158] especially as Londonderry may have set his
'heart' on a cabinet seat for the man who had been his daily
communicant 'on all the interesting matters of Internal
Policy'.[159] Liverpool might have welcomed this, but the
King was anxious to avoid any impression that the Canningites
were storming the closet. More particularly, Liverpool's
personal affection for Vansittart meant that his passing must
be engineered gently, so as not to wound, and 'Van's' major
condition was that Huskisson should not replace him.
Canning wrote to his ally, rather exasperatedly:

Once for all...*no power on earth could have moved Van to make room
for you*...I never doubted this; but if I had doubted, Van put it past
doubt in a   conversation...in which...speaking both kindly and handsomely of you, he said — without reserve — that to have made room for

155. Arbuthnot to Castlereagh, 14 Mar. 1819, Aspinall, *Correspondence of
Charles Arbuthnot,* 13-18.
156. Canning to Liverpool, 18 Dec. 1822, LP 38193 ff. 171-2.
157. Canning to Huskisson, 3 Oct. 1822, HP 38743 ff. 217-20, quoted in Brock,
op.cit. 163-4.
158. Ricardo to Trower, 30 Jan. 1823, Sraffa, op. cit. ix. 269-70; Huskisson to
Canning, 12 Jan. 1823, CP 68.
159. Liverpool to Sidmouth, 21 Nov. 1822, LP 38575 ff. 54-7.

you would have been, in his opinion and in that of his friends, a disgrace to which he could never have submitted.[160]

The proscription was hardly surprising, as Huskisson himself admitted.[161] He had conducted a systematic campaign against Vansittart's system, opposed him openly on the monetary question, and was wont to refer to the Chancellor, in the company of political gossips, as 'the real *blot* and *sin* of the Government'.[162]

In the event the Exchequer went to one who had hardly declared himself on the monetary question, Frederick Robinson, and who had threatened to retire from the government if not promoted.[163] His indolence was already known, but his pleasing manners and eloquent address made him a gratifying choice for the country gentlemen, essential in 1822. Moreover Vansittart liked him, and Robinson's succession was probably 'a very material ingredient in his decision' to retire.[164] So Robinson was selected, not for any professional attributes, but as a sop to 'Van' and to the squires. 'We all thought that the promotion of Robinson, connected as he was with Lord Londonderry, and *is* still in some degree with Vansittart, would take away all awkwardness from the arrangement in the eyes of the public, and remove any objection the King might have to it.'[165] 'Van's retreat is most handsomely covered and I am glad of it'.[166] Canning thought the arrangement tactically unavoidable, but was already planning with Liverpool that Huskisson should succeed in three years' time, when Robinson would surely be weary of arduous duty.[167]

160. Canning to Huskisson, 13 Jan. 1823, HP 38744 ff. 30-1.
161. Huskisson to Canning, 14 Jan. 1823, CP 68.
162. Croker to Peel, 16 Aug. 1822, *The Croker Papers. The Correspondence and Diaries of John Wilson Croker,* edited by L. J. Jennings (1885), i. 227-9.
163. Liverpool to Vansittart, 16 Dec. 1822, Vansittart MSS. 31232 f. 297.
164. Canning to Liverpool, 18 Dec. 1822, LP 38193 ff. 171-2; George IV to Liverpool, 2 Jan. 1823, LP 38575 ff. 82-3; Jones, *'Prosperity' Robinson,* 94-6.
165. Liverpool to Bathurst, 4 Jan. 1823, *Historical Manuscripts Commission, Bathurst,* 537.
166. Harrowby to Bathurst, 7 Jan. 1823, ibid. 537-8.
167. Canning to Liverpool, 18 Dec. 1822, LP 38193 ff. 171-2. Robinson's promotion may have suited Canning in that it would steal a little of the limelight from the latter's political rival, Peel. Thus Canning told Huskisson, 11 Aug. 1822, HP 38743 ff. 192-5, that it would be a 'great relief to me to have both Peel and Robinson to rely upon, *in situations of equal importance,* instead of dividing the debate with Peel alone' (my italics).

Robinson's appointment vacated the Board of Trade and
Huskisson succeeded happily to this,[168] but there was more
contumacious squabbling when he learned that he was not to
have the President's customary cabinet status. Only after a
very full airing of grievances did he obtain a promise of the
first vacancy or admission after one year. With his usual
slightly paranoiac sensitivity, Huskisson hinted that the
proscription was social; Mallet suspected that 'the *louche*
origins of Huskisson, the reports afloat as to the early part of
his life,[169] and his admirable pamphlet on the Bullion
Question in 1812 [*sic*], which the Monied Men of the City
will never forgive him, are insuperable obstacles to his promotion to a seat in the Cabinet.'[170] But the main explanation
was simply that, for reasons of pride, the King would not
accept a second Canningite into his cabinet in 1822.[171]

Nevertheless these events have led to a suggestion that
Robinson was more influential than Huskisson.[172] Whatever
the Exchequer and a cabinet seat represented, however, it
was not necessarily influence over policy. Cabinet was the
venue of *politicians,* often mere "ornaments", while policy
was decided by the *men of business,* and Liverpool thought
of Huskisson not as a Canningite politician but as a man of
business. Thus at one point Canning reassured Huskisson that
probably Liverpool 'would like *you* in V's room (if he is to
have any one) better than a *politician*'.[173] Economic policy
had never been formulated by the Chancellor of the
Exchequer, but by 'the sort of commission wch. has had to
decide upon the duties of his own office' (as Arbuthnot put

168. This annoyed Thomas Wallace, Vice-President of the Board of Trade, where
he had worked so assiduously as to render Robinson a 'cypher' ;   Arbuthnot to
Liverpool, 12 Jan. 1823, *Correspondence of Charles Arbuthnot,* 40. Wallace did
not mind serving under a peer, nor under the lethargic Robinson, but he knew that
he could never efface Huskisson.
169. i.e., his 'Jacobinism'.
170. Mallet, MS. Diary, 20 Jan. 1823, iv. 121-2. Ward to Copleston, 17 June
1822, *Letters of Earl Dudley to the Bishop of Llandaff,* 321.
171. Arbuthnot to Huskisson, ?6 Jan. 1823, HP 38744 ff. 13-14; Arbuthnot to
Bathurst, 12 Sept. 1822, *Historical Manuscripts Commission, Bathurst,* 532.
172. Jones, *'Prosperity' Robinson, passim.*
173. Canning to Huskisson, 3 Oct. 1822, HP 38743 ff. 217-20.

it), and Huskisson had long been a leading member. One of the secrets of Liverpool's political technique was to keep in the background those persons mainly responsible for making policy. In this way, the government could take credit for popular policies while shifting the blame when things went wrong; it could jettison policies without humiliation if they could be identified with some fringe member of the government. Peel was the front-man of resumption, and in 1821 Londonderry pretended to sympathize with the agriculturalists while Huskisson received the full measure of their resentment. To this extent Huskisson was justified in complaining that he was being saddled with work, responsibility, and power, yet deprived of tangible reward. His insistence on the cabinet was embarrassing, since his past services, which clearly entitled him to it, had rendered him unpopular with large sections of parliamentary opinion. Liverpool tried to keep him down, not because he was *un*important but because he was *too* important. Huskisson's eventual admission in August 1823 was an indication that the eighteenth-century game of cabinet politics, played with scant reference to economic and social problems, was no longer workable, but it was hardly a precondition of his influence. In January 1823 Bathurst remarked to Harrowby of Vansittart's deposition: 'Robinson's succession to the office is judicious, as it keeps more in the background *one* of the real objects of the Change, viz. Huskisson's promotion.'[174]

174. Bathurst to Harrowby, 5 Jan. 1823, Harrowby MSS. 1st series, XIV f. 123.

PART THREE

ADJUSTMENT TO PROSPERITY
1820 – 1830

VI

COMMERCIAL AND TARIFF REFORM
1820 – 1826

Our Fathers treated Industry and Commerce as they did their Children.
They wrapped and nursed them in swaddling cloaths; but these are now
exploded from the nursery as unfavorable to health and growth.
Huskisson to ————, 24 Dec. 1823, Bodleian MSS. Eng. lett. c. 144
ff. 109-11.

A 'system of kindness and conciliation'[1]

The work of Wallace, Huskisson and Robinson[2] was spectacular and controversial, and polarized opinion on the subject
of free trade, but it was largely a 'corollary' of monetary,
revenue, and agricultural policies, and it is in these that the
origins of the nineteenth-century drift towards free trade
must be sought. Formally, the free trade movement began
in 1820 with the London Merchants' petition and the first of
the Select Trade Committees, and is easily accommodated in
the so-called 'liberal awakening'. In reality, commercial
policy was untheoretical, and the timing of reform was
largely fortuitous.

It is now generally accepted that Tooke's description of
the London Merchants' Petition, as the 'originating impulse
to the movement' for free trade, is spurious. Its eloquent
'epitome' of the theoretical case for unilateral free trade
(based on comparative advantage and subject only to fiscal
necessity)[3] was a minority sentiment foisted by Tooke on

---

1. Joseph Hume in H. of C., 30 May 1828, 2 PD, xix. 904.
2. L. Levi, *The History of British Commerce and of the Economic Progress of the
British Nation, 1763-1870* (1872), 145-84; Clapham, *The Early Railway Age,*
311-36; A Brady, *William Huskisson and Liberal Reform* (1928), 73-131;
R. L. Schuyler, *The Fall of the Old Colonial System. A Study in British Free
Trade 1770-1870* (1945), 97-131; G. R. Porter, *The Progress of the Nation in its
social and commercial relations from the beginning of the Nineteenth Century to
the Present Day* (1836-8), section iv, 305-6.
3. The 1820 petitions from Manchester and from the Glasgow and Edinburgh
Chambers of Commerce were more traditional and less theoretical.

reluctant fellow-merchants, most of whom remained obstinately protectionist. 'There was nothing connected with the preparation or presentation of the Petition which could be construed into pressure on the Government', admitted its author. Moreover Liverpool, Castlereagh, Vansittart, and Robinson, having independently decided that reform was opportune, encouraged Tooke when the project seemed to be languishing. 'The simple truth is, that the Government were, at that time, far more sincere, and resolute Free Traders than the Merchants of London.'[4] With Samuel Thornton's help, Tooke inveigled many merchants into signing, probably by pretending that it was really a loyalist declaration against radicalism. 'It would divert you', he told Huskisson, 'if I were to tell you, as it does me upon recollection, how it came to be so signed as it was.'[5] Ricardo perceived at once that Alexander Baring, who presented the document to the Commons, was a 'professed...but lukewarm friend of free trade'. By 1826 Baring had become one of its most outspoken parliamentary enemies, delivering what Wilmot Horton called his 'nocturnal emissions' against Huskisson's policies.[6]

Eventually 196 signatures were obtained.[7] About half the Bank directors[8] (but not Harman's faction) signed, but most strikingly, sixteen of the twenty-nine officers of the Russian Company did so,[9] as well as several other Russian[10] and

4. Tooke and Newmarch, *A History of Prices,* vi. 331-44; T. Tooke, *Free Trade. Some Account of the Free Trade Movement as it originated with the Petition of the merchants of London* (1853). For complaints that Castlereagh had connived with Irving to promote the smaller, less specific London merchants' petition of 1819, see H. of C., 24 Dec. 1819, 1 PD, xli. 1571-3; Halévy, *The Liberal Awakening,* 121.
5. Tooke to Huskisson, 26 Feb. 1826, HP 38747 ff. 194-7.
6. Horton to Huskisson, 24 Mar. 1826, HP 38747 f. 191; Ricardo to McCulloch, 13 June 1820, Sraffa, *Works and Correspondence of David Ricardo,* viii. 197.
7. HP 38760 ff. 239-44.
8. Samuel, Stephen and A. H. Thornton, Henry Smith, William Ward, George Dorrien, Horsley Palmer, William Haldimand, Samuel Drewe, James Campbell, Robert Wigram, George Norman, Samuel Turner.
9. Tooke, Samuel, Stephen and C. G. Thornton, Stephen Cattley, T. F. Forster, James Gibson, John Harvey, W. Oughterlony, Thomas Raikes, the Rucker brothers, Thomas Solly, A. H. Thompson, Samuel Drewe, J. C. Weguelin.
10. e.g. William Sampson, Isaac Solly, Barth Jeffery, John White, George Warde Norman, George Norman.

north European[11] timber and general merchants. This, and Tooke's emphasis on timber, suggests that its propaganda masked a fairly traditional and particularist memorial on behalf of the north European merchants, whose main grievance — the preference on Canadian timber — was due for reconsideration in 1820. Indeed all mercantile free trade at this time was sectarian, in that its object was cheaper raw materials, or the abolition of some particularly annoying restriction or monopoly, such as the Corn Law. Countless pressure groups existed, but no unified commercial interest. Sugar merchants, for example, were divided into East and West Indiamen. Fine and coarse wool-growers disagreed as strongly as woollen and worsted manufacturers, and Edward Baines's 'only heresy as a Free Trader'[12] concerned the prohibition on export of British wool. London merchants could be more 'liberal' about the exportation of machinery than their counterparts in Manchester, who feared that mechanization would enhance the competitiveness of foreign cottons. The East India Company craved a free trade with respect to the West India sugar preference, while jealously guarding its own monopoly of the China trade. Judith Williams postulated a horizontal division between established merchants with vested interests to protect, and up-and-coming adventurers in search of new opportunities, who wished to ease restrictions and break monopolies.[13] This sometimes operated, but it was as often the large merchants with capital (the 'mighty athletes') who were best able to withstand the blasts of competition. One might keep down small rivals by monopoly or by freedom, and established merchants often looked to competition, as to 'dear money', as a guarantee of their superiority. On the other hand, adventurers, small men on the make, debtors, 'pigmy individual Traders',[14] might crave the flexible monetary policies

11. e.g. George Cowie, George Ranking, John H. Freese.
12. E. Baines (junior), *The Life of Edward Baines* (1851), 134 et seq.
13. J. B. Williams, *British Commercial Policy and Trade Expansion, 1750-1850* (1972), 439. Brougham in H. of C., 11 Feb. 1822, 2 PD, vi. 274 accused prosperous merchants of welcoming taxation as a means of stifling competition from lesser men.
14. Granville to Huskisson, 7 Apr. 1825, HP 38746 ff. 172-4, describing himself.

that frequently, as in Attwood's case, went with a protectionist attitude to trade. Most of the 1820 signatories were
established businessmen.

Protection was increased after 1815 to a peak in 1822,[15]
the eve of tariff reform. This fact alone gives subsequent
developments the appearance of a *volte-face*, but in fact the
increase was quite unintentional: tariffs had escalated since
Pitt's time, owing to the financial exigencies of war; in 1816
the loss of the property tax, which had fallen mainly on land,
left the tariff to bear the main revenue burden; the additional
duties of 1819 accentuated this bias;[16] and deflation raised
the value of specific duties in relation to the goods on which
they were levied. Indirect taxation was thus increased as a
proportion both of public revenue and of commodity prices.
Freer trade was impossible so long as tariffs bore such an
essential fiscal burden, and the reforms of 1823-6 had to wait
on revenue surpluses and relatively full employment. But
notwithstanding the fashionable new theories that attended it,
freer trade — like resumption — was regarded in official
circles as a return to pre-war normalcy. Robinson even said
that one of the 'first objects' of the war against Napoleon
had been to overturn the continental system of exclusion.[17]

The government's campaign against contraband reveals the
essential continuity of its fiscal motive. His biographer
endorsed the view that it was George Rose 'who first
conceived the idea of putting down smuggling, and improving

---

15. A. H. Imlah, *Economic Elements in the 'Pax Britannica'* (1958), 114-19
and *passim*.
16. These, and especially the additional 6*d.* per lb. on wool, have sometimes been
regarded as protectionist in inspiration (Gayer, Rostow and Schwartz, *Growth
and Fluctuation of the British Economy*, i. 156) but in fact they were merely
financial expedients. Ministers had steadily resisted Webb Hall's clamour for extra
protection to wool since 1816. J. Bischoff, *A Comprehensive History of the
Woollen and Worsted Manufactures* (1842), i. 450-2, Gayer et al., op.cit. i. 156
n.1, and Spring and Crosby, 'George Webb Hall and the Agricultural Association',
Journal of British Studies, ii (1962), 126 n.59, have all suggested that ministers
entered into a compact whereby the landed interest agreed to vote the £1,400,000
of malt duty in return for this boon to wool. This is possible — but opposition
M.P.s Western, Brand, J.P. Grant, Barham, Ridley, Newport, and Stanley all
opposed the extra taxation, despite the fact that they supported protection to
wool and had served on the Select Committee on wool in 1816.
17. H. of C., 28 Mar. 1816, 1 PD, xxxiii. 696.

the income of the state by decreasing the amount of duties exacted at the Customs House.'[18] Yet when Liverpool suggested this in 1814-15 Rose was sceptical, and instead recommended 'endeavouring to protect the present high Duties by active and immediate exertions by naval and military arrangements'.[19] He evolved a plan for using detective coastguards and naval vessels, which helped to meet a pressing problem of naval unemployment. But by 1817 the most urgent problem was revenue deficiency, and the ministerially-dominated Finance Committee of that year laid down an unambiguous blueprint for a controlled experiment in the administrative prevention of smuggling, to be followed in the event of failure by a 'theoretic' prophylactic:

It may be expedient, that under the present circumstances of the country the experiment should be fairly made to maintain the existing Revenue by such means as the Government may be able to apply to the counteraction of Smuggling, rather than have recourse immediately to considerable alterations in the Duties: but Your Committee cannot too strongly urge the necessity of not persisting longer in that experiment than a clear prospect of success will fully justify, and the propriety of having recourse in due time, in the event of failure, to the wisdom of Parliament for a commutation of the duties exposed to this danger, by the substitution of other sources of Revenue less obnoxious to it.[20]

This clearly has nothing to do with a liberal awakening. In the post-war years frantic attemtps were made to defeat illicit importation with martello towers, pilotage schemes, coastal blockades, and preventive guards;[21] this approach was undermined, however, by the move to retrench establishments after 1820, and also by such 'incidents' as the occasion in Sussex when a coastguard was judged to have murdered an innocent fisherman. M.P.s began to demand that smuggling be suppressed 'by other means than violence'.[22] One of the Treasury Commissioners, Charles Long, drafted a report on

18. *The Diaries and Correspondence of George Rose*, edited by L. V. Harcourt (1860), ii. 525.
19. Rose to Liverpool, 30 Dec. 1814, Rose MSS. 42774B ff. 331-2. See Rose's notes on smuggling prevention, LP 38262 f. 186.
20. CSC, *Fourth Report on the Income and Expenditure of the United Kingdom*, 1817, 124.
21. See the Liverpool Papers for several such plans, especially as connected with the Cinque Ports.
22. Fyshe Palmer in H. of C., 13 Apr. 1821, 2 PD, v. 217.

the cost-effectiveness of smuggling prevention, and admitted 'the difficulty of protecting the Revenue while the present high duties continue'.[23] As the revenue improved, tariff reform was adopted as the most eligible weapon of the law, especially for luxuries like lace and silks. When in 1825 Huskisson and Robinson spoke of removing the 'premium to the smuggler', and of discouraging lawlessness on the coast, these were not worthless debating points or sudden insights, but long-standing ambitions.[24]

Agricultural policy influenced the timing of commercial legislation in several ways. In 1820 Liverpool replied to the London petitioners that the Corn Law stood in the way of either unilateral or reciprocal free trade.[25] The gradual realization that autarchy was impossible, that foreign food would be needed, led to a greater emphasis on manufacturing exports simply as a means of remittance: the reduction of import duties would be a 'consequence' and not a 'concomitant' of agricultural policy.[26] Then, politically, it was necessary to 'soothe' landlords by dismantling some industrial protection before attacking the Corn Law.[27] 'Unnecessary and excessive protection [to cottons and woollens for example] is constantly thrown in our teeth by the Disciples of *Webb Hall*, and the advocates of extravagant duties on the productions of Foreign Agriculture'.[28] Finally, in the glut of 1820-2, farmers were unable to export their

23. *Twelfth Report of the Commissioners of Inquiry into the Regulations of the Customs and Excise,* 1822; LP 38290 ff. 255-60. This report was signed by Long, Somerset, Frewin, Herries, and W. J. Lushington. Vansittart probably had a hand in its composition, Arbuthnot to Liverpool, 5 Dec. 1821, LP 38290 ff. 119-21.
24. Huskisson in H. of C., 25 Mar. 1825, 2 PD, xii. 1207-9; *Speeches of William Huskisson,* ii. 342-3; Robinson in H. oc C., 28 Feb. 1825, 2 PD, xii. 734; Brady, op. cit. 116-18; L. Fisher, *Then and Now; economic problems after the war a hundred years ago* (1925), 13-15, 62-6; Brown, *The Board of Trade and the Free-Trade Movement,* 152-4. Liverpool to Herries, 26 Oct. 1823, Herries MSS. 57367 ff. 67-9; Dillon to CSC, *Report from the Select Committee on Import Duties,* 1840, QQ. 2827-31.
25. H. of L., 26 May 1820, 2 PD, i. 576-82.
26. See above, p. 150. Liverpool to Redesdale, 5 Sep. 1816, Redesdale MSS. D2002/C23: 'I think the true Policy for England would have been to protect Agriculture, and leave Manufactures to find their own level.'
27. Vansittart to Liverpool, 20 Dec. 1821, Yonge, *Life and Administration of Lord Liverpool,* iii. 164-5.
28. Huskisson to Finlay, 12 Feb. 1825, copy in HP 38746 ff. 134-6.

surplus owing to the huge price differentials between Britain and the continent. To prevent periodic grain redundancies, average production should be kept *slightly* below average consumption, and the difference annually imported. This, more than a concern for manufacturing exports, dictated ministerial progress towards free trade.

Imlah has shown that commercial reform was defensive and desperate, not done with the optimism of a 'mighty athlete' who no longer needed protection. As peace raised commercial rivals, Britain's war-time trading status seemed precarious. Thomas Wallace, who inaugurated commercial reform as Vice-President of the Board of Trade and chairman of the 1820-4 Trade Committees in the Commons, concluded from the fall in exports that Britain resembled 'a dying nation'.[29] Here freer trade was an employment policy, a cure for manufacturing depression and disaffection, a remedy for the disparity that all acknowledged between production and consumption. Liverpool recognized 'the great increase of our manufacturing population' and 'the dependence of a great part of the population on Foreign Demand'.[30] Though internal dealings might constitute the bulk of effective demand, foreign trade was the more dynamic or immediately expansible factor, especially when the state's finances were too depressed to permit cuts in excise and assessed taxes bearing on personal consumption. The main purpose of the trade committees of 1820-4 was certainly to discover and encourage new sources of commerce; but this must be distinguished from the tariff reductions of 1823-6, the aim of which was not to create outlets or 'force exports' (as protectionists alleged and Huskisson indignantly denied),[31] but to vet and stabilize any trade that the committees might have generated. Freer trade was a process of purification, a sieve to ensure that newly won commerce was 'natural', based

29. Wallace stated in H. of C., 12 Feb. 1823, 2 PD, viii. 100, that exports had fallen by £14,000,000 (official values) in 1815-19 and by a further £11,000,000 during 1819.
30. Liverpool to Grenville, 14 Nov. 1819, LP 38281 ff. 1-9. E. S. Cayley, *On Commercial Economy* (1830), 239, judged that whenever free trade created 'full employment' it was beneficial, and 'when it does not, it is detrimental'.
31. Huskisson in H. of C., 18 Mar. 1830, 2 PD, xxiii. 587-8. Indeed, Britain's overseas trade remained relatively static during 1815-50.

on comparative advantage for example, and not a product of speculation or of a peculiar temporary situation. In this sense tariff reform was a movement to reduce, at least to control, exports, rather than to expand them indiscriminately.

The official attitude was well expressed by the outgoing under-secretary at the War Office, Castlereagh's intimate, Edward Cooke, in an important memorandum for Liverpool in 1817:[32]

I consider our Commerce to rest upon five Principles. 1. the Encouragement of Home Manufactures & Market; 2d. Colonial Monopoly; 3d. Extent of Trade and Navigation; 4th. Support of a great Revenue; 5th. the Maintenance of a powerful protecting Marine.

When Baring and Brougham talk on the subject they generally consider [? tonnage] as Trade, and look merely to Quantity of Trade without reference to its Quality and its national or Political Relations... Now, I conceive, that...the natural Reflexion to make is, not, how our State of Commerce can be improved, but how it can be preserved.

Freer trade complemented convertibility in the attempt to eliminate commercial fluctuations. Huskisson publicly attributed these to 'our mercantile system, with its balance of trade, its balance of prohibitions and protections, and checks and bounties, and all the complicated and confused machinery by which the interests of commerce have been impeded instead of being promoted'.[33] Again, it was essential to make trade regular and not intermittent because the currency was extremely sensitive, under a metallic standard, to sudden variations in imports. This required either central control over commerce or, more practicably, greater freedom for it to find its level in the market.

British statesmen were clearly ambivalent in their attitude to Britain's economic achievements. Intensely proud of her industrial superiority, they nevertheless feared an international imbalance that would rebound to her disadvantage. Having gained most, Britain stood to lose most. Formerly, for example, ministers had thrilled to behold the margin of cultivation pushing ever upwards, and told themselves that even if this meant dearer food, other prices (including that of labour) would adjust, and that so long as internal equilibrium and domestic demand was maintained, all would be well. But in

32. 12 Sept. 1817, LP 38268 ff. 152-60.
33. H. of C., 15 Feb. 1822, 2 PD, vi. 422.

the glut of 1819-22, Britain's relative dearness prevented
corn exportation just as it attracted all foreign surpluses to
British warehouses. Internal equilibrium was clearly not
enough and ministers began to seek more harmonious
relations with the rest of the world. The government's freer
trade policy involved adherence to Malthusian fears of
periodic glut, and a hope that foreign trade would syphon off
industrial surplus, just as colonies would absorb redundant
population;[34] yet it was Ricardian rather than Malthusian
in that the object of increased trade was to restore external,
not domestic, equilibrium. Freer trade would increase certain
aspects of commerce but would also, in Huskisson's words,
disentangle Britain from those inefficient branches that
impeded rather than promoted economic well-being. It
would stabilize economic relations with the rest of the world.
The 'vaunted *Balance of Trade,* or the excess of our exports
above our imports', was not a national profit, but was 'only
capital sent out of the country for which no capital is
returned to it'.[35]

Fay contrasted Peel's administrative approach to free trade
with Huskisson's industrial and imperial vision.[36] Yet the
latters' vision remained agricultural — 'we must look to the
yeomanry' — and the spirit of his legislation was also administrative. For all Lansdowne's propaganda about buying in the
cheapest market, the inquiries of the trade committees were
almost entirely technical. The archetypal reform was the codi-
fication and consolidation of mercantile law, carried out for
Huskisson by James Deacon Hume, secretary of the Customs,
to encourage merchants to exercise their legitimate trading

34. See B. Semmel, *The Rise of Free Trade Imperialism. Classical Political
Economy, the Empire of Free Trade and Imperialism 1750-1850* (1970), 8-11,
130-57, for a valuable discussion of this point.
35. Huskisson, *The Question Concerning the Depreciation of Our Currency*
(1810), 58.
36. Fay, *Huskisson and His Age,* 123. Parnell caught the spirit of Huskisson's
policy in'Finance', *Edinburgh Review,* xxxiii (1820), 54-69: the Bank restriction
had spawned an over-production of goods and (worse still) had 'forced into
existence' a 'mass of manufacturing population...beyond the means of the
country, when it shall be restored to a healthy state of currency and capital, to
provide with employment'. Freer trade was the way to resolve this problem.

rights.[37] In this spirit, reform was inevitably cautious and piecemeal. 'It became us, therefore, to watch the issue of each experiment, and not to attempt too much at once, until we had felt our way, and until the public were prepared to accompany us in our further progress.'[38] It is misleading to suppose with Harriet Martineau that Huskisson 'opened his hand by one finger at a time, [simply] because the people or their rulers could not receive a handful of the truth about free trade'. Huskisson was genuinely feeling his way, and received truth was not at stake. Of course, he was unusually equipped for combat on a theoretical level, and deserved the compliment often made of having 'steered a steady course' between the extremes of abstraction and practicality:[39] 'If I deserve any portion of [merchant Kirkman] Finlay's Praise as a Minister, it is only that in which he gives me the credit of uniting some practical knowledge to theory: and if I have that knowledge in any degree it is because I am always desirous and disposed to listen to him, and such as him.'[40] Only later, when free trade had to be retrospectively defended, did discussions become dogmatic. The more theoretical Deacon Hume then claimed that he had dragged a cautious Huskisson behind him.[41] In reality Hume was useful to the minister — as were Lack, Jacob, Hill, Courtenay, Long, Harrison, and other officials, compilers of information but hardly partners in policy formation. Similarly Jones is probably correct in his view that, theoretically and emotionally, Robinson was a more consistent free trader than Huskisson. The latter shamelessly adopted doctrinaire arguments for purposes of debate. But it does not follow that Robinson contributed more to the origins of free trade, since that policy was not a dogmatic application of economic theory,

37. Fay, *Huskisson and His Age*, 276-96.
38. Huskisson in H. of C., 25 Mar. 1825, 2 PD, xii. 1197; *Speeches of William Huskisson*, ii. 328.
39. See the 1828 memorandum on Huskisson's principles in Herries MSS.
40. Huskisson to John Gladstone, 25 Mar. 1826, HP 38747 ff. 211-12.
41. C. Badham, *The Life of James Deacon Hume* (1895), 30, 308-9. For the routine work of Huskisson's Board of Trade see A. L. Lingelbach, 'William Huskisson as President of the Board of Trade', *American Historical Review*, xliii (1937-8), 759-74.

but a flexible adaptation of means to consistent pragmatic ends — food supply, monetary and economic stability. The overwhelming weight of evidence contradicts Jones's thesis, and endorses the unanimous contemporary view[42] that in 1823-6 the Board of Trade arrogated to itself much of the business traditionally associated with the Treasury.[43]

Despite the untheoretical nature of commercial reform and its dependence on other policies, ministers followed certain principles. They rejected the unilateralism recommended by the London merchants and based tariff reduction on bilateral reciprocity. In a sense this was a deflationary, post-Resumption version of the European war of retaliation that had been developing since 1815, and it led to a series of commercial treaties on the 'most favoured nation' principle.[44] As time went on, however, Huskisson looked more and more to a uniform tariff. Then came a desire to replace monopoly by preference, and also 'to lower, almost generally, the scale of our protecting duties, so as to make them really protecting, instead of prohibitory'.[45] There was Huskisson's desire also to tender indiscriminately, to all nations alike, equal facilities of commerce and navigation and equal inducements to bring goods, either for consumption or transit, to British ports.[46] He recommended that domestic industry should continue to be protected by duties that were countervailing in a very un-Ricardian sense — that is, that they should be sufficient to place the British manufacturer on a footing of fair competition with his foreign rivals, so as to

42. e.g. *Journal of Mrs. Arbuthnot*, i. 390-1; *The Greville Memoirs. A journal of the reigns of King George IV and King William IV,* edited by H. Reeve (1875), i. 258 (22 Dec. 1829).
43. Liverpool's correspondence with Herries suggests that the latter, as Treasury Secretary, played at least as important a role as Robinson.
44. Liverpool was sceptical: 'Few persons attach less real value than I do to Commercial Treaties, but it would be not true to say, that something may not occasionally be done to give a fillip to Commercial Enterprise.' Liverpool's observations on a commercial treaty with Portugal, 22 Jan. 1822, LP 38290 ff. 286-9.
45. Huskisson to Finlay, 12 Feb. 1825, copy in HP 38746 ff. 134-6.
46. Courtenay in H. of C., 12 Nov. 1830, 3 PD, i. 479, quoting a Board of Trade minute.

'excite his emulation and his industry',[47] and to 'excite emulation in our artizans'. Finally, Fay and Brady have explored Huskisson's ideas of colonial preference,[48] and the former has developed suggestive though questionable insights into his concept of informal empire, of an England that must be great or would be nothing, of free trade as the harbinger of imperial power. According to Fay, Huskisson's Smithian ambition was to establish habitual trade between industrial Britain and a primary-producing 'third world', and then to free that trade as internal trade between the agricultural and manufacturing sectors had been freed.[49] The remainder of this chapter will not attempt to elucidate these policies in detail, but will concentrate on certain salient aspects and illustrate the halting manner in which specific policies evolved.

'Warehouse of the world': the example of linen

Liverpool's government desired to render Britain the mart of nations, the Venice of her age, and *universi orbis terrarum emporium*.[50] It was anxious to promote entrepôt or transit trade, even if this was likely to be monopolized by foreign shipping. In the eighteenth century, certain commodities, like tobacco, had been allowed to enter Britain duty-free for re-exportation — simply as a concession to merchants, not to

47. Huskisson in H. of C., 18 Apr. 1826, 2 PD, xv. 349. Smart, *Economic Annals of the Nineteenth Century. 1821-30.* 385-6 and 289-90, points out that, in adjusting duties on woollens, earthenware, glass, and hardware, Huskisson had left foreign manufacturers on less than an 'equal footing'. For three of Huskisson's great speeches on free trade, see H. of C., 21 and 25 Mar. 1825, 23 Feb. 1826. 2 PD, xii. 1097-116 and 1196-222; xiv. 763-809; *Speeches of William Huskisson*, ii. 304-62, 465-530. Smart, op. cit. 271-85, 367-9.
48. Fay, *The Corn Laws and Social England*, 121-34; Brady, op. cit. 132-67.
49. J. D. Hume defined British policy as an effort to make colonies commercial as well as agricultural, especially the slave colonies where it was desirable to develop a white population. Hume's memorandum, 25 Aug. 1828, Peel MSS. 40333 ff. 32-4.
50. It also hoped 'that our Northern Colonies may become the entrepôts of American goods, for the supply of our Southern Colonies, instead of having such entrepôts established in neutral Islands in the West Indies.' Herries's memorandum on papers from Sir Howard Douglas with reference to a tonnage duty in New Brunswick on American ships, 15 Feb. 1830, Herries MSS. On departmental plans for a Jamaican free port entrepôt, see J. D. Hume's memorandum of 25 Aug. 1828.

render Britain the 'chief medium' of world trade. War and continental blockade transformed the entrepôt trade from a luxury into a necessity, a means of hoarding supplies. To promote it, the great Warehousing Act of 1803 allowed fifteen months' free deposit of goods in certain enumerated ports, and there were subsequent relaxations.[51] By 1815 the entrepôt trade had built up considerable vested interests (mainly dockers and shipowners), which now clamoured for legislative inducements in place of natural wartime demand. Thus in 1818 the Board of Trade, after extensive pressure from the Shipowners' Committee, recommended reducing rates of pilotage in the Cinque Ports so as to make British transit facilities more attractive.[52] Cash payments made it essential that commerce should be regular, and the ability to warehouse imports, until they were needed for consumption, would help. Accordingly, Wallace's Foreign Trade Committee of 1820 recommended the reduction of all charges (such as pilot, light, and harbour dues) that deterred foreigners from using British warehouses, and also an extension of the privilege of free bonding to include even manufactures whose importation for consumption was prohibited.[53] Emporium status would enable British merchants to fix world prices, while all witnesses agreed that transit trade was 'pure profit', attracting capital to England, winning rents for warehousemen and commission for merchants. Manufacturers benefited too because foreign merchants would make up assortments of cargo from local products. Transit might even redress the trade balance with European nations, enabling them to pay for British goods, and modifying the high exchange rates that were at present damaging Britain's export trade in colonial produce. Wallace summarized the policy: 'He wished to give

51. e.g. the 1815 Corn Law's warehousing clause. See above, pp. 25-6.
52. Lack to Liverpool, 12 Oct. 1818, LP 38273 f. 309; Buckle to Lack, 17 Aug. 1819; Buckle to Liverpool and Liverpool to Buckle, Aug. 1819, LP 38279 ff. 119, 121-13, 192. See the *Second Report of the Commissioners on the Customs and Excise (on the warehousing system) dated 3 Oct. 1818*, 9-12.
53. CSC, *Report on the means of maintaining and improving the Foreign Trade of the Country*, 1820, 3-15. See also CSC, *Report on the means of improving and maintaining Foreign Trade (Lights, Harbour Dues, and Pilotage)*, 1822 and CSC, *Three Reports on the means of improving Foreign Trade (Pilotage, Post Office Regulations, Ramsgate Harbour Dues, Light Duties, Ballast)*, 1824.

to the commerce of foreign nations the freest possible access
for the purpose of exportation from England. In short, he
was desirous of making this country the general depôt, the
great emporium of the commerce of the world.'[54]

But what happened when such principles clashed with
vested interests? The lobby most vociferously opposed to
warehousing policy was that of the Irish linen manufacturers,
who were strongly protected by both transit duties and
export bounties.[55] Nevertheless, in the south of Ireland the
industry was in permanent retreat, and even in Ulster it was
losing ground to English linens and Irish cottons.[56] Failure
of protection made the manufacturers all the more tenacious
of it, however. The 1803 Warehousing Act had included
foreign linens among the goods allowed to be freely deposited
in England, but seven years later, an *ad val.* duty of 15 per
cent was imposed on foreign (plain) linens re-exported from
warehouses. While the Orders in Council operated, the effect
of this was mainly fiscal, but their repeal opened up the
prospect of Germany supplying other nations directly with
its own linens, thereby threatening Britain's position as
keeper and carrier. The question therefore arose: should
Parliament abolish the transit duty and resurrect the free
warehousing system of 1803-10 in order to encourage the
deposit of foreign linens?

The Irish manufacturers' claim 'to a more than ordinary
protection' rested on an historical compact, according to
which Orange England had systematically set out to annihilate
Ireland's staple woollen manufacture in the interest of its
English rival, by treating Irish linens preferentially. In 1696,
the latter were allowed free entry into England, which
constituted a 25 per cent preference over foreign linens.
Later, foreign (but not Irish) linens entered into British
warehouses were charged a duty, not all of which was drawn

54. H. of C., 25 June 1821, 2 PD, v. 1292.
55. For background, see W. C. Gill, *The Rise of the Irish Linen Industry* (1924),
221-26, 227-44; E. J. Riordan, *Modern Irish Trade and Industry*, edited by
G.O'Brien (1920), 23 et seq; G. O'Brien, *The Economic History of Ireland from
the Union to the Famine* (1921), 315-36; J. Horner, *The Linen Trade of Europe
during the Spinning-wheel Period* (1920), 114-27.
56. Gill, op. cit. 303.

back on re-export. Meanwhile, the bargain had been sealed
by prohibitory duties on the export of Irish wool, and
accordingly linen replaced wool as the staple industry. British
and continental linen merchants naturally resented the charge
on foreign linens imported and re-exported. The 1803
Warehousing Act appeased them until 1810, when the Irish
preference was re-enacted. Irish manufacturers claimed that
the preference was a permanent peacetime asset, and the free
transit of 1803-10 a temporary wartime circumstance. English
merchants retorted that unrestrained equality was the norm,
and the measure of 1810 a mere wartime expedient. The
government also insisted that the protection was not
permanent, but was simply an encouragement to struggling
industry and one which shoul be withdrawn now that 'the
manufacture was no longer in its infancy'.[57] Protection to
infant industries always built up vested interests and
encouraged capitalists to invest, on the assumption that it
would be continued indefinitely. The only solution for a
parliament anxious to dismantle protection was to declare
prospectively a gradual withdrawal, as it eventually did in
the 1820s.

But for several years before that, the Board of Trade
vacillated mindlessly, the sport of every pressure group that
blew. In 1813 news reached James Corry, secretary of the
Irish Linen Board, that Vansittart felt 'kindly' to a repeal
of the transit dues.[58] Probably prompted by John Foster, a
Linen Board Trustee, the merchants and drapers of Antrim,
together with manufacturers in Glasgow and on the Clyde,
protested that repeal of the preference would hit Irish and
Scottish exports to South America and the West Indies,
markets which had compensated in part for the loss of
American custom.[59] Ministers succumbed to this pressure,

57. Hardwicke, 1802, cited by O'Brien, op.cit. 321 n.2. Grenville to Auckland,
15 Dec. 1806, *Historical Manuscripts Commission, Fortescue*, viii. 469. Vesey
Fitzgerald to Foster, 7 May 1813 and Foster to Fitzgerald, 13 May 1813, Fitzgerald MSS. 7818 pp. 247, 289-90.
58. Corry to Foster, 3 and 7 May 1813, Foster/Massereene MSS. D207/52/45;
D562/6630. See also Vesey Fitzgerald to Foster, 1 May 1813, Fitzgerald MSS.
7818 pp. 200-2.
59. B.T. 1/94 f 4; B.T. 5/24, 4; Dufferin to Foster, 13 May 1813, Foster/
Massereene MSS. D207/73/5; Corry to Peel, 1 Mar. 1814, ibid. D562/6313;
Corry to Foster, 20 Jan. 1814, ibid. D562/6639.

only to rouse English indignation in turn. In July 1814 the
Chairman of the Shipowners Committee, John William
Buckle, represented to the Board of Trade the fears of the
Brazil Committee of South American merchants, that unless
warehousing facilities were extended to include foreign linens
(and at once, while foreigners still possessed their war-time
habit of using Britain as an entrepôt), Germans and Russians
would blaze their own trails, and England would lose a
shipping monopoly that had made her 'the chief medium of
commercial intercourse' in Atlantic and Indian waters.[60] The
Government changed its mind again, and informed the Irish
of the Board of Trade's 'firm persuasion that the reasons
which originally existed for imposing the duty in question,
have totally ceased to exist; and that the continuance of such
a duty would be highly injurious to the present commercial
interests of the United Kingdom, generally, and to the Linen
Trade in particular.'[61]

Accordingly, in November and December 1814, linen
merchants, manufacturers, and bleachers in all the northern
counties of Ireland except Sligo — that is, in Antrim, Armagh,
Down, Tyrone, Londonderry, Donegal, Monaghan, Cavan,
and Fermanagh, as well as in Dublin, Belfast, Drogheda,
Glasgow, and Perth, sent strenuous representations to the
Linen Board, which itself dispatched a vigorous protest to
Chief Secretary Peel,[62] signed by Foster, Vandaleur, London-
derry, Peter la Touche, Granard, Leitrim, Sneyd, Massereene,
Westmeath, Dufferin, Maurice Fitzgerald, Beresford, Stewart,
Leslie, Brownlow, O'Neill, and thirty-two other influential
Trustees. (Corry was indefatigable in rousting them out —
one, Gore, was 'going to be married — but I have written to
him to sign first'.)[63] A defecting trustee was the controversial

60. Buckle to Board of Trade, 13 July 1814, CSC, *Report on the Foreign Trade
of the Country*, 1820, 122-3. As with corn (see above p. 5), the question of
protection united merchants and manufacturers in Ireland while it divided them
in Scotland. See the memorial of twenty-five Glasgow linen merchants, and
Finlay to Lack, 19 Nov. 1814, B.T. 1/94 ff. 1-3.
61. Becket to Peel, 27 Aug. 1814; Peel to Corry, 14 Sept. 1814; B.T. minute, 25
Aug. 1814; CSC, *Report on the Foreign Trade of the Country*, 1820, 124-7;
B.T. 5/24, 4.
62. CSC, *Report on the Foreign Trade of the Country*, 1820, 128-32.
63. Corry's memorandum in Foster/Massereene MSS. D562/6669.

Chief Justice, Lord Norbury. On 1 November he told Foster that England had compacted to continue the transit preference, on the strength of which great capitals had been invested, and that the Linen Board must wage 'a decent struggle before such a precious charge shall be ravish'd from Ireland'. But immediately afterwards, according to Corry, 'Peel...brought him completely round to his side',[64] and four days later Norbury wrote again to Foster:

You must put up your armour, as I foresee that the *transit duty* on foreign linens has most powerful opponents...

The Legislature can not preclude the British Merchant or foreign merchant from trading in a cheap article and taking it to every foreign port without touching in Gt. Britain or Ireland. The Acts relative to Transit are of late date, and seem to have originated from the nature of the War. But I am not strong enough to argue the propriety and justice of a continuance of the measure so as to reconcile it to the general principles of Commercial regulation.[65]

Despite Peel, however, Irish M.P.s constituted a phalanx of supporters whose feelings on corn, butter, or linen the government could not lightly disregard.[66] So the Board of Trade swung yet again. It told frustrated English merchants in 1815 that it meant, reluctantly, to 'acquiesce in the strong opinion expressed by the Linen Interest of Ireland' and to rescind the decision of the previous August to repeal the transit duty.[67] Even Peel admitted that it would 'be *impolitic* to effect [repeal] *at the expense of the clamour* and general dissatisfaction which it would inevitably produce' in Ireland.[68]

The issue was re-examined by the Commons Trade Committee of 1820. Here Irishmen claimed again that, in pursuing free transit, English merchants and shippers were selfishly attempting to transfer British capital out of Irish and into

64. Ibid.
65. Norbury to Foster, 1 and 5 Nov. 1814, Foster/Massereene MSS. D207/51/13, 14. Foster was doubtful of success at this time, seeing that 'many parts of Britain who used to concur with us in support of the Manufacture have got a second and a contrary Interest as Merchants'. Foster to Norbury, 2 Nov. 1814, ibid. 25.
66. P. J. Jupp. 'Irish M.P.s at Westminster in the early Nineteenth Century', *Historical Studies*, vii (1969), 65-80.
67. B.T. 5/24, 29-33 (8 Feb. 1815).
68. Peel to Becket, 28 Jan. 1815, CSC, *Report on the Foreign Trade of the Country*, 1820, 127.

foreign linens, in order that they themselves might exploit the consequent carrying trade. The Englishman George Ranking's argument, that this would in fact *benefit* Ireland by making her linens *more* competitive, assumed that additional capital could not lower unit costs:

'You mean, then, that from the withdrawing the British capital from the demand for Foreign linens...according to present law, lowers the price of Foreign linens to such a degree, that when they arrive at the Foreign port they undersell ours, whereas, that if British capital was in the market, that the price of them would be superior; that we could undersell them? — That is precisely my position.'[69]

More cogently, English spokesmen maintained that the transit duties deprived German manufacturers of the facility of making up assorted cargoes in the versatile English market. They were therefore compelled to send linens out to South America *in bulk,* which glutted those markets and damaged all producers equally, including the Irish.[70] Despite these arguments, the Committee, in recommending the removal of all restrictions on entrepôt, decided to exempt linens alone, since 'more than mere commercial considerations are connected' with Ireland's main industry. Then in 1823, heroic resistance by the Belfast Chamber of Commerce secured exemption of linens from the free public bonding provisions of the Warehousing Act for an indefinite period, though ministers could not promise 'that the matter will not be revised on some future occasion'.[71]

Navigation and monopoly: the examples of timber and sugar

All claims for preference faced a problem over quality. The Irish linen lobby had to establish on the one hand that their product was good enough to *deserve* — to profit from — to be

69. Ibid. 75.
70. Ibid. 77, 81-2.
71. Peel to Oriel, 18 Apr. 1823, Foster/Massereene MSS. D207/39/28; Corry to Oriel, 2 Apr. 1823, ibid. D562/6791. The Irish linen manufacture was also affected by proposals to abolish the Union duties and the guild-type restrictions on the manufacture, by the regulation of the West Indian colonial trade with the United States, and by efforts to repeal the bounty on British and Irish linens exported from England. The 'leading members' of the Board of Trade argued 'upon abstract principles, that Bounties were not consistent with sound policy.' Hadden to Marshall, 8 Jan. 1820, copy in Foster/Massereene MSS. D562/7165.

'capable of receiving' — preferential treatment, but also that it was not so good that it no longer *needed* it. In giving evidence on the reputation of Irish linens, Corry, Thomas Oldham (draper and exporter), and Joseph Stephenson (bleacher) were all alike self-contradictory. Canadian merchants demanding protection for the timber of the northern colonies against that of north Europe faced the same dilemma. After William Stewart had listed various uses for which Canadian was the most suitable of all woods, someone asked pertinently: 'Would not then the Canada timber continue to be employed for these purposes...even in the event of the duties on timber from the north of Europe being removed or diminished?'[72]

Favouritism to Canadian timber was not based on long-standing contractual justice, as with linens, but quite clearly on a wartime expedient. After 1807 Britain's customary supplies of Baltic timber for shipbuilding were virtually sequestered by the Continental System. In 1809, to attract alternative supplies, Portland's government suspended all duties on Canadian timber until 1820 and imposed a high 'countervailing' charge on foreign timber (41s. per load). The latter was raised in 1810, 1811, 1812, and 1813 so that by 1820 it amounted to 65s.[73] Meanwhile the real value of the preference increased as British freight rates fell towards foreign levels through excess shipping. The Board of Trade considered charging Canadian timber in 1817 and 1818, and there was diplomatic pressure for it to do so from Prussia and Sweden in 1818-19.[74] But although the infant industry argument hardly applied and although the government had always intended that the preference should be temporary, the fact remained that, in the cause of national defence,

72, LSC, *First Report from the Lords on the means of extending and securing the Foreign Trade of the Country*, 1820, 47.

73. G. S. Graham, *Sea Power and British North America 1783-1820. A Study in British Colonial Policy* (1941), 142-52; J. Potter, 'The British Timber Duties, 1815-60', *Economica*, new series, xxii (1955), 122-36.

74. Humboldt to Castlereagh, 9 Feb. 1818, and Castlereagh to Humboldt, 1 May 1818, A & P, *Correspondence with Foreign Powers relative to the Duties levied in England upon the importation of corn 1818-34*, 1839, 131-8. B. T. minutes, 4 Apr. 1818 and 7 June 1819; B.T. 5/25, 375-8.

considerable capitals had been invested in the Canadian trade
(more than £150,000 in Lower Canada alone). Moreover
Canning, like Huskisson later, was prevented by his Liverpool
connections from taking a 'pure view' of the case: 'I suppose
I must vote as my consituents may wish me — that, I take it,
will be for Canada, versus Norway'.[75] Inevitably the government compromised. Lansdowne's House of Lords Committee
of 1820 supported a material reduction of the foreign timber
duties, but in 1821 the less theoretical Commons' Committee
proved more sympathetic to the colonists.[76] Besides Canning
and Huskisson, it included Thomas Wilson,[77] and Marryat,
Baring and Gladstone, who were all involved in shipping and
treasured the North American trade for its carrying business.
Though both Committees summoned much the same body of
witnesses,[78] their Lordships concluded that the preference
was being wasted on a vastly inferior product, while the
Commons' Committee rested its alternative case on the
successful use of North American red and yellow pine in
shipbuilding. Eventually Wallace introduced a Bill (based on
the Commons' Committee's advice) to reduce the legislative
preference from 65s. to 45s. by imposing a 10s. duty on
Canadian timber and removing 10s. from the foreign impost.
Allowing for freight differentials, this would lower the real
preference to 30s. per load. Wallace heralded it as 'the first
step in receding from a system detrimental to our commercial
relations',[79] but to many it appeared as no more than a
'colonial job',[80] and certainly it was too slight a reform to
affect the disposition of the timber trade very seriously.
Baltic wood was preferred for most 'quality' purposes as it
had been, after an initial setback, even during the period of
high duties.

75. Canning to Huskisson, 8 Mar. 1821, HP 38742 ff. 187-97.
76. CSC, *First Report on the means of improving and maintaining the Foreign
Trade of the Country*, 1821.
77. Described in *Gentleman's Magazine*, new series xxxviii (1852), 637-8, as a
'superior merchant'.
78. Canada merchants Usborne, Bainbridge, and Stewart; North European traders
Tooke, Norman, Solly, Cowie, and Pelly; the shipowner Buckle; Canadian landlords; &c.
79. H. of C., 29 Mar. 1821, 2 PD, iv. 1501.
80. Lauderdale in H. of L., 22 May 1821, 2 PD, v. 882-3, 884-90.

Colonists offered a restrained defence of their preference, but on both sides the passion came from merchants, and especially from shipbuilders and owners. North European merchants engineered the famous London petition of 1820, while behind the scenes the Russia Company was frenetically memorializing the Privy Council.[81] Montrose and Leith likewise petitioned against the preference, but the other Scottish port of Grangemouth proffered rival petitions, one from its Baltic and the other from its Canadian merchants. Most commercial communities petitioned for the Canadas and against any alteration: Newcastle, Whitby, Hull, the Cumberland ports, Glasgow, Ayr, Kirkaldy, and Greenock. Liverpool merchants and shippers were mostly committed to the Atlantic trade, and in London the shipbuilders, the shipowners, Canada merchants, and foreign timber merchants each petitioned on its behalf. As a shipowner himself, Baring was present at their City Tavern Meeting of 16 May, where Buckle led the vociferous opposition to Tooke's London Merchant Petition (which Baring had presented) and the latter was forced to concede that he was more impressed than he had expected to be by the North American case.[82] The main parliamentary champion of colonial preference was Joseph Marryat, a vice-president of the Society of Shipowners, who castigated free trade as a formula 'to make rich countries poor, and poor countries rich',[83] He claimed that the colonies must be strengthened to protect them from predatory Yankees and to develop them as receptacles for British and Irish emigrants; and that as Canadians, unlike Europeans,[84] were forced to 'buy British' in British ships,

81. CSC, *First Report on the Foreign Trade of the Country*, 1821, Appendix 6, 171-2.
82. *The Times*, 17 May 1820.
83. H. of C., 29 Mar. 1821, 2 PD, iv. 1504. The debates of 1820-1 are excellently summarized in Smart, *Economic Annals of the Nineteenth Century, 1800-20*, 755-8 and Smart, *Economic Annals of the Nineteenth Century, 1821-30*, 24-33.
84. Norway was considered too poor to buy British manufactures in return for timber, and as she was also heavily indebted to England it was feared that she would use the timber trade merely to discharge her obligations. With Ricardian conviction, Lansdowne denied that this would signify, and averred that — whatever the immediate means of remittance might be — increased imports would always lead, before long, to increased exports. H. of L., 26 May 1820, 2 PD, i. 557.

they were entitled to their timber and corn preferences. (The latter was a dangerous argument for the shipping interest, since a desire to modify the preference might induce ministers to relax colonial restrictions on navigation.) The Baltic voyage being shorter, fewer ships would be required if the entire trade was transferred back to the North Sea, and British vessels would lose their monopoly under the stiff competition of cheaply freighted foreigners.[85] Tooke tried to console the doubters with the reflection that if British bottoms lost out, 'the freight to the foreigners must be paid by an exportation, direct or indirect, of some of our manufactures or productions.'[86] But the prospect of huge redundancies among sailors appalled ministers, and Marryat did not neglect to cite Adam Smith on the importance of defence over opulence and the need to maintain a large mercantile marine, trained in the broad and dangerous waters of the Atlantic. As Liverpool commented in another context, 'the great and favourite object of the policy of this country, for more than four centuries, has been to foster and encourage our navigation, as the sure basis of our maritime power'.[87] And so in fact the reform of 1821 was little more than a gesture of good will to foreigners and to David Ricardo.

Despite what Liverpool said about navigation, shipping was the interest most consistently hit by his commercial reforms. Marryat boasted of the number of ships employed in the Canada trade as a proof of its soundness and importance, but the Commons' Committee pointed out that many of these sailed at an enormous loss. Some weeding out was desirable, for excess shipping was not merely an evil in itself — it encouraged over-trading in commodities and was largely to blame for the general crisis of over-production. In particular, shipping was blamed for the great (but from the point of

85. British ships were then carrying most of the Russian trade (at a loss) but only about one-fifth of the Norwegian and Swedish. There was some doubt as to whether large 'Canadian' vessels could navigate Baltic waters.
86. CSC, *First Report on the Foreign Trade of the Country*, 1821, 58.
87. Liverpool's cabinet memorandum on the Spanish Colonies, 1824 in Yonge, op.cit. iii. 303. See Huskisson in H. of C., 12 May 1826, 2 PD, xv. 1144-89. The development of a professional navy was rapidly obviating the need to build up a commercial marine for war purposes. Williams, op. cit. 447.

view of profits, abortive) increase in the Canadian timber trade in 1818-19. Here a division appeared in the opinions of the colonial preference lobby. Shipowners usually ascribed this over-trading to the Canadian merchants' fears that they would shortly lose their legislative protection. The merchant John Bainbridge blamed the shippers, however, and suggested that a small 10s. duty on colonial timber (with nothing off the foreign tariff) would solve the problem 'because it would prevent the ships going out to the colonies without the intervention of a regular merchant'.[88] Among others, William Stewart, colonial timber merchant, complained that excess shipping had lowered freight rates and 'induced ship-owners to import on speculation'.[89] It was felt that since shipowners had to pay their apprentices anyway, they built and sailed ships even at a loss. 'The trade has been created by shipping, and the shipping has not been called for by the natural demand of the trade'.[90] Wallace himself announced that the enormous preference had over-stimulated colonial timber imports: 'The merchant who would regulate his proceedings by the real demand was thereby driven out of the market, and the trade was in consequence carried on by colonists and ship-owners.'[91] Here again, a move towards freer trade was conceived in terms of regulating and restraining rather than extending commerce.

Likewise Liverpool, denying that domestic consumption had insidiously declined,[92] attributed depression in the cotton trade to surplus navigation having overstocked the Indian market. Accordingly, Wallace's 1820 Committee

---

88. CSC, *First Report on the Foreign Trade of the Country,* 1821, 50. It would also encourage more discrimination with regard to quality in the importation of Canadian timber.

89. Ibid. 167.

90. Ibid. 140, 144, 46 &c. ' The ships have created the trade, and not the trade the ships.'

91. H. of C., 29 Mar. 1821, 2 PD, iv. 1502.

92. H. of L., 26 May 1820, 2 PD, i. 565-94. The shipowner Blanshard insisted that a trough in the cycle of consumption had at least prevented the usual 'cob web' type recovery: 'Within the last [six] months, the stagnation of trade in India has prevented freights from advancing in the manner expected from the reduced number of ships sent out.' CSC, *Report on the Foreign Trade of the Country,* 1820, 46.

recommended a significant modification of the shipowners' monopoly. The Restoration Navigation Code traditionally restricted the importation of European produce to ships from Britain and the producing country, and the importation of produce from the rest of the world to British ships only, travelling *directly* from the port of shipment to the United Kingdom. Faced by American, Prussian and Russian retaliation, successive governments had allowed certain exemptions (e.g. cottons), and in 1820 it was suggested that British ships should be permitted to load and introduce produce from any part of the world, irrespective of its place of growth or manufacture. In effect, non-British ships would become entitled to carry goods from (say) Asia as far as the Continent of Europe. Most merchants were well pleased by this proposal, but British shipowners complained that their higher freight rates would leave them with only the final instalment of importing cargoes across the Channel. Indian cargoes were mixed, the bulky goods (sugar, coffee, rice) destined for the Continent, the lighter, more valuable articles (cottons, indigo, dyewood, spices) bound for Britain. Most shippers diversified by carrying some of each type, and since the existing Navigation Laws forbade the importation to England of light goods via the Continent, England acted as entrepôt for the re-export of bulky goods to Europe, while English ships carried those goods over the long haul. If Wallace had his way, argued Buckle and Blanshard, Holland would take over much of this entrepôt trade, and 'we should lose the advantage of having London the emporium, which it is now.'[93]

Relying heavily on John Hall,[94] a London ship-broker and ex-merchant, Wallace's Committee concluded that these fears were groundless and that foreign ships would 'not habitually' displace British on the distant voyage, nor would circuitous trade often replace direct importation to England. An ingenious Committee member explained why he thought the light valuable goods would not be sent indirectly:

93. CSC, *Report on the Foreign Trade of the Country*, 1820, 43, 26-31.
94. Ibid. 49-60, 63-70; J. Hall, *Observations on the Warehousing System and Navigation Laws* (1821); J. R. McCulloch, 'Navigation Laws', *Edinburgh Review*, xxxviii (1823), 478-94.

Would not articles of great value and small bulk be precisely such as carriers, whose freight was cheaper, but inferior to our own, would be excluded from carrying; and would not the difference from the price of insurance, from the time taken for the voyage, the expenses of reshipment on the Continent, and the risk of trusting articles of value out of a merchant's own hands, be circumstances which would prevent such goods from coming indirectly?"[95] Since the valuable part of the cargo would come directly and the dross be sent circuitously, England would retain her entrepôt status. The reform would increase Euro-Asian trade and British shipping would share the benefits. Nevertheless, the possible threat of circuitous trade to British warehouses made it more than ever necessary to make British entrepôt more competitive by reducing harbour and other dues, and Wallace's Committee proceeded immediately to investigate these costs.

It is not true that this modicum of free trade passed without opposition,[96] though most of the dissent was expressed behind the scenes. Sheffield and George Chalmers attempted to raise a cry, and Buckle maintained relentless pressure. Wallace's 1821 proposal embodied an important concession to the shippers: Asian, African, and South American goods entering England after having been carried part-way in foreign bottoms, were to pay a discriminating duty, to prevent 'such importations from becoming an habitual trade'.[97] This was abandoned in 1822 in favour of a rule that such goods might enter from Europe for purposes of re-export only. It preserved Britain's transit trade, and it recognized that commerce had recovered while shipping had not; but it detracted greatly from the significance of the reform proposed in 1820, and it can hardly have signified as a gesture of reconciliation in the European war of retaliation. In 1823 unilateral gestures were abandoned for Huskisson's famous

95. CSC, *Report on the Foreign Trade of the Country*, 1820, 30. See Wallace in H. of C., 25 June 1821, 2 PD, v. 1289-99. There was much less opposition to the removal of restrictions on European trade, though John Nichol (Mediterranean merchant) and George Lyall (merchant shipper) feared that England might forfeit her monopoly of Levant trade and her entrepôt status between the Levant and Holland. CSC, *Report on the Foreign Trade of the Country*, 1820, 31-7.
96. Smart, *Economic Annals of the Nineteenth Century, 1821-30*, 101-6 — though this account is uncharacteristically inaccurate.
97. Wallace in H. of C., 25 June 1821, 2 PD, v. 1296.

Reciprocity of Duties Act, empowering the King in Council
to allow to the ships of any nation that would respond in
kind the privilege of transporting goods to the United
Kingdom on the same terms as British ships. This was the first
important violation of the Navigation Code.

Also behind Huskisson's relaxation of the Navigation Acts
was the wish to secure cheaper supplies from the United
States, to undo the consequences of the American Revolution,
and to re-establish the natural commerce between the United
States and the West India colonies. Liverpool's government
dealt lightly with, if it did not entirely exonerate, the East
India Company's monopoly of China trade, but the protecting
duty on West Indian sugar was then much more contentious,
as well as being complicated by non-commercial issues such
as slavery. To Ricardians the preference resembled the Corn
Laws, being a bounty granted to unsuitable West Indian land,
detrimental to consumers and to the comparatively advantageous lands of the East Indies. 'Interests are balanced',
ruminated Canning, 'and it must be decided one way or
other'.[98] John Gladstone, George Hibbert, Thomas Hodgson,
and Charles Ellis led a frightened but tenacious West India
lobby. East Indiamen claimed that several of their opponents
were also proprietors of East India Stock and could 'apply
their power, as such, against the interests of India to favour
the interests of the West Indies'.[99] Henry Goulburn was a
large and, like many others, fearfully indebted estate owner
in the West, and represented the protectionist case at the
centre of power. Reid and Whitmore were prominent in the
rival lobby, and Manchester, with its interest in the Indian
cotton market, took a contrary view to that of its commercial
neighbour. Led by G. W. Wood, the Manchester Chamber of
Commerce founded its case on the recent opening of the
West India colonies to some foreign trade, for which a
concession might be extorted on sugar, and on the continued
commercial restrictions placed on India. The discriminating
tariff was so heavy 'as entirely to prevent the use of the

98. Canning to Huskisson, 27 Dec. 1822, HP 38743 ff. 287-8.
99. Tucker to Huskisson, 27 Mar. 1823, HP 38744 ff. 179-88. See Hibbert to
Huskisson, 21 Mar. 1823, ibid. ff. 175-6.

coarser and medium [Indian] qualities, and to create frequent
and serious loss, even on the finest kinds'. This interdict in
turn prevented cotton merchants from 'obtaining return
investments exempt from loss'.[100] British sugar refiners also
claimed an interest in the question, since a bounty was granted
on the re-export of West Indian sugar that had been refined
in Britain, and Huskisson concurred with Hibberson, Chairman of Liverpool's East India Association, that it was 'rather
a question between the sugar refiners of Hamburg and
London than between the East and West India Interests'.[101]

Naturally Huskisson adjudicated in the most cautious
manner possible. The recent additional $5d$. duty should cease
and the remaining $10d$. should operate for the ten years that
were left of the East India Company's charter. This leniency
towards the West was necessary to enable it to make the
painful withdrawal, which must shortly be made, from
slavery. Indeed Charles Grant thought Huskisson's decision
too pragmatic — 'it goes to establish the Protection of the
West Ind^n monopoly as the *principle* and consequently any
relaxation as the exception. Whereas on all sound doctrine
— that monopoly should be the exception, and anti-monopoly
the principle — I do not know if I make myself intel-
ligible.'[102] Of course he did — but Huskisson was not much
concerned with sound doctrine. He knew that 'the country
will never be reconciled to the claim of a permanent monopoly', and in explaining this to Ellis he remarked significantly
on 'the necessity of gradually easing the W.I ^{ns}. from their
reliance on the perpetuity of the Protecting System. ...My own
conviction [is] that the boundary of monopoly is over-
production, which often makes it a curse instead of an

100. Manchester Chamber of Commerce MS. Proceedings, 2, 9 and 16 Apr.
1823, Volume I, pp. 154, 157-61, 163-4.
101. Hibberson to Huskisson, 17 May 1823 and Huskisson to Hibberson, 23 May
1823, HP 38744 ff. 218-22. A pro-West Indian memorandum of 1823 (HP 38761
ff. 95-100) argued: 'The effect then would be merely a transfer of the profit
from one class of home manufacturers to another. That is the superseding the
woollen manufactures, the staple of the Agriculture of the country, which are
largely exported to the West Indies, in favour of the cotton manufactures so
largely exported to the East Indies — and which in its raw state is not to any
great extent the produce of the colonies of Great Britain.'
102. Grant to Huskisson, 4 Apr. 1823, HP 38744 ff. 204-5; 206-9. C. H. Philips,
The East India Company, 1784-1834 (1940), 250.

advantage to those for whose benefit it is conferred (our Agriculturists for instance).'[103] Here again the key to government policy is to be found in the wish to eliminate unsound speculation and over-trading. This is why the Corn Laws, Navigation Laws and sugar monopoly were anomalies of more pressing importance than the East India Company's charter. *The boundary of monopoly was over-production.*[104]

As practical and gradual adjustments along traditional lines, Huskisson's tariff changes, unlike Canning's foreign policy and his own corn and currency measures, were generally approved in the cabinet. The diehards Eldon and Westmorland thought he moved too quickly even here, but Wellington, impatient of dogma, and the nation's 'protector against the political economists',[105] nevertheless regarded commercial reform in a mundane and favourable light: 'This I know, that this country was never governed in practice, according to the extreme principles of any party...[As to] liberal principles of commerce...[Huskisson] may have gone a little too far, or not far enough, in some cases; but this is very certain, that in principle he is right.'[106]

However, with the onset of depression in 1826 and ultratory violence against the government's economic policy generally, ministers were forced to defend their commercial reforms dogmatically, and 'free trade' was erected into a false symbol of the differences between traditionalists and the 'enthusiastick philosphers' of modernity. Political alliances were turned inside out by a chimera referred to as "Mr. Canning's system". In 1826 one part of the Whigs became 'His Majesty's Opposition' — for them 'Party there is none,

103. Huskisson to Ellis, 31 Mar. 1823, HP 38744 ff. 194-6. Ricardo in H. of C., 3 Apr. 1822, 2 PD, vi. 1448 'asked how the currency could be supposed to have affected [the West Indian cultivators]? Was it not notorious that their distress was entirely caused by over production?'
104. See the 18 Feb. 1823 memorandum on sugar in HP 38761 ff. 95-100 and 'Memorandum of an engagement agreed upon at Fife House on the 18th March 1823', ibid. ff. 103-4; also the memorandum in HP 38744 ff. 206-9 — 'is not the tendency of such a monopoly, overproduction? And is not this a parallel case to that of the Agriculturalist under the law of 1815?'
105. The phrase is Harriet Arbuthnot's, *Journal of Mrs Arbuthnot*, ii. 137.
106. Wellington, *Despatches, Correspondence, and Memoranda, 1819-31*, iv. 451-3 (20 May 1828).

and without it there can be nothing of what is called sport'[107] — while the most virulent abuse of government measures came from behind the Treasury Bench. 'The chief idol of the Tory party' was Lauderdale,[108] to whom Lansdowne and the Government seemed to be 'running a hard race who shall [?scratch] and [?dislimb] the country most',[109] while a Lansdowne-Canningite *rapprochement* grew every day more likely. In the countryside, the 1826 Election was virtually a plebiscite on 'Catholicism', but urban Tories often split acrimoniously over free trade.[110] Holland's verdict reflected a widespread contemporary opinion:

Elections in general are thought to have gone rather ill for government — not well for the Whigs, moderately for the Catholicks, but much in favor of that party, if party it be, which under various denominations of *monied men, commercial interests, radicals and political economists* seems in public opinion to be the ruling interest of the day.[111]

It was an incongruous grouping, but one that haunted the protectionist imagination. Wellington showed better insight, however, in discerning a horizontal division between rich and poor: 'Our Party consists of the Bishops & clergy, the Great Aristocracy, the landed Interest, the Magistracy of the Country, the great Merchants and Bankers, in short the *parti conservateur* of the Country.'[112]

107. Tierney to Holland, 23 Feb. 1826, HHP 51584 ff. 106-9.
108. Dudley to Helen Stewart, 21 Aug. 1827, *Letters to 'Ivy' from the First Earl of Dudley,* edited by S. H. Romilly (1905), 329; Colchester, *Diary and Correspondence,* iii. 363.
109. Lauderdale to Holland, 20 Feb. 1826, HHP 51692 ff. 145-7.
110. e.g. A. T. Patterson, *Radical Leicester, 1780-1850* (1954), 147-8.
111. Holland to Grey, 4 July 1826, HHP 51547 ff. 139-40.
112. Wellington to Mrs Arbuthnot, 20 Apr. 1827, *Wellington and His Friends,* edited by the seventh Duke of Wellington (1965), 74.

VII

THE PANIC AND ITS AFTERMATH
1825 − 6

What occasion was there for so much *secrecy* in the means which produced the *Distress*,...a literally *"hydrophobic"* dread of explanation or enquiry...among all Parties in Parliament?...If you can resolve this mystery, you will discover the cause which produced the death of Lord Londonderry, which has nearly produced that of Lord Liverpool, and which is *at this very moment*, cutting short the days of Mr Huskisson and Mr. Canning.

Thomas Attwood to Davenport, 26 July 1827, Davenport MSS., Attwood ff. 61-9.

The origins of a 'mental malady'

The events of the winter of 1825/6 mystified contemporaries. It was no longer possible to blame distress on transition to peace and loss of war-time demand, and there were no obvious explanations such as the war in 1793 and commercial uncertainty in 1719/20. Cyclical fluctuations in trade were familiar, but this was primarily a business depression resulting from the collapse of the capital market. Moreover the crash came abruptly, amid many visible signs of increasing real wealth and achievement. As late as September 1825, Canning saw only 'unexampled prosperity', and one pundit, admitting that 'absolute tests of full employment are difficult to obtain', lauded 1825 as a year 'when no honest man was without occupation'.[1] Essentially what happened to disturb this serenity was that two simultaneous booms − in foreign investment and in foreign trade − caused an external drain of specie from the Bank; while the collapse of those booms and resulting 'want of confidence', together with measures taken to mitigate the external drain, led to an internal drain as well.

The uncoordinated actions of government and Bank certainly precipitated the fatal booms in the first place.

1. [Daniel Hardcastle, jnr], *Banks and Bankers* (1842), 156; Canning to Plunket, 25 Sept. 1825, Stapleton, *George Canning and His Times*, 253.

Ministers had deliberately inflated in 1822 in order to revive 'dormant speculation'. The 'dead weight' annuity probably contributed significantly to expansion in 1823-5, years in which the Bank's holding of public securities increased by much more than its note issue. Twice ministers reduced interest on government securities, in 1822 and 1824, defying warnings from several Bank directors that it would throw too much capital on to the market.[2] Liverpool even considered covering expenditure in 1824 with an issue of exchequer bills, since these were bearing a high premium, and 'the general impression certainly is, that except for the Risk of War, some increase of our Unfunded Debt, would be advantageous to Commerce and Circulation.'[3] The extension of small notes[4] (which was to be the favourite scapegoat in 1826) was not inherently inflationary, but since the Bank had already collected the gold for paying them off, their sudden reprieve left it abnormally liquid. Finding themselves with a cash ratio of over 40 per cent, the directors also inflated by issuing £1,500,000 at 4 per cent on mortgages.[5] Though they did this 'entirely of their own free will, and without any suggestion or expression of a wish on the part of government',[6] ministers applauded the decision because it would benefit agriculture, and because it 'must ultimately help us in the reduction of the interest of the funded debt'.[7] Thus one inflationary measure was welcomed as facilitating another. The directors insisted that the experiment had only

2. Manning in H. of C., 23 Feb. 1826, 2 PD, xiv. 722-3; Palmer and Ward to CSC, *Report from the Committee of Secrecy on the expediency of renewing the Bank of England Charter*, 1832, QQ. 606, 1895-6; J. K. Horsefield, 'The Opinions of Horsley Palmer', *Economica*, new series, xvi (1949), 143-58.
3. Liverpool to Herries, 7 Nov. 1823, Herries MSS. 57367.
4. See above, pp. 159-61. I. Bowen, 'Country Banking, the note issues and banking controversies in 1825', *Economic Journal, History Supplement*, iii (1938), 68-88; J. K. Horsefield, 'The Bank and its Treasure', *Economica*, new series, vii (1940), 161-78, and Ashton and Sayers, *Papers in English Monetary History*, 50-65.
5. Clapham, *The Bank of England*, ii. 82-3.
6. Peel to Goulburn, 12 Nov. 1823, Goulburn MSS. II/14.
7. Herries to Liverpool, 11 Oct. 1823, LP 38297 ff. 54-5. See Liverpool to Herries, 11 Oct. 1823, Herries MSS. 57367; Robinson to Herries, 12 Oct. 1823, ibid. 57418 f. 68. Canning had toyed with a plan to advance money from the sinking fund for paying off mortgages contracted during the depreciation, LP 38291 ff. 384-94, 408-9; Canning to Liverpool, 21 Jan. 1823, CP 70.

involved a portion of their surplus profits, and had not raised the circulation at all,[8] but meanwhile they lent to the East India Company and stepped up their private discounting. Both government and Bank may have been justified in inflating, in view of the previous contraction, but they worked jealously apart, and together they over-stimulated a reviving economy.

Policies provided the opportunity for expansion; the country banks constituted a flexible capital market for turning facilities into facts. With the Bank of England accepting bills at longer dates, private bankers expanded their circulations. Later the Bank Court, the cabinet and many commentators held them chiefly responsible for the mania. They themselves retorted that the Bank had over-issued, and that 'necessarily the Country Bankers partook of that excess'.[9] They were probably right to see themselves as instruments rather than agents of speculation. But they competed irresponsibly for business, and many were personally too involved in the projects that they financed to assess their validity impartially.[10] Moreover, as the Bank of England's accommodation to industry was mainly through private banks rather than by direct discounting, its determination to accept only 'real bills', representing legitimate business, could seldom be applied.

The reduction of interest on government debt, and a shortage of opportunities for domestic investment in the period between the canal and railway building eras,[11] fortuitously deflected all this extra capital into foreign loans and joint-stock ventures overseas. (624 companies were

8. CSC, *Report on renewing the Bank of England Charter*, 1832, QQ. 1916-19, 1924, 1962-7, 2379-81.
9. Stuckey to CSC, ibid., Q. 1208; Beckett, Samuel Gurney and Harman to CSC, ibid., QQ. 1410-11, 3745, 2330.
10. Gladstone to LSC, *Report on the Circulation of Promissory Notes under the value of five pounds in Scotland and Ireland*, 1827, 143-4.
11. J. A. Cope, 'The British Economy in the Trade Cycle, 1820-30', University of Oxford unpublished B. Litt. thesis (1959), 251; but see Bowen, op. cit. 71-2.

formed with a capital of £372,000,000 in 1824).[12] Huskisson early predicted that the enormous number of foreign loans being contracted in London, for Europe and increasingly for Latin America, would 'turn out the most tremendous Bubble ever known'.[13] Liverpool warned Rothschild of a 'complication of Interests Political and Commercial as well as Financial', likely to arise from what Canning called the 'Jew loans' to South America, but despite Rothschild's assurances that neither he nor Baring would touch any such projects, between them they serviced £3,000,000 for Brazil and Buenos Aires in 1824-5.[14] Ministers dreaded that foreign loans would deprive Britain of money that she would need in wet seasons to purchase foreign food; yet ironically — and quite unintentionally — the loans to northern Europe were to facilitate the sudden, extraordinary purchases of 1828-31, 1839-40, and 1847, by creating readily negotiable assets in corn-growing areas that had no great marginal demand for British manufactures.[15] But though they did not welcome or approve of capital efflux, ministers probably encouraged it. The repeal of the Bubble Act in 1825 did nothing to inhibit the joint-stock boom, and dissentients like Wellington blamed Canning's policy of *recognition* for the storm of investment in South American mining companies.[16] Import speculation also revived in 1825, and Harman, Rothschild and the City merchants, and Wellington and Westmorland among ministers, complained that this was an artificial development caused by Huskisson's and Robinson's tariff reductions. In fact, though

12. H. English, *A Complete View of the Joint-Stock Companies formed during the years 1824-5* (1827); J. W. Gilbart, *The History, Principles and Practice of Banking*, edited by A. S. Michie, re-edited by E. Sykes (1922), i. 64; C. Fenn, *A Compendium of the English and Foreign Funds, and the principal Joint-Stock Companies* (1837), 59-61, 77-8, 88; Cope, op.cit. 252-6; C. K. Hobson, *The Export of Capital* (1914), 101; L. H. Jenks, *The Migration of British Capital to 1875* (1927), 40-64. The total projected amount of these loans was £52,994, 571 in 1818-25, and £50,544,571 in 1824-5 alone.
13. Fetter, *Development of British Monetary Orthodoxy*, 111-12.
14. Canning to Liverpool, 13 Dec. 1823; Liverpool to Canning, 14 and 25 Dec. 1823, CP 70.
15. Jenks, op. cit. 61-2 and nn. 57-8.
16. B. C. Hunt, *The Development of the Business Corporation in England 1800-67* (1936), 30-55; Palmer to CSC, *Report on renewing the Bank of England Charter*, 1832, Q. 606.

the warehousing and navigation policies may have contributed, a genuine running down of import stocks during 1824
was the main cause of this revival, and the tariff reforms
hardly affected the economy until after 1825.[17]

The years 1823-5 saw an ever-increasing facility of accommodation, falling interest rates, and a mounting circulation of
bills with little security. Despite some efflux of gold, the
exchanges were still at par in August 1824, at which point
the Bank suddenly stepped up its note issues. Huskisson,
Liverpool, and (most savagely) Tooke criticized it for inflating
when it should have done just the opposite. 'The Bank had
not kindled the fire, but, instead of attempting to stop the
progress of the flames, it supplied fuel for maintaining and
extending the conflagration.'[18] As the Bank's specie reserve
had increased by more than the circulation in 1822-4, the
directors claimed that, except in the first quarter of 1825 (by
which time the speculative mania was already uncontrollable),
they had not augmented their issues except on gold, like
good bullionists. They had expanded the circulation so as to
reduce the reserve to about one-third of their liabilities.
Anyway 'the gold would have circulated as coin, if notes had
not been issued upon it.'[19] In 1819 the government had
deprecated discretionary activity by the Bank, yet now
expected precisely such control. Unfortunately, the Bank's
circulation was too small in 1824 for much deflationary
manoeuvre — small that is in relation to its own reserve,
though, considering the extended country bank issues, it may
be that it was much too large. There was, in any case, no
tradition of central bank action to correct the vagaries of
private practice.[20]

17. Cope, op. cit. 59.
18. Tooke and Newmarch, *A History of Prices*, ii. 178-9; Gayer, Rostow and
Schwartz, *Growth and Fluctuation of the British Economy* , i. 206-7. The
opinions of Tooke and Huskisson on monetary matters were very close at this
time; Huskisson to Tooke, 8 Dec. 1825, HP 38747 ff. 143-4.
19. Norman to CSC, *Report on renewing the Bank of England Charter*, 1832,
QQ. 2558, 2550-2. The Bank's circulation rose from £17,700,000 on 3 Jan.
1822 to £19,300,000 on 1 Apr. 1824, while bullion stocks rose by £2,100,000.
20. Cope, op. cit. 243. In December 1824 and March 1825 the Bank sold
exchequer bills in a belated attempt to contract, and at the same time increased
its discounting to soften the pressure. Pressnell, *Country Banking in the Industrial
Revolution*, 482.

The panic

Cope estimates that September 1824 marks the point where
expansion became speculation.[21] Share prices shot up to a
peak in January 1825. But as depressing reports came home
of the performance of South American ventures, mining
shares plunged as rapidly, creating pressure on liquidity. This
was intensified in the spring as a glut in the American market
precipitated the collapse of the commodity boom.[22] Canning
insisted that the King's Speech in February should optimisti-
cally extol the prosperity and contentment that were diffused
through the nation.[23] But ministers sensed the cool change.
On 25 March Liverpool warned the public that speculation
was travelling 'beyond all bounds', and that when the
inevitable convulsion came, the government would on no
account rescue those who had gambled their ways to debt.
Making the same point a month later, Huskisson called on
country bankers to withhold advances from adventurers, and
on the Bank directors, who 'to a certain degree, were the
controllers of the currency, to watch with care and diligence
over the foreign exchanges'.[24] His statement may have
occasioned the first flutter, two days later, when consols fell
drastically to 91½,[25] and a group of directors retaliated by
warning Liverpool that unless he raised tariffs and restored
the balance of trade, the drain of gold would continue. By
May Huskisson was playing down the fall of the exchanges
and prophesying a speedy recovery;[26] Harman subsequently
criticized his 'florid picture' for having deadened the impact
of his earlier timely warning.[27] But the intention behind
Huskisson's change of attitude is obvious. While intimations
of disaster had been distant, it was correct to try to frighten
businessmen into a preventive caution; but once the first
drum beat had sounded in the market, it was surely wise to

21. Cope, op. cit. 258; Gayer *et al.*, op. cit. i. 184.
22. Gayer *et al.*, i. 175-7, 182-5; H. G. Macleod, *The Theory and Practice of
Banking* (1855), ii. 244-5; Tooke and Newmarch, op.cit. ii. 147-59.
23. 2 PD, xii, 1; Canning to Liverpool, 30 Jan. 1825, copy CP 71.
24. H. of L., 25 Mar. 1825, 2 PD, xii. 1194-5; H. of C., 28 Apr. 1825, 2 PD, xiii.
288.
25. *The Times*, 2 May 1825.
26. H. of C., 2 May 1825, 2 PD, xiii. 348.
27. CSC, *Report on renewing the Bank of England Charter*, 1832, Q. 2359.

try to stay the panic by brave music and reassuring words. Huskisson was attempting desperately to prevent an internal drain from reinforcing the emigration of specie.

That summer a series of incidents occurred involving country banks, the most notorious being at Bristol. September was a month of fevered rumours and some failures. The Bank was faced with 'the dilemma, of either continuing to discount, at the hazard of stopping itself; or of refusing to discount, and stopping the whole country'.[28] Choosing to protect their own reserves and leave the market to its fate, the directors sold almost £1,000,000 of exchequer bills, and rejected many bills drawn on Britain from Europe, as a result of mercantile 'wool gathering' and warehoused corn imports. The directors insisted under criticism that this was a 'forcible contraction' — effected by the public, not themselves — a response to the efflux of gold, just as the 1823-4 inflation had been in response to a growing reserve — and prompted by a consistent desire for a cash-ratio of one-third.[29] Huskisson and Liverpool certainly approved of the contraction — indeed they thought it long overdue, since specie loss combined with unfavourable exchange rates had indicated deflation somewhat earlier.[30] Huskisson was furious at the delay and believed 'that the Bank, in its greedy folly, was playing over again the game of 1817, and that in their consequences, the inordinate speculations, commercial and pecuniary, to which that game gave rise, would lead either to a second stoppage, or a serious revulsion, affecting public and private credit; and by its results the prosperity of our industrious classes'.[31] Huskisson's attitude to the Bank was contradictory. It was to manage its own concerns without expecting government

28. Hudson Gurney in H. of C., 27 June 1825, 2 PD, xiii. 1386.
29. Ward and Norman to CSC, *Report on renewing the Bank of England Charter,* 1832, QQ. 2051, 2552.
30. Ministers had only *in*flated in 1824 because the exchanges were favourable, and because the specie loss at that time was due to special payments (foreign loans), which could come from the Bank's vaults.
31. Huskisson to Canning, 4 Sept. 1825, HP 38747 ff. 76-80, Stapleton, *George Canning and His Times,* 225-7; Liverpool to [?], 3 Sept. 1825 and Liverpool to Lushington, 26 Nov. 1825, LP 38300 f. 172 and 38301 ff. 43-4; Liverpool to Bexley, 24 Nov. 1825, Vansittart MSS. 31232 ff. 343-4, Yonge, *Life and Administration of Lord Liverpool,* iii. 355.

help in a crisis, but was expected to curtail its profits in the national interest. Only Parliament had a right to discretion over monetary policy, but Parliament would not take the responsibility of interfering in the Bank's management. Finally, the directors were to let the circulation adapt strictly to the exchanges, while exercising contra-cyclical credit control at home.

There was a fundamental misunderstanding between government and Bank in September 1825. Liverpool and Huskisson thought the directors should guard against an external but not an internal drain, and they demanded deflationary action as an automatic response to the former. But when the Bank deflated in September, it was rather because an *internal* drain was threatening its reserves. Apparently, neither realized that to deflate at that moment would fatally accentuate the internal drain by fanning the alarm and pressing harder on liquidity. Just as money was becoming scarce and dear, the Bank sold securities and made it scarcer still.[32] Ministers were aware that a tightening policy would entail bankruptcies, but dismissed these as the just deserts of the improvident. As in 1819, they drew a rigid line between sound and rotten business, and did not perceive that the speculative disease had tainted so large a part of the business world that lack of confidence could escalate and ravage the solvency of the most innocent and fundamentally credit-worthy concerns. In their eyes, anyone who failed must *ipso facto* be a charlatan. Besides, in a crisis of over-production, a few salutary, exemplary failures would eliminate excess and bring 'ultimate good after some severe suffering'.[33] They did not realize that they were facing a new type of problem, and were confident that if only Canning kept the peace (which he did) and the crops were full (which they were), the crisis would pass naturally.[34] All that was needed was a touch of the deflationary, contra-

32. Ministers would have preferred the Bank to raise its discount rate. R. C. O. Matthews, *A Study in Trade-Cycle History. Economic Fluctuations in Great Britain 1833-42* (1954), 174.
33. Peel to Littleton, 23 Dec. 1825, Hatherton MSS. D260/M/F/5/27/2/110; Parker, *Sir Robert Peel,* i. 382-3.
34. Huskisson to Granville, 26 Apr. 1825, Granville MSS. 30/29/9/3 (No. 13) ff.

cyclical brake, in the same way that three years before a twist
of the throttle had overcome depression. The personal
distress involved in bankruptcies might create political
difficulties, but this was less important to government than
the need for specie and credit in times of war and famine.
Even as late as December 1825, ministers remained 'stone
blind, sand blind and gravel blind'[35] to the fact that the state
of the monetary system was itself threatening a fearful
dislocation, every bit as dangerous for their system of
government and the fabric of society as those great bogeys,
dearth and war.

Contraction by the Bank increased the pressure on private
banks clamouring for re-discount facilities. A rapid succession
of failures commenced in October, some of the most notable
being in the West Country, Lancashire and Yorkshire. Yet
until 12 December the Bank ignored ministerial pressure to
raise its discount rate to the 5 per cent maximum, preferring
to market more securities and to refuse accommodation outright. The Bank selected certain very large firms to refuse
accommodation to, including Barings and even Rothschild, in
the hope that since these houses were above suspicion, their
rejection by the Bank could hardly stigmatise them or frighten
their dependents. But in fact, repudiation of even these giants
probably spread the panic faster.[36]

Policy disputes in 1825

A coterie inside government circles, in close touch with the
foremost City financiers, had for some time been opposing
Huskissonian policies. The conflict was about power as much
as economic policy. Since 1819 Huskisson and Canning had
had policy-making more and more their own way, but knew
that their prestige was as vulnerable as the commercial upswing, and that certain colleagues — the peers especially —
would 'gladly seize upon any interruption (should any occur)
either to our political or our commercial prosperity, to
throw the blame of it on our Heads'.[37] The nucleus of
opposition to them was the Treasury, which (with the Bank)

35. T. Doubleday, *A Financial, Monetary and Statistical History of England
(1847)*, 280.
36. *The Times*. 26 Nov. 1825.
37. Huskisson to Granville, 26 Apr. 1825.

was the last institution to accept the tenets of classical economic policy in the nineteenth century, as it was the last to discard them in the twentieth. The organizer of discontent was the former political secretary at the Treasury, Arbuthnot, and its expertise came from his friends, the current joint-secretaries Herries and S. R. Lushington. Arbuthnot cordially detested the 'liberal tories', and kept up a rather effeminate, rarely effectual strain of intrigue. Herries, of course, was the intimate of Rothschild. They all resented the dominance of Huskisson and bullionism, but they were not indiscriminate inflationists. Herries stood out against Huskisson's extension of small notes in 1822, preferring to relieve debtors by a depreciation of the standard,[38] and other members of the group — Beeke, Spearman, and Bexley — also opposed that extension. Bexley, the former Chancellor of the Exchequer, blamed the 'multitude of collateral *bubbles*' on three 'liberal' policies: the abandonment of his own system of contracting annual loans, thereby freeing large amounts of capital; recognition of the South American states which had tempted the capital abroad; and 'the measures of Government in repealing prohibitions, and giving facilities to commerce', which, 'however judicious in themselves, had a direct tendency to promote the spirit of speculation.'[39]

Liverpool being lost to the Canningites, the dissenters bid hard for Wellington. Arbuthnot warned him in April that

Huskisson is one of the most dangerous men that ever was admitted into our councils. His hasty & sudden innovations in trade are sending all the gold out of the country; for in consequence of the reductions of duties, we are making everywhere extensive purchases, while not being met with equal liberality in any part of the Continent, our goods are not admitted in foreign ports on better terms than they were. The consequence is that trade is turning against us, & we are obliged to pay in gold. With all his liberalism in the H. of Cs., Baring is aware of this effect, & he is predicting gt. distress from diminished & diminishing circulation.[40]

A week later Herries reported that Huskisson's 'indecent

38. See above, pp. 160-61.
39. Bexley's memorandum, 11 Jan. 1826, LP 38371 ff. 83-93, Yonge, op. cit. iii. 358-61.
40. Arbuthnot to Wellington, 25 Apr. 1825, Aspinall, *Correspondence of Charles Arbuthnot*, 74.

presumption' had alarmed Rothschild and almost all the City merchants, since unilateral and unreciprocated free trade would drain the nation of specie. Lushington was sent off to sound out Robinson, and to urge him to 'stop [Huskisson] in his career', before he bankrupted everyone.[41] They soon discovered Robinson's impotence. Mrs. Arbuthnot was furious that the President of the Board of Trade felt fit to act without even consulting the cipher of the Exchequer: 'The arrangements of the trade of the country ought to be subordinate to the Finances and always have been hitherto, but Mr. Huskisson has quite emancipated himself from all such control and a pretty mess he has made!'[42]

Possibly these backroom rebels were associated with the 'cottage coterie' or *ultraciste* cabal directed against Canning's foreign policy.[43] The highest common factor was Rothschild, who opposed recognition of Latin America on both diplomatic and economic grounds. Politicians often regarded the policy of recognition as a bid to capture the commerce of the prospective republics, but Rothschild and several City merchants argued that it would in fact deprive Britain of a valuable bargaining counter, and that she should keep the promise of recognition constantly hanging over the Spanish colonies. *Maison Rothschild* was also 'la Haute Trésorerie de la Sainte Alliance',[44] and the opponents of Huskisson's economic and commercial policies – Wellington, Harrowby, Westmorland, Bexley, Herries – also stood for contacts with Metternich and the neo-Holy Alliance. 'Free trade' was, in part, an attempt to make the economy truly self-regulating and to rescue government from the strangling continental grasp of the financiers. Later on, of course, free trade came to be regarded as the paradigm of the 'international man' – of the cosmopolitan merchant, who promoted wealth but cared not where its bounty might be enjoyed; yet its origins were in nationalism and also (in a sense) in mercantilism.

The first serious policy clash between Huskisson and the rebels came in September 1825. It must be remembered that

41. *Journal of Mrs Arbuthnot*, i. 390-2.
42. Ibid. ii. 20.
43. H. W. V. Temperley, *The Foreign Policy of Canning, 1822-7* (1925), 240-54.
44. B. H. R. Capefigue, *Histoire des grandes operations financieres* (1856-60), iii. 103.

the government was even more anxious about its own solvency than the Bank's. By early September, exchequer bills were at a serious discount, and there was a real danger that, when the quarter-day came, many holders might wish not to renew but to cash them in. Liverpool was firm that a policy of dearer money was the only legitimate remedy, both for the general economic malaise and for making government securities more attractive to the public:

To meet however the embarrassments in which we may be shortly placed, I see no Remedy, but the Raising the Interest on Exch^r Bills. It is the Plain obvious and I may add *honest* Remedy. The interest on Exchequer Bills must be governed by the State of the Funds. If it is right to lower it when the funds have risen, it must be equally right to increase it when from any circumstances the Funds undergo a considerable, and as far as appearances warrant, an uncertain Depreciation. I see no objection to this but that it may add to the alarm, and in a small degree increase our estimates next year.[45]

Though in theory the floating debt provided ministers with a lever for influencing the general state of the money market, in practice the fear of a run on the Exchequer rendered use of this lever completely inflexible. So yet another deflationary brake was applied at an internally inopportune moment.

Liverpool deprecated any 'artificial contrivance, to augment the circulation and keep up the Funds'.[46] Now Bexley was (with his Treasury friends) the doyen of artificial contrivances, and he and Herries pressed for *inflationary* policies in September. Herries urged Robinson to raise the money that might be required to pay off exchequer bills, by borrowing from the Bank and funding private bills; or, better still, to prevent the bills' return by persuading the Bank or some individual financier — and there is no doubt as to who was in Herries's mind — to buy exchequer bills on the market and so keep them at a premium. At all events they should not deflate, by raising interest on the unfunded debt, in a season of narrowing accommodation. A 'rather fidgetty' Robinson scouted these suggestions, insisting that 'raising of the Interest would be the most legitimate mode of doing the

45. Liverpool to [?], 3 Sept. 1825, LP 38300 f. 172.
46. Ibid.

thing'.[47] He went so far as to add that if a limited number
of exchequer bills were cashed in it would be beneficial 'as
tending to diminish the general amount of bills in circulation,
and thereby to diminish the chance of being inconveniently
run upon hereafter'.[48] Here is concern for public solvency
and a complete blindness to Herries's anxieties over the
economy. As it happened, not many holders did present their
bills, but the problem of the floating debt was soon to recur.

Throughout September, October, and November, the
'common cant of the City', whose main spokesman was
Rothschild, was all for liberal discounting and for gearing the
circulation — not to the exchanges — but to the business
cycle, which just then was full. Thomas Attwood circularized
the London bankers to find support for a cheap money
campaign, and a protectionist *City Bulletin* was issued,
containing the oxymoronic lament that 'the scarcity of
money diffuses itself from the fountain head over the whole
community.' Huskisson thought that this, and the anonymous
letters sent to the cabinet ministers, were part of a move by
Rothschild to force suspension, and commented sardonically,
'I know of no one who would more rejoice at another Bank
Restriction. It would be the Messiah of the Jews. I hope it
will be as long in coming as any other Messiah they may have
hitherto been looking for.'[49] 'Rothschild has been involved
in all Villèle's ill-judged speculations', wrote Liverpool,
'and he is looking to extricate himself'.[50] Both ministers

47. Robinson to Herries, 16 Sept. 1825, Herries MSS. 57402.
48. Robinson to Herries, 18 Sept. 1825, Herries MSS. See Herries's interesting
letter to Peel, 10 Feb. 1835, Herries MSS., on how the problem of the exchequer
bills, and the delay in advertising them, contributed to the panic of 1825: 'The
enormous danger that *may* arise under this System was exemplified...in 1825.
...The Shock of Public Credit which produced such terrible results on that occasion
was increased by the course which the Treasury was compelled to adopt with
respect to the Exchequer Bills.'
49. Huskisson to Canning, 16 Nov. 1825, CP 68; Canning to Liverpool, 17 Nov.
1825, CP 71; Attwood's 'Resolutions for the Bankers of London', Wakefield,
Life of Thomas Attwood, 101-2; Huskisson to Hume, 9 Sept. 1825, HP 38747 f.
98.
50. Liverpool to Lushington, 26 Nov. 1825, LP 38301 ff. 43-4, referring to
Charles X's reduction of interest on the French National Debt in order to
compensate *émigrés*. This transaction entailed losses for the Paris Rothschild,
James. E. C. Corti, *The Rise of the House of Rothschild* (1928), 337-41, 350-3.

persisted in the belief that — in the words of an approved editorial — specie loss showed that 'we have been over-crammed with circulating medium, and ought to have less of it amongst us'. The cheapness of gold as compared with its value abroad proved that there was 'more than the *real* wants of society call for', and the selfish, dangerous, and speculative wants of voluble businessmen must be ignored. Facilities might postpone the reckoning, but 'If any crash is to come, the sooner it arrives the less terrible will be the ruin.'[51] In other words, governments should not accommodate the circulation to the domestic business cycle, as Attwood, Rothschild, and Herries were urging, but should endeavour to *prevent* excessive movements of that cycle. Steady exchanges would do what 'real bills' banking could not do — separate the sheep of enterprise from the goats of speculation.

The crash

The final crisis came on 12 December when Pole, Thornton & Co. of London fell, bringing down forty-three correspondent country banks. Pressnell explains this timing by 'an old weakness' — the need for the country banks to remit taxes to the government *before* the quarterly dividends on the funds could be paid.[52] Robinson 'funked' in adversity, earning the City's 'utmost contempt', but Huskisson stood 'firm, manly, and consistent'[53] — some said stubborn. Liverpool, Canning, Huskisson, Wellington, the Bank governors Buller and Richards, and the financiers Rothschild, Baring, and Irving, held hourly and angry consultations during the following panic-stricken week. Now ministers urged inflationary measures on the Bank — issue of exchequer bills, expansion of discounts and, for the first time since 1821, circulation of £1 notes. Fearful for his reserves, Buller demanded in return an authorization for suspension in case

51. *The Times*, 23 Nov. 1825.
52. Pressnell, op. cit. 477-500, especially 485. For full general narratives, see Macleod, op.cit. ii. 241-53; Tooke and Newmarch, op. cit. ii. 160-71; Clapham, *The Bank of England*, ii. 97-102; J. Francis, *History of the Bank of England, its times and traditions* (1847), ii. 1-26; Fetter, *Development of British Monetary Orthodoxy*, 111-18.
53. H. U. Addington to Vaughan, 2 Mar. 1826, Vaughan MSS. C.2.

the Bank ran dry, which ministers steadfastly refused.
Huskisson and Canning thought the Bank had devoutly
wished for this consummation all along. Canning told his
secretary that

It was quite obvious that the object of most of the old school of Bank
directors, was to force the Government to sanction a suspension of cash
payments, and therefore that they took no measures to provide for
such a crisis as the present, which they probably foresaw, thinking the
Government would held them. That such fools as ——— [? Harman]
had always been against Peel's Bill, but that if the Government once
sanctioned another suspension of cash payments we should never have
a tolerable currency again.[54]

Huskisson would never sanction a formal suspension, and
suggested instead that the Bank should, *in extremis,* pin a
notice to its door, promising to pay as soon as gold came in.
As Richards complained, 'the advice was given by Government and the responsibility would have fallen upon the
Bank.'[55] Restriction was almost conceded at a dramatic five-
hour cabinet meeting on the evening of Friday the 16th, Peel
having assembled troops to defend Threadneedle Street,[56]
but Canning and Huskisson just managed to beat off Wellington, who reluctantly advocated suspension. That night
Rothschild procured £300,000 gold for the Bank — Paris sent
£400,000 on the 19th — soon after it began to 'pour in from
all quarters' — and the crisis was over.[57]

The recovery owed much to the Bank's heroism in
financing the crisis at risk to itself at a time when country
paper had lost credibility. On the 16th it agreed to buy
exchequer bills, issue small notes and extend discounts.[58] Its
notes 'were received with acclamation, almost',[59] and its

54. Stapleton's memorandum, 27 Dec. 1825, Stapleton, op. cit. 227.
55. CSC, *Report on renewing the Bank of England Charter,* 1832, QQ. 5031-59,
2219-32.
56. See Peel's correspondence with Taylor, Henry Hobhouse, and Buller in Peel
MSS. 40384 ff. 16, 40-2.
57. Stapleton's memorandum mistakenly gives Monday the 26th as the date of
the crucial cabinet meeting; elsewhere he agreed with other authorities in assigning
it to a Friday. A. G. Stapleton, 'The Greville Journals', *Macmillan's Magazine,* xxxi
(1874-5), 156-7.
58. Peel to his father, 16 Dec. 1825, Peel MSS. 40384 ff. 10-11; Parker, op. cit.
i. 381.
59. Harman to CSC, *Report on renewing the Bank of England Charter,* 1832,
QQ. 2269, 2232, 2217.

circulation rose from £18,037,960 to £25,611,800 between
the 10th and the 24th.[60] A meeting of City merchants at
Mansion House, where Thomas Wilson carried resolutions
pledging those assembled to exercise mutual trust and
confidence, contributed to the recovery.[61] There was no
mutual confidence in government circles, however, for the
rebels were staging an open confrontation. They had captured
Wellington, who consulted Rothschild and commented later
that 'had it not been for most extraordinary exertions — above
all on the part of old Rothschild — the Bank must have
stopped payment.'[62] He defended the directors, and blamed
the crisis entirely on Huskisson's 'false policy' of 'encouraging foreign speculations & allowing the country banks to
inundate every district with one & two pound notes'.[63]

There has been some argument as to 'whether the Bank,
the Government, Attwood, Joplin, or Stuckey deserves the
credit'[64] for the dramatic turnabout in policy that led to the
Bank's acting in support of the market by increased issues
and credit after the 12th. Peel kept his colleagues informed
of provincial events and opinions, and from the Midlands
Calthorpe, Spooner, Attwood, and Peel's father begged for
monetary relaxation.[65] On the 16th and 17th Attwood met
the directors — at the cabinet's suggestion — but could not
persuade those 'timid and indecisive' men to discount
'irregular paper'. He also urged the issue of £1 notes.[66] But
evidently ministers were only interested in what he had to
say about the local situation, and would not even parley with
him on national policy. Another to claim credit for having
recommended liberal discounting was Vincent Stuckey,
formerly Huskisson's private secretary at the Treasury, now

60. Fetter, op. cit. 113-14.
61. *The Times,* 15 and 16 Dec. 1825.
62. Stanhope, *Conversations with the Duke of Wellington,* 22 Sept. 1839. 158-9;
Corti, op. cit. 349-50. See below, p. 236, for Huskisson's irritation at the important part played by Rothschild in 1825-6.
63. *Journal of Mrs Arbuthnot,*i. 426-9.
64. Fetter, op. cit. 116.
65. For this correspondence see Peel MSS. 40384, ff. 4-11, 67, 165 &c.
66. Attwood to Peel, 16 Dec. 1825, Peel MSS. 40384 f. 8; Attwood to his wife,
17 Dec. 1825, Wakefield, op. cit. 99.

a country banker and landowner who was described contemptuously by Beeke as 'a Philospher $K\varphi T' \epsilon\xi o\chi\eta\nu$ of the new school' who 'swears by Mr. Huskisson'.[67] Another claimant was Thomas Joplin in *The Courier*.[68] Later some directors demanded praise for having acted entirely of their own accord, but in fact, as Fetter shows, they had had to be goaded towards their central banking destiny.[69] The relevant point here is that whoever actually instigated the inflationary measures, the bullionist ministers — Liverpool, Canning, Huskisson, Peel, and Robinson — supported them vigorously.[70]

Why did these ministers 'about-turn', and recommend support of the market even to the point of risking the reserve? First, their advice to expand followed from a mechanical application of bullionist theory, the exchanges having turned back in favour. September's deflation, while it intensified internal panic, had succeeded externally (though no doubt the panic itself contributed to the up-turn). Canning told Stapleton that the loss of reserve was quite different from the drain of 1797, in that it was merely internal and there was now a rapid influx of gold. They had only to surmount the next few days and, as Peel said, 'keep the exchanges at least not unfavourable'.[71] Thus, in proposing expansion, ministers were hoping not — like Attwood, Rothschild, and Herries — to adjust the circulation to internal engagements and the domestic demand for money, but rather to achieve external balance. To ministers, the real hero of the recovery was September's deflation, working just in time, and not the Bank's lending in the last resort in December, which was only

67. Beeke to Bexley, 30 Aug. 1826, Vansittart MSS. 31232 ff. 354-7; CSC, *Report on renewing the Bank of England Charter*, 1832, Q. 5012.
68. *Courier*, 13 Dec. 1825; T. Joplin, *An Examination of the Report of the Joint Stock Bank Committee*, second edition (1837), 63-98; T. E. Gregory, *The Westminster Bank through a Century* (1936), ii. 149-50.
69. CSC, *Report on renewing the Bank of England Charter*, 1832, QQ. 602-5.
70. Peel to his father, 16 Dec. 1825. Cabinet minute, 15 Dec. 1825, Peel MSS. 38371 ff. 77-8.
71. Peel to Littleton, 23 Dec. 1825, Hatherton MSS. D260/M/F/5/27/2/110, Parker, op. cit. i. 382-3.

possible because September's deflation had succeeded.[72]
There was another, neglected reason for the switch to an
inflationary policy. The government insisted on one measure
above all, which the Bank directors most bitterly resented.
On 12 December it requested them to purchase £200,000
exchequer bills, and on the 13th another £300,000, though
they themselves would have preferred to increase discounts.[73]
Ostensibly this was to relieve the money market,[74] but
actually it was to rescue the Treasury. September's problem
of the floating debt had returned. On 23 November Buller
and Richards informed Robinson that if exchequer bills,
being still at a discount, were presented for payment, the
Bank would not have funds to cover them. Lushington
advised Liverpool to issue new bills at greater interest (rather
than pay off old bills or fund them) despite the likely effect
on the funds. On the 29th it was duly announced in the
Gazette that the exchequer bills were to be called in, and
an increased rate of interest (2d. per day instead of 1½d.)
offered on those that were re-issued, amounting to about
£300,000 on the whole four millions. Nevertheless, on 1
December, unadvertised exchequer bills were still at a
discount of 11s. and it became evident that nearly all the
floating bills were going to be presented for payment, notwithstanding the increased interest.[75] Ministers were therefore eager for the Bank to purchase exchequer bills, in order
to raise them to a premium and prevent their return. Some
very pertinent questions put to Harman in 1832 suggest how
significant this consideration was:

...You would think it imprudent for Government, at a time when

72. The Bank was gradually coming round to the government's opinion. In April
1827 Harman resigned from the Court; in December the Court, on Ward's initiative,
formally rescinded its notorious 1819 repudiation of exchange theory; and
subsequently the Bank did attempt to correct falling exchanges by selling
exchequer bills and by selling silver for gold in Paris (though not by varying Bank
rate). Horsefield, 'The Bankers and the Bullionists in 1819', *Journal of Political
Economy*, lvii (1949), 442-8; Clapham, *The Bank of England*, ii. 117.
73. CSC, *Report on renewing the Bank of England Charter*, 1832.
74. Herries and the 'coterie' must have supported this relief to the money market,
though most of them were now looking further – to a restriction on cash payments.
75. *The Times*, 24, 25 and 30 Nov., 2 Dec. 1825; Lushington to Liverpool, 25
Nov. 1825, LP 38301 ff. 37-9.

exchequer bills were at a discount, to commit itself by such an advertise-
ment [pledging to give money or new bills at the holders' option] ...,
without making an arrangement with the Bank, which should secure
that the exchequer bills should not fall to a discount? — [I take it for
granted, that if either a government or an individual have a call coming
upon them, it is their duty to provide means for discharging it.]
...If Government applied at that time to the Bank, to purchase
exchequer bills by an increased issue of Bank notes, did not the Government apply to the Bank to adopt a measure inconsistent with its own
security? — [It certainly was not a very desirable measure.] ...So that if
the Bank assisted to issue Bank notes by the purchase of exchequer
bills, in order to relieve the difficulty of Government, that might
endanger the security of the Bank, and if it refused that measure, it
might endanger the security of the Treasury? —[Yes] .[76]

The strategy succeeded. On the 20th the Bank's brokers
appeared on the market at 10 a.m. to buy exchequer bills,
and after only two hours the discount had fallen from 90s. to
20s. By the 21st exchequer bills were at par, and that
particular 'plague was stayed'. Ministers relaxed — Liverpool
retired to Coombe on the 22nd and Wellington to Sudbourne
— despite the fact that the Bank's reserve was still plummeting
(it touched a nadir at £1,027,000 on the 24th). Though
historians usually represent 1825 as a trial for the Bank and
the principle of convertibility, a still more vital concern for
ministers, though hardly one that they could confess publicly,
was their own solvency. And it is possible that their decision
to relax the currency in mid-December followed from the
need to settle the specific problem of the unfunded debt.

1826: the troubled aftermath

There was as much discussion as distress in 1826[77], but for
ministers it was a year to survive, not a time for reconstructing
economic policy. Their remedial legislation was merely a

76. CSC, *Report on renewing the Bank of England Charter*, 1832, QQ. 2188-
2209, 2051-6. G. W. Norman, *Remarks upon some prevalent errors with respect
to currency and banking* (1838), 64-5: 'It must not be forgotten that, during the
panic, Exchequer-bills were at a discount.'
77. For debates and legislation, see Clapham, op. cit. ii. 102-16; Smart, *Economic
Annals of the Nineteenth Century, 1821-30*, 336-57; Fetter, op. cit. 118-24;
Francis, op. cit. ii. 26-68; W. T. C. King, *History of the London Discount Market*
(1936), 35-101.

series of expedients (though this did not prevent their being puffed subsequently into precedents).

Convertibility had patently failed to discourage unsound flotations, so ministers sought a scapegoat in the banking system. First came a planned withdrawal of small country notes in favour of coin, both as a prophylactic — notes having led alternately to 'fictitious prosperity' and 'overwhelming distress'[78] — and as a social measure, since a run on the banks mainly hit poor noteholders, who could not hang on until the crisis was passed.[79] The main dilemma was that while the exchanges were satisfactory, country banks had monopolized provincial circulation, leaving the Bank of England merely 'the sole depository for gold'; so that when the exchanges fell and panic ensued, the Bank had been also 'the sole resort for obtaining it'. In other words, the Bank's specie reserve was at one moment too high, and its 'legitimate profit...curtailed', while at another its reserve was exposed to severe pressures. All the cabinet (except Bexley perhaps) seemed confident that the abolition of small notes would spread a future run for gold over a 'wider surface' than the Bank's reserve, and also 'cause such pressure to be earlier felt' and more quickly reversed.[80]

The government interdicted the stamping of any new small notes in February, but when Robinson moved the cessation of all existing small notes as from April 1829, there was a threatened combination against him of country bankers, 'paper gentry', and City merchants. With help from Brougham, Tierney, and most of the opposition, he carried it (222-39) against Baring's handful of 'commercial Whigs'.[81] But a few

---

78. Huskisson in H. of C., 18 Mar. 1830, 2 PD, xxiii. 582-3. This was not to isolate small notes as necessarily the cause of the mania; the point was that small notes fed on excitement, concealed a specie drain, and prevented any significant fall of exchange rates until after the excitement had become manic, and it was too late for precautionary action.
79. Liverpool in H. of L., 17 Feb. 1826, 2 PD, xiv. 455-7.
80. Liverpool and Robinson to B. of E., 13 Jan. 1826, LP 38371 ff. 94-106; 2 PD, xiv, 103-7.
81. Two-thirds of those who divided with Baring were merchants and bankers. Canning to Liverpool, 10 Feb. 1826, CP 72; Huskisson to Granville, 9 Mar. 1826, Granville MSS. 30/29/9/3/16 ff. 60-1. See Wellington, *Despatches, Correspondence, and Memoranda, 1819-31*, iii. 97, 116-18, 137.

Days later, possibly because the country bankers were
threatening to sabotage the measure by withdrawing all
their notes *at once*,[82] or possibly because of pressure from
Wellington, Bexley, Herries, and Lushington, Liverpool
announced in the Lords that the Bank of England might
continue to stamp new small notes until October 1826.
Canning had already defeated Hudson Gurney's amendment
to this effect in the Commons, and was 'thunderstruck' on
hearing of the proposed relaxation. His anger stemmed partly
from the humiliation of having to change tack in the
Commons, but also went deeper: 'The rise of the funds today
is in *my* mind, the reverse of a favourable symptom — It
clearly shows that the relaxation is held to be a relaxation *in
favour of the paper system*. This inference may be corrected
in argument: but the *impression* is made, and is indelible.'[83]
Canning knew that, in supporting the measure, many Tories
expected it to be inflationary, a prelude even to depreciation:
'It will require all our vigilance to falsify the hopes of our
supporters.'[84]

The proposal to extend the prohibition of small notes to
north of the border, where the banks had proved secure, set
all Scotland aflame.[85] Huskisson was not impressed by the
arguments of Walter [Malachi Malagrowther] Scott that the
stability of Scottish banks rendered regulation unnecessary:
Scotland, it is notorious, with banks perfectly solvent, has contributed
its full proportion of the undue facilities, which have produced the late
crisis. Both from London and Lancashire, the paper which could not
find discount in England was sent off to Scotland, where it met with
that accommodation; and now, upon the change, not that extravagant
accommodation only, but even the most cautious, is at once withheld,
to a much greater extent than in England.
This sudden veering about may be a very good manoeuvre to save
their own vessel, but it has been the cause of many wrecks here, and has
greatly added to the want of confidence and to the stagnation in the
commercial world.[86]

82. Smart, op. cit. 347-8; *The Greville Memoirs*, i. 79-81 (20 Feb. 1826).
83. Canning to Liverpool, 20 Feb. 1826, CP 72.
84. Canning to Liverpool, 21 Feb. 1826, CP 72.
85. Fetter, op. cit. 122-4; Smart, op. cit. 352-7.
86. Huskisson's 'Memorandum on Currency and Finance', 8 Feb. 1826, HP
38755 ff. 229-54. See Gurney in H. of C., 9 Feb. 1826, 2 PD, xiv. 148.

But Huskisson conceded that in the rude northern climate a wee 'paper dram'[87] might be required, as it was not in England, to tempt capitalists into business. Scottish politicians exerted their considerable influence, and after face-saving select committees had reported to each House, Liverpool agreed to exempt Scotland and Ireland from the interdict.[88]

If Scotland could not be assimilated to England, then English banking might be rendered more like the Scottish. Another remedial measure of 1826 was to invade the Bank's Charter to the extent of allowing joint-stock banks with an unlimited number of partners to practise, except within 65 miles of London. It would exclude the 'fictitious capitalists' from private banking, and it would bring a welcome gleam of publicity to play upon bankers' liabilities. There were feeble protests from the country banks and from the Bank directors, but although this combination had managed to defeat a similar proposal four years earlier, they were now, as Clapham observes, 'never so inert in the hands of ministers'.[89] Another proposal was to establish Bank of England branches. Liverpool had long wanted this, especially for Manchester where there were no local notes, and carried the plan in cabinet. In 1826 the younger Bank directors under Norman overcame the reluctance of Harman's faction at last, no doubt arguing that branches would compensate for the loss of provincial monopoly.[90] Bexley feared that they would compete unfairly with the country bankers, and Huskisson, who was more anxious to overhaul the currency than to tinker with banking, expected 'little or no good' from it.[91]

The most serious political crisis of 1826, however, involved a sin of omission. Bankruptcies intensified as firms that had

87. Huskisson to Abercrombie, 16 May 1826, HP 38748 ff. 35-7.
88. Colchester, *Diary and Correspondence*, iii. 433-4.
89. Peel to Littleton, 3 Jan. 1826, Hatherton MSS. D260/M/F/5/27/3/2; Parker, op. cit. i. 384; Herries MSS. II, 110-15; Clapham, op. cit. ii. 102-7; Smart, op. cit. 350-1; Pressnell, op. cit. 501-10; H. Burgess, *Circular to Bankers* (1827).
90. Norman, MS. autobiography, quoted in D.P. O'Brien, *The Correspondence of Lord Overstone* (1971), i. 6 and n.5; Harman to CSC, *Report on renewing the Bank of England Charter*, 1832, QQ. 2332, 2349.
91. Huskisson to Gladstone, 29 July 1826, HP 38748 f. 66.

held on during the liberal discounting of December now
faced falling markets.

Commissions in Bankruptcy recorded in *London
Gazette,* from Morgan, *The Theory and Practice
of Central Banking, 85*

	Jan-Mar.	Apr-Jun.	Jul-Sept.	Oct-Dec.
1824	264	270	184	281
1825	245	254	180	462
1826	824	824	368	574

Gladstone's Liverpool was typical, with 'Confidence greatly
diminished, money scarce and much wanted — prices of
goods still falling, and sales very difficult, not knowing whom
to trust, whilst the consumption of the Country is fast falling
off...more and serious failures are apprehended.'[92] Inevitably
merchants clamoured for relief, and especially for government
to relieve 'monetary famine'[93] by issuing exchequer bills to
distressed firms, as in 1793 and 1811. There were memorials
from all over Britain, the most formidable being a deputation
from the City under Baring, and another from Lancashire
under John Wood, Vice-President of Manchester Chamber of
Commerce.[94] All the merchant M.P.s and most of the gentry
supported an issue of exchequer bills; Arbuthnot also desired
it, and at first Canning believed it to be 'the only remedy to
which the moneyed world will look with confidence — and
confidence is the one thing wanting'.[95]

Backed by Huskisson and Peel, however, Liverpool firmly
refused. If the 'active circulation' needed an extra two
millions, he preferred the Bank to *buy* exchequer bills and
increase the circulation in doing so. Huskisson claimed that
this would 'throw a farther amount of currency into the
country, and thereby afford it relief'[96] more effectively than

92. Gladstone to Huskisson, 20 Jan. 1826, HP 38747 ff. 175-6.
93. Alexander Baring, Lord Ashburton, *The Financial and Commercial Crisis
Considered,* third edition (1847), 8.
94. *The Times,* 13, 14 and 15 Feb. 1826; A. Redford, *Manchester Merchants and
Foreign Trade 1794-1858* (1934), 76-7; Smart, op. cit. 326.
95. Canning to Wellington, 17 Feb. 1826, Wellington, *Despatches, Correspondence
and Memoranda, 1819-31,* iii. 116-17; Canning to Liverpool, 23 Feb. 1826, copy
CP 72.
96. H. of C., 14 Feb. 1826, 2 PD, xiv. 403.

issues of new bills direct to merchants. There was a confrontation on 23 February, when Wilson presented a commercial petition from London for an issue of exchequer bills, and was supported by the merchants, by the directors Pearse and Manning, and silently by 'every man of the old Pitt party'.[97] Canning was rightly convinced that ministers would only avoid humiliating defeat if they could persuade the Bank to lend to merchants on security of goods.[98] When it refused, Canning — tired of 'dealing gently with the Bank' — grew 'saucy', denounced the directors' obstinancy and, to Parliament's consternation, declared that ministers would resign rather than issue exchequer bills.[99] The government's existence depended on an 'absolutely hostile' Bank. Behind the scenes, on the 25th, Herries tried more persuasive arts. The directors objected that, without branches, they could hardly apply 'real bills' judgement in lending to merchants in Manchester and Glasgow, whereas exchequer bills could be issued through Commissioners with local knowledge of which were the creditworthy firms. Ministers retorted that as an issue of exchequer bills could only help if the Bank chose to cash them, 'the intervention of the Bank was in any event absolutely necessary.' The only real relief would come about by increasing the circulation, irrespective of how it was done,[100] and according to Tooke, an issue of exchequer bills would be less likely to effect that increase than Bank loans. For exchequer bills would call forth money from the hoards, and tide over the few recipients of them; but would probably not raise the total amount of circulating medium, nor give much general relief, as the Bank would reduce its issues to offset the extra money created.[101] In other words, specific accommodation to some would merely deprive others that were more deserving, and more likely to make

97. Croker to Wellington, 20 Mar. 1826, Wellington, op. cit. iii. 209-12; *The Croker Papers*, i. 314-17.
98. Canning to Liverpool, 23 Feb. 1826, CP 72.
99. H. of C., 23 Feb. 1826, 2 PD, xiv. 727-8; Canning to Liverpool, 24 Feb. 1826 CP 72.
100. Peel to Wellington, 3 Mar. 1826, Peel MSS. 40306 ff. 184-90, partly quoted in Parker, op. cit. i.395-8. Wellington, op.cit. iii. 143-5; *The Times*, 26 Feb. 1826.
101. T. Tooke, *Considerations of the State of the Currency*, second edition (1826), 160-8.

beneficial use of funds. There was no conception that accommodation might *create* new facilities.

At last, protesting, the directors agreed to lend up to three millions, on condition that the Bank's advances to government were reduced. In fact, only one and a half was actually lent, but the amount was less important than the psychological effect of lending any at all: 'If it is believed to be abundant it will really be so.'[102] This whole puzzling episode has never been explained satisfactorily. As Canning put it to a friend, it seemed absurd that a government could almost break up on whether an issue of exchequer bills to be cashed by the Bank was a better or worse method of relieving commercial distress than direct issues of Bank notes without exchequer bills. 'To be sure it would have been a mighty foolish kind of death'.[103] Historians of banking have explained the dispute in terms of the government pushing the directors into central bank responsibilities. Most contemporaries and political historians have explained it in terms of Liverpool's pledge of March 1825, vowing never to issue exchequer bills to merchants. Though Bank loans would come to the same thing materially, semantically Liverpool would not have to renege on that pledge.[104] 'I need not tell *you* all the reasons (very good ones) why the Government did not like to undertake an issue of Exchequer Bills', wrote Croker to Wellington on 20 March. He thought that exchequer bills might be justified 'as a *special* remedy, in a *special case*'. 'But Lord Liverpool, influenced, as the world said, by his pledge and prophecy of last year relative to the evils of overtrading, would not listen to it...Indeed, all that is *visible* [of the intrigue] to me is so very absurd, that I cannot but suspect that there were some better, or at least more important, reasons at bottom.'

Canning hinted at 'evil consequences, *both immediate, and remote,* which would attend the issue of Exchequer Bills

---

102. Herries to Littleton, 29 Mar. 1826, Hatherton MSS. D260/M/F/5/27/3/9.
103. Canning to Granville, 6 Mar. 1826, Stapleton, *George Canning and His Times,* 237-8; Croker to Wellington, 20 Mar. 1826; Tierney to Holland, 13 Mar. 1826, HHP 51584 ff. 110-13.
104. See above, p. 207. Halévy, *The Liberal Awakening,* 230; Burdett in H. of C. 28 Feb. 1826, 2 PD, xiv. 925-6.

by Government'.[105] The most cogent of the 'immediate' considerations relates to the market for public securities. As in September and December, there was a danger that exchequer bills, being again at a discount, might be presented for payment. On 16 February the Bank consented to the purchase of £200 - £300,000 at par, which was enough to raise all of them to par.[106] In this context, the difference between government issues of exchequer bills and the Bank's purchase of them from the Exchequer becomes obvious. At least it was very obvious to Peel, who wrote — 'There are 30 millions of Exchequer Bills outstanding. The purchases lately made by the Bank can hardly maintain them at par. If there were a new issue to such an amount as that contemplated — viz., five millions — there would be a great danger that the whole mass of Exchequer Bills would be at a discount, and would be paid into the revenue.'[107]

But was it merely a technical problem of public finance? To understand what made the exchequer bill market more important to ministers than rescuing troubled businesses, it is necessary to consider Canning's 'remote' consequences, and especially two related, semi-conscious assumptions concerning the performance of a capitalist economy and the preservation of social stability. Huskisson, Peel, and Liverpool withheld direct relief to bankrupts (as distinct from general relief through additional currency) *pour encourager les autres*. In peacetime, any cyclical failure must be the fault of businessmen themselves. To step in afterwards to save them would 'offer a bonus to extravagant speculation'.[108] Huskisson warned that if parties 'might always expect to obtain an asylum in government, it was as much calculated to encourage speculation as the poor-laws were calculated to encourage vagrancy, and to discourage honest industry'.[109]

105. Canning to Liverpool, 23 Feb. 1826, CP 72 (my italics).
106. *The Times*, 16, 21, 25 and 26 Feb. 1826.
107. Peel to Wellington, 3 Mar. 1826, Wellington, op. cit. iii. 144. The distinction was also obvious to Lauderdale; Lauderdale to Holland, 19 Feb. 1826, HHP 51692 ff. 138-41.
108. Robinson in H. of C., 23 Feb. 1826, 2 PD, xiv. 707.
109. H. of C., 14 Feb. 1826, 2 PD, xiv. 403.

Like smuggling, over-speculation must be rendered less *eligible* than honest, manly, cautious trading.

But in proffering these rational arguments, ministers betrayed an almost sadistic attitude. Even the unemotional King's Speech expressed pleasure in the thought that wild-cat speculations would be discouraged in future by 'the experience of the sufferings which they have occasioned'.[110] There was avid talk of punishing the guilty, and merchants responded with appropriate masochism — 'We shall be the better for passing through the ordeal'.[111] The events of 1825-6 encouraged the tragic fascination with business crashes that so affected the nineteenth-century mentality, the novelists' preoccupation, for example, with business misfortunes and their associated vortices of loss and destitution. Symbolic figures were Bulstrode, whose disgrace seemed to most Middlemarchers to have 'enveloped' everybody in financial contact with him, and to have 'blighted' each of his clients 'like a damaged ear of corn'; Melmotte, whose career illustrated the mindless, cyclical peregrinations of credit; above all Merdle, whose ramifying prosperity and enveloping collapse was described as a sorely contagious disease, an epidemic 'Bred at first...in the wickedness of men, and then disseminated in their ignorance...[but] communicated to many sufferers who are neither ignorant nor wicked'. The very word *inflation,* to describe the over-reaching, over-extended activity of the boom, invoked a tragic concept of sinful excess, and of pride (before a fall); while the cyclical inevitability that the bubble must eventually burst induced not only fatalism, but even a kind of glorification in purgative failure. In this mood, sharp economic recessions were almost welcomed, and popular abuse was concentrated on the upswing. Saving was still glorified as a consequence of protestant acquisitiveness, but no longer speculation. Possibly this explains the problem of Torrens,[112] who in 1826 abandoned his former 'real bills' doctrines and began instead

110. 2 PD, xiv. 1-2.
111. Gladstone to Robertson, 12 Jan. 1826, Checkland, *The Gladstones,* 155.

to praise *drones* as the heroes of the economy. As Hansen has put it, men 'feared the boom even more than the depression.'[113] In a twentieth century of genuine tragedy, these induced surrogates for tragic intensity survive in the works of Robbins and Hayek,[114] who regret the passing of the Victorians' short, sharp shock to business and condemn the modern preference for the 'lingering disease'; who would prefer an invigorating (and Darwinian) cold shower of failure to 'bankruptcy phobia' and the unmanly pampering of feeble businesses; and who object to Keynesian methods of lifting a depression for reasons that Huskisson would have endorsed — that money is a drug, and inflation an addiction, which can never be cured by further indulgence, but only by the excruciating agony of total and immediate withdrawal.

Bullionism had appealed to the landed interest in 1819 as an instrument of social stasis. So although it did agriculture no good, and despite the populist alliance on cheap money, the crash of 1825-6 was welcomed by those landlords who were not themselves involved, as a 'reckoning' for some of the bourgeois meteors launched in the early decades of the century. It would console what J. G. Lockhart called 'impatient poverty', and would deter those 'money-making appetites'[115], with their corollary — over-trading — which was the root of all 'the social and moral evils of the period'.[116] 'Our old traders did not make fortunes *in a minute*' moralized one High Tory, 'but they generally died rich, the result of constant moderate gains on regular

112. A problem discussed in L. Robbins, *Robert Torrens and the Evolution of Classical Economics* (1958), 86-90 (which discounts the charge that Torrens changed his mind in order to improve his chances of gaining official employment), and in D. P. O'Brien, 'The Transition in Torrens' Monetary Thought', *Economica*, new series, xxxii (1965), 269-301 (which stresses Ricardo's theoretical influence on Torrens).
113. See Peel to Littleton, 23 Dec. 1825, Hatherton MSS. D/260/M/F/5/27/110: 'We have been working too fast — building to fast.'
114. L. Robbins, *The Great Depression* (1934), 71-5; F. A. Hayek, *Prices and Production* (1931), 98-9.
115. Hardcastle, *Banks and Bankers*, 121.
116. J. Francis, *Chronicles and Characters of the Stock Exchange* (1949), 261.

trade'.[117] A great crash should check the 'gambling spirit' (in the funds and elsewhere) by men of no property. It should check what Metternich designated a bourgeois 'presumption' in the middle classes, with their constitutional maypoles beribboned in individualistic fallacies. It should emphasize the prudence of rural quiet and rest against what Dr. Tanner, in his interesting introduction to *Mansfield Park*, lists as the forward passions of the age — 'the new attitude abroad in the land — speculative, acquisitive, calculating, and irreverent', as personified by the Crawfords. Tanner makes a convincing case for this novel as an allegory in which virtuous tranquillity, enduring custom and tradition, in short 'The quiet thing!', finally defeat the forces of evil, whose two great symbols are 'speculation' and land 'improvement'.[118]

Was convertibility, joint-stock, publicity, and the refusal of relief to bankrupts a policy of keeping companies to the 'companied' classes, of pushing down little men? Thomas Attwood regarded his crusade as a fight for the underdog in all sectors of the economy, a horizontal campaign embracing town and country:

Above all things let the depreciation...be *carried far enough*. If the scale of justice *must* lean at all to one side, for God's sake, let it be to the side of money. Let it be in favour of the weak against the strong, of the Debtor against the Creditor, of the man struggling to raise his head above the waters, and not of the man who already stands upon firm ground. Of all the cruel and monstrous doctrines that ever were broached in political economy, the most cruel and preposterous is that, which seeking public plunder under the mask of public faith, pretends that the *raising of the value of money* is no greater injury and injustice to Debtors than the *lowering of such value* is to the *Creditors* in a Community.[119]

It would be profitless to speculate further on ministers' subconscious attitudes, but it is suggestive that in his most famous remark Liverpool could not forbear to sneer. His

117. Redesdale to Colchester, 23 Jan. 1828, Colchester, *Diary and Correspondence*, iii. 541.
118. Penguin edition of *Mansfield Park* (1966), Introduction, 7-36, and Chapter XXV.
119. Attwood to Davenport, 22 June 1826, Davenport MSS., Attwood ff. 43-52. Attwood, of course, did not put the blame on over-trading but rather on government and Bank operations, which had created a crisis of confidence out of nothing.

argument was reasonable — that private banking would be more secure if an unlimited number of wealthy men were allowed to form partnerships — but the tone was contemptuous: 'Any petty tradesman, any grocer or cheese-monger, however destitute of property, might set up a bank in any place.'[120] He clearly thought that if the government stood aside — relying on the gold standard, freedom to bank, freedom to invest in joint stock (with unlimited liability and no relief guaranteed to those who fell in the struggle) — in other words, 'where perfect liberty prevailed, each person having an equal right to invest his capital, *the wealthier must in time drive out the weaker and less solvent.*'[121] The confident assumption — never overtly stated — was that unsound, over-done speculation was only perpetrated by men of no capital or real worth. Liverpool had faith still in the power of bullionism to discriminate fairly between sound and unsound speculators, to perform its own automatic selection of 'real bills'.

120. H. of L. 17 Feb. 1826, 2 PD, xiv. 462.
121. Ibid. 461. (my italics).

VIII

BANKING AND FINANCIAL REFORM

Master of unbounded wealth, ... the arbiter of peace and war, ... the credit of nations depends upon his nod; ... ministers of state are in his pay. ... [Do] not allow the finances of this great country to be controlled any longer by a Jew.

T. H. Duncombe in H. of C., 18 Feb. 1822, 2 PD, xviii, 542–3.

Monetary policy and war

The events of 1825–6 prompted an urgent reappraisal of economic policy. Until about 1822 the main problem had been to return to peacetime normalcy, and the 1815 Corn Law was one of several expedients designed to control that deflationary transition. By 1823 normalcy appeared to have been achieved; the need now was for stability, and to this end Robinson and Huskisson tampered with the tariff and the navigation code. December 1825, however, shattered any illusions that convertibility and a more open trade would suffice to prevent financial crises, crises that crippled Britain's military and diplomatic strength. The paramount but unstated objective of subsequent policy was to put the British economy on such a footing that, if war broke out again, the nation could prosecute it without having to suspend cash payments, without storing up all the trauma of social dislocation and contractual injustice involved in abandoning a metallic standard and afterwards returning to it.[1] The prospect of military and therefore financial exertion was present throughout the 1820s: against Russia over Greece, France over Spain, Spain and Austria over South America, and the United States over trade.[2] It was largely to prepare the monetary and

1. Grenville thought that Pitt should not have suspended in 1797, Wellington that he should have resumed again in 1798; Gregory, *The Westminster Bank through a Century*, ii. 145; Stanhope, *Conversations with the Duke of Wellington*, 1 Nov. 1837, 111–12.
2. The United States was Britain's best customer, but custom only bred acrimony in the early nineteenth century.

financial systems for military and naval campaigns that ministers toyed with retrenchment, bimetallism, banking reform, and direct taxation.

The government recognized three different strategies for financing wars. It could sacrifice everything to maintain what it called 'public credit', so that it might borrow readily in an emergency.[3] Alternatively, it could ignore public credit but, by relieving industry of fiscal and other burdens, create private wealth that might be tapped in time of crisis. Then again, it could hoard a surplus of revenue against eventualities, as in a sinking fund. In the late twenties ministers moved towards the second of these solutions. Retrenchment would have been the obvious and most popular way of stabilizing the nation's finances, diminishing the debt and preparing the currency for sudden exertion, but since the only significant opportunity for retrenchment lay in cutting the size of the armed services, and since this would have defeated its own military and diplomatic purpose, ministers preferred to derestrict commerce and boost consumption. Free trade, later lauded as Cobden's engine of international peace and goodwill, was for the Tory governments of the 1820s an essential preparation for hostilities.

Huskisson was far from sure that the measures of 1826 and the government's ostentatious refusal to suspend cash payments would tie country bankers more closely to the exchanges. A lucid memorandum of February 1826, in which he proposed a bimetallic solution,[4] stressed the interdependence of diplomatic, financial, agricultural, and monetary policies. It commenced with a theme that was to recur frequently:

3. Ministers were particularly anxious about the unfunded debt in February 1826 because the outcome of Wellington's diplomatic mission to St. Petersburg was uncertain, and war still a possibility.

4. Huskisson's 'Memorandum on the Present State of the Country in respect to Currency and Finance', 8 Feb. 1826, HP 38755 ff. 229–54, printed in Wellington, *Despatches, Correspondence, and Memoranda, 1819-31*, iii. 98–104. Huskisson had been sympathetic to bimetallism since 1823 at least; Ricardo to Trower, 30 Jan. 1823, Sraffa, *Works and Correspondence of David Ricardo*, ix. 270; Huskisson to Peel, 24 Mar. 1828, HP 38755 f. 227.

In all the circumstances of this country there is nothing more calculated to create anxiety, and call for early consideration, than our want of adequate preparation in respect to the arrangement of our currency and finance, to meet those demands which war may at any time render necessary.

Our riches and power are greater than at any former period; but our wealth is a mine placed by the side of a volcano, and our strength may fail us at the moment when we may require its greatest exertion.

It is unnecessary to show that, in point of currency, the country is not prepared for the drain of war.

War would force the government to suspend cash payments lest shortage of money 'paralyse our exertions'. Huskisson doubted whether the economy could even meet a bad harvest without undermining the solvency of the Bank, since paying for irregular food imports out of a metallic circulation would cause monetary pressure and panic. An external flight, however caused, would lead to domestic drain. The danger might be reduced by substituting gold for paper, but this would also stifle legitimate enterprise. Huskisson concluded that the currency needed a 'broader foundation' — 'one sufficient to protect us, without violent fluctuations, not only from the effect of any extraordinary disturbance in the foreign exchange, occasioned by the course of commercial speculation, but also from the greater pressure which may be brought upon the money market by a bad harvest or a war' — and that bimetallism was most likely to provide this. He foresaw several advantages in the monetization of silver,[5] but the most important was that it would enable the country to meet an unfavourable exchange due to ordinary commercial fluctuation without too much strain on its stocks of gold bullion and coin; while at the same time 'It will afford a fund for the extraordinary occasions of dearth, armament or war... We shall be in a state to meet a war without incurring an act of bankruptcy.'

There were other reasons why the monetary system remained an inflexible instrument in times of crisis. First, the Bank had too many of its advances locked up in long annuities (such as mortgages and the Dead Weight), and it should be forced, by threats to its charter if necessary, to make more of its funds 'immediately available' for use in an

5. At the French ratio of 15½:1, leaving the gold content of the pound unchanged and slightly increasing the 1797 silver content.

emergency. Second, there was the unfunded debt, those thirty millions of exchequer bills 'unprovided for':

> In former periods of peace we had none... The whole of these thirty million are *virtually* payable on demand. Let it be considered how they would hamper us, even upon an armament, and much more upon the actual breaking out of a war. What a drag they would be upon any loan we might then be forced to make; how much a very great fall in the funds, besides creating real distress in many quarters, would, at the outset of a contest, or with the question still pending in negotiation, tell inconveniently upon public feeling, both at home and abroad.
>
> In possible contingencies, too, such an unfunded debt might make it very difficult to provide for the quarterly dividends. Its existence in its present amount is contrary to all sound policy in reference to our political situation, and in the end will prove the very reverse of economy.
>
> In my opinion, two-thirds of it ought to be reduced in this and the next year.

As well as guarding against military and diplomatic impotence, bimetallism appealed to Huskisson because silver was the 'great staple' of Spanish American commerce and the new republics' chief means of paying for British exports. Huskisson was here thinking less about exports than about how to obtain bullion, not simply to build up a treasure chest, but in order (as before) 'to make money as cheap as is consistent with the maintenance of [the standard]'.[6] He also hoped that a dual standard would attract capital to Britain, and that London might usurp the status of bimetallic Paris[7] as the pecuniary entrepôt of the world. (His unnecessary jealousy of Paris had been compounded by her having helped to bale out the Bank of England in December 1825).[8]

> France, not only by the amount of her metallic currency, but by her proximity to this country, and her position on the continent, and by the great public credit which she possesses, is become very much the centre (*the clearing-house*) of all the great pecuniary dealings to which commerce, exchanges, loans, and all the movements of the money-market, give rise between this country and the continent. The example

6. See above, p. 94. Huskisson detected a secular rise in world money values, which he feared might not be counteracted by increased credit facilities (bills, cheques, &c.), Huskisson to Canning, 16 Aug. 1826, HP 38748 ff. 117–19. He urged William Jacob to begin research on the production of precious metals.
7. France possessed a bimetallic *coinage*; Huskisson was here recommending a bimetallic *standard* with paper circulation.
8. See above, pp. 216-17.

of France in the last twelve years shows what great stability against ruinous fluctuations at home, and what power of adjustment in respect to foreign drains, she derives from her great metallic circulation. Neither invasion and the occupation of her capital and part of her territory, nor the payment of a very large foreign tribute, nor the disquietude which continued some years after the restoration of the Royal family, nor the Peninsular war,[9] ever for a moment deranged her currency, or brought great pressure upon her foreign transactions. The nearer, therefore, we can approximate to the state of France, without giving up the peculiar advantages of our circulating credit, the better. Finally, by placing herself outside the normal course of European financial transactions, which were conducted in silver, Britain had put herself 'at the mercy of a powerful house here [Rothschild], acting in concert with their connexions on the continent, and vested them with a power' that could be offered to hostile statesmen such as Metternich.

Though Huskisson arranged for the Bank to hold silver ready for immediate coinage in case all the small notes should disappear,[10] Wellington vetoed bimetallism in 1826.[11] Unlike Huskisson, he did not fear Rothschild, did not covet Latin-American trade, and considered that the growing productivity of New World silver mines rendered that metal 'useless as a measure of value'. He also supposed for a time that the varying agio on gold in bimetallic countries meant that there were constantly two prices current on the market, whereas Huskisson intended that whichever metal was momentarily cheaper should govern the standard. But before long Wellington was converted to the idea of a dual standard, on the grounds that it 'would enable the country to rest on the supply of one metal if the other failed'. Ironically though, whereas Huskisson hoped that bimetallism would limit Rothschild's influence, Wellington anticipated that it 'would put it in the power of the great men who have such masses of plate in their possession to send their plate in to the Bank at any extraordinary emergency of national credit' — as 'old Rothschild' had done in December 1825. He

9. Of 1823, presumably.
10. H. of C., 10 Feb. 1826, 2 PD, xiv. 243; Herries to Goulburn, 29 July 1829, Herries MSS. 57401 ff. 13–14.
11. Wellington to Peel, 18 Feb. 1826, Peel MSS. 40306 ff. 182–3, Wellington, op. cit. iii. 135–6; Wellington to Canning, 19 Feb. 1826, ibid. iii. 137; Wellington to Mrs Arbuthnot, 19 Feb. 1826, *Wellington and His Friends*, 55; Peel to Wellington, 10 Feb. 1826, Peel MSS. 40306 ff. 173–5, Parker, *Sir Robert Peel*, i. 394–5.

shared Huskisson's apprehension of famine, however, and in 1839 he was to argue that bimetallism would prevent a drain of either metal singly 'at any sudden pressure — such as may be feared this very year for the purchase of foreign corn.'[12]

In 1828 Wellington, Goulburn, Huskisson, Peel, Herries, and Hill devised a plan whereby both the Mint and the Bank might issue, against deposit of silver, notes that would be redeemable in silver only and eligible for all payments to the Treasury. The idea was that silver could be exported to correct a falling exchange without any run on gold, the bastion of the *internal* circulation.[13] Baring supported the plan before a committee of inquiry at the Board of Trade, arguing that the existing system would collapse in the 'day of trial' — in war, famine, or financial panic. Years later he said he thought that it was essential to 'enlarge as much as possible the base on which our paper must rest', since 'refined perfection' in a standard soon led to 'no standard at all', merely to a 'Birmingham mire of inconvertible rags'.[14]

Since the retirement of Harman, who had supported bimetallism,[15] the most influential director had been Horsley Palmer, Deputy Governor in 1828. He blocked the government's plan, arguing that the Bank already possessed sufficient silver bullion for the directors to raise exchange rates, procure gold from abroad, meet domestic panics and defeat 'combinations made to their prejudice'.[16] Wellington was unconvinced, having by now entirely accepted Huskisson's view that a foreign expenditure must derange the internal circulation, but he was politically anxious not to cross the Bank.[17] Probably Palmer saw bimetallism as a

12. Stanhope, op. cit., 22 Sept. 1839, 158—9.
13 Wellington to Peel, 4 Apr. 1828, Peel MSS. 40307 ff. 70—1; C.T., Report Book, 28 Apr. 1828, 91—6; Fetter, *Development of British Monetary Orthodoxy*, 124—6.
14. A & P, *Minutes of Evidence taken in 1828, before the Committee for Coin, at the Board of Trade*, 1830, 6—15; Ashburton, *The Financial and Commercial Crisis Considered*, third edition (1847), 37—40.
15. Baring in H. of C., 8 June 1830, 2 PD, xxv. 154.
16. A & P, *Minutes of Evidence in 1828 on Coin*, 1830, 15 — 16.
17. Wellington to Goulburn, n.d., Goulburn MSS.II/12; but see *A Political Diary, 1828—30*, by Edward Law, Lord Ellenborough, edited by Lord Colchester (1881), i. 83—7; Lauderdale to Page, 13 June 1828, Bodleian MSS. Eng. lett. b. 3 ff. 47—8.

deliberate threat to the Bank's chartered privileges, engineered
by its old enemy, Huskisson. It was sincerely believed in
Threadneedle Street that the government desired to establish
the Mint as a rival, Ricardian, and national bank, and that it
was secretly coining silver. It was to anticipate this non-
existent operation that in 1829 the Bank itself began to press
silver into circulation through its new branches.[18]

Huskisson's resignation in 1828 removed any chance that
Britain might go bimetallic. Herries was satisfied that all was
well with the currency, and thought that the dual standard
was simply another of Huskisson's injudicious relaxations
(like the small notes extension of 1822),[19] while Peel
believed naïvely that cessation of small notes was the one
thing needful.[20] Bimetallism finally stepped beyond the pale
in 1830 when it was embraced by Matthias Attwood. Whereas Huskisson's "limited bimetallism" would not have involved
a devaluation of the standard of gold, and was intended to
mitigate rather than to negate the effects of cash payments,[21]
Attwood moved for a dual standard that would be frankly
depreciatory.[22] Even Huskisson opposed, because it was linked
to anti-bullionist longings, and perhaps because he thought
that the most pressing problem was no longer shortage of
money but lack of incentive to industrial investment.[23]

18. Herries to Goulburn, 29 July 1829.
19. H. of C., 8 June 1830, 2 PD, xxv. 158–60.
20. See, for example, Ellenborough, *A Political Diary, 1828–30*, i. 187.
21. Huskisson could not conceivably have written the letter preserved among his papers (HP 38758 ff. 64–70) and attributed to him by Melville, *The Huskisson Papers*, 310–19 and Fetter, op. cit. 127. It was in fact written by the banker Farquharson to Robert Herries on 20 Dec. 1829, and contains an uncompromising attack on economic policy since 1819 – deploring the failure to reduce interest on the debt and to adjust private contracts equitably.
22. For an interesting discussion of the 1830 debates, see H. H. Gibbs, Lord Aldenham, *A Colloquy on Currency*, third edition (1894), 252–8.
23. Huskisson to Denison, 10 Jan. 1830, HP 38758 ff. 95–6: 'The real evil of the Country is not the want of money (of currency we have enough) but the want of profit in all the pursuits of industry. This is the reverse of a thriving state. It is one of great suffering, and which if continued, would lay the foundation of national impoverishment and decay.'

Bimetallism languished for fifty years. Fortified by gold dis-
coveries in three continents, and with a healthy balance of payments, monometallic Britain prospered well enough, though
the dual standard's few champions argued that it would have
mitigated the difficulties of 1847 and 1856, 1866 and 1890.

Horsley Palmer had obstructed bimetallism, but it was
probably he who formulated an alternative proposal for
monetary stability. In 1827 Huskisson sought James Pennington's advice on how to prevent 'too great facility of expansion
at one time' and 'too rapid contraction of paper credit' at
another.[24] Pennington suggested that instead of trying to
maintain a fixed ratio between specie reserve and issues, as
hitherto, the Bank should keep its government securities
steady at a fixed ratio, and then allow its notes to vary with
its bullion holding. Fetter speculates that ministers acted as a
channel through which Pennington's suggestion developed
into the 'Palmer Rule', as propounded before the 1832 Bank
Charter Committee — that when the circulation was 'full',
the Bank should have a bullion reserve equal to one-third of
the notes and deposits, and that these liabilities should then
fluctuate — in normal conditions — with the specie reserve.[25]
This interesting suggestion presupposes co-operation between
ministers and directors, whereas under Palmer the Bank
seemed (even to a sympathizer like Herries) to exhibit 'a
jealousy and suspiciousness, such as I have never witnessed'.[26]
There are indeed indications that the 'Palmer Rule' developed
in *opposition* to government policy. For many years Huskisson had been unhappy about the amount of public and other
long-term securities held by the Bank, for they threatened
the Treasury's finances and hampered the Bank's freedom of
action in a crisis. On 30 March 1827 he declared to a group
of directors that the Bank's holdings of permanent securities

24. Huskisson to Pennington, 1 June 1827, HP 38749 ff. 270—1; Pennington's
memorandum (1826), HP 38761 ff. 201—10; Pennington to Huskisson, 23 June
1827, HP 38749 ff. 319—24; R. S. Sayers, *Economic Writings of James Pennington*
(1963), xvii-xxii.
25. CSC, *Report on renewing the Bank of England Charter*, 1832, QQ. 72—95;
Fetter, op. cit. 129—33. Palmer retained a discretionary power to decide what
were "normal conditions" — hence Peel's desire for further restrictions on Bank
issues in 1844.
26. Herries to Goulburn, 29 July 1829.

like the 'dead weight' should be materially reduced. The following day Palmer replied that such holdings were harmless, whatever the state of the exchanges:

'I am of opinion that it will be more beneficial than otherwise, that the major part of the Bank issues should be upon Government securities and a given proportion of bullion to secure the convertibility, *varying the rate of interest* according to the undue increase or diminution of such proportion of the precious metals — and which a very small discount account will suffice to accomplish.'[27]

1827 marked a fresh start in Bank policy and not merely in respect to exchange theory. Under Harman, the Bank had frequently complained that its issues were locked up in government securities, whereas in 1827 Palmer moved towards his later 'rule' by recommending a high level of securities and variation of advances with holdings of specie. Palmer also requested that if the Bank was to continue as lender of last resort, it should be given some measure of control over all note issues.[28].

Palmer ought not to be rebuked for omitting bank deposits and bills of exchange from his calculations:

It is what I term collateral currency, such as bills of exchange, credits (and Country Bank issues so long as they exist) which govern prices; the most trifling demonstration of contracting on the part of the Bank puts an immediate check on that part of the circulation, and instead of the Bank being required to contract its issues, it is then called upon for a very great temporary extension to supply in part that which is withdrawn.

So the 'currency school' developed in opposition to the wish of Huskisson, Canning and Liverpool for a bank that would take no part in monetary management but be available for crises on some self-regulating basis such as bimetallism. Though Peel in 1844 was to utilize 'currency theory' to justify an *automatic* system of note issue, Palmer had initially developed the theory as an assertion of the Bank's right to 'manage', and of its power to control the private bank issues

27. Palmer to Huskisson, 31 Mar. 1827 (italics in original), and Palmer's 1827 memorandum, HP 38749 ff. 165–73.

28. As Fetter remarks, op. cit., 133, Pennington wanted the Bank of England to monopolise note issue and Palmer did not. However, in 1832 Palmer was constrained by political realities, and it is clear that in 1827 he too would have welcomed a monopoly. Failing that, either the Mint should control all issues, or else the private banks should compete for issues (in which case the Bank of England would not issue at all, and country banks would not be able to apply to it in a crisis).

and other 'collateral' currency. The fundamental issue turned once again on the exercise of power.

The Finance Committee of 1828 and the politics of retrenchment

Distress had reawakened 'morbid sensibility in the public mind' on the subject of retrenchment, a popular lust to curtail 'vainglorious establishments'.[29] In a memorandum of April 1827, Herries pointed out that, owing to the recent depression, the revenue surplus was too slight to meet the five millions annually appropriated to the sinking fund in 1823. He suggested drastic retrenchment and a revision of the sinking fund arrangements, as the only alternative to extra taxation (which was inconceivable during a depression) or to further loans and deficit financing. The new prime minister, Canning, pledged his government to the appointment of a public inquiry to settle the questions of expenditure and debt,[30] questions that played a conspicuous and ostensibly causative part in the political intrigues that occurred after the Canning bonfire had burned itself out.

First, the Canningite Whigs — Lansdowne, Tierney, and Carlisle — objected to the choice of Herries as Chancellor of the Exchequer (after Huskisson and Sturges Bourne had refused the post) in August 1827.[31] They complained that he was a 'Protestant', 'regarded somewhat favourably by the Tory opposition',[32] and a nominee of the King. George IV defended Herries's appointment on the grounds of expertise: 'The office requires ability & not aristocracy... The most valuable among you — Mr Huskisson was Secretary to the Treasury. . . The King will have those that are proper for

29. Huskisson to Adam, 6 Oct. 1827, HP 38751 ff. 136—8; *The Times*, 12 Oct. 1826; *Morning Chronicle*, 17 Oct. 1826; Liverpool to Herries, 18 Oct. 1826, Herries MSS. 57367 ff. 133—4; Robinson to Herries, 27 Sept. 1826, ibid. 57402 ff. 19—21.
30. E. Herries, *Memoir of the Public Life of John Charles Herries* (1880), i. 139—44; Aspinall, *Letters of King George IV*, iii. 291—2.
31. *The Greville Memoirs*, i. 109—13 (20 Aug. and 1 Sept. 1827); Herries, op. cit. i. 153—236; Jones, *'Prosperity' Robinson*, 152—68; Huskisson to Granville, 2 Sept. 1827, Granville MSS. 30/29/9/3/24; Huskisson to Goderich, 31 Aug. 1827, Ripon MSS. 40862 ff. 229—30.
32. Holland to Tierney, 22 Aug. 1827, Tierney MSS. 37 (C).

their business & if there be room after this — the Cabinet
may if they please look out for ornaments.'[33] Many thought,
plausibly, that Herries's promotion must have been urged by
Robinson (now Lord Goderich and Canning's successor as
prime minister) who, 'being totally deficient in financial
capacity could neither go on without Herries, nor did he wish
to expose to another Chancellor of the Exch: his inca-
pacity'.[34] Probably the Whigs' real objection was Herries's
intimacy with Rothschild, to whom he was said to have sold
Treasury secrets. The truth of this accusation is less significant
than the fact that many persons repeated it. Huskisson believed
that the dispute had 'reference to *another quarter'*, and
Viscount Granville remarked afterwards that a 'mysterious
individual...has raised Herries to the Chancellorship of the
Exchequer'.[35] It reflected fears not only of Rothschild
personally but of business interests generally. Huskisson's
desire to systematize sprang from no philosophical bent, but
from a determination to unshackle the administration from
what he honestly believed were dark, secret stock exchange
influences — to break from financial 'mystery' out 'into the
light'. Herries was the City's favourite, adept financially and
innocent of economic theory. Baring clearly believed him to
be the most susceptible Chancellor; Pearse of the Bank
assured him that 'if you will take the Chancellorship of the
Exchequer, it will tend more to raise the funds and give
financial confidence than the restoration of poor Canning's
life'; Irving wrote that 'with the exception of one, you have

33. George IV's August 1827 memorandum, Aspinall, op. cit. iii. 291–2. Peel disagreed with the King's high opinion of Herries and considered him fit only for
'mending the blunders in the Malt Bill'. Peel also thought that the Whigs' objections were merely tactical, and that they would later waive them in return for
Holland's admission to the government. Peel to Arbuthnot, 5 Dec. 1827, Aspinall,
Correspondence of Charles Arbuthnot, 95; Peel to Goulburn, 16 Sept. 1827,
Parker, op. cit. ii. 22–3.
34. H. U. Addington to Vaughan, 22 Feb. 1828, Vaughan MSS.C. 2; see Tierney
to Holland, 1 Sept. 1827, HHP 51584 ff. 134–6; Planta to Herries, 12 Aug. 1827,
Herries MSS.; *The Times*, 23 July 1827.
35. The King's physician Knighton was implicated in this **Herries/Rothschild**
cabal. Huskisson to Goderich, 29 Aug. 1827, Ripon MSS. 40862 ff. 227–8; *New
Times*, 25 Aug. 1827; *The Times*, 27 Aug. 1827; Herries, op. cit. i. 164–8,
227–30; *The Greville Memoirs*, i. 264–6 (9 and 17 Jan. 1830).

the voice of all the Bank.'[36] *The Times* remarked that the
funds rose when it seemed that Herries would be appointed
and fell when it seemed that he would not. (Huskisson was
too well aware of Rothschild's influence over the price of
stock to be impressed by this).

Herries was finally accepted by the Whigs, but he remained
'a live shell'[37] waiting to blow up the cabinet, and after
only four months of 'strenuous imbecility',[38] Goderich gave
up the ghost of Canning's ministry.[39] Herries and Huskisson
quarrelled over the mooted appointment of Althorp to the
chair of the Finance Committee, and Goderich refused to
coerce or continue without either man. But was this
economic dispute peripheral or central to the government's
undoing? Goderich later contended that it was 'sole cause',
while both parties agreed that it was not more than a relatively
'unimportant', 'immediate occasion'.[40] Herries claimed that
his authority had been slighted by Huskisson's having decided
on Althorp at Tierney's suggestion, without first consulting
himself. But for three weeks he seemed to have accepted
Huskisson's handsome apology of 30 November and only
took umbrage again on 21 December.[41] Secondly, Herries
apprehended that 'The alarm and distaste of those who
are opposed to Finance Committees as instruments of too
extensive and dangerous Reforms, will not be diminished
by the appointment of Lord Althorp, who is regarded as
the most prominent member of the most reforming
party in the House'.[42] Yet Herries had repeatedly urged
that the Committee should be no façade, but be seen

36 Pearse to Herries, Aug. 1827 and Irving to Herries, 31 Aug. 1827, Herries, op.
cit. i. 224–7, 220–1.
37. Palmerston's autobiography in Lord Dalling, *The Life of Henry John Temple,
Viscount Palmerston* (1871–4), i. 211. Palmerston thought that the King had
planted the bomb deliberately.
38. Horton to Littleton, 10 Jan. 1828, Fay, *Huskisson and His Age*, 87.
39. Jones, op. cit. 184–204.
40. Herries, op. cit. ii. 71–7; H. of C., 18 Feb. 1828, 2 PD, xviii. 503. Herries's
secretary, Spearman, also suggested that the Finance Committee was only a
pretext for the quarrel; Herries, op. cit. ii. 56–7.
41. See the correspondence in Buckinghamshire MSS. (Goderich), 0.34–49,
144–9.
42. And who had denounced the sinking fund. Herries to Huskisson, 29 Nov.
1827, HP 38752 ff. 100–2.

to be a genuine instrument of reform. Besides, as Huskisson
more subtly argued, the chair would fetter Althorp, 'invite
a reciprocity of confidence', and render him far less dangerous than if he were an irresponsible but leading member of
the committee, 'kept at a jealous distance by the Friends of
Government'.[43] Althorp alone cannot account for Herries's
intransigence. On 21 December Bexley, after a frank interview
with Goderich, was able to confirm Herries's suspicions that
the premier was negotiating to effect the entry of Holland
(a Whig and a 'Catholic') into the cabinet. Accordingly, after
further discussions with Knighton, Herries set out to break
up the government, and chose the Finance Committee as his
pretext.[44]

Like Herries, Huskisson assured the despised Goderich that
it was not the Finance Committee issue that had sounded
'the tocsin of your Administration'. He suspected that that
'rogue' Herries had been intriguing with Wellington since
before Canning's death. Feverish conversation with Anglesey
and de Walden persuaded Huskisson's never very phlegmatic
imagination of a deep malignity, 'an influence elsewhere', a
'fiendish', 'baneful and secret influence' near the King,
working to traduce and denigrate himself.[45] Knighton was
implicated in these terrors, and possibly Wellington, but the
central figure hovering in the background of Huskisson's
imagination was Rothschild. Historians should beware of conspiracy theories, but only a genuine if fantastical belief in
conspiracy can account for Huskisson's sudden collapse of
will in late December. Moreover it is hard fact that Herries

43. Huskisson to Herries, 8.00 a.m., 30 Nov. 1827, ibid. ff. 112–13; Buckinghamshire MSS. (Goderich), 0. 36; Huskisson's memorandum, 28 Dec. 1827, HP
38753 ff. 110–29.
44. Herries, op. cit. ii. 28–9, 45–52; Aspinall, *Letters of George IV*, iii. 352–3;
Herries to Bexley, 28 Dec. 1827, Herries MSS. 57403 ff. 169–79. When, during
January's recriminations, Herries complained of having been excluded from
negotiations, Goderich assumed that he was referring to the Finance Committee
chair, whereas in fact he meant Holland's entry into the cabinet.
45. Huskisson to Goderich, 11 p.m., 12 Feb. 1828, Melville, *The Huskisson Papers*,
291–2; Huskisson's memorandum, 28 Dec. 1827. Jones, op. cit. 198–9;
Huskisson to Granville, 15 Jan. 1828, Granville MSS. 30/29/9/3/35. Herries had
certainly maintained a correspondence with Arbuthnot and Holmes, to whom
he leaked secrets of the Canning and Goderich cabinets. Wellington continued to
despise Herries, nevertheless. See Herries MSS.

was in touch (indirectly through his secretary) with Nathan
Meyer at this time. Spearman reported on 31 December: 'He
[Rothschild] is very anxious that you should not stir' —
meaning presumably that Herries should not resign.[46] There
is an obvious motive and one that explains why Herries
selected the Finance Committee as his excuse. His business
contacts had been pestering him for some time with their
anxieties about his own retrenchment crusade, announced
under Canning. For example, the banker member for Bristol
wrote to him:

I am in almost daily communication with two or three of the largest
holders of English stock, and I observe that the great fear operating in
their minds is not so much the political state of the world as the
expected Finance Committee, which they fear may be so formed as to
recommend measures of finance of a very novel character. . . The great
stockholders above referred to put *all* their trust in you, and I can
assure you with truth that they would not at this moment hold any
English stock if you were not the Chancellor of the Exchequer.[47]

Like Rothschild, they dreaded a unilateral resignation by their
ministerial ally. In resisting Althorp, therefore, Herries —
and Bexley too — were representing the interests of their City
friends.

It was not only Huskisson who scented the presence of a
grey financial eminence; within a few weeks of the fall of
Wellington's government in 1830, a Whig Chancellor of the
Exchequer, Althorp himself, was to boast 'of ordering his
door to be shut against Rothschild'.[48] At all events, the
disputes of 1827 were about power, not policy. Huskisson
was prepared for Herries to have either the Exchequer or the
Finance Committee, but not both. Lord Redesdale suggested
that Huskisson, having exercised 'complete power' over
Liverpool and Robinson, and therefore over economic policy
itself, was now trying to supersede a Chancellor whom he

46. Spearman to Herries, 31 Dec. 1827, Herries MSS. 57374 ff. 56—8; this refers
to a memorandum of Spearman's conversation with Rothschild on the 30th . Fay,
Huskisson and His Age, 108—11, was probably wrong in thinking that Huskisson's
mysterious comment to Peel about Herries in Janury 1828 referred to the Rothschild connexion (it probably referred to the Herries/Knighton link), and he rather
underestimated how much deeper the differences between the two men went than
disagreement over Althorp and the Finance Committee.
47. Hart Davis to Herries, 26 Nov. 1827, Herries, op. cit. ii. 2.
48. Althorp to Arbuthnot, 13 Feb. 1831, Aspinall, *Correspondence of Charles
Arbuthnot*, 136.

could *not* dominate personally, by making him and Goderich 'ciphers in their departments, under the control of *his* [Huskisson's] Committee of Finance'.[49] In the same way, Wellington, when he became premier, objected to the Finance Committee as an independent power even more than he disliked its specific proposals. It was an affront to his authority, and a tool (he mistakenly thought) of Huskisson. He protested indignantly that 'he would have done the work [of retrenchment] himself', and done it better, and after it had functioned for only a session he allowed the Committee to drop quietly out of mind.[50]

Caring 'not for the dissatisfaction of ultra-Tories' and in the interests of 'efficient government',[51] Peel induced Wellington to offer Huskisson his post of Colonial Secretary in January 1828. The brief alliance of Peel and Huskisson in 1828 pointed to the 1840s and the Tory party split into ministerial élite and bucolic squires. Huskisson accepted office (to the dismay of many Canningites), Goulburn was made Chancellor, and thin-faced Herries was dispatched to the Mint. Huskisson commented sardonically that it had never been intended to leave Herries at the Exchequer, and that it was a 'good epigram' to make him succeed to Tierney's position.[52]

The Finance Committee, or Committee on Public Income and Expenditure, which exercised an influence similar to that of the May Committee a century later, has usually been regarded as a starting point. For Lucy Brown, it marks the point of departure for Whig economics (such as they were) in the 1830s; the triumph of the radical view of tax reduction as the first priority, against the Tory determination that public credit must be maintained in all circumstances. For Finer, it represents the first great instance of Benthamite influence working in government and administration, through 'philo-

49. Colchester, *Diary and Correspondence*, iii. 535—6, 538.
50. Littleton, MS. Journal, 20 Feb. 1828, Hatherton MSS. D260/M/F/5/26/7. Artuthnot to Peel, 10 Feb. 1829, Peel MSS. 40340 ff. 211—12; H. of C., 13 Feb. and 16 Apr. 1829, 2 PD, xx. 338—9; xxi, 886. To be fair to Wellington, his ministry did retrench effectively.
51. Peel to Gregory, 18 Jan. 1828, *Memoirs by Sir Robert Peel*, i. 15—17.
52 Huskisson to Granville, 18 Jan. 1828, Granville MSS. 30/29/9/3/36, copy in HP 38754 ff. 162—4.

sophic' officials like John Bowring.[53] At the time, Harriet Arbuthnot complained that 'The Finance Committee is filled with political economists who alarm the *illiberals*', while to the liberals themselves it signified victory in the old battle between 'cheap, economical, civil government' and 'large, expensive military government'.[54] It certainly encouraged Parnell's *On Financial Reform* (1830), Wade's *The Extraordinary Black Book* (1831), and the crusade against a despotic and dear government, which helped to precipitate the reform crisis of 1830–2. But the Finance Committee also marked a culmination of certain trends in policy, trends that were not to be resumed until after the Tories returned to office in 1841. And so, more relevant here than the measures of economy, such as superannuation reform, is its handling of the questions of free trade and debt management.

Peel superintended nominations to the Finance Committee and carefully balanced safety with appearance. It would contain five 'reformers' but, as Herries reassured him, 'Baring and Bankes would not lean to the subversion of our financial system altho' they would press the reduction of Establishments; and Maberly and Hume would in some material points counteract each other. Maberly will support Establishments and run at the Sinking Fund while Hume will be ultra violent against both.'[55] The most dangerous was Parnell, whom Peel appointed chairman – possibly so as to invite a reciprocity of confidence. The others were Althorp, Stanley, Newport, and Howick from the opposition; 'Huskissonites' – Tierney, Littleton, and Horton; Lowther, Knatchbull, Ward, Home Drummond, Palmer, and Ridley as ministerial supporters; and for the government, Goulburn, Herries, and Fitzgerald.[56] Brougham conceded that this was 'as fair a committee as he

53. Brown, *The Board of Trade and the Free-Trade Movement*, 12; S. E. Finer, 'The Transmission of Benthamite Ideas 1820–50', in *Studies in the growth of nineteenth-century government*, edited by G. Sutherland (1972), 30.
54. Russell in H. of C., 25 Apr. 1822, 2 PD, vii. 69, quoted in J. Prest, *Lord John Russell* (1972), 27.
55. Herries to Peel, 10 Feb. 1828, Peel MSS. 40395 ff. 219–21.
56. For Tierney's suggested 66 nominees in mid-November 1827, see HP 38761 ff. 269–70.

could desire...by one third fairer than any Finance Committee he had before seen', and publicly begged Huskisson to reconsider his refusal to serve, since 'the knowledge
of all other members of the committee combined was as
dust in the balance, compared with [his] resources.'[57]
Never proof against this sort of flattery, Huskisson relented.
The scene may well have been rehearsed in order to spite
Herries and also Wellington, who confessed to Peel that
he was 'a little uneasy about the composition of the Committee considering that you do not and Mr. Huskisson
does belong to it'.[58]

The only significant opportunity for retrenchment lay in
the military and naval estimates, and it was here that Tories
most dreaded the Finance Committee's power. Wellington
had been bewildered by Canning's combination of a bellicose
Near Eastern policy with military reductions in Gibraltar and
the Mediterranean. The Duke assumed that foreign policy
should adapt to the limits of a nation's power, and never
understood the mentality of statesmen who responded to a
reduction of material resources with an increased show of
power, concealing weakness beneath bluff and bluster.
Arbuthnot tried to convince Herries that his Finance Committee project was 'pregnant with danger': 'What I most dread
is the Finance Committee... How can the King consent to a
reduction of the army which is even now not equal to the
exigencies of our extended Empire? This is in truth most
disastrous.' Herries demurred on the grounds that retrenchments were unavoidable, and shortly after Arbuthnot wrote
again:

I am sure that immense reductions must be made. But I firmly believe
that by refusing grants for Bridges, Roads, &c. — by cutting off
immensely from Colonial and other Foreign Expenditure — and by
suspending works in the Naval Department — by putting an entire
end to the African Coast and Sierra Leone — and by some other savings
and improvements — we might get more than ever has been contemp-

57. H. of C., 15 and 18 Feb. 1828, 2 PD, xviii. 447–8, 557. Baring added that
the 'aggregate' of the financial knowledge of the other members 'bore no
proportion' to Huskisson's. Ibid. 447.
58. Wellington to Peel, 18 Feb. 1828, Peel MSS. 40307 ff. 50–1; Peel to Althorp,
17 Feb. 1828, Peel MSS. 40395 ff. 244–5.

lated. Let our army also be put upon a more economical footing in point of Cloathing and other matters; — but I think it must be insanity to weaken our Military Force at the very moment that we have embroiled ourselves by that fatal Treaty with Russia and France upon the affairs of Turkey.[59]

At this point Canning inconsiderately died — thereby cheating Arbuthnot of a vindictive triumph over him in Parliament — and Peel emerged as the strongest economizer in the Duke's cabinet. Backed by Goulburn, he threatened to resign unless his colleagues implemented a Finance Committee recommendation to suppress the office of Lieutenant-General. Wellington and Hardinge had argued forcibly against this proposal before the Committee, and, supported by Aberdeen and Ellenborough, the prime minister rejected Peel's demand, for the sake of both military efficiency and ministerial authority. Peel gave way in a huff, and Althorp denounced the Committee as a 'delusion', since it was evident that while ministers might sack the odd clerk or dockyard labourer, they would not obey instructions to abolish a *political* office.[60]

Yet in fact the Committee itself had doubts about military retrenchment. It had only just carried the vote on the Lieutenant-General. It was badly scared by Sir George Cockburn's evidence, which showed how much smaller was the difference between the British and foreign navies than most of its members had fondly imagined.[61] Thus the Committee reported that much of the annual expenditure was applied to charges of a fixed nature, and was not reducible by 'any measure of retrenchment that could immediately be adopted'. Besides, the object behind the government's new positive approach to retrenchment — to economical reform as a cure rather than a concession — was, by balancing the nation's books, to equip it for sudden military exertion. And though the point was not put, it would have been absurd to attempt this by a military purge, rendering the nation physically vulnerable at the same time as it made her

59. Arbuthnot to Herries, 29 and 31 July, 2 and 5 Aug. 1827, Herries MSS.
60. Althorp to Graham, 2 July 1828, Graham MSS., Bodleian Film 107, Bundle 2.
61. Littleton, MS. Journal, 27 Feb. 1828. Ellenborough, *A Political Diary, 1828–30.*, i. 32–3, 86, 153–7, 173; *Journal of Mrs Arbuthnot*, ii. 183, 196.

financially secure. Ultimately, Herries's recommendation that
'the Revenue. . . ought to be adapted to the Expenditure,
not the Expenditure to the Revenue', was impossible to
achieve.[62]

Hitherto Britain's main resource against sudden war was
the sinking fund. The theory was that, by upholding public
credit, it would facilitate government borrowing in a crisis.
More directly, it was a hoard of treasure that could be raised
in emergency.[63] In 1828 the Finance Committee put an end
to this Pittite machinery.[64] The orthodox line of criticism,
stemming largely from Hamilton, reached a climax with an
apparently influential pamphlet by Lord Grenville, who had
firmly supported the sinking fund from 1786 to 1822. He
now joined the chorus in protesting that only a *genuine*
surplus could support a sinking fund, and he added that the
present fund did not constitute a 'resource in unforseen
emergencies'. Grenville eschewed the moral question as to
whether a generation should finance its own wars or burden
posterity,[65] and argued that it was more important to cut taxation and the annual charge on the debt than it was to redeem
the actual capital of the debt.[66] More radically, Lauderdale
and Page urged that the sinking fund entailed 'compulsory' or
'forced parsimony', which shortened the circulation, and

62. CSC, *Fourth Report on Public Income and Expenditure (Revenue, Expenditure, and Debt)*, 1828, 27.
63. Robert Hamilton, *An Inquiry concerning the Rise and Progress, the Redemption and Present State, and the Management, of the National Debt of Great Britain
and Ireland* (1813), third edition (1814), 7, defined the fund's third principle as
being to raise a peace-time surplus to discharge the debts of previous wars or to be
a resource for affording future wars. A much-read anonymous, ministerial
pamphlet, *Administration of the Affairs of Great Britain, Ireland, and their
Dependencies* (1822), sixth edition (1823), 24-5, defined the fund as: a surplus
to give government 'a due weight and control in the money market', and
especially to uphold government credit 'under any casual deficiency of the
revenue'; a means for the eventual reduction of the entire Debt to three per cent
stock; and a fund of treasure, and of 'disposable income, for any emergency of
the state'. Ibid. 18–46.
64. Hargreaves, *The National Debt*, 135–56.
65. For which he was criticized by the Vice-President of the Board of Trade, T.
P. Courtenay, in his *A Letter to Lord Grenville on the Sinking Fund* (1828),
7–12. See J. M. Buchanan, *Public Principles of Public Debt* (1958), 31–47.
66. Lord Grenville, *Essay on the Supposed Advantages of a Sinking Fund* (1828),
5–13, 77–82, &c.

that it 'has the effect of forcibly converting a portion of the revenue into capital'. In a Keynesian-sounding phrase, they condemned the 'propensity to parsimony' as likely to impoverish everyone by diminishing production. Whenever a money economy replaced barter, the danger of parsimony increased because individuals could profitably invest capital as *rentiers* instead of in enterprise, and the state ought not to encourage such parsimony by a sinking fund.[67] Whereas Ricardo, assuming that supply created demand, mainly dreaded a shortage of *fixed* capital, and therefore of production, Lauderdale thought that too little *circulating* capital would stifle demand, diminish production, reduce profits from existing fixed capital, and deter investors. In other words, by adding to the fixed and taking from the circulating capital, the sinking fund was probably responsible for 'many of the effects hitherto attributed to Mr Peel's Bill, and other causes'. Above all, the enormous withdrawal of circulating capital in 1822–5, and its being forced on the market as fixed capital, had led to the fall of interest on fixed capital and consequently to the fatal bubble flotations and bankruptcies. Whereas in the 'orthodox' view it was cheap money that had stimulated over-trading and the emigration of capital, for Lauderdale the explanation lay in a failure of consumption and effective demand. In the Ricardian canon, sinking funds tended to compulsory saving and the diversion of wealth from 'unprofitable expenditure' to 'fixed' or 'productive capital',[68] but Lauderdale followed Malthus in thinking that 'progress' depended mostly on circulation (demand) and that an addition to the proportion of fixed capital would arrest it.

A swifter nemesis waited for the sinking fund in the growing disillusionment of ministers and officials. Canning wished to abolish it; Huskisson to re-define it;[69] Wellington to make it

67. Lauderdale to Page, 16 June 1829, Page MSS. ff. 65–70.
68. See, for example, D. Ricardo, 'Funding System', *Encyclopaedia Britannica Supplement* (1824), 421. Ricardo thus implied that sinking funds led to reduced taxation.
69. See above pp. 163–4.

a more efficient instrument of redemption; and Robinson to diminish its annual charge, since under the existing system of accumulation and redemption, 'the prospect of any relief to annual expense [is] so remote (for 10 or 15 years *is a remote* period with all the intermediate chances of war or armament).'[70] In 1823 Robinson had proposed that the fund should accumulate at compound interest until it amounted to one per cent of the total public debt. Initial progress being so slow, however, he now decided that it would be more beneficial to let the initial five millions wait only until it had climbed to twenty (as it already had), instead of to 1 per cent, and then to cancel those £20,000,000 of debt, setting free £600,000 every four years. But he was strongly in favour of maintaining a legally fixed surplus of revenue to constitute a 'sinking fund for war purposes'. Finally Herries, in his April 1827 memorandum, suggested that the only way to make good a deficiency in the legally appropriated amount of sinking fund, without extra taxation or borrowing, would be to abandon the obligation to buy a fixed amount of stock yearly *irrespective* of whether sufficient surplus existed. He repudiated the late Lord Londonderry's apprehension that public credit must necessarily suffer from the absence of a legally fixed annual surplus, so long as Parliament declared that it would continue to appropriate whatever it could of the five millions. Robinson's objection to Herries's plan showed unusual foresight. He abandoned the dogma of public credit, and argued that if Parliament merely applied genuine surplus, to no specified amount, then it would have difficulty in repudiating Radical demands for tax reductions to the amount of the current surplus. The main benefit of the fund, after all, had been that it had provided ministers with a justification for keeping up taxes.

The Finance Committee included some inveterate enemies of the sinking fund, such as Joseph Hume, as well as more guarded critics like Bankes and Parnell. The latter merely wished to repeal some of the taxes that impeded trade and manufactures, by 'suspending the Sinking Fund, till funds

70. Robinson to Herries, 22 Dec. 1826, Herries MSS. 57402 ff. 23–5; Robinson to Herries, 29 Nov. 1826, LP 38576 ff. 110–13.

could be got for it, without doing so much injury to industry'.[71] A private manuscript notebook of Parnell's provides a rare and fascinating glimpse at the course of the discussion in the Committee.[72] Nearly all the members were agreed that appropriation of five millions annually would not continue to answer. Ministers wished merely to lower the amount. On 23 June Goulburn moved that 'a fixed sum' be applied annually to the reduction of debt, funded or unfunded, whereupon Bankes proposed to substitute merely 'the surplus of the revenue' actually obtained, rather than a fixed sum. Goulburn's proposal was defeated by ten votes to nine[73], but when, two days later, Bankes's amendment was debated, Huskisson moved to apply 'a *permanent* surplus of the revenue' as distinct from simply any surplus that happened to occur. In other words, he was demanding that even though no fixed amount was to be set aside, Parliament must continue to vote sufficient taxes to ensure that there always would be some surplus. Like Robinson, he realized that the mere direction as to a surplus, without any measures to guarantee that there would always be one, must quickly lead to deficit. Huskisson's motion drew ten votes against ten, whereupon the chairman (probably Parnell, possibly Hume) cast a negative. Bankes's plain 'surplus of revenue' was then carried, but Huskisson managed to salvage some of the fund's lost ground by carrying a resolution,

That regard being had to the total amount and fluctuating nature of our Revenue, as well as to the necessity not only of carefully avoiding any addition to the public Debt but also reducing it as far as possible in time of peace, it will be expedient in estimating the supply and ways and means to include in balance of the latter a surplus of not less than three millions in each year.[74]

Whereupon Stanley clarified the opposition position by carrying a motion that in the case of an annual surplus amounting to less than these three millions budgeted for, 'the

71. H. Parnell, *On Financial Reform* (1830), 232–3.
72. This notebook is now in the possession of Lord Congleton (Parnell MSS.).
73. Hume, Parnell, Bankes, and Maberly must have been among the ten; the other six were probably Baring, Stanley, Althorp, Howick, Newport, and Tierney.
74. Parnell, MS. Notebook; Howick failed by 6 votes to 12 with a motion that the surplus to be applied should be the actual surplus of the previous year and not that estimated for the current year.

deficiency ought not to be supplied by borrowing.'

Huskisson, Maberly, and Hume then initiated a lengthy discussion about the dangers of possessing a large unfunded debt.[75] On 2 July Hume raised the question of whether the redemption of funded or discharge of unfunded debt should be given priority. The Committee decided that the latter was just as important, since although exchequer bills were currently at a high price, and the debt outstanding on them was insignificant, yet great 'embarrassment and loss...under certain circumstances, might arise from the existence of a large Debt payable on demand'. December 1825 and March 1826, and the continual fear of war, obviously prompted this advice.[76] Finally, on 3 July, at Althorp's suggestion, the Committee agreed to recommend that the surplus might be used to convert, with the owners' approval, permanent into temporary annuities.[77] The 'classical' theory of public finance had not yet developed to the point where it would seem axiomatic that it was in the state's best interest, as in that of an individual debtor, to have its debts in long rather than short annuities.

Bankes's 'surplus only' requirement, together with Huskisson's, Stanley's, Hume's, and Althorp's recommendations, were incorporated into the Committee's 4th Report, dated July 10th. [78] The commentary, apparently by Herries,

75. For a further suggestion by Huskisson in committee for reducing the unfunded debt, see Littleton, MS. Journal, 15 Feb. 1828. This scheme would have involved 'borrowing' the forty millions of stock belonging to Chancery suitors and replacing outstanding exchequer bills with it. 'I have talked of [this] fifty times to Lord Liverpool, but Lord Eldon would not hear of it. We'll make Lord Lyndhurst do as we like.'

76. Hume to Tierney, 1 July 1828, Tierney MSS. 38. In 1829 Goulburn proposed to convert three millions exchequer bills into 4 per cents, reducible in 1833, so as to lower the unfunded debt.

77. Althorp had withdrawn a suggestion that a part of each year's surplus should actually be offered as a 'bonus' (i.e. bribe) to whichever holder of perpetual annuities agreed to convert the largest amount into terminable annuities; Parnell, MS. Notebook.

78. CSC, *Fourth Report on Public Income and Expenditure*, 1828, 5–25. This Report also criticised the Dead Weight Annuity as an expensive and 'intricate contrivance' to provde a fixed sinking fund by fresh borrowing.

was perfunctory. It observed that only £3,495, 760 of debt
had been redeemed since 1816; that most of this had been
effected by the reduction of the interest on exchequer bills
and on 5 and 4 per cent stock, or by the cessation of terminable annuities; that very little had been achieved by the
application of a surplus directly to redemption. But it added
that 'it would be difficult to say that without the continued
application of a portion [of] the Revenue to the Redemption
of the existing Debt, that increased value of the public
securities would have been created, whereby this great alleviation of the public burthens had been affected'. In 1829,
amid radical gloating, Parliament acted on Herries's Report
and made an 'absolute break with the past',[79] replacing
the principle of the fixed sum and accumulation with that
of the accidental surplus.

Thus lived — thus died — the sinking fund. Never more did
sorrow light on it, or shame. It was not made the inner
weight to bear of twenty years unprecedented war. The
reaction against that 'glorious piece of nonsense'[80] undoubtedly went too far, however, and in this respect the fears
of Huskisson and Robinson were well founded. After a token
effort in 1829, governments succumbed to pressure to reduce
taxes rather than debt. Parnell's view became popular, that
the repeal and reduction of taxes on industry, of excise duties,
and of tariffs on raw materials, would do far more good in the
existing situation than debt reduction.[81] Annual surpluses
thus succumbed to popular clamour for tax relief, with the
inevitable consequence that when the revenue declined,
owing to trade depression, it led to prolonged deficit.[82] In
other words, there was no surplus in an average year to be

79. Smart, *Economic Annals of the Nineteenth Century 1821–30*, 449–51,
475–7. The Report also recommended that all funded debt redeemed by the
application of real surplus should be cancelled, thus lowering annual charge,
rather than that it should go on accumulating for a time (as it had since 1825),
with dividends of redeemed stock paying for further stock.
80. Leycester in H. of C., 11 July 1828, 2 PD, xix. 1667.
81. Parnell in H. of C., 11 July 1828, 2 PD, xix. 1676–7.
82. H. Parnell, 'Financial Measures of the late and Intentions of the present
Ministry', *Edinburgh Review*, lxxiv (1841–2), 507–9.

applied to a poor year. The old sinking fund of the Tories, however inefficient for debt redemption, had provided this resource. Its moral appeal, which lasted until the return of distress in 1826, provided an excuse for just sufficient taxation to cover the normal yearly fluctuations of revenue. But the government's perhaps hypocritical defence of the device on the wrong grounds — that is, as the agent of redemption — only led to its ridicule and condemnation by more utilitarian, earnest, and *literal* Radical financiers. Rather than appropriate a fixed sum and borrow to meet it in bad years, as the Tories had done, the Whigs of the 1830s — following Parnell and Poulett Thomson — abandoned fixity and squandered all their surpluses in tax relief. What was lost was not public credit as Londonderry had prophesied, but government solvency as Huskisson predicted in 1830, when he pleaded for the retention of a 'reasonable' surplus — 'I will not say upon the principle of a Sinking-fund, but as the necessary guard and provision against the effect of those fluctuations to which our public income is liable' — and against all 'incidents and casualties' which might arise.[83] In 1841 Peel had to choose between government loans or fresh taxes to balance the budget. Moreover, losing the sinking fund removed the most tangible weapon with which to finance war. Ministers had to trust that an unshackled manufacturing economy would create sufficient personal wealth to tax in emergency.[84] Retrenchment and the erosion of surpluses forced free traders to rationalize their policy as the bringer of peace. But pacific foreign policy followed from financial and commercial measures which had been partly motivated by the need to prepare, financially, for war.

83. H. of C., 18 Mar. 1830, 2 PD, xxiii. 597—8.
84. Prior to 1914 there was a similar clamour for bankers' reserves, or a war chest, independent of the vicissitudes of the Bank of England's reserve. L. S. Pressnell, 'Gold Reserves, Banking Reserves, and the Baring Crisis of 1890', in *Essays in Money and Banking in honour of R. S. Sayers,* edited by C. R. Whittlesey and J. S. G. Wilson (1968), 224—8.

A fiscal endorsement of free trade and the question of direct taxes

In 1820 Parnell had prophesied that tariff reduction would increase trade and with it fiscal revenue,[85] and T. P. Courtenay, who was privy to Huskisson's and Robinson's reforms of 1823—26, described them as an 'experiment of the effect of reduction upon the produce of the remainder'.[86] If so, the experiment was officially pronounced successful in a lengthy financial statement by Herries, which accompanied the fourth Report[87] of 1828. Herries was not reputed to be one of the 'liberal economists'; he had been hostile to most of the experiments of the mid-twenties, and his belated approval betrayed nothing of fervour or ideological conviction. Letting statistics argue for themselves, he demonstrated that 'there has been an increase of consumption, and an augmentation of receipts', indeed an 'almost uniform improvement' during 1826—7, in the case of most raw materials and manufactured articles. Furthermore, the 'fall of prices would seem to have been among the causes of the improvement'. Most striking was cotton-wool, where a 50 per cent cost reduction had led to huge increases in consumption.[88] Cheaper raw cotton and labour had enabled manufacturers to sell goods 'materially cheaper', and 'thus they have gained admission more freely into the foreign markets'. The Whigs' subsequent failure to provide a surplus to cover deficiency years was probably influenced by the Report's implication that, with reduction of the burthens pressing on industry and trade, the process might be carried to an indefinite extent without danger of deficit.

Herries's statement further observed that 'a less amount of capital has sufficed for carrying on a more extensive trade'. Lord Liverpool and his advisers held that capital ('Life Blood which animates and sustains our dense Population')[89] and

85. H. Parnell, 'Finance', *Edinburgh Review*, xxxiii (1820), 54—69.
86. Courtenay, op. cit. 107—8.
87. CSC, *Fourth Report on Public Income and Expenditure*, 1828, 27—37, embodying extracts from a statistical report by William Irving, Inspector-General of Imports and Exports.
88. West India sugar was an exception to this trend, owing to a crop failure.
89. Huskisson's memorandum, 18 Oct. 1826, HP 38761 ff. 211—48.

skill were more important than low costs to the success of
manufactures and conquest of trade. Cheapness they considered rather a symptom of failure than a prescription for
prosperity.[90] But after 1829 cheapness (with comparative
advantage as its corollary) gradually came to be regarded as
the essential ingredient of economic progress. It seems very
likely that in 1842 Peel, who expressed public disdain for the
Report and evidence of the Whigs' Select Committee on
Import Duties in 1840, was none the less influenced by the
more narrowly fiscal Report of Herries in 1828, with its
financial endorsement of tariff cuts.[91] The stumbling-
block for Peel was the question of wages. His fears of social
revolution were increasing, and from his point of view the
flaw in free trade, as understood by the Finance Committee,
was that wages would fall with the rest, indeed would lead
the dive into cheapness. The disclaimer — that the wages of
labour did *not* vary with the cost of subsistence — had to
wait for Cobden and for close empirical observation of the
effects of further tariff reductions.

In 1830, contemplating the low profit margins, the suffering, the lack of incentive to invest, the 'reverse of a thriving
state', Huskisson — now out of office — recommended further
tariff reform. He was goaded into this by dread of depression
rather than inspired by theories of wealth:

We now press too hard upon labour, and the Capitals employed in
productive industry. So long as we had cheap money, and were rendering it cheaper in each succeeding year, the evil of this pressure was
disguised and contracted; but the moment the progress of depreciation
ceased, it began to be felt. We are like the Opium Eater, but it does not
follow that we are to go back [to that] destructive habit. For a time
it deluded us as to our real situation, but having once made the effort
to leave it off, we must now get into a more healthy course.[92]

But he would only support, for example, malt and beer duty

90. See, for example, Herries's notes on 'Low Prices' in Herries MSS. v. 88; Herries
approved 'free trade as meeting this state of things'. In other words, free trade
was a response to cheapness rather than a device to create it.
91. Prest, *Lord John Russell*, 218, appears to endorse Russell's complacent view
that Peel's second ministry guided the ship with the charts left in the cabin by the
Whigs. But the real continuity lies between the Wellington and Peel governments,
with the Whig decade forming an hiatus in economic policy. N. Gash, *Sir Robert
Peel, the Life of Sir Robert Peel after 1830* (1972), 327–9.
92. Huskisson to Denison, 10 Jan. 1830 and Denison to Huskisson, 3 Jan. 1830,
HP 38758 ff. 95–6, 82–4.

reduction as part of a 'system'. What this meant he elucidated
in his great speech against Davenport's motion for a reconsideration of Peel's Bill. Here he claimed that the proportion
of the national income reserved for 'reproduction' ought to
be far greater than it was, in order to increase the comforts of
the labouring classes, who were 'the immediate instrument
of that reproduction', and also to augment the capitals
which called that labour into exertion (Ricardo's investment
fund). Both wages and the profits of productive capital were
at present too low. But there was simply too little public
revenue to enable the government, without a return to deficit
financing, to remit sufficient taxes to relieve distress, to
stimulate consumption and receipts, to achieve a 'cheerful'
and progressive, as distinct from a stagnant and declining,
state. Therefore some alternative source of revenue must be
found. And here, after much perambulation, Huskisson at
last trod, gingerly, on to the 'tender ground'. There must, he
said, be a redistribution of taxation, since it was doubtful
'whether we shall afford adequate relief, without removing
a larger amount of those taxes which press directly upon
income arising from capital engaged in industry, and upon
the income of labour to which that capital gives employment;
– transferring, as far as may be indispensable, the burthen
upon [i.e. on to] all that class of income which arises from
capital not so employed.'[93] At present, fully three-quarters of
the national revenue was levied on customs and excise, on
'productive industry', instead of on 'realised wealth'. That
'vortex' of 'gigantic speculation' – those foreign loans that
glutted London with money – those 'pursuits which, were
they multiplied even an hundred-fold, could never add the
value of one peppercorn to our national resources' – all
these were rampant while the labourers, who *did* have power
to enrich the community, were distressed, and while the
industrialists of Lancashire and Yorkshire wanted funds. In
future, taxation must be concentrated on fundholders, landlords, mortgagees, and annuitants.

Whatever they might say in the Commons, Liverpool and
his financial advisers had always regarded the income or

93. H. of C., 18 Mar. 1830, 2 PD, xxiii. 599.

property tax, not as a war-time expedient, but as a permanent
device to maintain the economy on a war footing. Castlereagh, for example, would have liked to have restored it in
1819 if politically possible. It was coveted for fiscal reasons
rather than as a device to facilitate tariff reform, and was
never even discussed on free trade or protectionist grounds.
Canning is normally thought of as a free-trader, though an intuitive rather than theoretical one, yet he was one of the few
ministers not to regret the income tax. 'Can you remit us any
more taxes?' he asked Liverpool while they were preparing for
the 1825 session. 'If so, I am for direct ones this session.' He
was not here protesting against free trade, but being a politician more than an administrator, he was eager to gratify the
parliamentary classes. Liverpool replied:

If we *could* do what we *ought* to do (do not be alarmed, I am not going
to propose it), we should make an augmentation in our direct taxes of
at least two millions; and, as a compensation, take off indirect taxes to
the amount of four of five millions. By such an arrangement we should
not materially reduce our revenue, and we should considerably increase
the wealth and resources of the country, by the relief which might be
afforded to commerce.[94]

Political dependence on the great landlords and capitalists
prevented this; but commercial and manufacturing depression
in 1826–30 revealed the fiscal unreliability of taxing consumption and trade for necessary revenue, and also ruled out
any extra indirect taxes to supply the deficit. Perhaps
Canning's death removed an obstacle to fiscal reform. At any
rate Goderich, Huskisson, and Herries were in complete
accord on the matter, and planned to substitute a property
tax for certain indirect taxes during 1828. Herries later
defined three motives: to tax 'accumulated wealth', since
the greatest national burthen was 'the charge of the accumulated debt'; to free British industry and commerce from the
duties that were impeding competitiveness in its 'growing
rivalry with the manufactures of the Continent'; and finally,
like George Harrison in 1819, to assuage 'public feeling'
by a gesture.[95] Wellington's appointment put an end to

94. Liverpool to Canning, 19 Oct. 1824, Yonge, *Life and Administration of Lord
Liverpool*, iii. 311; Canning to Liverpool, 17 Oct. 1824, CP 71.
95. Herries's 8 Nov. 1841 paper, sent to Peel, in Herries MSS. Herries, op. cit. ii.
1–2, 205–12; Fay, *Huskisson and His Age*, 115–16; see above p. 82.

Herries's suggestion, but in the course of his three sessions as premier, proposals for an income tax divided his cabinet. As usual, the battle was fought within, not between, the government and opposition parties.

With a certain amount of posturing, Peel emerged as the ministry's strongest tax reformer.[96] He kept saying how he wished to reach the 'great capitalists' — Rothschild, Baring, his own father — and the landlords, especially Irish absentees. His desire for an income tax was less narrowly fiscal than Herries's — he hoped that it would reconcile class antagonisms and enable Parliament to commute taxes bearing on industry and 'the comforts of the labouring poor'.[97] Peel and Huskisson were lucky in that social welfare and economic progress seemed compatible. They escaped the dilemma of twentieth century politicians who often wish to increase progressive taxation for social reasons, but who are convinced by classical economic theory that economic progress requires the taxation of consumption, and that direct taxation of the wealthy would impinge on saving and investment.[98] Peel and Huskisson saw investment as depending on manufacturers' profits, which required cheap raw materials; and just as tariffs had magnified inequalities, so a reduction of import duties, with an income tax to supply the necessary revenue, would both diminish inequality and stimulate investment. Unlike successive Labour governments, they never had to choose between increasing aggregate wealth and equalizing its distribution.

So were Peel and Huskisson touched by intellectual influences? Because Peel's 1842 income tax rendered further

96. Despite S. H. Northcote, *Twenty Years of Financial Policy, 1842–61* (1862), 29 and Torrens, *Life and Times of Sir James Graham*, ii. 206–7, who both believed that Graham had to cajole a reluctant Peel in 1842. See Gash, *Sir Robert Peel*, 298–305.
97. Peel to Arbuthnot, 16 Feb. 1830, Aspinall, *Correspondence of Charles Arbuthnot*, 124; Ellenborough, *A Political Diary, 1828–30*, ii, 203–16; Gash, *Mr Secretary Peel*, 615–8. Arbuthnot to Peel, 16 Feb. 1830, Peel MSS. 40340 ff. 218–19. Arbuthnot wanted a 'transposition of taxation' away from tariffs, mainly for political reasons — namely, that Parliament would insist on it if government did not act first.
98. E. F. Schumacher, 'Public Finance — its Relation to Full Employment', in *The Economics of Full Employment*, edited by F. A. Burchardt (1944), 86–7, 91.

instalments of free trade possible, and because classical
economists attacked indirect taxes so vigorously, it is often
assumed that income tax was an essential component of the
'classical' canon. Thus Semmel spoke of Peel in 1842 as
donning the mantle of Huskisson, Ricardo, and the 'liberal
economists'.[99] Yet it would be truer to say that Peel was
rejecting economic theory. Theoretically, the main point of
contention was whether the burden of taxation fell ultimately
on the landed interest, as Smith argued, or on the monied
power, as Ricardo insisted. Huskisson and Peel were attempting to break away from these vertical concepts and to reduce
taxes that fell on the poor, as the source of productive wealth
(and also of revolution). Shebab suggests a rising torrent of
educated opinion in favour of income tax in 1816—30, but his
list of (mainly anonymous) publications is meagre. [100] Adam
Smith had expressly opposed property taxes and ignored the
redistributive possibilities of fiscal policy.[101] There is a
strange notion that Ricardo favoured direct taxes 'very
decidedly',[102] yet though he advocated a once-for-all capital
levy, and though he deprecated taxes on consumption,
especially on necessaries, he looked to over-all fiscal reduction and retrenchment rather than to changes in the incidence
of taxation. All taxes reduced production and all were therefore unwelcome. In the early 1820s he regarded proposals to
revive the income tax as illegitimate attempts by the landed
interest to 'reach the stockholder'.[103] McCulloch con-

99. Semmel, *The Rise of Free Trade Imperialism*, 141.
100. F. Shebab, *Progressive Taxation. A Study in the development of the progressive principle in the British Income Tax* (1953), 72 and n. Perhaps the most
influential pamphlet was the anonymous *Three Letters of Paul Silent to his
Country Cousins* (1816).
101. W. Kennedy, *English Taxation, 1640—1799. An essay on policy and opinion*
(1913), 146—50 and *passim*.
102. B. E. V. Sabine, *A History of Income Tax* (1966), 53. R. Girardeau, 'La
théorie de l'impôt chez Ricardo', *Revue de Science et de Législation financières*,
xliii (1951), 319—31, suggests that Ricardo's *Principles* contained a covert plea for
an income tax, but the best authority, C. S. Shoup, *Ricardo on Taxation* (1960),
219—24, rejects this interpretation.
103. Ricardo to Trower, 14 Dec. 1822 and 28 Jan. 1820, Sraffa, op. cit. ix. 246—
77 and viii. 153-5. D. Ricardo, *On the Principles of Political Economy, and
Taxation* (1817), Sraffa, op. cit. i. 221. E. R. A. Seligman, *The Shifting and
Incidence of Taxation* (1899), 147—51. Initially, Cobden opposed Peel's 1842 tax
as an anti-millowner, anti-shopkeeper device: J. Morley, *The Life of Richard
Cobden* (1881), i. 240—1.

demned income taxes as inquisitorial; too easily evaded in the
non-agricultural sector; and — despite what Huskisson and
Parnell were saying — likely to discourage capital investment.
They merely inhibited demand for labour, and though they
might narrow the gulf between employer and labourer, the
absolute position of the working classes would worsen.
McCulloch thus disliked Peel's tax of 1842, and subsequently
Gladstone's tariff reductions and increasing reliance on the
single tax.[104] J. S. Mill preferred revenue tariffs on luxuries
to taxes on income,[105] and most subsequent 'classical' thinkers
agreed that economic progress required the taxation of consumption by non-protective indirect taxes and a minimum of
interference with capital investment.

Thus when in 1830 Huskisson and Peel, backed by Althorp,
Parnell, and Poulett Thompson, argued for an income tax,
they were not repeating the dogma of 'liberal economists'.
Like Ricardo and McCulloch, they spoke of not taxing
capital, of keeping up profits and maintaining an inviolate
fund for investment; but whereas the theorists considered indirect and assessed taxes optimal for growth and feared that
an income tax would jeopardize capital accumulation and
investment, the politicians took a directly contrary view. This
reflects the fundamentally different approach of Ricardo and
Huskisson. The former desired a maximization of exports, on
the basis of comparative advantage, in order to delay the
inevitable long-term pressures on money-wages and the
erosion of profits leading to a stationary state; it was essential
that food and raw materials should be cheap and that the
taxation of profits should be minimized. Huskisson did not
wish to force a maximum amount of exports, merely to
secure the optimal amount for a freely working market
system without serious fluctuations.

The only eligible influences in favour of income tax were
anti-Ricardian. Torrens maintained that it was the most
legitimate tax because it penalized *private* consumption but

104. O'Brien, *J. R. McCulloch*, 245–63.
105. J. S. Mill, *Principles of Political Economy* (1848), revised edition (1909),
Book V, Chapter vi, *passim* and 864–72; Book V, Chapter iii. section 5, 829–32.

not investment. Taxes on necessaries or *general* consumption
would amount to the taxation of wages, disturb the wage
fund equilibrium and retard national production.[106] In 1830
he was still denouncing the indirect taxes that 'palsied
industry' and 'suspended speculative demand', but he now
wished to confine direct taxation to 'dormant money
capitals' not destined for productive investment.[107] Torrens
was still outside the mainstream of Ricardian monetary and
fiscal policies, in so far as he thought that they should be
discriminatory and redistributive, a means of diverting
resources from the drones to the socially useful. But later, as
he adopted a more Ricardian monetary position, he
abandoned direct taxation. By 1852 he was condemning
income tax, unilateral free trade and other dogmas, which,
though wisely adumbrated by Huskisson, Peel had perpetrated
'with the headlong zeal of a recent pervert'. At the last
Torrens felt that revenue duties on luxuries were most con-
ducive to growth.[108]

Thomas Chalmers, 'the "McCulloch" of Malthusiansim',[109]
probably exercised a more significant influence over policy.
Like most economists, he held decided views on the vertical
incidence of taxation, and attacked the Ricardians for
supposing that the brunt fell on money and trade, rather than
land; but he differed from most economists in believing —
with Peel and Huskisson — that this issue was immaterial
compared with its horizontal incidence — 'the question
between the higher and the humbler classes in society'. An
income tax would command 'a fresh sentiment of gratula-
tion from the country at large', and would succeed in
'charming away a rancorous politics from our nation'. It
'would wrest their most formidable weapon from the hands

106. R. Torrens, *A Letter to Liverpool on the State of the Agriculture of the
United Kingdom, &c.* (1816),22 and n.; Shebab, op. cit. 66–9.
107. R. Torrens, *The Crisis and the Remedies* (1830); Robbins, *Robert Torrens
and the Evolution of Classical Economics*, 289–90.
108. R. Torrens, *Tracts on Finance and Trade, submitted to the electors* (1852),
No. 2. In particular Torrens thought that Peel had unwisely forsaken reciprocity
for unilateralism.
109. Schumpeter, *History of Economic Analysis*, 487. See below pp. 308–11 for
Chalmers's influence.

of demagogues. It were the grand specific. . . for appeasing the outcries of public discontent.' Nor could it harm land-lords, since ultimately they bore the burden of all taxation anyway. Chalmers opposed 'scurvy' Ricardian economics in believing that the aggregate of taxation was not yet as high as it ought to be — witness the widespread consumption of luxuries;   that the substitution of direct for indirect taxes would 'lower the money price of manufacturing labour and so, by cheapening, would enlarge our exports'; it would even encourage agriculture and provide employment for redundant or 'excrescent population'.[110] Peel and Huskisson were much closer to Chalmers on fiscal matters than to Ricardo.

Herries and Peel persuaded Goulburn to budget for a reduction of duties on beer, hops, and sugar, and to tax the revenue of all landed and fixed property and of all funds and offices, while sparing the profits of trade and land occupation. Wellington, Ellenborough, Rosslyn, and, more guardedly, Bathurst, Melville, and Lyndhurst opposed this in cabinet, and Peel and Herries grudgingly gave way. Ellenborough objected that it would be inequitable to tax land and funds, but not professions and trades, and would inflame bitterness between town and countryside. This was to regard social divisions as based vertically on sectors, rather than on horizontal classes, as Peel and Huskisson were beginning to do.[111] Thus when Goulburn announced in Parliament that he would not resort to an income tax because it would mean 'transferring the charge from the shoulders of one party to those of another', he did not mean that it would redistribute wealth in favour of the poor — Peel's main argument in its favour — but that it would switch taxation from one section of the establishment to another.[112] The July revolution and the Last Labourers' Revolt were to open Ellenborough's eyes to

110. T. Chalmers, On Political Economy, in connexion with the Moral State and Moral Prospects of Society (1832), in Chalmers, Works (1849), xx. 119—29. See Chalmers to Wilberforce, 25 June 1822, Wilberforce MSS. A Selection from the Correspondence of Thomas Chalmers, edited by W. Hanna (1853), 97—9.
111. Like McCulloch, Ellenborough claimed that an income tax would harm the poor by reducing the demand for labour. Ellenborough, op. cit. ii. 209—13.
112. H. of C., 15 Mar. 1830, 2 PD, xxiii. 309.

the horizontal divide and to convince him that, however oppressive an income tax might prevent anarchy.[113]

Wellington was the insuperable obstacle. As guardian of the landed interest, he opposed a measure that he thought would punish the gentleman with £1,200 a year, and he was also anxious 'to get the City of London with the Government as Pitt had'.[114] Preferring to meet financial exigency through bargains with the mighty, he wished to renew the Bank's Charter in 1829, four years before it was due to expire, and to 'give the Bank every possible advantage resulting from the transmission of the Revenue and keeping the publick money, making the Bank pay handsomely for the same'.[115] He reckoned that he might raise enough in this manner to cover a reduction of the sugar, tobacco, and other duties against which public opinion was moving; or, as Ellenborough surmised, he might even persuade the Bank to manage the debt *gratis*. Likewise he proposed a premature renewal of the East India Company's Charter, flouting the widespread unpopularity of the Company's China trade monopoly, because 'he thinks he could get the Company to take Ceylon off our hands, and thus save £100,000 a year.'[116] Here motivation reverts to the problem of power. Wellington longed to escape from the *system-builders*, to avoid government 'machinery' such as the property tax, and to restore the old personal and political relations between the Treasury and the City as they had flourished in good Vansittart's goldless days, before the triumph of Huskisson and the *system*. He longed to resurrect what Huskisson himself condemned, in a portentous phrase, as 'the encroachments of power, and the errors of empiricism',[117] to leave

113. Ellenborough, op. cit. ii. 346 (24 Aug. 1830).
114. Ibid. i. 212, and ii. 138. Rothschild and Harriet Arbuthnot both thought that he succeeded in this aim. *Journal of Mrs Arbuthnot*, ii. 200.
115. Wellington to Goulburn, 6 Sept. 1828, Goulburn MSS. II/12. He was still toying with the idea of a bargain in 1830; Wellington to Goulburn, 20 Aprl 1830, ibid. Ellenborough, op. cit. i. 185, thought that the Duke was 'sacrificing future advantage for present profit, and all to make a good financial show next year' (1 Aug. 1828).
116. Ellenborough, op. cit. i. 184; *Journal of Mrs Arbuthnot*, ii. 201, 286.
117. H. of C., 18 Mar. 1830, 2 PD, xxiii. 584. Huskisson saw 'enlightened public opinion' as the 'shield' with which to protect the nation from these arbitrary powers of darkness.

the light and return to financial 'mystery and darkness'.

The Whigs were equally divided on direct taxation, Poulett Thomson, Althorp, Howick, and Parnell being favourable, Baring, Spring Rice, Grey, Palmerston, and Brougham decidedly hostile.[118] In his first budget, Althorp was to move 'exactly in the wrong direction' (according to Herries) by surrendering the house and window taxes and imposing a duty on raw cotton.[119] In Whig — Radical mythology, 1816's triumph over 'corruption' remained the most encouraging memory of the bleak years, and it may have inhibited tax reform in the 1830s. Nothing was done until Peel re-entered office in 1841 to face the accumulated deficits of spineless finance. His government reverted to direct taxation in 1842 in order to put Britain on a war footing, not by enabling her to finance hostilities directly, but because the substitution of an income tax for tariffs would rescue the state's finances, increase private wealth and 'establish the practicability of carrying on new wars without adding to the debt, and wholly by war taxes'.[120] Cobden condemned the income tax initially as a military weapon, but in Gladstone's subtle hands it became a temporary engine of peace, vetting foreign policy and limiting national aggression to just and moral causes. For once a nation has to pay for its own wars by current taxes, instead of dumping the burden on to posterity by loans,[121] its representatives become less irresponsibly bellicose. By the 1850s, therefore, it is fair to see income tax and free trade as pacific and cosmopolitan. But neither adjective fits Tory financiers of the 1820s, and their fiscal policy was designed to equip the economy for battle without resorting to disastrous expedients like Bank restrictions and loans. Peel,

118. D. Le Marchant, *Memoir of John Charles Viscount Althorp, third earl Spencer* (1876), 238—9; Mitchell, *The Whigs in Opposition*, 227—8.
119. Herries's 8 Nov. 1841 paper; L. Brown, *The Board of Trade and the Free-Trade Movement*, 46—56; S. Buxton, *Finance and Politics, 1783—1885* (1888), i. 32—4; Aspinall, *Correspondence of Charles Arbuthnot*, 136.
120. Parnell, *On Financial Reform*, 266—9.
121. O. Anderson, 'Loans versus Taxes: British Financial Policy in the Crimean War', *Economic History Review*, 2nd series, xvi (1963—4), 314—27.

with his sensitive social conscience, was the link between Canningite chauvinism and Gladstone's *pax Britannica.*

THE FIRST ASSAULT ON
THE CORN LAWS 1825−1828

When the last bill was passed [1828], Huskisson said to me you will
have two more changes − if Peace continues. In two or three years' time
you will pass a Law for a Free Trade under a 10s duty and then, in a
few years more, you will pass another to reduce that Duty yearly till it
comes to nothing, and you will not feel the change by the increase of
trade it will cause you and the consequent improvement in prices.
Littleton to Leigh, 26 June 1832, Fay, *Huskisson and His Age*, 342.

Intimations of famine

Carlyle misled his readers when he described the landed
establishment as anchored on the scaly rind of a slumbering
leviathan, which without warning suddenly dived under on
the repeal of Catholic and Nonconformist disabilities.[1] No
doubt the horrid face of that High Tory monster *was*
intolerance, but its vulnerable underbelly − financial greed
− had been rumbling for some time. In the second half of the
1820s, the agricultural proto-populist movement of 1821-2
re-emerged to demand reform of the constitution, of taxation
and especially of the currency: 'Prices had fallen, poor-rates
had risen, rent and tithe were not elastic enough, and the
farmer's fat sorrow had become lean; he began to speculate
on causes, and to trace things back to that causeless mystery,
the cessation of one-pound notes.'[2] During 1824-5 even
Sinclair had begun to think that cash payments had, after all,
been successfully resumed,[3] but panic and the depression of

1. T. Carlyle, 'Signs of the Times', *Edinburgh Review*, xlix (1829), 439-59.
2. George Eliot, *Felix Holt, the Radical*, Chapter III. Though not officially banned
until 1829, many small notes were withdrawn from 1826 onwards.
3. *The Late Prosperity, and the present adversity...discussed, in a correspondence
between Sir John Sinclair and Mr. Thomas Attwood* (1826), 1-6.

1826 immediately revived agricultural anti-bullionism.[4] Its new prophet was the Radical estate improver from Cumberland, Sir James Graham, whose immensely influential *Corn and Currency* (1826) was consciously designed to educate the country gentry out of their reliance on protection, and to inculcate instead desire for retrenchment, free trade, free banking, small notes, currency reform, and the taxation of annuitants. He passed a sombre and misleading judgement on resumption:

The capitalist and the economist ruled the day; and an administration, more connected with annuities than with land, possessed of few acres, and haunted by general principles, introduced, in 1819, a measure which will render that year memorable in the history of our misfortunes, if it be not the real date of our decline.[5]

Reaction against the 'fatal measure of having cut up the currency by the roots'[6] contributed largely to the ultra-Tory revolt against the Duke of Wellington in 1830.[7] Malcontent ultras regarded rotten boroughs as havens for the 'march of intellect men' — Ricardo's disciples — and wanted a reform that would strengthen landed representation and secure, among other things, a permanent reprieve for small note circulation. While the ultra leaders Knatchbull and Vyvyan debated whether or not the Duke was 'wobbly' on cash, Grey pretended to have an open mind.[8] The backwoods subscribers to *Blackwood's* were instructed by its anti-Ricardian economist, David Robinson, to regard gold at 77s. 10½d. as the root of the social and political catastrophe.[9]

4. See, for example, C. C. Western, 'A letter to the Earl of Liverpool, on the cause of our present embarrassment and distress, and the remedy', *The Pamphleteer*, xxvii (1826), 219-38.
5. J. R. G. Graham, *Corn and Currency; in an address to the landowners* (1826), 37-8; W. T. Mc. Torrens, *The Life and Times of Sir James R. G. Graham* (1863), i. 182-94.
6. S. E. Brydges, *To the worthy freeholders of the County of Kent*(1831).
7. D. C. Moore, 'The other face of reform', *Victorian Studies*, v (1961-2), 7-34.
8. H. M. Knatchbull-Hugessen, *Kentish Family* (1960), 182; B. T. Bradfield, 'Sir Richard Vyvyan and the fall of Wellington's government', *University of Birmingham Historical Journal*, xi (1967-8), 141-56; M. Brock, *The Great Reform Act* (1973), 132.
9. Especially *Blackwood's*, xix (1826), xxvi (1829), xxvii (1830), passim. H. Perkin, *The Origins of Modern English Society, 1780-1880* (1969), 237-52. *Blackwood's* continued to recommend the repeal of Peel's Act until the 1850s, but the *Quarterly* never went so far, its panacea for distress being emigration. Johnston, *British Emigration Policy*, 132-3.

Peel realized that it was the kernal of agriculture and Radical discontent, and 'seemed to think there would be an entirely new [political] combination, of which the currency questions would be the basis.'[10]

Meanwhile on protection, agriculturists were now wholly defensive. They preferred to 'cling to the present system with all its inconveniences rather than trust to the Honor or Candour of their opponents if the principle of duty is admitted' — i.e. once the question had been stirred again.[11] Fifty-nine petitions were sent to the Commons in 1826, 587 in 1827, all from lords and occupiers, all deprecating *any* change in the Corn Law. Curwen's 'conversion' to this static position is noteworthy. As late as 1822 he had been a high protectionist, but in the mid-twenties, after converting many acres to pasture, he abandoned his arable ambitions. His biographer comments that it was 'a sad retreat from high farming', and attributes it to high labour costs and low prices.[12] But the fundamental reason was a growing conviction that autarchy was impossible. 'I [once] thought England might have gone on increasing her production almost to an unlimited extent', proclaimed a disillusioned Curwen sadly in 1827. He had 'once thought Great Britain could produce corn for itself, but he now thought otherwise'. 'We had all or most of us at least ploughed too much', exhausting soil in the process and diminishing returns. He now acknowledged, a year or two after ministers had done so, that self-sufficiency could not allay famine.

Liverpool's government was increasingly alarmed about the prospect of famine. Most agriculturists thought its concern one-sided: 'That man has the intellect of a fool, and not of a statesman, who can look at this nation in the present moment without discovering that a glut in any commodity is as destructive as a scarcity, and that all trading systems and all governments, ought to guard as much against the one as the other.'[13] However, Liverpool recognized 'no ground

10. Croker to Hertford, 25 Mar. 1833, *The Croker Papers*, ii. 205; G. S. R. Kitson Clark, *Peel and the Conservative Party* (1929), 107-9.
11. J. L. Foster to Oriel, 25 Apr. 1825, Foster/Massereene MSS. D207/74/148.
12. E. Hughes, *North Country Life in the Eighteenth Century*, ii (1965), 223, 231-2, 283-9.
13. *Blackwood's*, xix (1826), 311.

whatever...*(except in a case of absolute Famine)* for the Interference of the Crown' in the workings of the corn market. Even when mercantile frauds looked like opening the ports to oats, Liverpool refused to act. For how could a government possibly justify an intervention that went 'not to save the people from starving, but to benefit the Farmers by preventing oats being too cheap'?[14] In April 1825, however, Huskisson persuaded the cabinet that it must interfere at last, by letting bonded corn on to the market. A bill was passed in May permitting the admission, in two instalments, of all corn warehoused in England before 1822,[15] at a duty of 10s. instead of the 17s. stipulated by the still inoperative Law of 1822.

Despite what Fay wrote and some contemporaries thought, Huskisson did not do this to gratify merchants with corn deteriorating in warehouses. He insisted that they abide by the outcome of their speculations, and he was very curt to a deputation from his own constituency that requested duty-free importation out of bond.[16] Nor for that matter did he do it to appease agriculturists, though naturally they were delighted by a measure that would keep prices below 80s. and the ports shut. As usual Huskisson was looking farther ahead than his critics. He was already planning to reduce protection in 1826 or 1827, and was therefore alarmed by the huge mass of corn that, despite the denials of Whitmore and the free traders, was languishing in continental ports. This surplus must be brought 'by degrees...to its fair level'. It must be excluded from England, not to maintain the existing Law, but to attack it more effectively. In a year or two 'that artificial mound which had accumulated in the foreign corn countries, in consequence of our own corn system, would be in some degree diminished',[17] depriving British farmers of a

14. Liverpool to Grant, 15 Aug. 1824, LP 38299 ff. 61-2; Liverpool to Herries, 21 Aug. 1824, Herries MSS. 57367 ff. 78-9.
15. Calculated at 400,000 qrs. in the case of wheat. Smart, *Economic Annals of the Nineteenth Century, 1821-30,* 303-4, states incorrectly that the act was to apply only if the price reached 70s.
16. H. of C., 28 Apr. 1825, 2 PD, xiii. 282; Huskisson to a Liverpool deputation, 1 May 1825, HP 38746 ff. 193-5, Melville, *The Huskisson Papers,* 183-5.
17. H. of C., 28 Apr. 1825, 2 PD, xiii. 281.

cogent argument against freer trade. Meanwhile the Bonded
Corn Bill would ensure that 'much of the accumulated corn
in this country would be disposed of before the arrival of the
period when the corn laws must come under the revision of
parliament'.[18] Finally, Huskisson would by then have lowered
manufacturing tariffs even further, exposing the Corn Law as
a single naked anomaly. In these ways, a measure of protection
to agriculture in 1825 'would tend greatly to facilitate the
arrangements which might be hereafter made on the general
subject of the Corn Laws'.[19]

Immediate consumer interests also dictated the admission of
bonded corn. In the stormy spring of 1825 it seemed likely
that food supplies would run short, raising prices to the high
seventies but not beyond. Without some inducement to the
owners of bonded corn to admit their produce before the
next harvest, or before the next quarterly average could be
announced on 15 August, there might well be a hiatus in
food supply. 'His sole object was to keep down the price of
corn, and to prevent it from rising to an unreasonable extent,
in the interval between this period and the next harvest.'[20]

Obviously it was essential to know exactly how much corn
was waiting to flood in from Europe. On 20 June 1825, the
Board of Trade, 'by desire of Lord Liverpool and Mr Huskisson', resolved to send William Jacob, the Receiver of Corn
Returns, to the continent to find out. He was to report in
time for the next session on the general state of agriculture in
the corn-exporting countries, but particularly on the amount
of surplus bonded for exportation and how it was likely to be
affected by corn law revision.[21] Jacob reported on 21
February 1826 to the effect that the European surplus,
actual and potential, was minimal. Even 'If a duty in this
country of 10s. or 12s. per quarter was imposed, it would not
allow of such a profit, on the supposition of the price being

18. Ibid. 283.
19. H. of C., 2 May 1825, ibid. 340.
20. Ibid. (my italics).
21. B.T. 5/33, 454-5, 461-3 and *passim*. Jacob to Napier, 22 June 1825, Macvey
Napier MSS. 34613 f. 320. For further government enquiries into foreign
agriculture, see A & P, *Accounts and Papers relating to corn and grain*, 1826,
15-452.

from 60s. to 64s. as to induce any great exertions to increase cultivation in the bordering districts on the Vistula.'[22]

This document had an immediate vogue and was frequently alluded to in debates. Most agriculturists detested it as an 'ex parte' inquiry by a convert to economic liberalism.[23] Most free-traders welcomed it. Whatever Jacob's intentions, his emphatic assurance that exclusion from the British market was causing a contraction of North European cultivation reinforced Whitmore's two cardinal contentions — that the Corn Law was prejudicing England's reserve food supply, and that British farmers no longer needed protection against foreign competition. But when in April, on the basis of Jacob's findings, Whitmore moved to reduce agricultural protection, the government opposed and defeated him (250-81).[24] Huskisson explained that 'it would be impossible to legislate wisely, unless the currency, which was the soul and element of the prices, should have been first disposed of'.[25] Another reason for procrastinating on corn was that an Election was due after the end of the session, and ministers dared not brave just yet the landlords' displeasure.

That appeared to be the end of the corn question for 1826, when ministers suddenly introduced another temporary measure to admit bonded corn, and also to endow themselves with a discretionary power to import further foreign wheat by Order in Council during the dissolution. Both protectionists and free-traders regarded this as a ruse by Canning and Huskisson 'to get rid of the whole system of Corn-laws by a side-wind',[26] and after the Irish protectionist members had gone down, confident that the issue would not be broached until the Election was over. In fact, however, Canning only

22. A & P, *Mr Jacob's Report on the Trade in Corn, and on the Agriculture of the North of Europe*, 1826; printed in 2 PD, xv. 396-489 and in a special supplement to *The Times*, 27 Apr. 1826; Smart, op. cit. 382; Barnes, *A History of the English Corn Laws*, 190-1.
23. e.g. Robertson and Wodehouse in H. of C., 2 May 1826, 2 PD, xv. 800-2 and 827-8; *Blackwood's, xx (1826)*, 359-85.
24. H. of C., 18 Apr. 1826, 2 PD, xv, 318-71; Smart op. cit. 382-6; Barnes, op. cit. 189-90.
25. 2 PD, xv. 346; *Speeches of William Huskisson*, ii. 547-8.
26. Lethbridge in H. of C., 2 May 1826, 2 PD, xv. 787-8; see Holme Sumner in H. of C., 8 May 1826, ibid. 977; *Journal of Mrs Arbuthnot*, ii. 25-6.

agreed reluctantly, and in deference to his chief, whose motive was (as usual) pragmatic. 'Ld. Liverpool suddenly took fright, lest the harvest shod. be unproductive, and the price of corn shod. become excessive, suddenly proposed to the Cabinet [on 2 May] (wch. had been summoned for anor. purpose) the admission of foreign corn to a certain extent, and prevailed on Canning...to that effect, without having advised with a single individual out of doors'.[27] Since the rejection of Whitmore's motion — possibly because of it — there had been serious riots in Manchester and other manufacturing areas. On May day Lord King presented a petition from the distressed weavers of Manchester, which broke away from the traditional attack on mechanisation, and instead condemned agricultural protection as the source of their suffering. In reply Liverpool announced portentously that 'the time, and the events which have recently happened, render a revision of the existing laws which regulate the price of food absolutely necessary.'[28] On the following day he announced his decision on bonded corn to the cabinet.

It was not, as in 1825, that there was any danger of the ports opening to the detriment of farmers. Nominally prices were much lower than then, but considering the extreme decline in wages, they were 'greater in reality'. Ministers therefore decided to admit bonded corn in order to keep prices within the range of the distressed manufacturing labourers, and to arrogate further powers over importation as a means of moderating prices during the summer.[29] It is more difficult to say whether ministers accepted the Lancashire weavers' view that corn imports would resuscitate cotton exports. Huskisson did say that 'if a foreign demand could be created, either by the purchase of [foreign] corn, or by any similar measure, relief would be administered to the cotton manufacturer'. But he only used this proto-Cobdenite argument defensively, when British manufacturers were depressed.[30] Ministers thought that the Bonded Corn Bill might

27. *The Diary of Henry Hobhouse (1820-27)* , edited by A. Aspinall (1974), 120.
28. H. of L., 1 May 1826, 2 PD, xv. 746-8; Canning in H. of C., 1 May 1826, ibid. 764-6; Smart, op. cit. 387-8; Colchester, *Diary and Correspondence*, iii. 426.
29. Huskisson in H. of C., 2 and 8 May 1826, 2 PD, xv. 818-20, 995; *Speeches of William Huskisson*, ii. 558-60, 572.
30. Brady, *William Huskisson and Liberal Reform*, 66.

jerk the economy out of a standstill, but they did not therefore
suppose that corn law reduction could render Britain an
industrial workshop. They were not even implying that
protection had impaired Britain's export performance in the
first place, simply that temporary relaxation might stimulate
a non-speculative recovery. So long as commerce was
flourishing the price of grain had been immaterial, but in the
present context cheap food might help to restore commerce:
'The evil under which the country now laboured, arose from
over-trading, and a want of credit; and the only way in which
it could be remedied, was by creating such a demand as
would lead to the renovation of credit'. Foreign demand was
important because distress was greatest in the export-based
cotton industry, but it was also necessary to regulate
domestic demand. Having sold bonded corn, merchants
would buy limited amounts of fresh foreign corn to refill the
warehouses; this would create a small demand for cottons,
'that demand would create credit, and the beginning of credit
would be the termination of the existing distress'.[31] All this
had virtually nothing to do with prices.

Temporary and 'temporizing' it might be, but inevitably
everyone saw the Bill as a tilt at the Corn Laws, and the
'land', led by the Duke of York, 'rallied in the most boisterous
manner'. Grey, Lauderdale, and Russell led many Tory peers
and squires in an agricultural revolt against the Bill, while
Tierney and the more 'liberal' Whigs supported ministers. In
the divisions, government 'beat the *land* black and blue',[32]
until Creevey was jubilant: 'The charm of the power of the
Landed Interest is gone; and in a new Parliament Canning
and Huskisson may effect whatever revolution they like in
the Corn Laws.'[33]

Yet Huskisson really had no relish for chastising the land.
His concern was with the consumer and public order. In the

31. Huskisson in H. of C., 2 May 1826, 2 PD, xv. 824-5, 817-18.
32. 185 to 58 and 167 to 51 in H. of C., 166 to 67 in H. of L. Maxwell, *The
Creevey Papers*, ii. 101. What Whigs feared most was the dictatorial nature of the
new discretionary power to import grain during the dissolution, and they managed
to limit this power of importation to 500,000 qrs.
33. Ibid. Canning to Liverpool, 2 May 1826, CP 72. *Some Official Correspondence
of George Canning*, edited by E. J. Stapleton (1887), ii. 47-8, 52-3; Tierney to
Holland, 4 May 1826, HHP 51584 ff. 121-2; Colchester, op. cit. iii. 429-30;
Journal of Mrs Arbuthnot, ii. 25-6.

summer of 1826 occurred another of famine's alarms. As late as 8 August the harvest promised to be 'excellent, and well got in',[34] but a melancholy report from Goulburn on the state of the Irish potato threw ministers in a panic. Peel fretted about the difficulty of transporting supplies from Europe, even if any could be procured, and Huskisson was alarmed by 'sombre' reports on the performance of oats in the industrial west of Scotland and England:

Unfortunately that deficiency is most alarming in those crops which are the food of the lowest classes — potatoes and oats. It is further unfortunate that the falling off is likely to be the greatest in the parts where the lowest classes most abound...

In this state of things, seeing the price of oats at this time considerably above the *highest* price of our *present* corn law, and having now the certainty that, by the working of that Law, our ports *must* remain shut till 15th November (when the season [i.e. ice] will have closed them against any intercourse with the north of Europe), my opinion, founded on these and other circumstances, is that some *immediate* measures ought to be taken.[35]

By 20 August, it was clear that potatoes had begun to recover, but oats looked like being one-third below average. So on 29th, the cabinet decided to issue an Order in Council on 1 September, opening the ports for oats, oatmeal, rye, beans, and peas (but not for wheat or barley, which were sufficient) at a duty to be specified thereafter. This Order contravened the Act of May 1826, which had empowered the government to import additional wheat only,[36] and it was therefore necessary to call Parliament before Christmas to indemnify ministers and to fix retrospective duties on the corn imported. By the time it met, it was evident that the administration had over-reacted, that the potato crop was sufficient, while the unhampered 'Course of the Law...would

34. Liverpool to Canning, 8 Aug. 1826, CP 72; Liverpool to Peel, 4 and 10 July 1826, Peel MSS. 40305 ff. 190, 195-6; Liverpool to Herries, 9 Aug. 1826, Herries MSS. 57367 f. 116.
35. Huskisson to Peel, 18 Aug. 1826, HP 38748 ff. 124-6, Melville, op. cit. 202-4 (misdated); Robinson to Peel, 21 Aug. 1826, Peel MSS. 40388 ff. 305-6, Jones, *'Prosperity' Robinson*, 126-7; Huskisson to Canning, 11 Aug. 1826, CP 68; Peel to Huskisson, 17 Aug. 1826, Peel MSS. 40388 ff. 265-74; Peel to Goulburn, 14, 17, and 19 Aug. 1826, Goulburn to Peel, 25 Aug. 1826, Goulburn MSS. II/16.
36. Smart, op. cit. 387-91, and Barnes, op. cit. 191-3, both assume, wrongly, that the Order of 1 Sept. 1826 was in pursuance of the powers granted to ministers by the Act of May 1826.

1

78 PART THREE

have allow'd the importation [of oats] in November'.[37] The
odious Arbuthnot claimed that scarcity 'would not be thought
to exist at all, were it not necessary for every one in this
Country to be swelled out with beef and pudding and strong
liquours'.[38] The implication was that Liverpool, Peel, Huskisson, and Canning had taken advantage of a momentary panic
to undermine the Corn Laws. The suspicion was increased by
an incident at Manchester, where Huskisson was alleged to
have hinted from the hustings that a free corn trade was
imminent.[39] Wellington was incensed, and *Blackwood's*
called for Huskisson's proscription.

The three emergency measures of 1825-6 intensified
passions on both sides of the corn law debate. Yet in 1826
two opposed extremists made significant admissions:
Lethbridge still disputed Whitmore's central argument 'that
a scarcity was about to take place', but conceded that '*if* that
fact could be sufficiently proved, it would furnish a forcible
reason against the principle upon which the existing system
of our Corn-laws rested'; Whitmore still maintained, against
Lethbridge, 'that in the usual state of the country, taking one
year with another, the produce was not equal to the
consumption'; but he conceded that '*if* the contrary were the
fact, and *if* the produce could be proved to exceed the
consumption, there would not be any occasion for a revision
of the Corn laws'.[40] These were isolated insights, but coming
from two men who normally argued in ideological terms,
they indicate that Huskissonian empiricism was advancing.

The Corn Law of 1828

The suspensions and temporary measures of 1825-6
underlined the need for a permanent Corn Law, and Liverpool

37. Bathurst to Harrowby, 14 Sept. 1826, Harrowby MSS. 1st. series, XIV ff.
127-8; Ellice to Durham, 8 Sept. 1826, Durham MSS.
38. Arbuthnot to Herries, 26 Aug. 1826, Herries MSS. Henry Hobhouse commented, just as crassly, that 'Wheat is of no use in Ireland, where the peasantry
will not eat it' — but no doubt wheat *is* an acquired taste. *The Diary of Henry
Hobhouse*, 123.
39. Melville, op. cit. 204-8; Brock, *Lord Liverpool and Liberal Toryism*, 223-4.
For a similar incident, see Wellington, *Despatches, Correspondence, and
Memoranda, 1819-31*, iii. 342-4.
40. H. of C., 2 May 1826, 2 PD, xv. 786, 802.

hoped that the new Parliament would co-operate. The
Election was held to have strengthened the 'free trade'
interest, amorphous though that was.[41] Yet protectionist
clamour against Huskisson personally was so strong that
Liverpool arranged for himself and Canning to 'take the lead',
so as to 'obviate much jealousy and prejudice', and carry
more authority than if it was merely 'a *Department Question*'.
To keep him 'as much as possible in the background',[42]
Liverpool circulated Huskisson's crucial memorandum of 18
October 1826[43] to a few colleagues only — Canning, Peel,
Wellington, and later Robinson.[44] It began by listing seven
important and familiar objections to the existing Law:

(1)   the sudden transition at 80s. unsettled all parties.

(2)   the quarterly average was liable to fraud.

(3)   temporary (contingent) prohibitions deranged foreign
trade and the exchanges.

(4)   prohibition up to a high price maximised price
fluctuations (leading alternately to agricultural expansion and
contraction), and aggravated the plight of consumers in a
scarce year, and of producers in an abundant year.

(5)   foreign farmers had already 'considerably curtailed'
cultivation because of exclusion from Britain, thereby
depriving British consumers of any resource in a future run of
bad harvests.

(6)   British farmers were liable to exhaust their stocks in
an effort to keep the ports from opening, which meant that
the ports were unlikely to open until such time as foreign
stocks were inadequate, or until after ice had closed the
northern shipping ports.

(7)   prohibition deprived foreigners of the means to pay
for British goods and forced them to manufacture, while dear
food, having plunged the labourer 'lower in the scale of

41. e.g. Holland to Grey, 4 July 1826, HHP 51547 ff. 139-40.
42. Liverpool to Canning, Oct. 1826 and 10 Feb. 1827, Yonge, *Life and Administration of Lord Liverpool*, iii. 450-2. See *Journal of Mrs Arbuthnot*, ii. 79.
43. HP 38761 ff. 211-48; LP 38371 ff. 182-217. See also Huskisson's memorandum of 21 Feb. 1827, HP 38762 ff. 1-17.
44. Liverpool to Huskisson, 25 Oct. 1826, HP 38748 ff. 184-6, Melville, op. cit.
210-11 and Yonge, op. cit. iii. 429-30; Huskisson to Canning, 18 Oct. 1826,
HP 38748 ff. 182-3, Melville, 209-10.

subsistence', finally 'curtailed profits' and drove capital out of Britain.[45]

To these seven arguments Huskisson added an eighth ('of equal importance to me'), which was obviously prompted by memories of December 1825:

The two difficult questions of our corn laws and our currency have frequently been discussed together, but their relation to one another has generally been considered as confined to the influence which the contraction or expansion of the currency has upon the price of corn. I think there is a further consideration involved.

My position is this — that with a prohibition of corn up to a *high scarcity price*, this country cannot, under the present system of Banks and paper credit, maintain, for any length of time, a metallic currency, either at the *existing*, or at any other *fixed* standard of value.

The implications of this were grim for those agriculturists that demanded an increase, *either* of protection, *or* of the circulation, for Huskisson now wished to reduce protection in order to safeguard the fixed money settlement of 1819. He thought the Corn Law had sparked off the inflationary spiral of 1823-5, dear food having extended the circulation, which in turn pushed up all other prices[46] and fed over-speculation:

A rise of price, first produced by Monopoly, creates a demand for an extension of circulating credit, which, in its turn, becomes the occasion of a further rise of price, the one and the other operating alternately as cause and effect, till every part of our circulation, from that of Bills of Exchange to that of the Bank of England, is proportionately increased. Our paper circulation is like a series of concentric circles; — the outward is formed of Bills of Exchange, the inward of the notes of the Bank of England. When the wants of commerce, or the spirit of over-trading, force out an increased issue of circulating credit, the outward circle is the first to expand. When the increased issue begins with the wants of government — i.e. an increase of Bank advances — the expansion commences at the inward circle. But in both cases the others speedily follow, so as to retain their relative proportions; — and in both cases the effects are the same.

45. See also Huskisson in H. of C., 28 Apr. 1825, 2 PD, xiii. 286. Canning's and Liverpool's observations on a Prussian proposal for reciprocally freer exchange between 'workshop' Britain and 'primary producing' Prussia, bear out the view expressed above, p. 115, that ministers were more concerned to *keep* Germany supplying corn than to increase Britain's export markets. H. of L., 11 May 1826, 2 PD, xv. 1094; C. P. Villiers, *Free Trade Speeches* (1883), i. 213-15.
46. Though 'labour, being every where a *ready money* commodity, is the slowest to participate in [inflation], and the last admitted to its full share in the altered value of money.'

The corn monopoly of 1815 had been devised for a period of Bank restriction, when prices could rise indefinitely without detriment to the currency. But as a consequence of Peel's Act, bullion was the only commodity in England that could not partake of an inflationary price rise. Huskisson continued:

The consequence is that, as soon as the rise has reached the great articles of mercantile speculation, the import of which is not prohibited, they are eagerly bought up in foreign countries, and of course paid for in the only commodity which has not risen in England...To be consistent, therefore, with our system, if we keep our present prohibition of corn, we must reimpose the restriction on cash payments. In the present value of money a monopoly of the corn market, up to the price of 80s a quarter, and the continuance of a great paper circulation, constantly convertible into coin at a *fixed* standard, are, I will venture to say, for any considerable number of years, incompatible.

Unable to deny to Attwood and Graham a connexion between circulation and price, Huskisson here turned their arguments about, asserting that corn prices controlled the circulation, which in turn regulated other prices. He ignored their condemnation of the secular fall in prices since 1818, and blamed the moderate and temporary recovery of 1823-5 for the dangerous currency inflation of those years.

Moving to remedies, Huskisson concentrated on the need to prevent unilateral price movements. Unlike the Attwoods, he maintained that external equilibrium was the essential requirement of sound policy, from which internal stability would follow. 'Our first step must be to establish a sympathy between the price of *British* and *Foreign* Grain, so that, either in rising or falling markets, both should obey the same impulse, however different the range of the orbits in which they move. To effect this we must substitute habitual freedom of intercourse for habitual prohibition.' He followed this with three admittedly compromise principles:

(1)   that the British farmer was entitled to 'countervailing' protection to the amount of his 'special burthens' *vis-à-vis* other domestic interests.

(2)   that the British farmer was entitled to no protection at all once corn had touched a scarcity price.

(3)   that to offset the occasional sacrifice of (2), the British farmer was 'equitably entitled, in years of extraordinary abundance, to have that protection occasionally increased

beyond what mere compensation for special burthens would require'.

Liverpool entirely agreed that since the consumer had to be protected against prices rising too high, agriculturists must be protected against them falling too low.[47] This ruled out the imposition of fixed duty, since no duty could be imposed at high prices unless it was so small as to be nugatory at low.[48] Huskisson therefore suggested once more a sliding scale or 'floating duty', with wheat paying 20s. p. qr. at 55s. or below, and 1s. less for every shilling rise in price. This seemed applicable to the present 'limited demand' for European corn, though he realized that when, in future, a more 'extended demand' existed, the scale would have to be reduced (as it was in 1842). Following conversations with several 'dreadfully alarmed' Kentish farmers, Liverpool amended the scale slightly, to apply a 40s. duty at 50s., then dropping by 2s. for each shilling price rise. 'I think the *main points* are these. — That 60s is, as matters now stand,[49] a *remunerating price,* and that *beyond* 65s the monopoly ought to cease, and the foreign corn flow into the country with a moderate duty.'[50] Huskisson welcomed this scale, whereby foreign corn should 'occasionally ooze out' of bond above 60s., and flow out in considerable quantities above 65s.[51] Westmorland was scandalized, but the entire cabinet had agreed to the scale by 22 November. It was more lenient to agriculture than many of them had expected. In Canning's words, it 'cast the balance of principle in favour of trade and the balance of price in favour of agriculture'.[52]

Robinson contributed an unhelpful memorandum recommending import duties as a means to raise revenue and

47. Liverpool's memorandum, ?Nov. 1826, LP 38371 ff. 230-7.
48. Fay, *The Corn Laws and Social England,* 82, suggests, ingeniously but implausibly, that ministers rejected a fixed countervailing duty because it would have been 'grounded on quicksand', that is, it would have had to be lowered as 'special burthens' on agriculture were lowered.
49. i.e. taking into account the appreciation of money and reduction in taxation since 1815.
50. Liverpool to Huskisson, 25 Oct. 1826, HP 38748 ff. 184-6, LP 38302 ff. 83-6; Melville, op. cit. 210-11; Yonge, op. cit. iii. 429-30.
51. Huskisson to Robinson, 20 Nov. 1826, HP 38748 ff. 192-3, Melville, op.cit. 211-13.
52. See *Journal of Mrs Arbuthnot,* ii. 55-7.

promote emigration.[53] He told Herries that he looked 'to a new source of Revenue (altho' not to be made prominent in the House of Commons) from a sound revision of the Corn Laws'.[54] (It could hardly be 'made prominent' since revenue duties would not also be protecting). He admitted that his scheme 'was much objected to'. It is very unlikely that, apart from Bexley, Robinson's colleagues thought of a new Corn Law in fiscal terms — Wellington expressly denied it — and they do not seem to have taken Robinson's vagary at all seriously.[55]

When, after deliberately building up suspense, Canning revealed the government's proposals, murmurs of relief passed audibly over the land. The alterations were certainly 'not so great as apprehended'.[56] Scotland was reported as being 'almost without an exception, satisfied';[57] Irishmen considered it a 'decided victory' for agriculture;[58] and even Lowther thought the move to freer trade 'so diluted, that... the country gentlemen will have little cause to cavil'.[59] Canning's main defence of the Bill was that it would establish a 'sober, regular course' of trade without the present 'perpetual jirks and impulses arising out of extraordinary emergencies'. It would equalize prices and prevent alternate 'drought' and 'deluge'.[60] The Bill seemed certain to pass when on 1 June Wellington moved that 'foreign corn in bond should not be taken out of bond until the average price of corn should have reached 66s'. With the votes of former ministers — Eldon, Bathurst, Melville, and Westmorland, who had all reluctantly agreed to the measure in November — he

53. Robinson to Peel, 17 Sept. 1826, enclosing 'Suggestions on Emigration and Corn Laws', Peel MSS. 40389 ff. 55-64.
54. Robinson to Herries, 29 Nov. 1826, LP 38576 ff. 110-13.
55. Bathurst MSS. Loan 57/19; Wellington, *Despatches, Correspondence and Memoranda*, iii, 432-7; Jones, op. cit. 127; Robinson to Peel, 12 Mar. 1827, Peel MSS. 40392 ff. 269-70; Colchester, op. cit. iii. 532.
56. Jonas Asplin's diary, 3 Mar. 1827, in *Essex People 1750-1900*, edited by A.F.J. Brown, Chelmsford (1972).
57. Cockburn, *Letters chiefly connected with the Affairs of Scotland*, 173-4.
58. J. L. Foster to Oriel, 2 Mar. 1827, Foster/Massereene MSS.D207/74/240.
59. Aspinall, *Letters of George IV*, iii. 202. See Holland to Grey, 2 Mar. 1827, HHP 51547 ff. 167-8; and Hallam to Farr, 26 Mar. 1827, 'Unpublished letters of Arthur Henry Hallam from Eton', edited by N. Zamick, *Bulletin of the John Rylands Library*, xviii (1934), 37-8.
60. H. of C., 1 Mar. 1827, 2 PD, xvi. 770-1. For the debates, see Smart, op. cit. 407-22.

carried the amendment (78-74); whereupon ministers abandoned the Bill, and passed a third temporary Warehoused Corn Act, allowing the 560,000 qrs. in bond in to home consumption on the same terms as they would have enjoyed if Wellington had not wrecked the main Bill.

The interesting question here is Wellington's sincerity. He claimed that he thought he had Huskisson's prior consent to the amendment, and it is possible that their semantic misunderstanding on this point was genuine.[61] Too unsubtle to be devious, he nevertheless possessed, as Canning complained, a 'marvellous capacity for reading letters in his own sense'.[62] He had long been brooding on the warehouses as vehicles for 'speculative frauds in the corn trade', and rightly disputed Huskisson's view that the proposed weekly (as distinct from quarterly) averages would be less susceptible to them.[63] In March and April he had sat on a Select Committee of Lauderdale's to inquire into quantities of bonded grain and shipping costs. The nineteen witnesses (mainly merchants and factors) were agreed on two points: that Jacob had greatly underestimated Europe's agricultural potential and over-rated her production costs; and that weekly averages would 'open a massive door to fraud'.[64] They convinced Wellington that 'the warehouse system...must be reformed', since although a certain amount of abuse was unavoidable, warehouses afforded 'the ready means of immediately taking advantage of the success of the frauds committed in making the averages'.

61. Even so, Wellington breached etiquette by quoting Huskisson's letter in the upper house without permission, and he was plainly being factious in persisting with his amendment after the government's opposition to it had become known. See Ellenborough's admission, referred to in Gladstone's memorandum of 21 Jan. 1842, Gladstone MSS. 44819 ff. 74-6, *Historical Manuscripts Commission, W. E. Gladstone* (1972), ii. 168.
62. Canning to Goderich, 6 June 1827, A Aspinall, *The Formation of Canning's Ministry, February to August 1827* (1937), 292.
63. Wellington to Huskisson, 28 Mar. 1827, Wellington , *Despatches, Correspondence, and Memoranda*, iii. 612-13; Wellington in H. of L., 1 June 1827, 2 PD, xvii, 1096-7; Wellington to Goderich, 5 June 1827, Buckinghamshire MSS. (Goderich) D/MH/G G.11.
64. LSC, *Report on the price of shipping foreign grain from foreign ports*, 1827.

'Was the Committee of the House of Lords to be considered as nothing?'[65]

Huskisson flatly rejected Wellington's first proposal, which was to 'put the warehouses here and in Holland upon the same footing' by charging a duty on the entry of corn into bond. In a letter of 24 May Wellington suggested another scheme, whereby so long as corn was below a certain level, no foreign corn should be removed from a British warehouse until all the corn previously stored in that warehouse had been removed, or the owners' written consent obtained. The advantage of a chronological withdrawal from bond was that merchants with recent speculative purchases would be unlikely to manipulate a fraudulent opening of the ports, since not for some time would they be able to benefit from it.[66] Huskisson pointed out that this plan was administratively impracticable. Besides, he was as suspicious of farmers as the Duke was of merchants, and objected that an agriculturist might, by warehousing a single bushel, hold up all subsequent bonders of corn in the same warehouse. But at this point Huskisson added an ambiguous rider. He too had been pondering the warehousing problem, with reference not to mercantile abuses but to Westmorland's complaint that the proposed Law would give as much priority to freshly-imported corn as it would to corn that had been bonded for years. Huskisson admitted the injustice of this, and with his mind on Westmorland's problem rather than on Wellington's, he wrote back 'hastily' to the Duke:

Had your proposal been that no corn bonded after the passing of the present bill should be allowed to be entered for home consumption till the average price had reached 66s; and that thenceforward all corn so bonded, or thereafter imported, should come under the regulations of the bill, individually I should not object to such a proviso. It would ensure that no quantity beyond that now in bond should be thrown upon the market, unless, in spite of that quantity, the price reached a level which might fairly be taken as an indication of our being in want of a further supply from abroad.

65. Wellington to Goderich, 8 June 1827, Ripon MSS. 40862 ff. 210-14, Aspinall, *The Formation of Canning's Ministry,* 292-5; Wellington to Huskisson, 4 June 1827, HP 38749 ff. 293-7.
66. Wellington to Huskisson, 24 May 1827, HP 38749 ff. 264-6.

But I am afraid that even this amendment would be fatal to the Bill in our House.[67]

The ambiguity here was whether this referred to a permanent, statutory arrangement or to a temporary expedient. Having stated 'an evil permanent in its nature and...proposed a permanent remedy',[68] Wellington assumed that Huskisson's counter-suggestion was also permanent. But Wellington's proposal had superficially recalled Westmorland's short-term objection, and Huskisson admitted that

What was uppermost in my mind when I threw out this [counter] suggestion was the inconvenience which might arise from letting into consumption further supplies of wheat, hereafter to arrive, until the greater part of the quantity *now in bond* should have been disposed of...In writing the unlucky paragraph...I was no longer thinking of 'the permanent evil', your remedy for which I had discussed in the former part of my letter.[69]

The . keyword was 'thenceforward', which had different meanings according to whether the clause was to operate permanently or temporarily. To the Duke, 'thenceforward' referred permanently to 66s., so that *whenever* wheat was cheaper it might not be taken from British warehouses, but thenceforward (meaning at or above 66s.) it might. For Huskisson, 'thenceforward' referred to one single point in time — when corn next reached 66s. Until then, corn already bonded before the passing of the Bill might be withdrawn from the warehouses, but not corn bonded since its passing; after the price had once reached 66s., corn might be let out freely without distinction.[70]

It may have been genuine miscomprehension. The Duke honestly did not 'consider the amendment as proposed by me

---

67. Huskisson to Wellington, 24 May 1827, copy HP 38749 ff. 282-3. The last sentence should have given Wellington pause if, as he claimed, he was really trying to secure votes for the Bill, and not to wreck it altogether.
68. Wellington to Huskisson, 4 June 1827.
69. Huskisson to Wellington, 5 June 1827, copy HP 38749 ff. 299-302.
70. Jones, *'Prosperity' Robinson*, 147, in his anxiety to inculpate and discredit Huskisson at every opportunity (thereby boosting Robinson's claims to pre-eminence), misinterprets this incident, and argues that in the sentence of 24 May beginning 'Had your proposal been that no corn bonded after the passing of the present bill...' (above, p. 285), Huskisson really meant to write 'before' instead of 'after'. In fact, 'before' is precisely what Huskisson did *not* mean.

to be at all contrary to the principle of Lord Liverpool's measure'.[71] Protection to him meant securing a certain price, and warehousing posed a threat to this ambition.[72] His amendment probably aimed a deliberate 'death blow to the warehousing of foreign corn in this Country'.[73] Huskisson was not concerned about prices in themselves, but warehousing was essential to his policy of safeguarding food supplies, and of importing regular quantities of wheat annually for the sake of exchange stability.

The battle had to be fought again in 1828, this time inside the cabinet. High Tories were amazed by Huskisson's inclusion in the Duke's administration: 'This Machiavelian parvenu was the primum mobile of all the Æolian system. Is the Duke to be converted to his theory? Or do they suppose at Apsley House that Huskisson is to give his tacit consent to the break-up of his own system?'[74]

On 10 March, Huskisson and his ally, Charles Grant (President of the Board of Trade), suggested a scale similar to that of 1827, whereupon the premier countered with a much more protective scale and a surcharge on warehousing.[75] Huskisson held out against raising the pivotal point of the scale to 64s., but conceded that if 200,000 qrs. of wheat should enter in any twelve consecutive weeks while the average price was at or below 64s., there might be a 25 per cent increase of duty until wheat had averaged 66s. or more for a period of six weeks. ('That is, it might be permanent', noted Ellenborough in his journal.) Peel, Goulburn, Melville, Ellenborough, Bathurst, Lyndhurst, Aberdeen, Dudley, and Palmerston eagerly agreed, and condemned Wellington's insistence on discriminating — as he had attempted to do in 1827 — against corn warehoused in England and in favour of corn coming straight from foreign ports. 'The Duke will not

71. Wellington to Huskisson, 4 June 1827; *Journal of Mrs Arbuthnot,* 17 June 1827, ii. 126-7; Wellington to Grant, 7 Mar. 1828, copy HP 38755 ff. 145-6.
72. As Fay, *Huskisson and His Age,* 134, perceptively wrote, Wellington simply saw a 'citadel to defend', which 'the enemy [foreign corn] threatened to infiltrate'.
73. Huskisson to Melville, 6 June 1827, copy HP 38749 ff. 305-6.
74. Londonderry to Harriet Arbuthnot, 17 Jan. 1828, Aspinall, *Correspondence of Charles Arbuthnot,* 98.
75. Wellington to Grant, 7 Mar. 1828. See Table 3, below.

yield, though all were against him...He feels he is looked up
to by the great landed interests, and he is afraid of being
reproached by his friends.'[76] In fact, many agriculturists
would probably have preferred Huskisson's proposal to his
own. More pertinent was the Duke's determination to
maintain his authority in cabinet, and his 'pre-scientific'
and 'impatient practicality incident to military insight',
which made him hostile to anything that emanated from a
'theoretical political economist' or 'literary statesman', such
as he conceived Huskisson to be.[77]

Eventually Huskisson and Wellington agreed on a formula
— to impose a 5s. surcharge in place of the extra 25 per cent
duty — but now Grant held out unilaterally, saying he was
pledged to the 1827 Bill, that the new proposal was 'a
practical change of the pivot' upwards, and that the temporary
surcharge might last indefinitely.[78] He insisted that it should
operate for a maximum of sixteen weeks, and rejected Peel's
suggestion for it to terminate (come what may) each New
Year's Day, since this would simply dump corn on the January
markets. On the 27th Huskisson and Wellington agreed to
abandon the idea of temporary extra duties for a rather
steeper scale (25s. at 62s., rising and falling in shilling stages),
but Grant still prevaricated. *He* was expendable, but —
lamented Huskisson — *his* resignation would 'bring *my*
publick life to a close in Bitterness'. For Huskisson would
have to go too (or else alienate the Canningites for ever),
and since he would then have to vote for almost *any* Corn
Bill in preference to the existing Law, his going would look

76. Ellenborough, *A Political Diary, 1828-30*, i. 51-69; Palmerston's journal in
Dalling, *Life of Viscount Palmerston*, i. 231-44.
77. *The Collected Works of Walter Bagehot*, edited by N. St. John-Stevas, iii
(1968), 332; T. E. Kebbel, *Essays upon History and Politics* (1864), 219. Ellenborough to Peel, 14 Mar. 1828, Peel MSS. 40396 ff. 47-8.
78. Grant to Peel, n.d., Peel MSS. 40396 f. 87. Grant also opposed a proposal to
restore Irish corn to the averages.

Plans for permanent scales of duties on corn, 1828

Price of British wheat p. Imperial quarter	Bill of 1827		Grant's & Huskisson's original plan, put to Cabinet on 10 Mar.		Wellington's original proposal, put to Cabinet on 10 Mar.		Grant's scheme of 25 Mar.		Wellington's proposal agreed to by Huskisson on 27 Mar. & by Grant on 28 Mar.		Benett's plan of 25 Apr. approved by Huskisson and Grant		Act of 1828	
s.	s.	d.	s.	d.	s.	d.	s.	d.	s.	d.	s.	d.	s.	d
49					40									
50					40									
51					38									
52	40	8	40	8	36							38	8	34	8
53	38	8	38	8	34							38	8	33	8
54	36	8	36	8	32							38	8	32	8
55	34	8	34	8	30							38	8	31	8
56	32	8	32	8	29							36	8	30	8
57	30	8	30	8	28					30		34	8	29	8
58	28	8	28	8	27					29		32	8	28	8
59	26	8	26	8	26		(?)29			28		30	8	27	8
60	24	8	24	8	25		(?)27			27		28	8	26	8
61	22	8	22	8	24		(?)25			26		26	8	25	8
62	20	8	20	8	23		23			25		24	8	24	8
63	18	8	19	8	22		21			24		22	8	23	8
64	16	8	18	8	21		19			23		20	8	22	8
65	14	8	17	8	20		17			22		18	8	21	8
66	12	8	16	8	18		15			21		16	8	20	8
67	10	8	10	8	15		13			20		14	8	18	8
68	6	8	6	8	12		11					12	8	16	8
69	4	8	4	8	7		9					10	8	13	8
70	2	8	2	8	2	6	7					(?) 7	8	10	8
71	1		1		2	6						(?) 4	8	6	8
72	1		1									(?) 1	8	2	8
73														1	

(Wellington's original proposal column) plus 2s. 6d. surplus duty on corn bonded in U.K.

A few parts of the above scales are estimates of what their authors intended.

like a deliberate attempt to wreck the Duke. On the 28th Grant capitulated under pressure.[79]

79. Huskisson to Charles Grant, 14, 20, 25, and 27 Mar. 1828; Huskisson to Robert Grant, 21 Mar. 1828; Charles Grant to Huskisson, 17, 19, 21, 24, and 27 Mar. 1828; Peel to Huskisson, 25 Mar. 1828; Huskisson to Peel, 27 Mar. 1828; HP 38755 ff. 155, 187-9, 265, 273-4; 203; 160-1, 178-83, 205, 256, 277; 275. Charles Grant to Huskisson, 25 Mar. 1828; Goulburn to Peel, 30 Mar. 1828; Huskisson to Peel, 29 Mar. 1828; Peel MSS. 40396 ff. 85-6; 40333 ff. 6-9; Peel to Goulburn, 29 Mar. 1828, Goulburn MSS. II/17. Gash, *Mr Secretary Peel*, 465-8.

The 1828 Act is invariably depicted as a copy of Canning's 1827 Bill amended to satisfy protectionist prejudices. Wellington's struggle against Huskisson and Grant supports this view. But the (albeit perfunctory) debates in Parliament suggest that the reality was more complex. Initially (in March), opinion was divided along such lines as these: agriculturists (including Benett) welcomed the Bill as at least an improvement on the previous year's, while free-traders like King and Whitmore were indignant about the additional duties offered at and around the pivot point. If Canning's scale had been 'bad enough', this was 'too bad'.[80] But in late April, the chief opposition to the Bill came from a group of agriculturists led by Benett and Western, while free-traders silently acquiesced. Benett had noticed that although the Bill offered more protection than that of 1827 when the price was 60-64s.,[81] it offered less at the more crucial prices of 52-58s. Stanley complained that it gave 'prohibition when we did not want it, and protection when we needed it least'.[82] To rectify this anomaly, Benett moved an amendment for a steeper scale, giving more protection when the price was in the fifties, and less when it was in the early sixties. Huskisson and Grant wished to adopt this alternative, possibly because they thought that not much European wheat could afford to arrive at less than 58s. anyway. Again Wellington held out, this time against the agriculturists — since it would be unbecoming for a government to submit to all the 'conundrums' of its friends[83] — and the amendment was defeated 230-32.

Technically, the 1828 Law failed as utterly as that which it replaced. Huskisson hoped that a graduated scale with weekly averages would steady the course of trade while discouraging combination and fraud.[84] Weekly price variations should be

80. Smart, op. cit. 438-44.
81. At which price no corn had entered in 1827.
82. H. of C., 22 Apr. 1828, 2 PD, xix. 25.
83. Ellenborough, op. cit. i. 90-1. For Wellington's expectations of the 1828 Law's effects, see Wellington to Kenyon, 5 Apr. 1828, Kenyon MSS. In Parliament he still spoke the language of 1815 — viz. the need to prevent the decultivation of poor soils and the dangers of famine if Britain depended on Europe.
84. Huskisson's 18 Oct. 1826 memorandum. HP 38761 ff. 211-48. Liverpool's Nov. 1826 memorandum. LP 38371 ff. 230-7.

too small for merchants to speculate on, and the scale should encourage necessary importations while checking redundant consignments. The 1827 scale might have succeeded, but the 1828 Law removed its essential feature — gradualness — and substituted some sharp jumps in the scale (13*s*. 8*d*. duty at 69*s*., 1*s*. at 73*s*.).[85] As prices crept up, importers were to hang on to their corn, despite the consumers' very real need for it, until it could be entered at the nominal charge, when they all suddenly flooded the market together. The profits this brought were uncertain and risky, and did not encourage foreign cultivators. Holders of domestic grain, if they had sufficient capital, would likewise withhold their produce from the market until 71*s*. or 72*s*., confident that importers would not release their wheat until 73*s*. Moreover the prospect that a slight price fall at these high levels might raise the duty considerably, was a deterrent to importation from remote areas with large transport costs. All foreign cultivation, therefore, but especially in these distant lands, became speculative and chancy. Thus the Bill had precisely the opposite effect to what was intended. British farmers who could not afford to exploit the Law by hanging on sold cheaply, while consumers paid dear; foreign agriculture was discouraged, Europe became the source of sudden importations ruinous to agriculturists, but not of steady surpluses necessary to consumers; fluctuations in the amount and cost of importations were greatly intensified, and these sudden inundations had to be paid for largely in bullion (as in 1830, 1831, 1838, and 1839).[86] At least Huskisson would have

85. A corresponding sliding scale of export bounties would have made the 1828 Law more logical. Brady, *William Huskisson and Liberal Reform*, 69-70, suggests (implausibly) that Huskisson saw the sliding scale as a method of *combining* autarchy and agricultural protection with industrial expansion and encouragement of trade.

86. This is interestingly discussed, with some inaccuracies, in A. Marshall, *Industry and Trade* (1919), 735-9. See Tooke and Newmarch, *History of Prices*, iii. 20-51 and v. 168-74; Matthews, *A Study in Trade-Cycle History 1833-42*, 35-7; Brady, op. cit., 70-1; J. R. McCulloch, *A Dictionary, Practical, Theoretical, and Historical of Commerce and Commercial Navigation* (1882), 442-4; Fay, *The Corn Laws and Social England*, 84-6; J. R. McCulloch, *Statements illustrative of the Policy and Probable Consequences of the proposed repeal of the existing Corn Laws, &c.* (1841), 10; D. Salomons, *Reflections on the operation of the present Scale of Duty for regulating the importation of Foreign Corn* (1839), passim.

perceived these inadequacies and would have adapted the scale to new market conditions long before 1842.[87]

Jacob's Europe and free trade

The Corn Law of 1828 was the first step in applying a policy that had been formulated as long before as 1821. Yet historians often ignore the 1821 Report, and regard the 1827 Bill as marking the origin of a timid approach to free trade, inspired by Jacob. Smart, Barnes, and Fay all emphasized the seminal role of Jacob's Report in the deliberations leading up to the government's initiative in 1827.[88] Broadly, their interpretation was that the high protection imposed in 1815 followed from the conviction that an abundance of cheap corn lay waiting abroad, eager to pour into this country once its legislative defences were down; but that in the mid-twenties Jacob, formerly a firm protectionist himself, was able to demonstrate that European farmers were not, and never would be, able to compete with their English counterparts, and that the vigorous blasts of freer trade could be safely extended to agriculture.[89] Freer corn proceeded from strength, from invulnerability to competition, rather than from any inadequacies of protection. Fay's Huskisson was 'ever a learner', and Jacob one of his crucial teachers. This interpretation supplemented the view, current in the 1940s and 1950s, that the nineteenth-century corn laws were nugatory, having little effect on prices, because there was no cheap foreign corn to exclude; and that their real significance was in symbolizing a struggle for power between landlords and manufacturers.

This thesis has been ably controverted by Susan Fairlie,[90] who reasserts the practical effects of the 1815 Corn Law in

87. Huskisson in H. of C., 25 Mar. 1830, 2 PD, xxiii. 916; *Speeches of William Huskisson,* iii. 555.
88. Smart, op. cit. 382; Barnes, *A History of the English Corn Laws,* 190-1, 287; Fay, *The Corn Laws and Social England,* 80.
89. This interpretation draws support from Parnell's recantation over the Corn Laws, though it is unlikely that any of his avowed reasons — Jacob on Europe, Ricardo on profits and rent — was relevant to government policy. H. of C., 9 Mar. 1827, 2 PD, xvi. 1101-2; Smart, op. cit. 414-5; Barnes, op. cit. 194-5, 215; Semmel, *The Rise of Free Trade Imperialism,* 138.
90. S. Fairlie, 'The Nineteenth-Century Corn Law Reconsidered', *Economic History Review,* 2nd series, xviii (1965), 562-73.

protecting farmers against European surpluses that were still much more than minimal. Following Professor Matthews,[91] she contends that Jacob's diagnosis of the failure of continental agriculture was premature by about a decade and a half. In 1819-26 and again in 1831-8 there really were European gluts, which the corn laws really did exclude. Though she underestimates the non-economic and irrational aspects of the corn law debate so rightly stressed by Miss Kemp,[92] Dr. Fairlie's analysis certainly clarifies the actions of Peel after his apprehension of the *actual* extinction of European surpluses after about 1840, and of the need to harness extra-European supplies against the possibility of famine. However, Dr. Fairlie perpetuates the tradition that the Corn Law of 1815 was rationally based on the need to protect farmers against more competitive rivals in Europe.[93] She agrees with Fay that Jacob's Reports then pointed away from protection by playing down foreign competition, but contends that ministers substantially retained protection because they were better informed than Jacob of conditions abroad. Yet protection was not always a rational response to European circumstances. Protectionists were primarily concerned with social balance inside Britain, and only indirectly with the external situation. Likewise in 1815 ministers were attempting to regulate the *internal* balance of investment (in favour of agriculture), rather than simply to discriminate against foreigners. European grain was cheap and *potentially* competitive, but its surpluses were too unreliable and slight to be allowed to become an integral part of food supply. And since a very small importation (like a slightly too bountiful harvest) could have a disproportionate effect on prices owing to the inelasticity of demand, all outside grain should be embargoed until prices had risen. Jacob himself stressed the effect of market psychology on price, and thought the 1815 Corn Law essential for

91. Matthews, op. cit. 35-7, 40.
92. B. Kemp, 'Reflections on the Repeal of the Corn Laws', *Victorian Studies*, v. (1961-2), 189-204.
93. 'The British nineteenth-century Corn Laws only made sense on the assumption that there was abundance of cheap corn in Europe which, in free trade conditions, would tend to flood the British market, undercutting British farmers and lowering the price of British bread.' Fairlie, op. cit. 562.

confidence and agricultural expansion. The move towards freer trade in 1821 followed from ministers' conviction that, notwithstanding Jacob, European surpluses could and must become an integral part of supply after all, just as 1846 followed from Peel's realization that even these supplies would not be sufficient proof against famine. Barnes, Fay, and Fairlie all forget that as early as 1821, with European glut a notorious fact and Jacob still agog for protection, Liverpool's government agreed on a gradual reduction of the Corn Law, and on encouraging more regular importation. Its desire to reduce protection preceded intimations from Jacob that Europe could no longer compete.

When Fairlie suggests an analogy with France, Switzerland, the Netherlands, Spain, Portugal, Sweden, and Sardinia, it is with states that had traditionally suffered a deficit of corn and had always encouraged imports. In the early nineteenth century these nations became convinced that, as a result of wartime improvements, they could become self-sufficient for the first time, if only their farmers were protected against the cheap corn of Russia and northern Europe. Consequently after 1819, with the onset of glut, all these states turned to import restrictions and export bounties.[94] Britain's position was different, however, for she was in the reverse process of losing confidence in her own traditional powers of self-sufficiency (despite the temporary abundance of the early twenties), and facing a future of dependence. The prospective reduction of her import restrictions planned at that time aimed to safeguard against a growing threat of starvation.

Jacob's opinions did not in fact somersault, but must appear remarkably consistent once it is accepted that for him — as for Liverpool and Huskisson — protection had been only a means to an end. Like them, Jacob moved from high protection in 1814-15 to free trade in 1826-8, but unlike them, he did not abandon autarchy. His initial protectionism, far from being based on Fairlie's 'abundance of cheap corn in Europe', was based on its absence. Nor was his contempt for the continent's agricultural prospects a product of a 'collective

94. Ibid. 566.

but temporary period of scarcity' in the mid-twenties, as is often assumed.[95] As early as 1814 Jacob was denigrating the actual and potential capacity of Europe's peasant cultivation, even supposing a perpetual demand from Britain. The whole world could not supply three weeks' consumption. English agriculture, on the other hand, could boast the turnip and — owing to its structure — was amenable to capitalization;[96] it only required parliamentary protection 'to the great producers of corn, to the *bad* farmers',[97] and the day would come when Britain nourished Europe. This vision, which Jacob never abandoned, made him favour protection in 1814 to sustain the marginal farmers, those heroes of the cold clay and light sand who provided one-eighth of subsistence. Against the objection that protection was unnecessary if there were no foreign supplies available to force down prices, Jacob retorted that 'opinion' was a more potent short-term factor in price than the realities of supply and demand. An erroneous belief in the immensity of continental stocks was frightening British farmers into premature sales of their own corn, whereas if they had known the truth, they would have held back until the market was more favourable.[98]

It was to dispel this myth of foreign competition that Jacob set out for Europe in 1819. Understandably, his message that no surpluses existed and that an open British market would not create any, failed to convince either Huskisson or the agriculturists during the universal glut of 1821.[99] By 1826, however, when Huskisson sent him off again, the situation in north Europe was much more corroborative of his preconceived thesis of scarcity. In 1827 the Board of Trade dispatched him to Germany, Denmark, and the

95. Ibid. 564.
96. W. Jacob, *Considerations on the Protection required by British Agriculture, and on the Influence of the Price of Corn on Exportable Productions* (1814), 30-61; Jacob to CSC, *Report on Petitions complaining of the depressed state of Agriculture,* 1821, 368-9.
97. W. Jacob, *A Letter to Samuel Whitbread* (1815), 25.
98. Jacob, *Considerations on the Protection required by Agriculture* (1814), 55-7. Thus this was hardly a 'novel' view in 1828, as Barnes, op. cit. 208-9, supposed.
99. See above, pp. 114-15. W. Jacob, *A view of the agriculture, manufactures, statistics, and state of society of Germany, and parts of Holland and France, taken during a journey through those countries, in 1819* (1820).

Netherlands, and in his Second Report he attempted finally to expose the myth of abundance. He said that at each empty granary he had been told that abundance awaited him a few miles farther on — yet he had never found it. Jacob also attacked once more the view of protectionists and free traders alike that Corn Law reduction would stimulate production abroad and create abundance in the future.[100]

Jacob abandoned protection in favour of open trade (subject to heavy duties in 1821 and without duty in 1828), not because of the European situation but simply because it had failed *internally*. Prices and production had fallen at home, and he took up free trade to restore them, not (like Huskisson) to facilitate imports.[101] For the only way to disabuse farmers of the myth of European abundance was to open the trade. Also, by disastrously accentuating price fluctuations, 1815's contingent prohibition had quite unintentionally mimicked the old, outmoded laws against regraters and forestallers, and discouraged domestic farmers from hoarding their grain — thus it was jeopardizing supply and making prices over-sensitive to seasonal crop differences.[102] Jacob's chief complaint was against the warehousing clause, which was intended to steady prices, create a reserve food supply, and attract capital to the growth of and trade in British corn. He alleged that it was destructive of all these ends, and that because of it 'the attention and capitals of the great speculators has been withdrawn from the English

---

100. A. & P, *Second Report [to Board of Trade] respecting the Agriculture and Trade in Corn, in some of the Continental States of Northern Europe,* 1828, printed in W. Jacob, *Tracts relating to the Corn Trade and Corn Laws* (1828), especially 108-9. Jacob did recognize the agricultural potential of new lands like America and Australia, but he did not think that Britain would ever have to import food from them. CSC, *Report on the present state of Agriculture in the United Kingdom,* 1833, QQ. 202-4; Jacob, *Tracts relating to the Corn Trade,* 134.
101. Even in 1815 Vansittart had objected to Jacob's preference for high prices. Vansittart to Huskisson, 19 Jan. 1815, HP 38740 ff. 42-3, Melville, op. cit. 97-8.
102. Jacob, *Tracts relating to the Corn Trade,* 130-1; ibid. 89-91 noticed that during the 1820s, the stocks of wheat left on hand at the beginning of each harvest had steadily declined.

to the foreign grain',[103] which was a cheaper and more profitable investment. Formerly large dealers had acted as middlemen, who kept prices steady by selling a little at one time and buying at another. But the speculators' present involvement in foreign corn deprived those farmers who could not afford to hoard of a ready demand, and so precipitated them on losing markets:

The few farmers that can afford to speculate on their own productions, and who have acted on the plan of selling one half their growth as soon after harvest as their threshing machines can beat it out, and have reserved the other half till the next harvest, have not been losing by it; but all others who have carried a regular periodical quantity, through the whole year, to the markets have suffered most severely from the low prices it has yielded.

Liverpool and Huskisson refused to trust food supply to the self-interest of middlemen, who might be unenlightened and unscrupulous, and they also rejected state-controlled granaries and distribution. Jacob insisted that neither the warehouse nor the granary but the barn was the proper antidote to famine, since farmers were 'the only natural preservers of the surplus'.[104]

Thus in 1826-8 Jacob recommended free trade, as in 1814 he had recommended protection, on the premise that Europe's powers of supply (and competition) were mythical. He continued to want higher prices and domestic expansion. So when Whitmore and the 'orthodox' free traders made use of Jacob's Reports, they were disingenuously selective. They conveniently stressed Jacob's indication that the 1815 Corn Law had depleted surpluses abroad and stocks at home, in order to argue that protection was jeopardizing security against famine, and also that free trade could be attempted without danger to British agriculturists. So doing, they ignored Jacob's equally emphatic assertions that, even with

103. Jacob to Huskisson, 1 May 1821, HP 38742 ff. 210-23; Jacob to CSC, *Report on Petitions complaining of the depressed state of Agriculture*, 1821, 361. He was echoed by two farmers, Ellman junior and Thomas Orton, ibid. 118-24, 130-2. The merchant Samuel Kingsford, who had been a most influential witness in 1814, complained in 1821 of 'The Capital of our *Corn Merchants* being *locked up* in *Bonded Wheat*'. Kingsford to Liverpool, 26 Feb. 1821, LP 38289 ff. 81-2. See Whitmore in H. of C., 18 Apr. 1826, 2 PD, xv. 324-7.
104. Jacob, *Considerations on the Protection required by Agriculture* (1814), 97-101, 107-12.

the encouragement of the British market, northern Europe would *never* be able to supply Britain — presumably because his pessimism undermined their vision of a Europe that would victual Britain in return for her manufactures. Whitmore cited Jacob to argue that unless Parliament acted, foreign surpluses would shrivel, despite Jacob's belief that it was beyond the power of any legislation to keep that surplus from being extinguished by population pressure abroad.

What ministers thought is unrecorded, but probably Huskisson, Liverpool, and Peel reacted to Jacob as Baring did. Unlike Whitmore and his cohorts, Baring voiced doubts about Jacob's First Report, since he did not agree that Britain could 'grow corn enough for its own consumption'. He accepted

that the supply which could now be sent to England from the Continent was not very great. But he differed entirely from Mr. Jacob as to the supply which might be furnished to this country in a very short period. The supply of which Mr. Jacob spoke was what he saw in warehouses in different places;...But, when the foreign growers put their seed in the ground next year, knowing that England could not do without them, they would take care that there should be an abundant supply.[105]

Ministers did not share Whitmore's passion for comparative advantage. As late as 1825 they still declined to apply a policy that had been in the pipeline since 1821, because of abnormal foreign surpluses that might abuse any relaxation. Huskisson accepted Whitmore's claim that the Corn Law was discouraging European production, but not his opinion that it had already exterminated all competition. After Jacob's Report of 1826, however, this second contention could be accepted too. The Report also corroborated the view of Tooke, who influenced policy far more than Jacob, that protection was unnecessary because Europe could not increase her supplies without raising prices to the British level. Probably Huskisson, who knew from consular reports that stocks were dwindling, commissioned Jacob's Report with every intention of exploiting its foregone conclusion for the purpose of undercutting protectionist opposition in Parliament. Who

105. H. of C., 8 May 1826, 2 PD, xv. 987. Baring concluded that the Corn Law should be reduced at once (1826) while foreigners' stocks were low and they would be unable to exploit that reduction. Agriculturists retorted that even if Europeans could not compete at once, they would with encouragement soon be able to do so.

better to send than this eccentric with the *idée-fixe*? For Huskisson it was a propaganda rather than fact-finding mission. 'I believe it has produced the effect designed by it', commented Jacob, 'that of allaying the fears of the great Landholders who were alarmed by the unascertained surplus of the continental countries'.[106]

But it is virtually certain that, like Baring and as in 1821,[107] ministers repudiated Jacob's view that Europe would never be able to increase her surpluses. Jacob's brief (drafted by Huskisson's secretary at the Board of Trade, Thomas Lack) implied affirmative expectations, in requesting him to discover 'what increase of cultivation would be likely' and what 'additional quantities...might be imported...from Poland'. Later, Huskisson faintly praised his emissary's 'diligence and ability', adding that the Report 'was not, perhaps, quite perfect'.[108] The correspondence and memoranda of Liverpool and Huskisson in the autumn of 1826 indicate that, notwithstanding Jacob, both anticipated 'considerable importations' when the price was above 65s. Moreover Huskisson's acolyte, Deacon Hume, continued to deride Jacob's prophecies, and to advocate comparative advantage, decultivation of 'virtually sterile' soils, and constant food imports.[109] It is true that Huskisson was 'ever a learner',[110] but Jacob was his tool, not his teacher.

The real significance to ministers of Jacob's First Report must have been its message that the Corn Law was *causing* agricultural decline in Europe. For, premature or not, this

---

106. Jacob to Napier, 24 June 1826, Macvey Napier MSS. 34613 ff. 346-9.
107. See above pp. 114-15.
108. H. of C., 18 Apr. 1826, 2 PD, xv. 345.
109. H.B.T. [J. D. Hume], *Letters on the Corn Laws, and on the Rights of the Working Classes, &c.* (1834), second edition (1835), 37 *et seq.* See Brown, *The Board of Trade and the Free-Trade Movement*, 23 and n., 172-3 and n., 211-12, on Jacob's lack of influence over the Board in the 1830s. The 'Controversy between Mr. Senior and Colonel Torrens, respecting the effect of the Corn Laws', MS. memorandum, ?1832, preserved among the miscellaneous papers of T. H. Villiers, MS. Clarendon Deposit c. 548, turns on this question of the accuracy of Jacob's prophecy. Senior contended against Torrens *for* an import duty on corn and *for* the accuracy of Jacob's pessimistic observations with respect to Europe's agricultural supply potential.
110. Fay, *The Corn Laws and Social England*, 80.

undermined the 1814 Report's contention that prohibition could *not* have this effect, that habitual exclusion would not render food imports less available in a *crise des subsistances,* since there was nothing for foreigners to do except grow food, and send their puny surpluses sporadically to England. Jacob showed the need for encouragement to the agriculturists of northern Europe, not to stop them spinning and weaving but to keep them sowing and hoeing. Reciprocity treaties and Corn Law reductions were to keep Europe agricultural rather than to prevent her from industrializing.

Jacob switched from protection to freer trade in the certainty that British agriculture could only benefit from the competition (such as it was) of uncapitalized and backward foreigners. Ministers had no such chauvinist illusions, but agreed that freer trade would benefit, by stimulating, the *best* British farmers. Jacob at least appreciated that the European economy was to some extent autonomous, while ministers often argued as though it depended entirely on the encouragement granted or withheld in the British market.[111] But they were more realistic about Britain's own supply potential — and about the future. Liverpool warned that no Corn Law could be permanent, since Prussia and Poland would eventually industrialize and cease to provide. Then, extra-European food would be needed, and the sliding scale of duties would have to be lowered.[112]

In abandoning autarchy, ministers no more intended to deflate than they had in adopting bullionism. Price was an

111. The movement of corn prices was much the same in all European countries, whether they exported regularly to Britain or not. Fairlie, op. cit. 563-7.
112. H. of L., 25 Apr. 1825, 2 PD, xiii. 148. On the fact that after 1830, 'concern about an independent supply slowly faded away', being hardly mentioned in the 1846 debates, Olson comments: 'Laissez faire sentiments achieved a remarkable ascendancy as time passed, and some ardent free traders doubted that even the exigencies of war could restrain "natural" market forces or nullify the law of comparative advantage.' M. Olson, *The Economics of Wartime Shortage* (1963), 36-7. More pertinently, an independent supply was no longer feasible by the 1840s, and *laissez-faire* ideology, in so far as it influenced politicians at all, probably followed from this hard fact. Incidentally, Lucy Brown, op. cit. 205, is surely mistaken in supposing that autarchic arguments in favour of protection were rare before the 1830s and commonplace in the 1840s.

emotive issue, but the Law of 1815 was not a high price policy, nor that of 1828 a low.[113] 60s., which was considered a fair price in the later year, was not so far from the 80s. maximum of 1815, in view of the intervening currency appreciation and remission of taxes. Ministers simply wanted steady and reliable prices, yet never achieved them. When in 1826 Liverpool said 'that in any law to be adopted you must legislate with reference to price',[114] he acknowledged that the 1815 policy of attempting to renumerate farmers by a combination of prices and yields, being based on expectations of agricultural expansion, had broken down. Farmers had most needed high prices in the very years when obligations to the consumer had disallowed them — that is, when yields were low. Temporary measures had been devised to prevent prices rising excessively, but none to stop them falling. Huskisson vainly hoped that the sliding scale would base remuneration simply on prices, that it would secure supplies in lean seasons and profits in full ones. When, long after Liverpool and Huskisson had predicted, the Corn Laws were entirely repealed, this was done not to lower but to stabilize prices, not to sell commodities but to cultivate supplies.[115]

---

113. See *Speeches of William Huskisson,* iii. 257 for the minister's expectation that the new scale would at least maintain prices.
114. Liverpool's MS. memorandum, 1826, LP 38371 ff. 230-7.
115. The problem of manufacturing exports had, of course, become more important by 1846, when Peel had not only to safeguard food supplies but also to enable the labouring poor to pay for them, which required steady employment opportunities.

CONCLUSION

THE ECONOMICS OF LIBERAL TORYISM

The most liberal policy has been carried into our foreign relations, darkness and Intricacy have been banished from the Finances. The laws are becoming less complex — and the Wisdom of the Philosopher is adopted as the rules of the Merchant.
Sydney Smith to Huskisson, 15 Mar. 1826, HP 38747 f. 209.

Economic policy was dominated by the need to secure food supplies and stable employment for a rapidly growing population. Ministers supported high protection so long as this appeared to be the best guarantee of subsistence. When the 1814–15 price fall threatened heavy losses on wartime agricultural investment, massive decultivation, and a flight of capital from the land, ministers stepped in to prevent an inappropriate diversion of funds to industry, and also to exclude foreign surpluses that were large enough to have ruined farmers, but too slight to feed consumers. They assumed that, thus encouraged, British (and Irish) farmers could feed the nation, but they persevered in warehousing, despite its unpopularity, as a contribution to subsistence that alien governments could neither tax nor withhold. By 1821 intimations that autarchy was after all impossible, reinforced as they were by diminishing returns theory, and increasing confidence in Europe's food supply potential, led ministers to advocate a *gradual* resort to free trade in corn. Then in 1826 Jacob demonstrated that conditions were favourable for beginning such an experiment, since the abnormal post-war glut had rotted away, and also that if it were not begun immediately, European agriculture might dwindle beyond recovery. Meanwhile the restored gold standard, being acutely sensitive to commercial fluctuations, dictated regular annual imports, with warehouses to ration supplies, rather than spasmodic importation in the wake of harvest failure.
 This contradicts Fay's opinion that Huskisson mainly

desired the expansion of industry and commerce, and that cheap foreign food was an 'incidental bye product'.[1] When ministers said that England should take Germany's corn to prevent her from industrializing, they were thinking less of British exports than of keeping Germany agricultural for the sake of food supply. Measures to make exports more competitive, such as lowering tariffs on raw materials, were prompted by the potential need for food imports. Ministers did not expect freer trade in corn to cheapen food appreciably, since with population growth it would increase demand for corn, so neither could they expect it to make exports more competitive; but they did suppose that food imports would boost sales of goods on a basis of reciprocal trade. This is clear from one of Huskisson's objections to prohibitory corn laws[2] : that they checked manufacturing exports, not by enhancing their costs but by withholding from foreigners the means of payment. They bestowed on foreign manufactures a bounty, which was measured less by the increased price of corn here than by its depressed price abroad. So freer trade would maintain English and raise foreign prices, thus protecting farmers everywhere.

Official policy was not transformed by free trade ideology. Possibly Canning, with an emotional need to feel *avant-garde*, and Robinson, 'prepossessed with his own opinions and impatient of contradiction', were more abstract than pragmatic thinkers.[3] But the contemporary caricature of Huskisson as a utopian doctrinaire, 'a projector from disposition', was absurdly misplaced.[4] Lacking political though not intellectual confidence, Huskisson was unusually anxious to emphasize his own rigid consistency, while his schematic intellect liked to tie the various fragments of policy into a single coherent explanation. This was misleading, since the main purpose of

---

1. Fay, *Huskisson and His Age,* 251.
2. See above, p. 279.
3. And after all, Canning was less disposed to tariff reform than Liverpool, Huskisson, Peel, and eventually even Herries. See above p. 260. Of course, free trade was soon to become — notwithstanding its pragmatic origins — an ideological fixation, and to remain so long after it had ceased to be in Britain's best interests.
4. Bathurst to Arbuthnot, 16 Sept. 1827, Aspinall, *Correspondence of Charles Arbuthnot,* 94.

theory was to justify, not originate, measures. Physiocratic doctrine was borrowed to justify the Corn Law, Ricardian jargon later to denounce it.

W. R. Brock's structural view that the Tory government abandoned high protection as a consequence of switching the basis of its support from the landlords to the representatives of finance, industry, and commerce is also suspect. The City possessed most power in the early protectionist days before Vansittart's departure, and Huskisson's quarrels with Herries were fundamentally about the need to eradicate such unconstitutional influence. But stable employment was a major aim of policy, and ministers came to recognize — especially after Peterloo — the error of their initial assumption that the best opportunities for growth were to be found in the agricultural sector. They turned instead to the towns, as the more likely mass opiate. In Deacon Hume's words,

We have long passed that point up to which the prosperity of a country is based upon its land. Our trade has outgrown our agriculture, because it has led to an increase of population which the land can neither profitably employ nor plentifully feed. What it is to have a redundant population the landed interest well know, and the more trade is cramped the more redundant will a given population prove to their cost. I know they think that there is a circle of employment to be found in the HOME TRADE, in which the same internal elements of prosperity may be perpetually revolved and improved — that as mouths increased in number bread would get dearer, rents would rise, expenditure enlarge, home trade flourish, and the power of the people to pay for the bread increase with its price.

England, with her population rise, had undergone a transition (obscured by long war and the difficulties of adjustment to peace) 'from the practice of exporting corn, to the practice of exporting manufactures':

If the increase of population should not comprise a new body of manufacturers, capable of supplying commodities for the foreign market, besides having mouths enough to consume all the home-grown corn; then, not only would the import trade be lost, but the home trade and the agricultural would languish together, and the country would become little else than one great poor-house.

On the other hand, if the additional population consists chiefly of manufacturers, who produce commodities suitable to foreign markets, and the export of those commodities materially exceed in quantity the corn which had formerly been exported, in return for the imports —

the case of the country is thenceforth entirely changed, and its future prosperity will be based upon trade, and not upon land; and no imaginable measure can be so injurious to land as that which may impede the progress of trade.[5]

Even the bulk of the landed interest, after Webb Hall, abandoned dreams of agricultural expansion (coupled with industrial recession) for defence of the *status quo,* and active hostility to the Corn Law passed into urban hands.

It is not possible to explain economic policy in this period with reference to material interests and pressure groups. There were, as elsewhere, declining artisans, deluded debtors, and rampant creditors, who gave a terminology to economic debate. But the 'interests' were usually too many and too divided to exercise much influence, so that to describe politics in the period between patronage and parties as those of *interest,* is like supposing that a multiplicity of political factions adds up to *party politics.* Ministers liked to conciliate interested opinions, if it was possible to do so without disrupting policies,[6] but the lobbies never dictated to them.

Gladstone once suggested that the Whigs and Reform delayed the repeal of the Corn Laws by a decade,[7] and he was probably correct. Liverpool, Canning, Huskisson, Peel, Robinson, Vansittart, Sidmouth, and even Wellington were economically more 'liberal' than Grey, Brougham, Holland, Lauderdale, and Russell, though this was less for humanitarian reasons than to allay revolutionary discontent. While both parties wished to appease the lower classes, the Whigs could not afford concessions on economic policy because their only hope of winning office was by economic bribes to the country gentry, who held the balance of power and for the

5. H. B. T. [J. D. Hume], *Letters on the Corn Laws* (1835), 44—5 (original italics).
6. e.g. in 1820 ministers considered allowing a drawback on exports of woollen manufactures, 'not from any opinion such a drawback is necessary, but in order some degree to meet the *Feeling* which exists in the manufacturing districts', but they eventually decided against it. Liverpool to Lascelles, 8 Jan. 1820, LP 38282 ff. 146—7. Canning and Huskisson worked assiduously for Liverpool town on such issues as the Law of Merchant and Factor, but Merseyside's interest in Latin American trade almost certainly counted for little in Canning's policy of recognition. Professor Wilson's remarks about the role of interest groups in policy formation during the later seventeenth century apply with similar force to the 1820s. C. Wilson, *England's Apprenticeship, 1603—1763* (1965), 165—8.
7. Gladstone in *Nineteenth Century,* ii. (1877), 540, and reprinted in W. E. Gladstone, *Later Gleanings* (1898), i. 136.

most part regarded the Tories as natural ministers. The Tories, on the other hand, could not make political concessions because their monopoly of landed support depended on their stand against 'Reform'. Liverpool relied on the squires' hatred of political reform in pressing them to accept inimical economic measures that might help to stave off revolution. Peel was to gamble on the same strategy in 1846, but forgot that with 'Reform' out of the way, the Whig bogey could no longer be held *in terrorem* over his backbenchers.

Economic policy, though largely empirical and untouched by abstract dogma, did have an ethical content. Industrial and commercial progress both inspired and terrified. Economic growth had proceeded so far that a recoil to pre-industrial levels would be catastrophically disruptive. It was essential not to let the economy retrogress, but also to keep growth within legitimate bounds. Liberal Tories rejected utilitarian economics, which simply sought to maximize wealth and happiness, for a romantic belief in *naturalness*. Agreeing with Ricardo that international equilibrium was essential to a right distribution of wealth, Liverpool, Huskisson, and Canning nevertheless shared what Keynes called Malthus's 'vaguer intuitions' that there was such a thing as natural and therefore 'effective demand', as a 'natural surplus' and '*un*natural demand for labour'.[8] To overstep the natural level of economic activity would inevitably cause over-production and gluts.

Liberal Tories saw the need to come to terms with the fashionable science of political economy, but remained suspicious of Ricardo and the 'illuminati' of the *Edinburgh Review,* Coleridge's 'contemptible democratical oligarchy of glib economists',[9] who seemed to be controlling the destinies of the nation. Ministers were influenced here by a group of clergymen who saw it as their duty to emancipate scientific economics from the Devil and to assert the 'connexion of Political-Economy with Natural Theology'.[10]

8. Malthus to Ricardo, 16 July 1821, Sraffa, *Works and Correspondence of David Ricardo,* ix. 20; J. M. Keynes, *Essays in Biography, (1933),* (1961 edition), 103.
9. T. Allsop, *Letters, Conversations and Recollections of S. T. Coleridge* (1864), 86.
10. R. Whately, *Introductory Lectures on Political-Economy* (1832), 59.

For if what the dismal science said about the earth and about man was true, it showed the Creator in a very unfavourable light. What was needed was an optimistic or at least consolatory version of the science. And so when Nassau Senior resigned from the Oxford Chair of Political Economy in 1829, Richard Whately was elected; he had no obvious professional qualifications, but was persuaded that as a prominent Christian he might be able to rescue economics 'permanently from disrepute'.[11] On Whately's elevation to Dublin, Frederick Denison Maurice let himself be proposed (unsuccessfully) on the grounds that no one else was ready to come forward and argue that 'political economy is not the foundation of morals and politics, but must have them for its foundation or be worth nothing.'[12] The most thorough of these clerical economists, however, was Thomas Chalmers, Professor of Moral Philosophy at St. Andrews, 'the favourite child of whose intellect' was to reconcile the truths of Christianity and commerce. This he did — despite his fear of 'secular contamination' from the 'encroachments' of commercial 'earthliness'[13] — in his *Bridgewater Treatise* of 1833.[14]

Chalmers, the friend of Wilberforce, 'McCulloch of Malthusianism', 'second most influential Scotsman of his generation' and 'greatest preacher of his age', was an inspiration to the Liberal Tories. His preaching moved Canning and Huskisson to rapture, sometimes even to tears, especially the influential *Astronomical Sermons* of 1817, which denied the apparent 'infidelity of natural science'.[15]

11. E. J. Whately, *Life and Correspondence of Richard Whately*, (1866), i. 66–7.
12. Maurice to Hare, 29 Nov. 1836, *The Life of Frederick Denison Maurice* by F. Maurice, London (1884), i. 210. Maurice had even fewer qualifications than Whately: 'I shall of course endeavour to master the details of the subject — with its principles, alas! I am not acquainted.' Ibid. He was turned down by the Puseyites, not because of his unfitness for the job but because of his views on baptismal regeneration.
13. Hanna, *Memoirs of the Life and Writings of Thomas Chalmers* (1849–52), iii. 93–4.
14. T. Chalmers, *On the Power Wisdom and Goodness of God as manifested in the adaptation of external nature to the moral and intellectual constitution of man* (1833).
15. T. Chalmers, *A Series of Discourses on the Christian Revelation, viewed in connection with the Modern Astronomy* (1817), 21.

Chalmers, who preferred the intuitive perceptions of Hutche-
son and Adam Smith to the rationality of David Hume, was
to all intents and purposes a Canningite in politics — that is
to say, he opposed Reform and opposed retrenchment
(which would merely inhibit consumption), but supported
Catholic Emancipation, the property tax, and — though a
physiocrat — free trade in corn. Above all, he endorsed
Malthus's condemnation of Speenhamland, as having transformed charity from a thing of loving tenderness to 'a matter
of angry litigation'.[16] (Whately for one was a more cynical
less-eligibilist: 'If good boys have a larger slice of cake than
the rest, this does not indeed increase the amount of cake,
but it may increase good conduct.')[17]

The main threat that orthodox political economy posed to
Christian belief was its 'principle of population'. Churchmen
had blithely assumed, with Paley, that an increasing population demonstrated the fact that a nation was happy and
contented, when suddenly Malthus's ecological prognostica-
tions challenged belief in a beneficent God. Malthus himself
in his second edition, John Bird Sumner, Whately, and
Copleston all attempted to square their belief in a good God
with the fact of pestilence by emphasizing that, thanks to the
preventive check to population growth, and thanks to the
fertilizing of every sterile promontory, wars and famines need
never occur again.[18] Chalmers, however, preferred to argue
that this ecological predicament provided a rare opportunity
for the exercise of moral freedom. The present generation of
paupers was peculiarly blessed, since hunger would *force* it to
be moral, that is to elevate 'mind' above 'passionate flesh',
reflection above sensuality. Fear of death did not preclude

16. T. Chalmers, *On Political Economy, in connexion with the Moral State and Moral Prospects of Society* (1832), 403–4.
17. *Life of Richard Whately,* i. 77.
18. Whately, *Introductory Lectures,* 164–6; Whately to Senior, 1835, *Life of Richard Whately,* i. 301; J. B. Sumner, *A Treatise on the Records of the Creation. . . . and the Consistency of the Principle of Population with the Wisdom and Goodness of the Deity* (1816); R. A. Soloway, *Prelates and People,* 93–106. All this Christian apologetic helped to create a climate of optimism about the possibility of agricultural expansion, and this in turn helped to prepare for the 1815 Corn Law.

freedom of choice. It followed that only *Christian* economists, like Malthus himself, and not mere *political* economists, could convince workers that sexual abstention would lead to spiritual (and eventually financial) regeneration:

Politcal economy is but one grand exemplification of the alliance, which a God of righteousness hath enlisted, between prudence and moral principle on the one hand, and physical comfort on the other. However obnoxious the modern doctrine of population, as expounded by Mr. Malthus may have been, and still is, to weak and limited sentimentalists, it is the truth which of all others sheds the greatest brightness over the earthly prospects of humanity — and this in spite of the hideous, the yet sustained outcry which has risen against it. This is a pure case of adaptation, between the external nature of the world in which we live, and the moral nature of man, its chief occupier.

In this way Science had revealed a link between 'the economy of outward nature' and 'the economy of human principles and passions'.[19]

Chalmers believed in preventive checks to speculation as well as to population. After the 'population principle', the most unchristian postulate of orthodox political economy was its notion of 'economic man', motivated entirely by self-interest — by profit and pleasure.[20] Now Chalmers was absorbed by the problem of financial speculation and the possibility of inculcating a commercial morality; he was also feelingly eloquent on the miserable uncertainties facing the nineteenth-century businessman, who must feel himself to be 'floating on an ocean of contingency, on which, perhaps, he is only borne up by the breath of a credit that is fictitious and which, liable to burst at every moment, may leave him to sink under the weight of his overladen speculation'.[21] Chalmers distinguished bluntly between 'natural' trade, which was beneficial, and 'excrescent trade. . . the blotch and distemper of our nation'. But he also believed

19. Chalmers, *On the Power Wisdom and Goodness of God,* ii. 49–50. See Chalmers, *On Political Economy,* 28; T. Chalmers, *The Christian and Civic Economy of Large Towns,* i. (1821), 3–24.
20. One utilitarian solution was to marvel at God's skill in making self-interest turn out to be enlightened. Whately, *Introductory Lectures,* 59–64; Chalmers, *On the Power Wisdom and Goodness of God,* ii. 33–51; T. Chalmers, *The Application of Christianity to the Commercial and Ordinary Affairs of Life* (1820), 76.
21. Chalmers, *The Application of Christianity to Commerce,* 275.

that 'spiritual discipline' was capable of restraining the appetite that urged men to get rich *too* quickly, and could reduce man's acquisitive instincts to 'the standard of the gospel':

An affection for riches, beyond what Christianity prescribes, is not essential to any extension of commerce that is at all valuable or legitimate; and, in opposition to the maxim, that the spirit of enterprise is the soul of commercial prosperity, do we hold, that it is *the excess of this spirit beyond the moderation of the New Testament*, which, pressing on the natural boundaries of trade, is sure, at length, to visit every country, where it operates with the recoil of those calamities, which, in the shape of beggared capitalists, and unemployed operatives, and dreary intervals of bankruptcy and alarm, are observed to follow a season of overdone speculation.[22]

Chalmers seems to have regarded bankruptcy, with its harsh punishment, as a positive check, devised by God, to force businessmen into adopting the preventive or moral check of moderation. Fear of debt would make the middle classes moral, as fear of death from hunger elevated the poor. This connection was never explicitly made but it can be glimpsed in later writers, who often wrote about bankruptcy in Malthusian terms — as of Bulstrode *blighting* his clients like 'a damaged ear of corn' and of Merdle's *pestilential* collapse. Anyway Liberal Tories, following Chalmers and other clerical economists of evangelical bent, attempted to solve the problem of over-production, not by seeking new outlets for the export of commodities, capital, and Christians (since informal or free trade imperialism, as Chalmers knew, could only delay the problem), but by regulating production morally, through the application of Christian conscience. It followed that the Usury Laws, which imposed artificial restraints on financial greed, should be abolished, since it was only by being tempted to speculate wildly that one *could*, in conscience, abstain.

22. Ibid. iii-vi (my italics). See T. R. Malthus, *Principles of Political Economy considered with a view to their practical application* (1820), 495: 'When profits are low and. . . capital is flowing out of the country, . . . is it not contrary to the general principles of political economy . . . to recommend saving, and the conversion of more revenue into capital? Is it not just the same sort of thing as to recommend marriage when people are starving and emigrating?'

Coleridge made the same diagnosis of social ills when he denounced the excesses of the "commercial spirit". However, he abhorred the callous Liberal Tory injunction to 'let things find their own level', and wanted to correct the passion for speculative excess by intervention and leadership: 'the Spirit of Commerce is itself capable of being at once counteracted and enlightened by the Spirit of the State, to the advantage of both. . . If we are a Christian nation, we must learn to act nationally as well as individually as Christians.'[23] But the Liberal Tories were less mystical about the state and did not relish intervention. Their aim in removing protections and monopolies was to strip the economy down to its natural state, based on man's appetite for profit and aversion from loss, on 'goading men to be good' through fear of the consequences, as one of Liberal Toryism's last and truest votaries was to put it later. They finished up with a competitive model that in most practical essentials resembled Ricardo's. But whereas the classical economists wanted free trade in order for the economy to grow and to avoid the terrors of a stationary state, the Liberal Tories like Liverpool, Huskisson, and Peel, who implemented free trade, really saw society as a stationary, self-acting, and unprogressive model, whose beneficent workings (once human excrescences had been eliminated) would illuminate the wisdom and glory and goodness of its Creator. Whereas Ricardians welcomed bankruptcies as weeding out the economically inefficient, in order that the 'worthy' might expand more confidently, Liberal Tories wanted to promote, not growth, but the fear of God among businessmen.

It may seem fanciful to suggest that Huskisson 'turn'd, without perceiving his condition, Like Coleridge, into a metaphysician'. Nevertheless, his economic philosophy rested on the conviction that free trade, convertibility and unlimited liability (the last in the shadow of the Marshalsea) would somehow promote sound, moral enterprise while repelling speculation; and would in consequence help to keep the social engine ticking over. The famous peroration of 1810

23. S. T. Coleridge, *Lay Sermons*, edited by R. J. White (1972), 169–70, 202–8, 223,228.

has been cited as proof of his desire for economic growth; yet he extolled only 'Legitimate commerce...put in motion by capital, the *genuine* growth of progressive accumulation'.[24] His competitive individualism was based on an evangelistic scheme of morality. Economic life was a state of moral trial, avarice an original economic sin, and economic man in a condition of probation. It was a system of temptation and retribution, of conversion and self-restraint, whose sanction was the shame and pains of debt, and whose hope lay in the atoning sacrifice of bankrupts. Only the internal check of individual conscience could permanently remove the twin evils of procreation — leading to overpopulation — and of speculation, leading to gluts. Thus Peel could say in 1826 that 'Much good, after some severe suffering, will prevail'. Such assumptions, latent in Huskisson and Peel, became explicit with Gladstone, who, in shuffling off his early Coleridgean coils in favour of the retributive, atonement-oriented theology of Bishop Butler and Thomas Chalmers, became as it were the last Liberal Tory. For him, 'Religion and Christian virtue, like the faculty of taste and the perception of beauty, have their place, aye and that the first place, in political economy, as the means of creating *and preserving* wealth.'[25]

To think like this was not to be 'haunted by general principles'.[26] 'High' and 'Liberal' tories shared the same social and economic vision, which was essentially retrograde, and differed mainly in their methods. Where 'Highs' relied on the 'spirit of state', on contacts with the powerful, 'Liberals' — who did not have such contacts — rejected 'empiricism' for a belief that the economy could be self-acting, mechanical. They moved towards free trade simply

---

24. Huskisson, *The Question Concerning the Depreciation of Our Currency* (1810), 153.
25. [Gladstone], 'Course of Commercial Policy at Home and Abroad', *Foreign and Colonial Quarterly Review*, i (1843), 253.
26. The charge was Graham's, see above, p. 270. But as Graham drifted into liberal toryism in the thirties, so he abandoned his cynicism for a belated Butlerianism. See *The Gladstone Diaries*, edited by M. R. D. Foot and H. C. G. Matthew, iii. 555-7.

as a means to get this static model working without friction. They lacked any mercantilist belief in the power of the state to organize men's lives beneficially, and thought that the *summum bonum* must take care of itself; but like mercantilists, they saw the main task as being to *preserve* wealth, which was limited, against predatory foreign competition. Even after Peterloo and the brutal facts of food supply had forced them to concentrate on the performance of manufacturing exports, their ambition remained simply to maximize employment opportunities within the context of what was conceived to be a finite international economy. In a sense, liberal tory economic policy ceased when, in mid-century, liability for debt was limited, evangelical morality was ditched, and an idea of progress replaced the previous conception of a static, self-regulating economy.

SELECT BIBLIOGRAPHY

All books are published in London unless otherwise stated.

MANUSCRIPTS

British Museum, Additional Manuscripts
Huskisson Papers
Liverpool Papers
Peel Papers
Vansittart Papers
Herries Papers (unsorted)
Ripon Papers
Rose Papers
Aberdeen Papers
Auckland Papers
Wellesley Papers
Thomas Grenville Papers
Hardwicke Papers
Arthur Young Papers
Macvey Napier Papers
George Chalmers Papers
Broughton Papers
Holland House Papers
Robert Wilson Papers
Newcastle and Pelham Papers
Treasury Secretaries' Correspondence

British Museum, other series
Bathurst Papers (Loan 57)
Hertford Papers (Egerton Manuscripts)

Public Record Office, London
Board of Trade Records
Colchester Papers
Ellenborough Papers
Granville Papers

Public Record Office, Northern Ireland
Foster/Massereene Papers
Chilham Papers
Charles Ryle Fay Papers

County Record Office
Addington Papers, Devon
Buckinghamshire Papers, Buckinghamshire

Goulburn Papers, Surrey
Hatherton Papers, Staffordshire
Tierney Papers, Hampshire

State Paper Office, Dublin
General private correspondence, 1815—21

Bodleian Library, Oxford
Page/Lauderdale Correspondence
Clarendon Deposit
Burdett/Coutts Papers
Graham Papers (microfilm of Netherby Manuscripts)

Business Records
Bank of England Records
Manchester Chamber of Commerce Proceedings, Manchester Central
    Library
American Chamber of Commerce (Liverpool) Record Books, Brown,
    Picton, and Hornby Libraries
Liverpool Parliamentary Record Office Papers, Brown, Picton, and
    Hornby Libraries

Other Collections
Canning Papers, Leeds Public Library (Harewood Manuscripts)
Castlereagh Papers in the possession of the Marquis of Londonderry, at
    Mount Stewart, County Down
Wellington Papers in the possession of the Duke of Wellington at
    Stratfield Saye
Harrowby Papers in the possession of the Earl of Harrowby at Sandon
    Hall, Staffordshire
Henry Parnell Papers in the possession of Lord Congleton at Ebbes-
    bourne Wake, Wiltshire
John Louis Mallet Diaries in the possession of Mr. Philip Mallet
Kenyon Papers in the possession of Lord Kenyon at Gredington, Salop
E. D. Davenport Papers in the John Rylands Library, Manchester
Brougham Papers in University College, London
Charles R. Vaughan Papers, Codrington Library, All Souls College,
    Oxford
Newport Papers, Queen's University, Belfast
Newport/Grenville Correspondence (microfilm copy from Newport
    Manuscripts in the William R. Perkins Library, Duke University)
Vesey Fitzgerald Papers, National Library of Ireland.

BIOGRAPHIES, MEMOIRS, AND COLLECTIONS OF DOCUMENTS

The Correspondence of Charles Arbuthnot, edited by A. Aspinall,
    Camden 3rd Series, lxv (1941).
The Journal of Mrs Arbuthnot 1820—30, 2 vols., edited by F. Bamford
    and the Duke of Wellington (1950).

C. M. Wakefield, *Life of Thomas Attwood (1950)*.

D. Le Marchant, *Memoir of John Charles, Viscount Althorp, 3rd Earl Spencer* (1876).

A. Aspinall, *Lord Brougham and the Whig Party*, Manchester (1927).

C. New, *Life of Henry Brougham to 1830*, Oxford (1961).

Buckingham and Chandos, *Memoirs of the Court of England during the Regency, 1811–20*, 2 vols. (1856).

——, *Memoirs of the Court of George IV, 1820–30*, 2 vols. (1859).

The Formation of Canning's Ministry, February to August 1827, edited by A. Aspinall, Camden 3rd Series, lix (1937).

W. Hinde, *George Canning* (1973).

A. G. Stapleton, *George Canning and His Times* (1859).

——, *The Political Life of George Canning*, 3 vols. (1831).

Some Official Correspondence of George Canning, edited by E. J. Stapleton, 2 vols. (1887).

Memoirs and Correspondence of Viscount Castlereagh, edited by C. W. Vane, Marquis of Londonderry, 12 vols. (1848–53).

W. Hanna, *Memoirs of the Life and Writings of Thomas Chalmers*, 4 vols., Edinburgh (1849–52).

A Selection from the Correspondence of Thomas Chalmers, edited by W. Hanna, Edinburgh (1853).

A. M. W. Stirling, *Coke of Norfolk and His Friends*, single volume edition (1912).

The Diary and Correspondence of Charles Abbot, Lord Colchester, edited by Charles, Lord Colchester, 3 vols. (1861).

The Creevey Papers, edited by H. Maxwell, 2 vols. (1903).

The Croker Papers. The Correspondence and Diaries of John Wilson Croker, edited by L. J. Jennings, 3 vols. (1885).

Letters of the Earl of Dudley to the Bishop of Llandaff, edited by E. J. Copleston (1840).

H. Twiss, *The Public and Private Life of Lord Chancellor Eldon*, 3 vols. (1844).

A Political Diary 1828–30 by Edward Law, Lord Ellenborough, edited by Lord Colchester, 2 vols. (1881).

The Letters of King George IV, 1821–30, edited by A. Aspinall, 3 vols., Cambridge (1938).

W. T. Mc. Torrens, *The Life and Times of Sir James R. G. Graham*, 2 vols. (1863).

J. T. Ward, *Sir James Graham* (1967).

The Greville Memoirs, a Journal of the Reigns of King George IV and King William IV, edited by H. Reeve, 3 vols. (1875).

E. Herries, *Memoir of the Public Life of John Charles Herries*, 2 vols. (1880).

The Diary of Henry Hobhouse (1820–27), edited by A. Aspinall (1947).

J. C. Hobhouse, Lord Broughton, *Recollections of a Long Life*, edited by Lady Dorchester, 6 vols. (1909–11).

H. R. V. Fox, 3rd Baron Holland, *Further Memoirs of the Whig Party 1807–21* (1905).

Memoirs and Correspondence of Francis Horner, edited by L. Horner, 2 vols. (1843).

C. Badham, *The Life of James Deacon Hume* (1859).

The Speeches of William Huskisson, with a 'Biographical Memoir' by J. Wright, 3 vols. (1831).

C. R. Fay, *Huskisson and His Age* (1951).

——, 'Huskisson and Irish Affairs', typescript in Christ Church Library.

The Huskisson Papers, edited by L. Melville (1931).

C. D. Yonge, *The Life and Administration of Robert Banks, 2nd Earl of Liverpool*, 3 vols. (1868).

H. L. Bulwer, Lord Dalling, *The Life of Henry John Temple, Viscount Palmerston*, 3 vols. (1871–4).

Memoirs by Sir Robert Peel, edited by Earl Stanhope, 2 vols. (1856–7).

N. Gash, *Mr Secretary Peel. The Life of Sir Robert Peel to 1830* (1961).

——, *Sir Robert Peel. The Life of Sir Robert Peel after 1830* (1972).

C. S. Parker, *Sir Robert Peel*, 3 vols. (1891–99).

The Works and Correspondence of David Ricardo, edited by P. Sraffa, 10 vols., Cambridge (1951–5).

W. D. Jones, *'Prosperity' Robinson, the Life of Viscount Goderich, 1782–1859*, London and New York (1967).

The Diaries and Correspondence of George Rose, edited by L. V. Harcourt, 2 vols. (1860).

R. Rush, *Memoranda of a Residence at the Court of London*, 1st series, Philadelphia (1833) and 2nd series, 2 vols., Philadelphia (1845).

——, *Memories of the Court of London, 1819–25* (1873).

G. Pellew, *The Life and Correspondence of Henry Addington, 1st Viscount Sidmouth*, 3 vols. (1847).

P. Ziegler, *Addington. A Life of Henry Addington, 1st Viscount Sidmouth* (1965).

The Correspondence of Sir John Sinclair, with reminiscences, 2 vols., London and Edinburgh (1831).

Memoirs of the Life and Works of Sir John Sinclair, edited by J. Sinclair, 2 vols., London and Edinburgh (1837).

R. Mitchison, *Agricultural Sir John* (1962).

Memoirs of the Political and Literary Life of Robert Plumer Ward, edited by E. Phipps, 2 vols. (1850).

1st Duke of Wellington, *Supplementary Despatches, Correspondence, and Memoranda, 1797–1818*, 15 vols. (1858–72).

——, *Despatches, Correspondence, and Memoranda, 1819–31*, 7 vols. (1867–78).

Philip Henry, Earl Stanhope, *Conversations with the Duke of Wellington 1831–51* (1888).

Lady Elizabeth Longford, *Wellington: Pillar of State* (1972).

J. G. Gazley, *The Life of Arthur Young, 1741–1820*, Philadelphia (1973).

HISTORIES OF ECONOMIC POLICY

General

A. W. Acworth, *Financial Reconstruction in England, 1815–22* (1925).

A. Brady, *William Huskisson and Liberal Reform* (1928).

L. Brown, *The Board of Trade and the Free-Trade Movement, 1830–42*, Oxford (1958).

A. H. Imlah, *Economic Elements in the 'Pax Britannica'. Studies in British Foreign Trade in the Nineteenth Century*, Cambridge, Massachusetts (1958).

A. L. Lingelbach, 'William Huskisson as President of the Board of Trade', *American Historical Review*, xliii (1937–38), 759–74.

D. C. M. Platt, *Finance, Trade, and Politics. British Foreign Policy, 1815–1914*, Oxford (1968).

B. Semmel, *The Rise of Free Trade Imperialism. Classical Political Economy the Empire of Free Trade and Imperialism 1750–1850*, Cambridge (1970).

W. Smart, *Economic Annals of the Nineteenth Century, 1801–20* (1910).

—, *Economic Annals of the Nineteenth Century, 1821–30* (1917).

Money and Banking

T. S. Ashton and R. S. Sayers, *Papers in English Monetary History*, Oxford (1953).

J. Bonar, 'Ricardo's Ingot Plan', *Economic Journal*, xxxiii (1923), 281–304.

I. Bowen, 'Country Banking, the Note Issues and Banking Controversies in 1825', *Economic Journal, History Supplement*, iii (1938), 68–88.

E. Cannan, *The Paper Pound, 1797–1821* (1919).

J. H. Clapham, *The Bank of England*, 2 vols., Cambridge (1944).

A. Feavearyear, *The Pound Sterling. A History of English Money*, Oxford (1931).

F. W. Fetter, *Development of British Monetary Orthodoxy, 1797–1875*, Cambridge, Massachusetts (1965).

—, *The Irish Pound, 1797–1826* (1955).

—, 'The Politics of the Bullion Report', *Economica*, new series, xxvi (1959), 99–120.

H. H. Gibbs, Lord Aldenham, *A Colloquy on Currency*, third and revised edition (1894).

J. K. Horsefield, 'The Bankers and the Bullionists in 1819', *Journal of Political Economy*, lvii (1949), 442–8.

—, 'The Opinions of Horsley Palmer', *Economica*, new series, xvi (1949), 143–58.

320 SELECT BIBLIOGRAPHY

E. V. Morgan, 'Some Aspects of the Bank Restriction Period, 1797–1821', *Economic Journal, History Supplement*, iii (1939), 205–21.

——, *The Theory and Practice of Central Banking, 1797–1913* (1943).

R. S. Sayers, 'The Question of the Standard, 1815–44', *Economic Journal, History Supplement*, iii (1935), 79–102.

E. Wood, *English Theories of Central Banking Control, 1819–58*, Cambridge, Massachusetts (1939).

Agriculture

D. G. Barnes, *A History of the English Corn Laws from 1600 to 1846* (1930).

S. Fairlie, 'The Nineteenth-Century Corn Law Reconsidered', *Economic History Review*, second series, xviii (1965), 562–73.

C. R. Fay, *The Corn Laws and Social England*, Cambridge (1932).

C. R. Fay, 'Price Control and the Corn Averages under the Corn Laws', *Economic Journal, History Supplement*, i (1926), 149–54.

W. F. Galpin, *The Grain Supply of England during the Napoleonic Period*, New York (1925).

W. E. Minchinton, 'Agricultural Returns and the Government during the Napoleonic Wars', *Agricultural Historical Review*, i (1953), 29–43.

R. Mitchison, 'The Old Board of Agriculture (1793–1822)', *English Historical Review*, lxxiv (1959), 41–69.

D. C. Moore, 'The Corn Laws and High Farming', *Economic History Review*, second series, xviii (1965), 544–61.

J. S. Nicholson, *The History of the English Corn Laws* (1904).

M. Olson, *The Economics of Wartime Shortage, a history of British food supplies in the Napoleonic War and in World Wars I and II*, Durham, North Carolina (1963).

S. and B. Webb, 'The Assize of Bread', *Economic Journal*, xiv (1904), 196–218.

Finance and Taxation

S. Buxton, *Finance and Politics, 1783–1885*, 2 vols., Farnsworth (1888).

E. L. Hargreaves, *The National Debt* (1930).

A. Hope-Jones, *Income Tax in the Napoleonic Wars*, Cambridge (1939).

B. E. V. Sabine, *A History of Income Tax* (1966).

E. B. Schumpeter, 'English Prices and Government Finance, 1660–1822', *Review of Economics and Statistics*, xx (1938), 21–37.

E. R. A. Seligman, *The Shifting and Incidence of Taxation*, New York (1899).

F. Shebab, *Progressive Taxation, A Study in the Development of the Progressive Principle in the British Income Tax*, Oxford (1953).

J. M. Sherwig, *Guineas and Gunpowder, British Foreign Aid in the Wars with France, 1793–1815*, Cambridge, Massachusetts (1969).

N. J. Silberling, 'Financial and Monetary Policy of Britain during the Napoleonic Wars', *Quarterly Journal of Economics*, xxxviii (1924), 214–33 and 397–439.

Commercial Policy

F. Lee Benns, *The American Struggle for the British West India Carrying Trade, 1815–30*, Indiana (1923).

J. H. Clapham, 'The Last Years of the Navigation Acts', *English Historical Review*, xxv (1910), 480–501 and 687–707.

G. S. Graham, *Sea Power and British North America 1783-1820. A Study in British Colonial Policy* (1941).

L. Levi, *The History of British Commerce and of the Economic Progress of the British Nation, 1763–1870* (1872).

J. Potter, 'The British Timber Duties, 1815–60', *Economica*, new series, xxii (1955), 122–36.

R. L. Schuyler, *The Fall of the Old Colonial System. A Study in British Free Trade 1770–1870*, New York (1945).

Great Britain and the Colonies, 1815–65, edited by A. G. L. Shaw (1970).

V. G. Setser, *The Commercial Reciprocity Policy of the United States, 1774–1829*, Philadelphia (1937).

E. Williams, *Capitalism and Slavery* (1964).

J. B. Williams, *British Commercial Policy and Trade Expansion, 1750–1850*, Oxford (1972).

Social Policy

J. H. Clapham, 'The Spitalfields Acts, 1773–1824', *Economic Journal*, xxvi (1916), 459–71.

M. W. Flinn, 'The Poor Employment Act of 1817', *Economic History Review*, second series, xiv (1961), 82–92.

H. J. M. Johnston, *British Emigration Policy 1815–30: 'Shovelling out Paupers'*, Oxford (1972).

J. R. Poynter, *Society and Pauperism. English Ideas on Poor Relief 1795–1834* (1969).

THE THEORY OF ECONOMIC POLICY

R. D. C. Black, *Economic Thought and the Irish Question 1817–70*, Cambridge (1960).

M. Blaug, *Economic Theory in Retrospect* (1961).

——, *Ricardian Economics: a Historical Study*, New Haven (1958).

M. E. A. Bowley, *Nassau Senior and Classical Economics* (1937).

E. Cannan, *A History of the Theories of Production and Distribution in English Political Economy from 1776 to 1848.* (1893).

S. G. Checkland, 'The Prescriptions of the Classical Economists', *Economica*, new series, xx (1953), 43–70.

——, 'The Propagation of Ricardian Economics in England', *Economica*, new series, xvi (1949), 40–52.

The Classical Economists and Economic Policy, edited by A. W. Coats (1971).

B. A. Corry, *Money Saving and Investment in English Economics, 1800–50* (1962).

——, 'The Theory of the Economic Effects of Government Expenditure in English Classical Political Economy', *Economica*, new series, xxv (1958), 34–48.

F. W. Fetter, 'Robert Torrens, Colonel of Marines and Political Economist', *Economica*, new series, xxix (1962), 152–65.

S. L. Levy, *Nassau Senior, 1790–1864*, Newton Abbot (1970).

R. G. Link, *English Theories of Economic Fluctuations, 1815–48*, New York (1959).

R. L. Meek, *Economics and Ideology and other essays* (1967).

W. C. Mitchell, *Types of Economic Theory, from mercantilism to institutionalism*, 2 vols., New York (1967–9).

D. P. O'Brien, *J. R. McCulloch. A Study in Classical Economics* (1970).

M. Paglin, *Malthus and Lauderdale, the Anti-Ricardian Tradition*, New York (1961).

Proceedings of the Political Economy Club, iv and vi (1882, 1921).

L. Robbins, *Robert Torrens and the Evolution of Classical Economics* (1958).

——, *The Theory of Economic Policy in English Classical Political Economy* (1952).

J. A. Schumpeter, *History of Economic Analysis* (1954).

B. Semmel, 'Malthus: *Physiocracy* and the Commercial System', *Economic History Review*, second series, xvii (1965), 522–35.

C. S. Shoup, *Ricardo on Taxation*, New York (1960).

R. A. Soloway, *Prelates and People. Ecclesiastical Social Thought in England 1783–1852* (1969).

G. S. L. Tucker, *Progress and Profits in British Economic Thought, 1650–1850*, Cambridge (1960).

J. Viner, *Studies in the Theory of International Trade* (1937).

D. Winch, *Classical Political Economy and Colonies* (1965).

WORKS RELATING TO THE ECONOMIC BACKGROUND

General

M. C. Buer, 'The Trade Depression following the Napoleonic Wars', *Economica*, i (1921), 159–79.

S. G. Checkland, *The Rise of Industrial Society in England, 1815–85* (1964).

J. H. Clapham, *An Economic History of Modern Britain., i. The Early Railway Age, 1820–50*, Cambridge (1926).

J. A. Cope, 'The British Economy in the Trade Cycle, 1820–30', B. Litt. thesis in the University of Oxford (1959).

F. Crouzet, *L'économie britannique et le blocus continental, 1806–13*, 2 vols., Paris (1958).

A. D. Gayer, W. W. Rostow and A. J. Schwartz, *The Growth and Fluctuation of the British Economy, 1790–1850*, 2 vols., Oxford (1953).

R. M. Hartwell, *The Industrial Revolution and Economic Growth* (1971).

E. J. Hobsbawm and G. Rudé, *Captain Swing*, Woking &c. (1969).

P. Mathias, *The First Industrial Nation. An Economic History of Britain, 1700–1914* (1969).

R. C. O. Matthews, *A Study in Trade-Cycle History. Economic Fluctuations in Great Britain, 1833–42*, Cambridge (1954).

G. O'Brien, *The Economic History of Ireland from the Union to the Famine* (1921).

A. J. Peacock, *Bread or Blood, a study of the agrarian riots in East Anglia in 1816* (1965).

G. R. Porter, *The Progress of the Nation in its social and commercial relations from the beginning of the nineteenth century to the present day*. (1836–8).

J. Potter, 'Atlantic Economy, 1815–60: U.S.A. and Industrial Revolution and Great Britain', in *Studies in the Industrial Revolution*, edited by L. S. Pressnell (1960), 236–80.

W. W. Rostow, 'Adjustments and maladjustments after the Napoleonic Wars', *American Economic Review*, xxxii (1942), supplement 13–23.

W. Schölte, *British Overseas Trade, 1700–1930s* (1938), translated by W. O. Henderson and W. H. Chaloner, Oxford (1952).

N. J. Silberling, 'British Financial Experience, 1790–1830', *Review of Economics and Statistics*, i (1919), 282–97.

T. Tooke and W. Newmarch, *A History of Prices and of the State of the Circulation from 1792 to 1856*, edited by T. E. Gregory, 6 vols., (1928).

Agriculture and rural pressure groups

L. P. Adams, *Agricultural Depression and Farm Relief in England, 1813–52* (1932).

J. D. Chambers and G. E. Mingay, *The Agricultural Revolution, 1770–1880* (1966).

R. E. Prothero, Lord Ernle, *English Farming, Past and Present*, 5th edition (1936).

S. Fairlie, 'The Corn Laws and British Wheat Production, 1829–76', *Economic History Review*, 2nd series, xxii (1969), 88–116.

G. E. Fussell, 'The Dawn of High Farming in England', *Agricultural History*, xxii (1948), 83–95.

—— and M. Compton, 'Agricultural Adjustments after the Napoleonic Wars', *Economic Journal, History Supplement*, iii (1939), 184–204.

N. Gash, 'Rural Unemployment, 1815–34', *Economic History Review*, vi (1935), 90–3.

D. B. Grigg, *The Agricultural Revolution in South Lincolnshire*, Cambridge (1966).

Land, Labour and Population in the Industrial Revolution, edited by E. L. Jones and G. E. Mingay (1967).

D. Spring, 'Early Fitzwilliam and the Corn Laws', *American Historical Review,* lix (1954), 287–304.

——, 'Lord Chandos and the Farmers, 1818–46', *Huntington Library Quarterly,* xxxiii (1969–70), 257–81.

—— and T. L. Crosby, 'George Webb Hall and the Agricultural Association', *Journal of British Studies,* ii (1962), 115–31.

F. M. L. Thompson, *English Landed Society in the Nineteenth Century* (1963).

Merchant and business organization and opinion

M. W. Beresford, *The Leeds Chamber of Commerce,* Leeds (1951).

A. Briggs, 'Thomas Attwood and the Economic Background of the Birmingham Political Union', *Cambridge Historical Journal,* ix (1948), 190–216.

N. S. Buck, *The Development and Organisation of Anglo-American Trade, 1800–50,* Yale, New Haven (1925).

S. G. Checkland, 'The Birmingham Economists, 1815–50', *Economic History Review,* 2nd series, i (1948), 1–19.

——, 'American versus West Indian Traders in Liverpool, 1793–1815', *Journal of Economic History,* xviii (1958), 141–60.

——, 'John Koster, anti-Bullionist', *Manchester School,* xx (1952), 714–202.

——, *The Gladstones. A Family Biography, 1764–1851,* Cambridge (1971).

Liverpool and Merseyside, edited by J. R. Harris (1969).

E. Helm, *Chapters in the History of the Manchester Chamber of Commerce* (1897).

R. W. Hidy, *The House of Baring in American Trade and Finance, English merchant bakers at work, 1763–1861,* Cambridge, Massachusetts (1949).

R. A. Humphreys, 'British Merchants and South American Independence', *Proceedings of the British Academy,* li (1965), 151–74.

A. Redford, *Manchester Merchants and Foreign Trade 1794–1858,* Manchester (1934).

D. M. Williams, 'Merchanting in the First Half of the Nineteenth Century, the Liverpool Timber Trade', *Business History,* viii (1966), 103–21.

R. G. Wilson. *Gentlemen Merchants. The merchant community in Leeds, 1700–1830,* Manchester (1971).

G. H. Wright, *Chronicles in the History of the Birmingham Chamber of Commerce, 1813–1913, and of the Birmingham Commercial Society, 1783–1812* (1913).

Banking and finance

B. H. R. Capefigue, *Histoire des grandes opérations financières,* 4 vols., Paris (1856–60).

S. G. Checkland, 'The Lancashire Bill System nd its Liverpool Prota-
gonists, 1810–27', *Economica*, new series, xxi (1954), 129–42.
Count E. C. Corti, *The Rise of the House of Rothschild* (1928).
G. H. Evans, *British Corporation Finance, a study of preference shares,
1775–1850*, Baltimore (1936).
L. H. Grindon, *Manchester Banks and Bankers*, Manchester (1878).
C. K. Hobson, *The Export of Capital* (1914).
J. Hughes, *Liverpool Banks and Bankers, 1760–1887* (1906).
B. C. Hunt, *The Development of the Business Corporation in England,
1800–67*, Cambridge, Massachusetts (1936).
L. H. Jenks, *The Migration of British Capital to 1875* (1927).
W. T. C. King, *History of the London Discount Market* (1936).
L. S. Pressnell, *Country Banking in the Industrial Revolution*, Oxford
(1956).

POLITICAL STUDIES

A. Aspinall, 'The Canningite Party', *Royal Historical Society Trans-
actions*, 4th series, xvii (1934), 177–226.
——, 'Canning's return to office in September 1822', *English Historical
Review*, lxxviii (1963), 531–45.
——, 'The Coalition Ministries of 1827', *English Historical Review*, xlii
(1927), 201–26 and 533–59.
——, 'English Party Organisation in the early nineteenth century', *English
Historical Review*, xli (1926), 389–411.
——, 'The Last of the Canningites', *English Historical Review*, l (1935),
639–69.
B. T. Bradfield, 'Sir Richard Vyvyan and the Country Gentleman,
1830–34', *English Historical Review*, lxxxiii (1968), 729–43.
——, 'Sir Richard Vyvyan and the Fall of Wellington's Government',
University of Birmingham Historical Journal, xi (1967–8), 141–56.
A. Briggs, 'The Background to Parliamentary Reform in Three English
Cities', *Cambridge Historical Journal*, xiii (1952), 292–317.
M. Brock, *The Great Reform Act* (1973).
W. R. Brock, *Lord Liverpool and Liberal Toryism, 1820 to 1827* (1941).
G. S. R. Kitson Clark, *Peel and the Conservative Party* (1929).
J. E. Cookson, *Lord Liverpool's Administration: the Crucial Years,
1815–1822*, Edinburgh and London (1975), – (not consulted).
P. Fraser, 'Public Petitioning and Parliament before 1832', *History*, xlvi
(1961), 195–211.
E. Halévy, *A History of the English People in the Nineteenth Century*,
translated by E. I. Watkin, 6 vols., second (revised) edition (1949–
52).
H. Martineau, *History of the Thiry Years Peace*, 4 vols. (1877).
A. Mitchell, *The Whigs in Opposition, 1815–30*, Oxford (1967).
D. C. Moore, 'The Other Face of Reform,' *Victorian Studies*, v (1961–
2), 7–34.

H. W. V. Temperley, *The Foreign Policy of Canning, 1822–27* (1925).
E. P. Thompson, *The Making of the English Working Class* (1963).
S. Walpole, *A History of England from the Conclusion of the Great War in 1815*, 5 vols. (1878–86).
C. K. Webster, *The Foreign Policy of Castlereagh, 1812–22*, 2 vols. (1925).

For an extensive selection of the voluminous pamphlet literature dealing with economic policy problems in this period, and for a complete list of relevant official papers (Select Committee and Commissioner Reports, &c.), see the bibliography of A. J. B. Hilton, 'The Economic Policy of the Tory Governments, 1815–30', University of Oxford D.Phil thesis (1973).

INDEX